Pros and Cons

Pros and Cons

Social Policy
Debates of Our Time

S. Clara Kim
University of Dayton

Allyn and Bacon

Boston ∎ London ∎ Toronto ∎ Sydney ∎ Tokyo ∎ Singapore

Series Editor: *Jeff Lasser*
Series Editorial Assistant: *Susan Hutchinson*
Production Administrator: *Laurel Ibey*
Electronic Composition: *Cabot Computer Services*
Composition Buyer: *Linda Cox*
Manufacturing Buyer: *Suzanne Lareau*
Cover Administrator: *Jennifer Hart*

Copyright © 2001 by Allyn and Bacon
A Pearson Education Company
160 Gould Street
Needham Heights, MA 02494

Internet: www.abacon.com

Library of Congress Cataloging-in-Publication Data

Kim, S. Clara
    Pros and cons : social policy debates of our time / S. Clara Kim.
      p. cm.
    Includes index.
    ISBN 0-205-29840-0 (pbk.)
    1. United States—Social policy—1993–. 2. United States—Social
conditions—1945–. I. Title: Social policy debates of our time. II. Title.
HN59.2.K56 2000
306'.0973—dc21   99-087087
                                                      CIP

Printed in the United States of America

10 9 8 7 6 5 4 3 2 1   04 03 02 01 00

To My Parents

CONTENTS

Preface   xiii

1 Abortion   1

Religious Views on Abortion   3   /   Public Opinion about
Abortion   4   /   Extent of Abortion in the United States   4   /
Women Have the Right to Choose Abortion   5   /   The Fetus has
the Right to Life   6   /   Abortion Violates the Sanctity of Human
Life   7   /   Abortion May Be Immoral, But Should Not Be Ille-
gal   8   /   An Unwanted Pregnancy Justifies an Abortion   9   /
Abortion Is Sometimes a More Responsible Choice Than Child-
birth   10   /   Adoption Is a Better Option Than Abortion   11   /
Legal Access to Abortion Is Necessary for Sexual Equality   12   /
Illegal Abortions Are Dangerous   13   /   Government Should
Guarantee Easy Access to Abortion   14   /   Abortion Is Justified in
Rape Cases   15   /   Government-Funded Abortion for the
Poor   16   /   Mandatory Waiting Period   18   /   Parental
Consent (or Notification) Laws   19   /   Requiring Consent from
the Father of the Fetus   20   /   Late-Term Abortions (Partial Birth
Abortions)   21   /   When Should the Fetuses Be Given the Right to
Life?   22   /   References   24

2 Affirmative Action Policy (Race-Based)   27

Affirmative Action Is a Compensatory Remedy for Past Racial
Injustice   29   /   Affirmative Action Provides Minorities with
Opportunities That Did Not Exist Before   30   /   Affirmative
Action Helps Create Minority Role Models   32   /   Affirmative
Action Promotes Diversity and Pluralism   32   /   Affirmative Action
Is Unfair; It Is Reverse Discrimination   34   /   Affirmative Action
Outlived Its Usefulness: It Is Time to Put an End to It   36   /
Affirmative Action Undermines the Quality of the Workforce
38   /   Affirmative Action Stigmatizes Minorities   39   /
Affirmative Action Increases Racial Tension   40   /   Affirmative
Action Does Not Solve the Real Source of the Problem   41   /
Affirmative Action Helps Those Who Do Not Need Help, and Does
Not Help Those Who Do   44   /   Class-Based Affirmative Action
Should Replace Race-Based Affirmative Action   46   /
Affirmative Action Should Be Voluntary, Not Forced   46   /
References   47

3 The Death Penalty   50

American Public Opinion About the Death Penalty   51   /   The
Death Penalty in Other Countries   51   /   Punishment Should Fit
the Crime; Capital Crimes Justify Capital Punishment   52   /   The
Death Penalty Is a Necessary Restitution for the Victim and Victim's
Family   53   /   The Death Penalty Is "Cruel and Unusual"; It
Violates Human Dignity and the Criminal's Right to Life   54   /
The Death Penalty Does Not Deter Crime   56   /   Swifter
Execution of Death Penalty Would Increase Deterrence Effect
58   /   Greater Certainty of Execution Would Increase Deterrence
Effect   59   /   The Death Penalty Is Applied Unfairly to African
Americans   60   /   The Death Penalty Is Applied Unfairly to the
Poor   62   /   Innocent People Can Be Executed   63   /   The
Death Penalty Costs More Than Life Imprisonment   65   /
Criminals Are the Victims of Circumstances   67   /   The Death
Penalty Promotes Violence by Sending a Message to the Public That
Killing is Acceptable   68   /   The Majority of Americans Support
the Death Penalty   69   /   The United States Is the Only Western
Industrialized Society That Allows the Death Penalty   70   /   Life
Imprisonment Is a Better Option Than the Death Penalty   71   /
References   72

4 Gun Control   75

Gun Ownership in the United States   75   /   Extent of Gun
Violence in the United States   75   /   Types of Gun Control
76   /   History of Federal Gun Control Laws   76   /   State and
Local Gun Control Laws   78   /   Public Opinion about Gun
Control   78   /   The Right to Bear Arms Is Protected by the
Second Amendment   79   /   Guns Are No Longer Needed in
Modern Societies   80   /   Guns Don't Kill; People Kill   81   /
Easy Access to and Availability of Guns Increase Violence   82   /
Easy Access to and Availability of Guns Increase Suicide Rates
83   /   Easy Access to and Availability of Guns Increase Gun-Related
Accidents   84   /   Guns Are Not an Effective Means of Self-
Defense   85   /   Gun Control Takes Guns Away from Law-Abiding
Citizens Only, Not Criminals   88   /   Gun Control Measures Are
Effective in Other Countries   89   /   Targeted Gun Control versus
General Gun Control   91   /   Assault Weapon Ban   93   /
Handgun Ban   95   /   Brady Law   95   /   We Need Stricter Gun
Control Measures   96   /   Federal Gun Control Laws versus State
and Local Laws   98   /   We Need to Regulate the Gun
Manufacturing Industries   99   /   References   100

5 Health Care Reform   104

Our Health Care Costs Too Much   105   /   The Third-Party
Indemnity Insurance System Is Responsible for High Health Care
Costs   106   /   We Spend Too Much on Administrative
Costs   107   /   The Fee-for-Service System Is Responsible for High
Health Care Costs   107   /   High Physicians' Income Is
Responsible for the High Cost of Health Care   108   /   We Have
Too Many Specialists   109   /   Too Many Malpractice Lawsuits
Drive the Cost of Health Care Up   110   /   Too Many People Are
Uninsured   111   /   Health Care Costs Rose Because of Cost-
Shifting   112   /   The Development of Medical Technology
Justifies the High Costs   113   /   Good Quality Care Justifies High
Cost   114   /   Managed Care: Is It a Good Option?   115   /   The
Managed Care System Cuts Health Care Costs   116   /   Quality of
Care Suffers under Managed Care   117   /   Managed Care Creates
Competition   119   /   Managed Care Exacerbates Problems of
Inequality in Health Care   121   /   Doctors Are Not Happy with
the Managed Care System   122   /   Managed Care Provides
Preventive Care   123   /   Managed Care Plans Provide Limited
Choices for Their Members   123   /   Managed Care Reform: Is It
Necessary?   124   /   Underwriting and Preexisting Condition
Exclusions   127   /   Cost-Sharing   129   /   Health Care
Rationing   130   /   Health Care Reform: What Are the Options?
132   /   Universal Equal Care versus Tiered System   132   /
Private, Competition-Based Systems versus Public, Government-
Controlled Systems   134   /   National Health Insurance (NHI)
(Single-Payer Plan)   136   /   National Health Service (NHS)
(Socialized Medicine)   138   /   Mandated Employer-Based Health
Insurance   140   /   Mandated Individual (Consumer)-Based Health
Insurance with Medical Savings Account   142   /   References   144

6 Human Cloning   148

Religious Groups' Views on Human Cloning   150   /   Cloning
Methods: How Is It Done?   150   /   Use of Human Cloning
Technology in Four Areas   151   /   Whole Human Cloning
152   /   Tissue and Organ Reproduction   154   /   Genetic
Engineering   155   /   Transgenics (Cloning of Animals with
Human Genes)   156   /   It Is Too Early to Allow Human Cloning
158   /   Human Cloning Is Too Risky   159   /   Human Cloning Is
Morally Wrong   160   /   People Should Not Play God   161   /
The Identity Right and Individuality of the Clone Will Be Violated

161 / Cloning Is a Form of Asexual Reproduction That Can
Take Males Out of the Reproductive Process 162 /
References 163

7 Physician-Assisted Suicide   165

Physician-Assisted Suicide in Other Countries 166 / Public's,
Medical Professionals', and Religious Groups' Views on Physician-
Assisted Suicide 167 / How Often Is PAS Requested and
Performed? 167 / Physician-Assisted Suicide Is a
Constitutionally Protected Fundamental Right 168 / A Refusal
of Unwanted Medical Treatments to Hasten Death is Legal, Why
Not Physician-Assisted Suicide? 169 / We Need a Better Way of
Dying Than Needless Pain and Suffering 170 / The
Netherlands Has Successfully Allowed Physician-Assisted Suicide for
More Than Twenty-Four Years; Why Can't We? 172 / Suicide
Is Morally Wrong under Any Circumstances 173 / Christian
Theology Demands Respect for Life and Recognizes That Human
Life Is Sacred 174 / Potential Risks from Allowing Physician-
Assisted Suicide Are Greater Than the Benefits 174 / Physicians
Should Always Be Healers, Not Killers 176 / Hospice Program
Is a Better Option Than Physician-Assisted Suicide 177 / Better
Care of Terminal Patients Should Be the Answer, Not Physician-
Assisted Suicide 178 / Predicting Terminal Illness Is Never
Accurate 179 / The Decision to End One's Life Is Often an
Irrational One 180 / Legalizing Physician-Assisted Suicide Will
Lead to Widespread Suicide Attempts 181 / References 182

8 Social Security Reform   184

What Are the Problems with Our Social Security System? 185 /
What Are the Causes of the Social Security Problems? 185 / Is
This Social Security Problem a Crisis? 187 / Do We Need a
Major Overhaul or Minor Adjustments? 188 / Minor
Adjustment Options 191 / Social Security Payroll Tax Increase
191 / Raising (or Removing) Income Cap Subject to Social
Security Tax 192 / Reducing Social Security Benefits 193 /
Means-Tested Benefit Cuts 194 / Reduce Cost-of-Living
Adjustments (COLA) 195 / Increase of Retirement Age 196 /
Use of the Federal Budget Surplus 197 / Prevention of Social
Security Surplus Diversion 197 / Privatizing Social Security as a
Major Reform Option 198 / Full versus Partial Privatization
199 / Substitutive versus Supplementary Personal Accounts
200 / Mandatory versus Voluntary Personal Retirement

Accounts   201   /   Centralized versus Decentralized Management
of Personal Accounts   202   /   Privatization of Social Security: Is It
a Good Idea or a Bad Idea?   203   /   Many Other Countries Have
Successfully Privatized Their Pension Systems. Why Can't We?
203   /   Privatization Provides Greater Control over Our
Retirement Plans   204   /   With Privatization, We Can Get Higher
Rates of Return on Our Investment   206   /   Administrative Costs
Are Too High under a Privatized System   207   /   Private
Management of Retirement Funds Is Too Risky   209   /   Social
Security Is More Than Just Retirement Savings: It Is a Social
Insurance Program   210   /   Privatization Will Undermine the
Redistributive Function of Social Security   212   /   The Costs of
Changing to a Privatized System (Transition Costs) Are Too High
214   /   Privatization Would Be Good for the Economy   216   /
Privatization Will Prevent Government Diversion of Social Security
Surpluses   217   /   Privatization Would Hurt Women   218   /
Privatization Would Hurt Low-Income People   220   /
Privatization Would Encourage People to Work Longer   221   /
Centralized Investment of Social Security Trust Funds   221   /
Centralized Investment Would Bring Higher Rates of Return Than
Treasury Securities, with Lower Risks Than Private Accounts
222   /   Centralized Investment Is Dangerous to the Economy
224   /   Centralized Investment Will Be Affected By Political
Influence   225   /   References   226

9   School Voucher Programs   230

Types of School Choice Programs   231   /   Existing School Choice
Programs   231   /   Our Public Education System Has Failed; We
Need a Major Reform   232   /   School Vouchers Give Parents of
All Income Levels Freedom of Choice   234   /   Vouchers Increase
Parental Involvement in Children's Education   235   /   Vouchers
Foster Competition and Accountability   237   /   Competition Can
Be Created within the Public School System   240   /   Vouchers
Violate the First Amendment Requirement for the Separation of
Church and State   241   /   Private Schools Are Better Than Public
Schools   243   /   Government Vouchers Will Entail Government
Regulations   244   /   Vouchers Will Intensify the Existing
Inequalities and Segregation among Schools   247   /   Vouchers
Would Cost Too Much   250   /   It Is Better to Improve Public
Schools Than to Support Private Schools with Vouchers   251   /
The School Effect Is Limited   254   /   Private Schools Cannot
Accommodate All the Voucher Students   255   /   Voucher
Programs Will Strengthen the Inner-City Community   257   /
Means-Tested Vouchers   258   /   Vouchers Must Be Means-
Tested   258   /   Means-Tested Vouchers Have Been Successful
260   /   References   261

10 **Welfare Reform**   **266**

Welfare Discourages Work and Creates Dependency   268   /
Welfare Pays Too Much   269   /   Welfare Costs Too Much
Taxpayers' Money   270   /   Welfare Mothers Should Work
271   /   Welfare Encourages Illegitimate Births   272   /   Welfare
Destroys Family Values   273   /   Poverty and Economic Injustice
Should Be Blamed, Not Welfare   275   /   Reform Costs More
Than the Welfare Benefits   276   /   We Must End Welfare
Benefits to All Able-Bodied Adults   278   /   Welfare Reform Will
Increase Poverty   279   /   Innocent Children Will Suffer under
Welfare Reform   279   /   Welfare Reform Efforts Have Been
Successful   281   /   Private Charity Welfare versus Government
Welfare   282   /   Work Requirements (Workfare) in Exchange for
Welfare Benefits   284   /   Welfare-to-Work Partnership Program
285   /   Time Limits on Welfare Benefits   286   /   Family (Child)
Cap   288   /   References   289

Index   **291**

PREFACE

We hear about anti-abortionists' bombing of abortion clinics and murdering of abortion doctors. Yet, the majority of Americans support women's right to terminate pregnancies. Whose right is more important—the unborn fetuses' right to life or women's right to have control over their bodies and their lives? When does a fetus become a person with the right to life? Under what circumstances and up to what stage of pregnancy should abortion be allowed, if allowed at all?

After thirty years of implementation, voters in California (in 1996) and Washington (in 1999) decided to end the affirmative action policy in admissions to higher educational institutions. In 1996, the U.S. Court of Appeals sided with the earlier Texas state court ruling that race can no longer be used as an admission factor. Numerous lawsuits filed against colleges and universities challenge the racial preference in admissions. Is this the beginning of the end of affirmative action in the United States? What are the goals of affirmative action, and have we achieved those goals? Is it time to end affirmative action, or do minorities still need it? Is affirmative action the right way to redress the past discrimination and injustice minorities have suffered?

As of 1999, there are 3,517 death row inmates in thirty-eight states that permit capital punishment. Each year, these states execute over fifty inmates, and the number is growing. At the same time, we hear about innocent people, wrongfully convicted of crimes that they did not commit, being released from death row. Between 1973 and 1993 at least forty-eight people on death row were released after they were found to be innocent. Illinois has exonerated almost as many men (nine) on death row as it has executed (eleven). Nevertheless, the majority of Americans support the death penalty. Is the death penalty the right way to deal with capital criminals despite the possibility that innocent people can be executed and the claims that it applies unfairly against minorities and the poor? Is the death penalty effective in deterring capital crimes?

Even after the deadliest school shooting incident in Littleton, Colorado, in April 1999, where twelve students and a teacher were killed, Congress is reluctant to pass stricter gun control laws. Why do some Americans feel so strongly about the right to own firearms despite the high rates of gun-related violence, crime, accidents, and suicides? Are guns an effective means of self-defense? Would controlling guns reduce the problems of gun violence in our society?

We spend far more on health care than do other industrialized societies, and we have the highest-quality medical technology in the world. Ironically, however, we also have the highest number of people who are uninsured or underinsured among industrialized societies. Our health care costs are too high, health care administrative processes are too complex and wasteful, and our health care is not distributed equally to everyone who needs it. What are the causes of the high and rising health care costs in the United States? Does high-quality care justify the high cost of care? Is managed care a good option? What about National Health Insurance (single-payer plan) as Canada has, or National Health Service (socialized medicine) that the British have? Could mandated employer-based insurance be a viable option?

Since 1997, when Scottish scientist Ian Wilmut and his colleagues cloned a sheep named Dolly from a single adult cell, the possibility of human cloning has become closer to reality. What is wrong with cloning humans? Wouldn't human clones be like time-delayed identical twins? The techniques used in cloning can be very helpful in many areas of medicine and biotechnology. However, if those techniques are misused or abused, they could bring about serious ethical and social problems. Should we ban human cloning to prevent abuses despite the potential benefits?

Should we allow terminally ill but mentally competent patients to end their lives with the help of doctors? In 1994, Oregon voters approved legalization of physician-assisted suicide; in 1997, the Supreme Court dismissed the lawsuit that had kept the law tied up in federal court since 1994. During the first year under the nation's only assisted-suicide law, in 1998, fifteen terminally ill patients ended their lives with the help of their doctors. Refusing unwanted medical treatments to hasten one's death is considered legal; why not requesting doctors' assistance to hasten death? Why must terminally ill patients suffer the agonizing pain during the last days of their lives against their will? The Netherlands has successfully allowed physician-assisted suicide for more than twenty years; why can't we? What are the potential drawbacks of allowing physician-assisted suicide?

We pay more Social Security taxes than ever before in history. Nevertheless, according to the Social Security trustees' estimate, the Trust Funds will run out of money in 2034, and the majority of baby boomers will not be able to receive what they contributed to the system when they retire, unless the tax rate is increased substantially. What are the causes of Social Security's shortfall despite the heavy taxes? We cannot continue to raise taxes when they are already high enough—12.4 percent. Social Security taxes are a heavier burden than income taxes for about 75 percent of the taxpayers. Should we continue to raise taxes? Or, should we change the current pay-as-you-go system of Social Security into a funded system with private savings as many other countries have already done?

Our public schools spend twice as much money to educate children as private schools do, yet the academic performance of the public school students has not improved for over three decades. In fact, the outcome of the public education in many large inner-city areas has deteriorated as indicated by high dropout rates, falling test scores, deplorable levels of course failure and retention in grades, low levels of graduation and basic skills achievement. These inner-city public schools are not only failing in their educational mission but are increasingly becoming breeding grounds for a host of social problems, including crime, drug abuse, gang activities, pregnancy, and violence. Could private school voucher programs be an answer to these problems? Could vouchers foster market-type competition among private and public schools, providing incentives for better performance and improved academic achievement? Florida became the first state to provide statewide vouchers to allow students to attend private and parochial schools at the taxpayers' expense. Should other states follow this path?

Welfare spending in the United States increased more than eight times since it started in 1965. Nevertheless, the number of people living in poverty has increased, and their economic situation is worse than before. The number of out-of-wedlock births and single mothers on welfare has increased, and their duration on welfare is getting longer. Does welfare discourage work, create dependency, and encourage illegitimate births? Or, is it the changes in the economic structure that are to be blamed for the increased poverty and welfare dependency? Is welfare the right way to help the poor? How can we encourage welfare-dependent people to become self-sufficient without hurting their innocent children? How effective has the latest welfare reform been since it started in 1996?

These are some of the policy issues of our time that affect our lives or concern our moral grounds one way or the other. As citizens and as voters, we need to be better informed about these issues. Understanding both supporting and opposing views of the arguments always helps us make sound and fair judgments. It is my modest wish that readers will find this book helpful in making such judgments.

Acknowledgments

I would like to thank my daughter, Emilie Kim, for undertaking the laborious task of proofreading and editing the whole manuscript; my friend Marilyn Fischer for her editorial help and valuable comments; and my husband, B. Justin Kim, for his loving support. Thanks also go to the following people, who reviewed the manuscript: Jon Johnston, Pepperdine University; William Patterson, Clemson University; and Adam Shapiro, University of North Florida. I also thank Allyn and Bacon's editor-in-chief, Karen Hanson, for recognizing the potential of this book; production coordinator, Laurel Ibey; copyeditor, Kathy Deselle; and editorial assistants, Susan Hutchinson and Heather Ahlstrom, for their wonderful work and cooperation.

S.C.K.

CHAPTER

1 Abortion

From the late nineteenth century until the 1960s, virtually every state had laws prohibiting abortion unless the procedure was absolutely necessary to save a woman's life. Women who had money traveled abroad to obtain safe abortions in countries where the procedure was legal. Women who could not afford to leave the country ventured into back alleys for clandestine illegal abortions. Women too poor or afraid to seek any assistance resorted to self-induced abortions, and many paid with their lives. As early as the 1940s, physicians who had experience treating the victims of illegal and self-induced abortions began to see the issue as a public health problem. Lawyers, physicians, and activists lobbied state legislatures to adopt abortion law reform. Throughout the first half of the twentieth century, abortion laws became more liberal. In 1960, the American Medical Association observed that laws against abortion were unenforceable. In 1971, the American Bar Association officially supported women's right to choose abortion up to the twentieth week of pregnancy. In 1970, Alaska, Hawaii, New York, and Washington legalized abortions for any reason up to a legally determined time in the pregnancy. New York, which passed the most liberal law of the four, permitted abortion for any reason up to twenty-four weeks (after that only to save the mother's life) (Wilder 1998, 77; Dwyer and Feinberg 1997, 204; Solinger 1998, xi–xii; Siegel et al. 1986, 5–6).

On January 22, 1973, the Supreme Court made a landmark abortion decision. In *Roe v. Wade* and *Doe v. Bolton*, the Court, in two 7–2 decisions, ruled that the abortion laws that prohibited abortion except to save the life of the mother violated the "due process" clause of the Fourteenth Amendment, which protects the right to privacy against state action, including a woman's right to terminate her pregnancy. The Court decided that during approximately the first three months of pregnancy (first trimester), the decision to abort must be left up to the woman and her physician; during the second trimester, the state may regulate abortion procedures in ways that are reasonably regulated to maternal health; during the final trimester, the state may regulate and even forbid abortion except when necessary in the judgment of physicians to preserve the life or health of the mother (Siegel et al. 1986, 7). The central holding in *Roe* was that the state may not unduly interfere with the right of a woman to choose an

1

abortion before the fetus becomes viable (able to survive outside of mother's womb), yet has an interest in protecting the life of the unborn fetus after viability (Dwyer and Feinberg 1997, 208). Many people consider this time-based restriction an ideal compromise that could protect older fetuses and still safeguard the rights of the vast majority of women seeking abortions (Cozic and Petrikin 1995). The immediate effect of the *Roe* decision was to overturn forty-six of the fifty states' laws governing abortion. As a result, the number of abortions increased rapidly; almost one million abortions were performed annually until 1976, an estimated 300,000 of those with the support of federal funding (Siegel et al. 1986, 23; Dwyer and Feinberg 1997, 205).

In September 1976, Congress, pressured by the anti-abortion forces, decided that federal funds shall not be used to perform abortions except when the life of the mother would be endangered if the fetus were carried to term. The passage of this Hyde Amendment and the increasing stringency of its requirements have led to a drastic decline in the number of abortions paid for by the federal government through the Medicaid program. In 1980, the Supreme Court put an end to federally funded abortions, and this decision was followed by campaigns in many states to prohibit state funding of abortions. As of 1996, nine states refuse to use Medicaid funds to pay for abortions except when the woman's life is endangered; twenty-two states fund abortion only in cases of rape, incest, or when the woman's life is in danger. Seventeen states and the District of Columbia fund abortion in almost all circumstances (Costa 1996, 107; Siegel et al. 1986, 28).

Since the *Roe* decision, pro-life forces began to organize against liberal abortion laws. Throughout the 1980s, their vigorous lobbying efforts restricted the use of public funds to support abortion services as well as to limit access to abortions. In the 1989 *Webster v. Reproductive Health Services* case, the Supreme Court upheld a Missouri statute stating "human life begins at conception" and placed restrictions on access to abortion; the Court came within one vote short of overturning *Roe v. Wade* (Solinger 1998, xiv). The *Webster* decision, whether it was explicitly intended as such by the Court, was widely interpreted as a sign that states could permissibly legislate a variety of restrictions on abortion, and many states reacted this way. From 1989 until 1992, more than 700 anti-abortion bills were introduced in state legislatures across the country (Dwyer and Feinberg 1997, 208; Solinger 1998, xiii). Louisiana declared all abortions illegal except when the life of the woman is in danger or in case of rape or incest (Dwyer and Feinberg 1997, 208). Thirty-one states have laws that require a woman to give an "informed consent" before having an abortion. In many of the states, the woman must receive a lecture and state-prepared materials on fetal development, parental care, and adoption (Costa 1996, 106). As of 1998, thirty-seven states have laws on the books that require parental notification or consent before a minor can obtain an abortion; these laws are enforced in twenty-nine states (Kolbert and Miller 1998, 104; Whitman 1998). Three states have gag rules that prohibit health care providers who are employed by the state or by entities receiving state funding from counseling women about abortion or referring them to abortion services (Costa 1996, 105; Dwyer and Feinberg 1997, 207).

In 1992 the Supreme Court, in the case of *Planned Parenthood v. Casey*, upheld the *Roe v. Wade*'s ruling that a state could not forbid a woman to have an abortion prior to fetal viability. However, the Court ruled in favor of a right of states to attempt to dissuade a woman from abortion at any time during pregnancy, so long as they did not impose an "undue burden" on the right to an abortion. The Court allowed states to require informed consent and a mandatory twenty-four-hour waiting period for a woman seeking an abortion, and also noted that the stage at which the fetus can be considered viable must be changed. Medical science has advanced the ability of the fetus to survive outside the womb from about twenty-eight weeks at the time of the *Roe* decision to twenty-three or -four weeks, with possible further progress to come.

The anti-abortion movement has gained increasing support, and its activities have been sometimes violent. Abortion clinics have continued to be the site of pro-life demonstrations and the target of attacks. In the early 1990s, a number of abortion doctors and clinic employees were killed or wounded, and clinics were bombed.

Religious Views on Abortion

The Roman Catholic Church maintains a strong anti-abortion position. Pope Paul VI in 1968 declared abortion a "supreme dishonor to the Creator" and claimed that "from the moment of its conception life must be guarded with the greatest care, while abortion and infanticide are unspeakable crimes." The Eastern Orthodox Church, despite its schism with the Roman Church, maintains the same anti-abortion position (Siegel et al. 1986, 3).

While the Roman Catholic Church and evangelical Protestants have been highly visible in opposing abortion, scores of religious groups are fervent defenders of abortion rights. Some thirty-five Christian and Jewish organizations, for example, are members of the Religious Coalition for Abortion Rights, a grass-roots lobbying group formed in the 1970s to counter Catholic and evangelical anti-abortion efforts. More and more, churches are finding their adherents divided over the issue of abortion. The Presbyterian Church, the United Methodist Church, and other mainline denominations that stand officially in favor of abortion rights face a growing tide of dissent within their ranks. Among those officially opposed to abortion, such as Catholic, Southern Baptist, and Mormon churches, leaders are hearing increasing arguments among members who are uncomfortable with rigid anti-abortionism (Sheler 1992).

Public Opinion about Abortion

The data compiled from various polls clearly indicate that the majority of Americans do not want to ban abortion. In most polls, about six in ten Americans oppose a constitutional amendment to outlaw abortion. Gallup Polls in 1995 and 1996 found that between 48 and 56 percent considered themselves pro-choice and 33 and 40 percent considered themselves pro-life. In a 1996 Louis Harris and Associates survey, 49 percent said they tended to support pro-choice groups more, and 38 percent said they tended to support pro-life groups more (Ladd and Bowman 1997, 7).

At the same time, surveys suggest that most Americans do not want abortion to be legal in all cases. The majority want abortion to be legal only under certain circumstances (Ladd and Bowman 1997, 10). According to a Gallup survey, 73 percent of Americans support prohibition on abortion after the first trimester of pregnancy. Even among those who strongly identified themselves as pro-choice, 46 percent agreed that abortion should be limited to the first trimester (Helmer et al. 1993).

In both National Opinion Research Center and Gallup surveys, the majority of Americans support legal abortion when the woman's own health is seriously endangered by the pregnancy. Around eight in ten consistently support abortion if there is a strong chance of a serious defect in the baby. Roughly eight in ten support abortion if the pregnancy is the result of rape. However, the public is deeply divided about legal abortion simply as a form of birth control (e.g., inconvenience, financial burden, broken relationship). Nearly three-quarters support laws requiring a woman who is seeking an abortion to wait twenty-four hours before having the procedure done. Seven in ten support spousal notification and parental consent when minors are seeking an abortion. Large majorities support laws requiring doctors to inform patients about alternatives to abortion (Ladd and Bowman 1997, 8–9).

Extent of Abortion in the United States

Roughly 1.4 million women have abortions each year. The rate of abortions increased from 17 abortions per 1,000 women aged 15 to 44 in 1974 to 25 per 1,000 in 1980. From 1980 through 1990, the number of abortions remained relatively stable at 23–24 per 1,000, with year-to-year fluctuations of 5 percent or less. Since 1990, the number has decreased by 15 percent. Among women aged 15 to 44, there were 20 abortions per 1,000 women in 1997, the lowest rate since 1975: The abortion ratio was 305 legally induced abortions per 1,000 live births (Costa 1996; Waldman et al. 1998; Cooper 1997; CDC 1998). According to Lisa Koonin, chief of surveillance in the Centers for Disease Control's Division of Reproductive Health, possible reasons for the decline include reduced access to abortion services, attitudinal changes concerning the decision to have an abortion, and an overall decline in birthrates caused by the reduction in the proportion of women of reproductive age (Cooper 1997; Whitman 1998). According to the Guttmacher Institute's report, about half of the nation's pregnancies are unintended, and 43 percent of American women will have at least one abortion before turning 45 (Guttmacher Institute in Whitman 1998).

Most abortions (89 percent) are performed within the first twelve weeks of pregnancy; at least half are performed within the first eight weeks. Approximately 6 percent are performed between thirteen and fifteen weeks and 4 percent between sixteen and twenty weeks. Around 1 percent of abortions are performed after twenty weeks (Costa 1996, 147). Eighty-two percent of the women who had an abortion were unmarried or separated, and 44 percent have had at least one previous abortion (Waldman et al. 1998).

According to a survey of women who had an abortion in 1987, 76 percent said they were concerned about how having a baby could change their lives (e.g., having a baby would interfere with work, school, or other responsibilities, and not being able to afford a child); 51 percent had problems with a relationship or wanted to avoid single parenthood. Thirteen percent cited health of the fetus; 7 percent the health of the mother; 1 percent rape or incest (Waldman et al. 1998).

Pro-abortion (pro-choice) and anti-abortion (pro-life) arguments are summarized in the following sections.

Women Have the Right to Choose Abortion

Pro-Choice

The Constitution gives women a fundamental right to terminate their pregnancy. Our law affords constitutional protection to personal decisions relating to marriage, procreation, contraception, family relationships, child rearing, and education. We must recognize the rights of women, married or single, to be free from unwarranted governmental intrusion into matters so fundamentally affecting a person as the decision whether to bear or beget a child (O'Connor et al. 1992).

The choice of abortion is an exercise of liberty, autonomy, and the right to bodily integrity. Autonomy consists of the ability to control one's life, the right to make decisions about the most intimate matters of one's life without undue interference. Women have a right to bodily integrity, that is, a right to determine what happens in and to their bodies. A woman's bodily integrity is violated if she is forced to continue with an unwanted pregnancy (Wenz 1992, 47; Brody 1997; Fried and Ross 1995).

By restricting the right to terminate pregnancies, the state forces women to suffer the pains of childbirth, and in most instances, provide years of maternal care (Justice Blackmun in Hittinger 1995). The pregnant woman's suffering is too intimate and personal for the state to interfere and impose other people's moral convictions upon her (O'Connor et al. 1992). Our constitution protects rights of privacy. A woman's right to terminate her pregnancy is one of these rights of privacy (Justice Blackmun in Wenz 1992, 17; Savoy 1995; Sumner 1981; Dwyer and Feinberg 1997, 203).

Pro-Life

People do not have the right to do anything that may be necessary for them to retain control over the uses of their bodies. For instance, it is wrong for anyone to kill another human being (Brody 1997). The right to bodily integrity should not be confused with a right to do whatever one wishes with one's body (Dwyer 1997, 8). Women may have a right to determine what happens in and to their bodies but not when it involves killing of another human being. In abortion, the woman is not only making a decision about her own body but also about the life of another. What entitles her to make such a decision? Is the right to bodily integrity stronger than the right to life? How is it that the word "liberty" must be thought to include the right to destroy human fetuses? (Scalia 1995; Dwyer 1997, 8). There are many forms of conduct that are equally "personal, intimate, and private" as abortion, such as homosexual sodomy, polygamy, adult incest, and suicide. All of these are equally intimate and deeply personal decisions involving personal autonomy and bodily integrity, yet they are not entitled to constitutional protection, and have long been criminalized in American society. Why should abortion be an exception? (Scalia 1995).

The Fetus Has the Right to Life

Pro-Life

The fetus is a person with a right to life; a woman's right to autonomy does not outweigh the fetus's right to life. A person's right to life is stronger and more stringent than the mother's right to decide what happens in and to her body. The fetus is already on the path to human life; it has an interest in developing its capacities. The test of a civilized society is how it treats the most vulnerable group of people, such as the old and sick, the young and ignorant, the poor and disabled, the homeless and despised, and the dispossessed and imprisoned. Of all, the unborn child is the most vulnerable. Abortion is a particularly heinous crime because it kills the most vulnerable and innocent human being who has yet to be born (Paul II 1997; Dwyer 1997).

Pro-Choice

A fetus develops in, and only in, the body of an individual woman. At least in the early stages of its development, a fetus is a being whose existence and welfare are biologically and morally inseparable from the woman in whose body it develops. The moral standing of a fetus depends on its relationship with the woman who bears it and who acts as its moral guardian. In considering whether abortion is ever justifiable, therefore, we must examine the rights and responsibilities of the pregnant woman, not the fetus (Mackenzie 1997; Dwyer 1997, 2).

Having a right to life does not guarantee having a right to use another person's body, even if one needs it for his life. No one has a right to use another person's body as a life-support system without the person's consent. The only way one can have the right to use another person's body is by having been invited to use it by that person. The unborn person is given a right to its mother's body only if her pregnancy resulted from a voluntary act, undertaken in full knowledge of the chance that a pregnancy might result from it. Abortion is like refusing to allow one's body to be used as a life-support system. One may be morally obligated to help others in need but is not legally obligated to sacrifice herself (Thompson 1971; Savoy 1995; Gert 1995).

In abortion decisions, therefore, women's right to bodily autonomy must always prevail over any rights that may be claimed on behalf of the fetus. Fetal rights are weaker and more easily annulled than the rights of full-fledged people. The overall physical and social well-being of women must take priority over any subordinate processes, such as reproduction. Freedom and autonomy of living women always outweigh the rights of the unborn fetus (Thompson 1971; Kaplan 1998, 65; Warren in Mackenzie 1997, 176; Jaggar 1998, 344).

Abortion Violates the Sanctity of Human Life

Pro-Life

Human life has an intrinsic and innate value. Human life is sacred just in itself, and the sacred nature of a human life begins when its biological life begins, even before it has movement, sensation, interests, or rights of its own. Human life is sacred and inviolable; once a human life has begun, it is very important that it flourish and not be wasted. Abortion unjustly violates the rights and interests of the fetus; it fails to respect the sanctity of human life (Dworkin 1997).

The unborn is, from the moment of fertilization, a potential person. An early fetus may not look like a human, but it has all the potential to become a unique human being with full moral status. Potential people are still invaluable resources that are not to be squandered. Fetuses have a valuable future, a future like that of a normal person, a future like ours. This reason is sufficient enough to make the killing of any creature that has this potential property morally wrong. The state has an important and legitimate interest in protecting the potentiality of human life (Scalia 1997; Marquis 1989).

Pro-Choice

Nobody disagrees with the fact that human life is sacred and has an intrinsic value. The fetus, however, is not a person from the moment of conception; early fetuses do not have a life of their own. The early fetus is only a bit of tissue that is physically inseparable and indistinguishable from the woman's body. Embryos at the eighth week are only about three-quarters of an inch long and weigh three-hundredths of an ounce (Costa 1996, 182). An early fetus is no more a human than an acorn is an oak tree (Thompson 1971; Wenz 1992).

Whether abortion is against the interest of a fetus must depend on whether the fetus itself has interests at the time the abortion is performed, not whether interests will develop if no abortion takes place. The rights of any actual person invariably outweigh those of any potential person, whenever the two conflict. A living woman's right to liberty, health, happiness, and freedom outweighs whatever right to life even a hundred potential people may have by virtue of potential personhood (Warren 1997).

Abortion May Be Immoral, But Should Not Be Illegal

Pro-Choice

Even if it cannot be morally justified, abortion must be an option legally available to all women. Some people may find abortion offensive to their basic principles of morality, but that cannot control our policy decision about abortion. Society's obligation is to define the liberty of all, not to mandate one's moral code (O'Connor et al. 1992). The choice to abort a fetus or not is a moral decision that should belong only to the mother. Because it is the woman's body that carries the fetus and upon which the fetus depends, she has certain rights to abort the fetus that no one else may have. A pregnant woman may make a morally wrong decision concerning abortion, but the fact that she knows her own desires, capacities, and circumstances better than anyone else means she is more likely than anyone else to make the right decision (Jaggar 1998, 344; Dworkin 1993).

Abortion for an unwanted pregnancy may be a self-centered, callous, and immoral decision. However, no one is required to make large sacrifices to sustain the life of another who has no right to demand them. There is no law that requires a person to be a Good Samaritan, or even a minimally decent Samaritan (Thompson 1971). One may be morally obligated to help others in need but is not legally obligated to sacrifice oneself (Savoy 1995). Laws cannot function simply to enforce morality (Jaggar 1998, 343). Nobody knows for certain when life begins. People should be allowed to follow their own moral convictions and religious values in the abortion issue.

Pro-Life

The problem of abortion is as much a legal and public policy issue as it is a moral issue. What one thinks about the moral permissibility of abortion will always affect how one thinks about what the state should do by way of regulating abortion (Dwyer and Feinberg 1997, 203). There is a clear distinction between our duty to save one's life (which is a moral issue) when we do not have to, and our duty not to take it (a legal issue). Abortion is taking a life away from a person, and, therefore, it is a legal issue. The mother, in order to regain control over her body, has no right to abort the fetus from the point at which it becomes a human being (Brody 1997).

Abortion is a legal and policy issue as well as a moral issue because it involves a third party who must perform it. No one can force doctors or anyone else to perform abortion against their moral conscience when they believe it kills fetuses.

An Unwanted Pregnancy Justifies an Abortion

Pro-Choice

No one is for abortion. Everyone is much more for family planning. Once an unwanted pregnancy occurs, however, there should be an alternative, including safe and legal abortion (Weddington in Siegel et al. 1986, 64). There is no fail-safe method of contraception. Unplanned pregnancies can occur to any woman. According to the Alan Guttmacher Institute, a leading abortion research institute, 43 percent of unintended pregnancies occur in women using birth control (Savoy 1995). No one should be morally responsible for the consequences of an action if she has taken reasonable precautions against those consequences occurring. Abortion must therefore always remain available, not only as a backup method of birth control but also so that women can change their minds about giving birth if their life circumstances unexpectedly change in the course of their pregnancies (Jaggar 1998, 353).

According to family planning advocates, most women do not use abortion as a birth control method. Typically, a woman has thirty or more fertile years, which translates to about 400 chances to get pregnant during her lifetime. Therefore, it should not be considered unusual for a woman to make a mistake or experience birth control failure at least once during those years (Roleff 1997, 102).

The birth of a child can be a source of great joy to a woman who wanted a child. However, it can be a nightmare for a woman who for whatever reason does not want to have a child at a particular time or under particular circumstances. The effects of an unwanted pregnancy on the mother and other family members can be so overwhelming in some cases; it could seriously strain family resources or ruin one's career. In such cases, forcing a woman to continue a pregnancy is extremely cruel and sadistic. It will affect her entire life, and no woman's life should be twisted or ruined in such a way simply due to failed birth control. No child should be born unwanted. No woman should be forced to choose between compulsory motherhood and a back-alley abortion (Dworkin 1993; Savoy 1995; Jaggar 1998; ACLU 1992; Sumner 1981).

Pro-Life

Many women who opted abortion for their unwanted pregnancy but could not obtain abortion later report how glad they were that they did not have an abortion, and how much they love and enjoy the child they gave birth to, despite the difficulties they had to endure. Many others who chose to terminate their unwanted pregnancy later regretted that they had done so and wished that they had given birth to the child instead (Waldman et al. 1998). The birth of a child, under any circumstances, is a gift from God, and should be taken as a priority in everyone's life. Even if one cannot raise the child she gives birth to, there are many others who would be eager to adopt and raise the child. Abortion as a form of birth control cannot be justified.

Legalized abortion as a form of birth control would encourage people to engage in irresponsible sexual behavior and be disrespectful of the sanctity of human lives. The government should not support a policy that encourages people to become irresponsible for their behavior and disrespectful of human lives.

Abortion Is Sometimes a More Responsible Choice Than Childbirth

Pro-Choice

Birth is not always the right choice. In fact, under some conditions, choosing to give birth may be socially dysfunctional and morally irresponsible. When it comes to abortion, the decision is not just whether a woman wants to carry out the pregnancy, but whether a woman is willing and prepared to assume responsibility of being a parent for a lifetime—the financial, emotional, social, and moral responsibilities of a parent. For a variety of reasons, a woman might be unable to meet these obligations. Perhaps she is too young, too old, too poor, or perhaps she is in an abusive relationship and fears for her safety. Choosing an abortion in such conditions might well be the responsible course of action for the woman concerned (Mackenzie 1997; Wolf-Devine 1989; Ross 1982; Muller 1995).

Sometimes, it is a more responsible decision for a woman to choose abortion than to have an unwanted, unloved, and uncared-for child. It is not the decision to abort but the decision to have a child that must be treated with sufficient gravity in our society (Muller 1995). A growing consensus holds that unsocialized and mistreated children are at the heart of our social deterioration. They are more likely to be involved in violent and criminal activities and they lack the discipline needed to learn in school and to function in the workplace (Muller 1995). Studies have found that children of unwed teenage mothers are more likely to be abused, neglected, and abandoned (King 1996, 127), and they are more likely to drop out of school, use drugs, and become juvenile offenders, unemployed, and convicted of serious crimes (Zuckerman 1994). It is more important to minimize the birth of children to women who are unprepared to provide the familial structure needed for children to become stable and responsible adults than to minimize abortion (Muller 1995).

A typical child in a middle-income family requires a twenty-two-year investment of over $1.45 million. The child's unit cost rises to $2.78 million for the top-third income bracket and drops to $761,871 for the bottom-third income bracket (Longman 1998). Considering the high and rising cost of raising a child in modern societies, a decision to have a child must follow a serious commitment to support the child financially and emotionally. Having a child without such commitment and preparation is a morally irresponsible decision.

Pro-Life

There are only two possible ways for women to get pregnant. Either they are raped, in which case they have no causal responsibility for the existence of the fetus, although they have a moral responsibility toward it, or they are not raped, in which case they are held to be fully responsible, in both a causal and moral sense (Mackenzie 1997, 179). By engaging in sexual intercourse, a woman knowingly risks becoming pregnant, and that in choosing to take this risk, she must be responsible for the life she creates (Gert 1995). People need to take responsibility for their sexual actions. People who are old enough to have sex voluntarily know that conception is possible when they have sex. A responsible person would think twice about having unprotected sex. If a human life is created as a result of unprotected sex, the person should take responsibility of either raising the child or giving it up for adoption. A human life is too sacred to be destroyed simply because one made a mistake or because one was careless. Abortion is refusing to take that moral responsibility and, therefore, is always an irresponsible behavior.

Adoption Is a Better Option Than Abortion

Pro-Life

There is no reason for unwanted pregnancies to be terminated when there are many people who are able and eager to adopt children and provide a good home for them. Many people wait years for the opportunity to adopt a child. Adoption not only gives infertile couples an opportunity to raise a child but also gives women considering abortion a way to solve their problem of an unwanted pregnancy while sparing the life of the child. Furthermore, adoption allows couples who are not capable of reproducing to experience the joy of raising a child that they cannot enjoy otherwise. The fact that one cannot provide adequate care and love for her child cannot be a legitimate reason to kill the child when there are many others who are anxious to provide love and care for the child. The needless destruction of a viable infant deprives others of a source of great pleasure and satisfaction (Warren 1997).

Pro-Choice

Giving up a child for adoption for most women is a decision that is even more difficult to make than having an abortion. An embryo or an early fetus is easier to give up than a full-term baby, who is part of you and who looks like you. There are women who are utterly devastated by the thought of a child, a bit of themselves, put up for adoption and never seen or heard of again. They may want not merely that the child be detached from them, but more, that it be destroyed (Thompson 1971). Abortion is a matter of not wanting there to be a future child, so intimately related to oneself, for which one either has to take responsibility or to give up to another (Mackenzie 1997, 190).

No woman should be forced to have babies for infertile couples. Furthermore, if one is not going to keep the child, one should not be forced to go through the pain and inconvenience of pregnancy and birth, as well as the heat from the community and families that scorn an unwed mother.

Indeed there are many infertile couples wanting to adopt babies. However, most couples seeking adoption are white and want white infants with no obvious birth defects. There are an equal number of unwanted or abandoned children waiting to be adopted in foster homes, who are either of minority origin or are simply too old to be adopted (Smolowe 1995). Clearly, adoption cannot be a solution for unwanted pregnancies.

Legal Access to Abortion Is Necessary for Sexual Equality

Pro-Choice

Men and women are situated differently with respect to procreation. While it is possible for men to evade or even remain unaware of the consequences of their actions that result in pregnancy, the same is not true for women. Women cannot escape from becoming responsible for what was after all a joint action. Furthermore, because our society's prevailing gender norms assign women the primary responsibility for the care and well-being of their offspring, the birth of children affect the lives of their mothers far more significantly than it affects the lives of anyone else (Jaggar 1998; Mackenzie 1997).

When women are prohibited from controlling their reproductive lives and required to assume responsibilities of rearing children, they are forced to make sacrifices of their career, sexual freedom, employment, education, and social and recreational activities. Genuine equality between men and women requires that women be able to make and act on their own decisions concerning reproduction, including having access to safe contraception and abortion on demand. A policy that prevents women from obtaining abortion serves to perpetuate women's oppression and is for that reason impermissible (Markowitz 1990; Jaggar 1998).

The ability of women to participate equally in economic and social life has been greatly facilitated by their ability to control their reproductive lives (O'Connor et al. 1992). There is no fail-safe method of contraception. Therefore, the only way, other than abortion, that women could participate equally with men in economic and social life would be to submit to sterilization or to live as secular nuns. Legal access to abortion allows women to have sex for pleasure as men have always done. Life, liberty, and the pursuit of happiness must include the right to sexual happiness as well (Savoy 1995).

Pro-Life

The issue here is not sexual equality but sexual responsibility for both men and women. Whoever wishes to have sexual intercourse, regardless of whether male or female, must take responsibility of his or her action. If pregnancy occurs, even if it is unplanned or unwanted, both men and women must be equally responsible for protecting that life, and giving it the best chance of survival and fulfillment as possible. Legal access to abortion will encourage people to become irresponsible for their sexual activity. Sexual inequality existed in the past not because abortion was illegal but because of the traditional values and economic activities that required a large family. Genuine sexual equality can be achieved not through legalized abortion but through acquiring equal access to education and employment opportunities.

Illegal Abortions Are Dangerous

Pro-Choice

Legal access to abortion is indispensable to women's health. When safe and affordable abortions are unavailable, women often seek to terminate their pregnancies by resorting to ill-equipped practitioners or other methods that threaten their health and even their lives (Jaggar 1998, 349). Historically, women have been terminating unwanted pregnancies for centuries, whether or not it was legal. The decision of whether to have a child is so profound and life-altering that women have risked their lives in order to make it for themselves (Wilder 1998, 73). Experts estimate that 200,000 to 1.3 million illegal abortions were performed in the United States annually from the late 1940s until early 1950s (Solinger 1998, xi). Illegal abortions occurred largely outside of sterile medical settings, such as private homes and the back room of a drug store. About half of the women who sought illegal abortions reported medical complications afterward, including excessive hemorrhaging, infection, and sterility. They also reported that they worried about the possibility of dying, becoming sterile, or getting hurt and arrested (Jaggar 1998, 361). The number of abortion-related deaths has declined dramatically since abortion became legal in 1973. Based on the Centers for Disease Control figures, there was a decline from an average of 364 deaths per year from 1958 to 1962 to eleven in 1981 and eighteen in 1982 (Costa 1996, 152).

Pro-Life

The majority of the pre-*Roe* era abortion-related morbidity was associated with self-induced procedures, not those performed by back-alley practitioners. In fact, during the four years just prior to the *Roe* decision in 1973, Jane, an underground collective of laywomen in Chicago, Illinois, provided more than 11,000 abortions without any major complications. The dangers of back-alley abortions were exaggerated by the pro-choice advocates (Solinger 1998).

While being preoccupied with the issue of easy access to abortion, the pro-choice advocates have ignored the more important issue of preventing abortion. We need to focus on the prevention of abortion by emphasizing sexual and medical education and by making contraceptive options readily available to people including young teenagers. Legalizing abortion should not be the goal, preventing abortion should be the goal.

Government Should Guarantee
Easy Access to Abortion

Pro-Choice

It is hard to say that women have a real choice to abortion if they have no way of reaching an abortion facility or paying for abortion services (Jaggar 1998, 350). In light of two new Supreme Court decisions expanding the scope of constitutionally permissible restrictions, many states have enacted laws that placed increasingly burdensome obstacles in the path of women seeking abortions. Mandatory waiting periods, biased counseling requirements, parental consent laws, and limiting public funding are just a few examples. Compounding the problem, the number of abortion providers continues to decline. Many physicians, under the threat of death and violence, abandoned their abortion practices; hospitals stopped providing abortion; and many medical schools stopped teaching the procedure (Wilder 1998, 74). In 1991, only 13 percent of the nation's obstetrics and gynecology residency programs required training in first-trimester abortion, and only 7 percent in second-trimester training. Access to abortion has been limited to such an extent that there are no abortion providers in 84 percent of the counties in the nation, forcing many women to travel hundreds of miles to obtain their medical care. In addition, abortion providers are being driven out of business by the high cost of protecting their clinics, their staffs, and themselves from violent attacks by abortion foes. The limited access to abortion will result in longer delays for women seeking to terminate their pregnancies. Late abortions involve greater health risks and higher costs than early abortions (Kaplan 1998, 40; NWLC 1994; Wilder 1998; Whitman 1998).

Pro-Life

It is the doctors who voluntarily refuse to perform abortions not because they are afraid of terrorist attacks, but because it is against their moral conscience. Hospitals are unwilling to allow their facilities to be used for abortion and to train their medical staffs for abortion because abortion is immoral. Neither the government nor any woman can force the doctors to perform what they consider murder against their will.

Physicians are, and should always be, trained and socialized to save and preserve lives and not to do any harm or cause death. This is an important professional commitment physicians must adhere to. The state must not break down this barrier and place upon doctors the burden of destroying life, which is a conflict of interest.

Although it is true that 84 percent of counties lacked abortion facilities in 1992, 70 percent of women of child-bearing age lived in counties with facilities in 1992. The other 30 percent were concentrated in rural counties. Stories about long commutes in sparsely populated states like North Dakota have become news media staples, although only about 8 percent of the women who got abortions in 1992 drove more than 100 miles, according to the Guttmacher Institute (Whitman 1998).

Abortion Is Justified in Rape Cases

Pro-Choice

Requiring a woman to bear a child conceived in rape is especially destructive to her self-realization because it frustrates her creative choice not only in sex but also in reproduction as well. The raped woman has already suffered immensely from the act of rape and the physical and psychological after-effects of that act. It would be particularly unjust for her to have to live through an unwanted pregnancy owing to that act of rape. Even if the fetus is at a stage of viability, therefore, the mother has the right to abort it. The fetus has no right to be in that woman's body: The mother has not given the unborn person a right to use her body for food and shelter. It was put there against her will as a result of an act of aggression upon her by the rapist. Its continued presence is an act of aggression against the mother, and therefore, aborting the fetus is a justifiable act (Thompson 1971; Brody 1997; Dworkin 1993).

Pro-Life

However unjust the act of rape, it was not the fetus who committed or commissioned it. The injustice of the act, then, should in no way impinge upon the rights of the fetus, for it is innocent. However unfortunate and unjust that circumstance of rape may be, misfortune and the injustice are not sufficient causes to justify the taking of an innocent human being's life as a means of mitigation. The fetus has not committed the act of aggression against the rape victim; the mere presence of the fetus in the mother, no matter how unfortunate for her, does not constitute an act of aggression by the fetus against the mother (Brody 1997). Why should an innocent fetus be made to forfeit its right to life and pay with its life for the wrongdoing of someone else? The fetuses have a full right to life; the moral standing of a fetus is not dependent on how it came into existence. A fetus is a person regardless of how it came to existence and abortion is murder. The fetus conceived as a result of rape has the equal right to life as other fetuses. Rape does not justify an abortion, at least from the point at which the fetus is a human being (Sloan and Hartz 1992; Dworkin 1997; Brody 1997).

Supporting and opposing views on various laws related to abortion are discussed in the following sections.

Government-Funded Abortion for the Poor

Supporting View

Women's health care needs cannot be met unless their reproductive health care is included. Reproductive health care needs cannot be met unless abortion is included. In order to protect women's health, it is essential to cover the entire continuum, including abortion services, in a national health care plan, including Medicaid cases (NWLC 1994).

Whether abortion ought to be subsidized by government medical insurance is a question of social justice that cannot be answered without investigating the moral basis of compulsory social welfare programs in general. However, once a society has installed such a program, there is no justification for omitting abortion from the list of services covered by it. If abortion should be omitted on the ground that most pregnancies can be easily avoided, then treatment for lung cancer must also be omitted because most cases of lung cancer can be even more easily avoided. No rational legislator would seriously consider denying public funding for the medical treatment of injuries resulting from failure to use seat belts as a means of promoting highway safety or denying smokers treatment for lung cancer as a way of discouraging the use of tobacco (Savoy 1995; Sumner 1981).

Denying public funding for abortion or excluding abortion coverage from national health care discriminates against indigent women. Out-of-wedlock birth and early pregnancy pose serious problems for lower-class women in their effort to achieve self-sufficiency and economic independence. Punishing poor women for bearing children without providing them the same family planning options that middle- and upper-class women have is unjust. White, college-educated women give birth to only 4 percent of all illegitimate children; women with family income of $75,000 or more give birth to only 1 percent. The reason why rich and better-educated women do not have children out of wedlock is not just because they cannot collect welfare benefits for doing so. They have a deep understanding of how an unwanted pregnancy could impinge on their standard of living (Savoy 1995; Mencimer 1994).

Welfare reform is based on the idea that the government should help people become self-sufficient and make better lives for their families. Providing a range of reproductive health alternatives for poor women is one way to help them to be responsible. If we want to end welfare, the smartest step would be to repeal the Hyde Amendment. That move would likely have far greater effects on welfare rolls than the kinds of expensive and ineffective welfare-to-work programs (Mencimer 1994). If abortion were fully funded in every state, the Guttmacher Institute estimates that the net savings for the nation as a whole over a two-year period would total between $435 million and $540 million, four to six times the $95 million to $125 million it would cost to publicly fund abortions for all Medicaid-eligible women who want one (Mencimer 1994).

Objectors to public funding for abortion may argue that making tax money available for such highly controversial purposes forces taxpayers who are morally opposed to abortion to violate their consciences. However, abortion is not the only controversial issue when compared with many other purposes for which tax money is spent, such as support for controversial research programs and military adventures (e.g., human embryo research, genetic engineering, animal experimentation, nuclear and chemical weapons production). The mere fact that some citizens experience intense objections to a certain policy is not a sufficient reason to abstain from the policy. If it were, then every public policy would be vetoed by individuals who happen to feel strongly about something (Jaggar 1998; Carlin 1993).

Opposing View

The fact that women have a legal right to abortion does not mean that the state must fund such procedures. You may have a legal right to drive a motor vehicle, but the state is not obligated to buy you a car (Dwyer 1997, 1). The government must not use tax money for a procedure so many taxpayers find objectionable, if not abhorrent. The government has no right to use people's tax money to pay for something that many people consider to be a crime of murder. Government funding of abortion is offensive to pro-lifers in their essential capacity as citizens. It makes them unwilling partners in a collective crime. Pro-lifers believe that a program of government subsidies and mandated private-sector subsidies for abortion compels them to participate in the violation of a negative precept of morality, and not just any negative precept but a very serious one—"Do not commit unwarranted homicide" (Carlin 1993).

Mandatory Waiting Period

Supporting View

The waiting period before abortion gives the woman and her family members time to reflect on their decision, to explore alternative options, and make sure the decision is the right one for them. Many women who terminated their pregnancy regretted their decision later. Many others who did not terminate their pregnancy later reported how glad they were that they decided to have the child. Having an abortion involves not just terminating a pregnancy, but terminating a life of a human being. It is a decision that should not be taken lightly.

The Supreme Court justices, in 1992, ruled that imposing a mandatory twenty-four-hour waiting period in which a woman may reflect on her decision does not constitute a substantial obstacle to abortion. Requiring a pregnant woman to be informed of the risks of and alternatives to abortion is permitted under the *Roe v. Wade* decision and does not violate a woman's constitutional rights (O'Connor et al. 1992).

Opposing View

Mandatory delay (waiting period) laws have forced many women to substantially delay or even forgo the abortion procedure. A shortage of physicians forces many women to travel long distances to obtain the procedure and makes it necessary for most clinics to schedule abortion procedures only one or two days each week. Therefore, mandatory delays of only twenty-four hours may routinely result in actual delays of ten days to two weeks. While serving no health purpose, these requirements increase the cost of the procedure and force a woman to take extra time off from work, arrange child care, and remain away from home overnight or pay for another round-trip to the clinic (Kolbert and

Miller 1998, 100). The state does not have a right to further its interest in protecting potential life by simply wearing down the ability of the pregnant woman to exercise her constitutional right (Stevens 1992).

The delay requirement is based on the belief that the decision to terminate a pregnancy is presumably wrong. States may not presume that a woman has failed to reflect adequately merely because her conclusion differs from the state's preference. A woman who has, in the privacy of her thoughts and conscience, weighed the options and made her decision cannot be forced to reconsider, simply because the state believes she has come to the wrong conclusion. There is no legitimate reason to require a woman who has already agonized over her decision to leave the clinic or hospital and return again another day (Stevens 1992).

Parental Consent (or Notification) Laws

Supporting View

Parents are legally responsible for their teenagers and therefore have a right to know if their daughter is planning to have an abortion. No other medical procedure can be performed on a teenager without a parent's knowledge and consent, and abortion should not be an exception (Washington 1994). Most schools require parental consent to give children medicine, take them on field trips, or dismiss them early from class. Parental consent is required for activities that involve much less risk than abortion, such as ear piercing and participating in sports. When it comes to abortion, however, even a stranger can take our daughters with no repercussions whatsoever (Rep. Ileana Ros-Lehtinen in Superville 1998). Abortion can be medically risky and can have a psychologically damaging effect on women. When minors are involved, parental rights must override abortion rights and privacy rights.

Opposing View

Parental consent laws are unconstitutional and can be detrimental to the life and well-being of pregnant teenagers. These laws would force teens who fear telling their parents about their pregnancy to delay abortion, seek unsafe, back-alley abortions, or encourage them to travel to a state without mandated parental involvement. Because young girls are especially reluctant to seek treatment for problems related to sex or sexuality, confidentiality is a vital component in encouraging them to seek prompt medical care. Teenagers, more than any other group, tend to deny pregnancy and to delay abortion regardless of whether parental involvement is required. Teens who do not seek parental guidance regarding abortion are often physically and emotionally abused by parents, or even victims of incest. These laws unnecessarily increase their anxiety and lengthen delays. Later abortions involve greater health risks and are more expensive than earlier procedures (Superville 1998; Coburn 1996; Center for Population Options 1995).

No state has a law requiring a young woman who decides to bear a child to inform her parents, nor to receive their consent to continue a pregnancy, although having a child entails a great deal more parental support and involvement than having an abortion (Center for Population Options 1995). If a woman is mature enough to be a mother, she is also mature enough to decide not to be one (Jaggar 1998, 341; Sumner 1981).

Requiring Consent from the Father of the Fetus

Opposing View

There is no justification for restricting a woman's access to abortion by requiring the consent of the father of the fetus (Sumner 1981). Because of the particularity of the woman's situation in pregnancy, in cases of conflict over abortion, ultimately it should be up to the woman to decide whether she will choose abortion. The decision to have a child has more far-reaching implications for women than it does for men. After birth of a child, men may assume parental responsibility. Nevertheless, prior to birth, the decision should be made solely by the pregnant woman (Mackenzie 1997; Jaggar 1998, 346).

In 1992, the Supreme Court, in the case of *Planned Parenthood v. Casey*, invalidated Pennsylvania's requirement that a married woman notify her spouse before obtaining an abortion. Arguing that many women are vulnerable to physical and psychological violence at the hands of their husbands, the Court deemed that this provision imposes an undue burden on married women seeking abortions (Dwyer and Feinberg 1997, 209).

Supporting View

If women are allowed to choose abortion without the consent of the father of the baby, men should have the right to refuse to support the child they did not choose to bring into the world. A man who chooses not to support a child resulting from an unplanned pregnancy, which a woman decides to carry to term, is often indicted as a member of the class of deadbeat dads and remanded with severe prejudice and even criminal charges. The consideration that militates against allowing a man's power over his partner's decision of whether to become a parent, therefore, does not provide a justification for denying a man the power to control his own destiny as a parent and to choose whether he will support the child his partner unilaterally decides to bear (Savoy 1995). If we give women the right to murder a fetus without the consent of the father of the fetus, why can't men abandon children they did not want to have in the first place?

Late-Term Abortions
(Partial Birth Abortions)

Opposing View

Late-term (post-twenty-week) abortions do not remove nonviable tissues but kill babies. Late-term abortions have the same moral status as infanticide, except in the cases in which the mother's life is at risk (Sumner 1981; Shafer 1995). The so-called (by pro-lifers) partial birth abortion (technically called intact dilation and extraction, or D&X) is a procedure so disquieting that even pro-abortion rights Democrat Senator Daniel Patrick Moynihan has described it as "too close to infanticide" (Lavelle 1998). This procedure, used in pregnancies too advanced to be terminated by suction, involves bringing the fetus feet-first into the birth canal, puncturing its skull with a sharp instrument, and sucking out its brain tissue through a catheter. According to the *U.S. News & World Report*'s survey of eighteen clinics, about 7 percent of abortions performed in their clinics were D&X. Another method that is more widely used is dilation and evacuation (D&E), in which the fetus is cut into pieces with serrated forceps before being removed bit by bit from the uterus (Lavelle 1998).

Only 9.4 percent of the late-term abortions at clinics that responded to the *U.S. News* survey were done for medical reasons, either to protect the mother's health (a rare situation) or, more commonly, because of fetal defects such as spina bifida and Down Syndrome. About 90 percent of the post-twenty-week abortions were classified by the clinics as "nonmedical" (Lavelle 1998).

The experience of observing late-term abortions has been so disturbing that many doctors who have seen the procedure have refused to participate in abortions again (Meyer and DeWolf 1995). Furthermore, post-twenty-week procedures are four times more costly, seven times more likely to lead to medical complications, and far more physically and emotionally traumatic to the woman (Lavelle 1998).

Any woman who has become pregnant due to incestuous intercourse or rape will have ready access to an early abortion. If she declines this opportunity and if there is no evidence of genetic abnormality, she may not simply change her mind later (Sumner 1981). There is no reason why women should wait until the third trimester and have their viable fetus killed. This is clearly an inhumane and immoral case of infanticide.

Supporting View

Late-term abortions are rare and, when they do occur, it is frequently because the mother's life is in danger or because the parents have discovered late that their prospective child suffers from a serious birth defect or malformation (Muller 1995). Indeed, the total number of abortions performed after twenty-four weeks is small. Only two clinics in the country even perform third-trimester abortions, and only three or four doctors in the country perform legal, late-term abortions (Alter 1996). Though no one has reliable figures, experts estimate that partial-birth abortion accounts for perhaps 600 of the 1.4 million abortions performed in the United States each year (Gibbs 1996).

Even in normal (nonmedical) cases of pregnancy, late-term abortions must be available in some extreme cases. There are situations in which women find out that they are pregnant late in their pregnancy. It happens more often with very young teens with irregular menstrual periods, women in their late forties who mistakenly thought they had entered menopause, and poor or working women whose delay was caused by problems in arranging the abortion and raising the money. Forcing them to go through pregnancy, childbirth, and parenting is too cruel and inhumane (Lavelle 1998).

When Should the Fetuses Be Given the Right to Life?

When it comes to abortion, the most important issue is defining when the fetuses have rights and interests of their own, equal to those of other members of the community, including the interest in remaining alive. How far into a pregnancy should the line be drawn between when an abortion is justifiable and when it becomes impermissible? There are roughly five different views regarding when a fetus should be given those rights: 1) at conception; 2) at eight weeks; 3) at twelve weeks (first trimester); 4) at twenty-four weeks (second trimester); and 5) at birth.

At Conception

Human life is sacred and inviolable at every moment of existence. From the time the ovum is fertilized, a life is begun that is neither that of the father nor the mother; it is rather the life of a new human being with its own identity (Paul II 1997). By the time the embryo is implanted in a womb, which is approximately fourteen days after its conception, it is an identifiable living organism that already contains all the genetic codes that are unique to that individual person. The fetus has characteristics that no other person has and will never be duplicated. The fetus is already whoever he is going to become and the fetus's subsequent development is simply a process of achieving, a process of becoming the one it already is. Therefore, all the other stages of fetal development, such as quickening, gaining sentience, and brain-wave activity are just improvements of a person that already exists. A fetus, from the moment of its conception, is a full moral person with rights and interests equal in importance to those of any other member of the moral community. The government has a responsibility to protect a fetus from the moment of conception; abortion cannot be justified at any time during pregnancy (Brody 1997, 80; Dworkin 1993).

At Eighth Week

The fetus is not a person from the moment of conception. A newly fertilized ovum or a newly implanted clump of cells is no more a person than an acorn is an oak tree. A woman should be allowed to have an abortion until the point in pregnancy when there is medical evidence of brain activity. The universally accepted medical and legal definition of the end of life is the irreversible cessation of all functions of the brain, as measured by a flat electroencephalogram (EEG). Conversely, the presence of brain-wave activity is a "vital sign" of life. Brain-wave activity is consistently present by the eighth week after conception (Helmer et al. 1993).

Furthermore, eight weeks is designated by scientists as the end of the embryonic period and the beginning of the fetal period. By then, every internal organ and external feature found in an adult human being has been established. The heart, kidneys, liver, stomach, and other organs are functioning, and all external bodily parts are formed (Helmer et al. 1993).

At the End of the First Trimester (Twelfth Week)

No one can pinpoint a precise moment of when the fetus becomes a human being with a right to life. However, it surely is not a human being at the moment of conception and it surely is one by the end of the third month. The fetus becomes a human being with a right to life sometime between the second and twelfth week after conception. Abortions are, therefore, morally impermissible after that point except in abnormal or medical cases (Brody 1997).

The spinal cord makes its first appearance during the third week, and the major divisions between forebrain, mid-brain, and brain-stem are evident by the end of the eighth week. Although one may detect brain-wave activity at the end of the sixth week, the fetal brain does not develop sufficiently to support spontaneous motion until sometime in the third month after conception. While the state may not regulate abortion during the first trimester of pregnancy, it may restrict or even prohibit abortions in the second and third trimester (Brody 1997; Callahan 1970, 373; Dwyer and Feinberg 1997, 203).

At the End of the Second Trimester (Twenty-Fourth Week)

An adequate abortion policy should be a conjunction of a permissive policy for early abortion and a moderate policy for late-term abortions. For that purpose, the upper limit of permissive abortion must be located sometime near the end of the second trimester (Sumner 1981). The most often cited criterion for drawing the line between permissible and impermissible abortions is the viability of the fetus. A fetus is said to be viable if it is able to survive outside its gestational mother's womb. The viability, therefore, means the earliest age at which any fetus has been known to survive outside its gestational mother's womb (Gert 1995). Abortion is morally permissible prior to viability, but it is impermissible after viability. This is the position the Supreme Court maintained in *Roe v. Wade* and *Planned Parenthood of Southeastern Pennsylvania v. Casey.* The Court ruled that the state's interest in protecting fetal life becomes compelling after viability (Dwyer 1997, 6; Helmer et al. 1993).

Another criterion often used in drawing the line between permissible and impermissible abortion is sentience. Sentience is the capacity for feeling, that is, the ability to experience sensations of pleasure and pain. The threshold of sentience falls sometime in the second trimester (Sumner 1981). An adequate neural substrate for experienced pain does not exist until about the seventh month of pregnancy (thirty weeks). The cortical maturation beginning at about thirty weeks is a reasonable landmark for sentience. Since we wish to use extreme caution in respecting and protecting possible sentience, a provisional boundary at about twenty-four weeks should provide safety against reasonable concerns. This time is coincident with the present definition of viability (Grobstein 1988, 55, 130).

At Birth

An organism possesses a serious right to life only if it possesses a certain property. These properties include consciousness, sentience, the presence of self-concept and self-awareness, and developed capacities to reason, to communicate, and to engage in self-motivated activity. Any creature that lacks these traits is not a person and does not have a right to life. Fetuses are not persons because they do not have these traits, and thus they do not have a serious right to life (Warren 1997; Tooley 1972).

Even after birth, an early infant's life is so critically dependent on the care of other existing persons that killing it is not much different from allowing it to die because there is no one else who is willing and able to provide such care. Most human societies, from those at the hunting and gathering stage of economic development to the highly civilized Greeks and Romans, have permitted the practice of infanticide under such unfortunate circumstances. It would be considered a serious lack of understanding to condemn them as morally backward for that reason (Warren 1997).

REFERENCES

Alter, Jonathan. 1996. "When facts get aborted." *Newsweek.* 7 October.
American Civil Liberties Union (ACLU). 1992. "Reproductive freedom—the right to choose: A fundamental liberty." *ACLU Briefing Paper No. 15.*
Brody, Baruch. 1997. "Against the absolute right to abortion." Pp. 88–97 in *The problem of abortion.* 3d ed. Edited by Susan Dwyer and Joel Feinberg. Belmont, Calif.: Wadsworth Publishing.

Callahan, Daniel. 1970. *Abortion: Law, choice, and morality.* New York: Macmillan.

Carlin, David R. 1993. "Paying for abortion." *America.* 20 November.

Center for Population Options, (The). 1995. "Laws should not require parental involvement in abortion decisions." Pp. 105–12 in *The abortion controversy*, edited by Charles P. Cozic and Jonathan Petrikin. San Diego, Calif.: Greenhaven Press.

Coburn, Jennifer. 1996. "Parental consent puts teens in a bind." *San Diego Union-Tribune.* 10 January.

Cooper, Mike. 1997. "U.S. abortion rates lowest since mid-1970s." *Yahoo News.* 5 December.

Costa, Marie. 1996. *Abortion: A reference handbook.* 2d ed. Santa Barbara, Calif.: ABC-CLIO.

Cozic, Charles P., and Jonathan Petrikin, eds. 1995. *The abortion controversy.* San Diego, Calif.: Greenhaven Press.

Dworkin, Ronald. 1997. "Abortion and the sanctity of life." Pp. 127–54 in *The problem of abortion.* 3d ed. Edited by Susan Dwyer and Joel Feinberg. Belmont, Calif.: Wadsworth Publishing.

———. 1993. *Life's dominion.* New York: Alfred A. Knopf.

Dwyer, Susan. 1997. "Understanding the problem of abortion." Pp. 1–20 in *The problem of abortion.* 3d ed. Edited by Susan Dwyer and Joel Feinberg. Belmont, Calif.: Wadsworth Publishing.

———, and Joel Feinberg. 1997. "A short history of abortion in the United States and Canada." Pp. 203–12 in *The problem of abortion.* 3d ed. Edited by Susan Dwyer and Joel Feinberg. Belmont, Calif.: Wadsworth Publishing.

Fried, Marlene G., and Loretta Ross. 1995. "Abortion rights should not be restricted." Pp. 90–94 in *The abortion controversy*, edited by Charles P. Cozic and Jonathan Petrikin. San Diego, Calif.: Greenhaven Press.

Gert, Heather J. 1995. "Viability." *International Journal of Philosophical Studies* 3:133–42.

Gibbs, Nancy. 1996. "Politics and principle." *U.S. News & World Report.* 30 September, 30.

Grobstein, Clifford. 1988. *Science and the unborn.* New York: Basic Books.

Helmer, Steven R., Richard G. Wilkins, and Frank H. Fischer. 1993. "Abortion: A principled politics." *National Review.* 27 December.

Hittinger, Russell. 1995. "The Supreme Court's *Casey* decision should not be obeyed." Pp. 121–28 in *The abortion controversy*, edited by Charles P. Cozic and Jonathan Petrikin. San Diego, Calif.: Greenhaven Press.

Jaggar, Alison M. 1998. "Re-gendering the U.S. abortion debate." Pp. 339–55 in *Abortion wars*, edited by Rickie Solinger. Berkeley, Calif.: University of California Press.

Kaplan, Laura. 1998. "Beyond safe and legal: the lessons of Jane." Pp. 33–41 in *Abortion wars*, edited by Rickie Solinger. Berkeley, Calif.: University of California Press.

King, Bruce. 1996. *Human sexuality today.* Upper Saddle River, N.J.: Prentice-Hall.

Kolbert, Kathryn, and Andrea Miller. 1998. "Legal strategies for abortion rights in the twenty-first century." Pp. 95–110 in *Abortion wars*, edited by Rickie Solinger. Berkeley, Calif.: University of California Press.

Ladd, Everett C., and Karlyn H. Bowman. 1997. *Public opinion about abortion.* American Enterprise Institute for Public Policy Research.

Lavelle, Marianne. 1998. "When abortion comes late in a pregnancy." *U.S. News & World Report.* 19 January, 31.

Longman, Philip. 1998. "The cost of children." *U.S. News & World Report.* 30 March, 51–58.

Mackenzie, Catriona. 1997. "Abortion and embodiment." Pp. 175–93 in *The problem of abortion.* 3d ed. Edited by Susan Dwyer and Joel Feinberg. Belmont, Calif.: Wadsworth Publishing.

Markowitz, Sally. 1990. "Abortion and feminism." *Social Theory and Practice* 15:1–17.

Marquis, Don. 1989. "Why abortion is immoral." *Journal of Philosophy.* LXXXVI(4):183–202.

Mencimer, Stephanie. 1994. "Ending illegitimacy as we know it." *Washington Post National Weekly Edition.* January, 17–23.

Meyer, Stephen C., and David K. DeWolf. 1995. "Fetal position." *National Review.* 20 March.

Muller, Jerry Z. 1995. "The conservative case for abortion." *New Republic.* 21–28 August.

National Women's Law Center (NWLC). 1994. "Abortion and national health care reform." Pp. 1–4.

O'Connor, Sandra Day, Anthony Kennedy, and David Souter. 1992. *Planned Parenthood of Southeastern Pennsylvania v. Robert P. Casey.* 112 U.S. 2791.

Paul, II, John. 1997. "Abortion is immoral." Pp. 17–22 in *Abortion: Opposing viewpoints*, edited by Tamara L. Roleff. San Diego, Calif.: Greenhaven Press.

Roleff, Tamara L., ed. 1997. *Abortion: Opposing viewpoints.* San Diego, Calif.: Greenhaven Press.

Ross, Steven. 1982. "Abortion and the death of the fetus." *Philosophy and Public Affairs* 11:232–45.

Savoy, Paul. 1995. "Abortion is a moral choice." Pp. 46–54 in *The abortion controversy*, edited by Charles P. Cozic and Jonathan Petrikin. San Diego, Calif.: Greenhaven Press.

Scalia, Antonin. 1995. "The Supreme Court erred in reaffirming *Roe v. Wade*." Pp. 115–20 in *The abortion controversy*, edited by Charles P. Cozic and Jonathan Petrikin. San Diego, Calif.: Greenhaven Press.

Shafer, Brenda. 1995. "What the nurses saw." *National Right to Life News.* 18 July.

Sheler, Jeffrey L. 1992. "The theology of abortion." *U.S. News & World Report.* 9 March.

Siegel, Mark A., Donna R. Plesser, and Nancy R. Jacobs. 1986. *Abortion: An eternal social and moral issue.* Plano, Tex.: Information Aids.

Sloan, Don, M.D., and Paula Hartz. 1992. *Abortion: A doctor's perspective, a woman's dilemma.* New York: D. I. Fine.

Smolowe, Jill. 1995. "Adoption in black and white." *Time.* 14 August 146(7):55–51.

Solinger, Rickie, ed. 1998. *Abortion wars.* Berkeley, Calif.: University of California Press.

Stevens, John Paul. 1992. *Planned Parenthood of Southeastern Pennsylvania v. Robert P. Casey.* 112 U.S. 2791.

Sumner, L. W. 1981. *Abortion and moral theory.* Princeton, N.J.: Princeton University Press.

Superville, Darlene. 1998. "Bill restricts abortions." *Dayton Daily News.* 16 July.

Thompson, Judith Jarvis. 1971. "A defense of abortion." *Philosophy and Public Affairs* 1(1):47–66.

Tooley, Michael. 1972. "Abortion and infanticide." *Philosophy and Public Affairs* 2:37–65.

U.S. Centers for Disease Control (CDC). 1998. "Morbidity and mortality weekly report: Surveillance summaries." 47(ss-2):31–68.

Waldman, Steven, Elise Ackerman, and Rita Rubin. 1998. "Abortion in America." *U.S. News & World Report.* 19 January, 20–31

Warren, Mary Anne. 1997. "On the moral and legal status of abortion." Pp. 59–74 in *The problem of abortion.* 3d ed. Edited by Susan Dwyer and Joel Feinberg. Belmont, Calif.: Wadsworth Publishing.

Washington, Adrienne T. 1994. "Ask a kid: Parents need abortion notice." *Washington Times.* 11 March.

Wenz, Peter S. 1992. *Abortion rights as religious freedom.* Philadelphia, Pa.: Temple University Press.

Whitman, David. 1998. "Abortion: The untold story." *U.S. News & World Report.* 7 December, 20–23.

Wilder, Marcy J. 1998. "The rule of law, the rise of violence, and the role of morality: Reframing America's abortion debate." Pp. 73–94 in *Abortion wars*, edited by Rickie Solinger. Berkeley, Calif.: University of California Press.

Wolf-Devine, Celia. 1989. "Abortion and the 'feminine' voice." *Public Affairs Quarterly* 3:81–97.

Zuckerman, Mortimer. 1994. "Starting work as we know it." *U.S. News & World Report.* 4 July, 72.

2 Affirmative Action Policy (Race-Based)

Affirmative action (abbreviated AA) policy applies to a variety of steps taken to ensure that various minority groups in our society are not informally discriminated against in their access to employment, contracting, and educational opportunities. Minority groups include women, veterans, people with disabilities, and the economically disadvantaged, as well as some racial and ethnic minorities, particularly African Americans, Hispanics, and Native Americans.

Since AA was first introduced in an executive order by President Johnson in 1967, it has gone through many changes. As of 1999, AA refers to specific guidelines and rules applied to all government-contracted industries and other private industries with fifty or more employees to recruit, hire, and promote disadvantaged groups in order to ease the discriminating practices currently existing as well as those that existed in the past. Colleges, universities, and professional schools also use similar policies in admitting students. In the area of contracting, the government is required to set aside a certain percentage of contracts for minority-owned firms or firms that can show a disadvantage.

In most cases, AA is not a quota system; it calls for "a plan," "a good-faith effort," or "setting of broad numerical goals or a timetable" for hiring or admitting minorities until the composition of the workforce or student body more or less reflects that of the surrounding area from which the workers or students are drawn.

Since its inception, AA has been a controversial issue and has become considerably more so since the 1980s, leading to increasing public opposition to AA. In response to the public's strong negative reaction to AA, the Reagan administration dropped the requirement for goals and timetables for many industries, and the Bush administration announced its opposition to minority scholarships for college students. Although President Clinton has reinstated a pro-affirmative action position, public view against AA is growing, and many conservative legal groups are putting together a well-planned litigation strategy designed to end AA.

Until 1990, the Supreme Court had been supportive of AA. Although the Court does not support quotas, the use of racial preference for valid social and educational purposes of achieving diversity was declared legal in 1978 (the

Bakke v. University of California case). If there is sufficiently strong evidence of discrimination, even a quota system is legally permissible (e.g., the *Weber v. Kaiser Aluminum and Chemical Corp.* case in 1979); and the courts can even order such a system (e.g., the *Sheet Metal Workers v. EEOC* case in 1986). By 1990, African American college enrollment reached 11.3 percent, which is about the same proportion of the African American population in the United States. As minorities' enrollment in higher education and employment status improved, public opposition to AA grew, and the Supreme Court reacted accordingly. In 1990, in *Richmond v. J. A. Croson Co.*, the Supreme Court ruled minority set-aside programs unconstitutional unless specific industrywide discrimination can be proved. In 1995, in *Adarand Constructors v. Pena*, the Supreme Court issued a "strict scrutiny" standard for proving race-based discrimination, critically undermining AA policy (ACLU 1997).

In 1996, in *Hopwood v. University of Texas School of Law*, the U.S. Court of Appeals ruled that race can no longer be used as an admission factor (overriding the *Bakke* decision), and as a result, Hispanic admission dropped 64 percent and African American admission, 88 percent in just one year (ACLU 1997). In the same year, the anti-AA initiative, Proposition 209, narrowly passed in California. Within a year the number of African American freshmen at Berkeley's undergraduate program declined 57 percent, the number of Hispanics, 40 percent; the drop at UCLA was 43 percent for African Americans and 33 percent for Hispanics; law school enrollment of African Americans dropped nearly 72 percent, and of Hispanics, 35 percent (ACLU 1997; Reibstein 1997). However, the overall drop in non-Asian minority enrollment in eight University of California campuses was far less dramatic. The California university's official admission numbers of the 1998 fall freshmen class showed only 675 fewer non-Asian minority students spread over the eight campuses, so the new freshmen admissions are 15.4 percent non-Asian minority, compared with 17.6 percent for the 1997 freshmen class, a decline of 2.2 percentage points. This indicates that many minority students who had been pushed onto faster-track schools such as Berkeley and UCLA now attend less competitive colleges within the university system (Leo 1998; Krauthammer 1998; Wood 1998). In 1999, voters in the state of Washington also banned the use of race in college and professional school admissions, and its impact on minority enrollment is yet to be seen.

In order to battle the state prohibition against AA, public universities in California and Texas are struggling to find ways to remain racially diverse. The University of California is considering a proposal by the Latino Eligibility Task Force to eliminate SAT scores from admission decisions in order to boost Hispanic enrollment. The public universities in Texas have already dropped standardized tests for many applicants in order to comply with the state law passed in 1997, which requires automatically admitting those who finish in the top 10 percent of their high school regardless of their SAT scores. This top 10 percent law is a way of countering the effects of the court decision in 1996 outlawing AA at universities (Cloud 1997). By deemphasizing standardized tests and giving more importance to other qualities of the applicants, such as leadership skills, community service, work experience, and special disadvantages they had to overcome, many public universities in these states are able to maintain similar enrollment rates of non-Asian minority students as before (Leo 1998).

The decisions in Texas, California, and Washington have the potential to impact college admission policies nationwide. In 1998, a lawsuit was filed against the University of Michigan by the Center for Individual Rights, a Washington-based conservative public interest firm, on behalf of a white honor-roll student who alleges she was denied admission because of her race. A similar lawsuit is pending against Bowling Green University in Ohio. If these cases reach the high courts, it could result in a far broader ruling that would rewrite the rules governing admissions to the nation's higher education institutions in general.

What are the arguments surrounding AA? Why do we need it? Has it been effective? Is it time to put an end to it? The following sections summarize proponents' and opponents' arguments about the most controversial form of AA, the race-based preferential treatment.

Affirmative Action Is a Compensatory Remedy for Past Racial Injustice

Supporting Affirmative Action

AA is one of the most effective tools for redressing the racial imbalance caused by our nation's long-standing discrimination against minorities and for leveling what has been an uneven playing field for the entirety of our nation's existence (ACLU 1997). African Americans have suffered discrimination and oppression for more than 200 years, and this past experience has left them in a disadvantaged position politically, economically, socially, and psychologically. As a result, they are not equally prepared to compete with whites. The only way to undo the harmful effects of past discrimination is to provide racial preference in hiring and admissions. The goal of preferential treatment is to compensate their disadvantages and to level the playing field. Equal treatments of the unequals will only perpetuate and aggravate the inequality (Schwartz 1994, 220; Cruse in Lipset 1995).

Opposing Affirmative Action

In order to compensate for past racial injustice, remedies should apply only to the actual victims, and not to all members of a given category. Group-focused remedies, such as AA, are not only unfair but also are crude and ineffective ways of compensating the injustice of the past. Racially preferential treatment to higher education, for instance, helps middle- and upper-class minorities who do not have any disadvantage and had not been discriminated against rather than those who have obvious disadvantages regardless of race. For instance, a daughter of an African American surgeon in Manhattan gets preferential treatment over the son of a poor, white, West Virginia coal miner (Reiland 1996). What we need is a "victim-specific" remedy that is based on individual disadvantage only, not on race as a group. Race is not an accurate or appropriate proxy for such a disadvantage. Not all African Americans have suffered or are suffering from a disadvantage; it is not only African Americans who had been discriminated against in the past (Graglia 1995, 148; Carnoy 1994, 190; Newt Gingrich in his speech in 1996).

While rewarding those with no obvious disadvantage, AA forces white males who are not guilty of discrimination to unfairly pay the price for past discrimination that they had nothing to do with. Slavery occurred before they were born. It is not fair for the present generation of whites who have nothing to do with the slavery to "continue to pay a price for the ancient wrong committed by their forefathers" (Bob Dole in his speech in 1994). No one is against racial equality. However, racial equality must be achieved without violating people's individual rights and freedom. What we need is a plan that would provide help for the disadvantaged *individuals*, regardless of race, to work out their problems through individual improvement and mobility, than to provide a package deal of preferential treatment for all members of a group (Lipset 1995). Under our Constitution, there cannot be such a thing as "a creditor" or "a debtor race" (Justice Scalia in Reiland 1996).

Another liability of AA comes from the fact that AA indirectly encourages African Americans to exploit their own past victimization and experience of injustice as sources of power and privilege. By encouraging African Americans to believe that victimization justifies preference, AA nurtures a "victim-focused identity" in African Americans, which is the very condition they should try to overcome. The real power comes from taking responsibility for one's own educational and economic development, not from claiming power or preference solely based on past victimization (Steele 1994, 213–4).

Affirmative Action Provides Minorities with Opportunities That Did Not Exist Before

Supporting Affirmative Action

Without AA, minorities' access to higher education and professional jobs will be greatly limited regardless of their qualifications. For instance, many universities in the past officially or unofficially limited the number of Jewish, Asian, Hispanic, female, and Catholic students' enrollment: African Americans were simply barred (Monk 1994, 209). Many minority professionals say that they would not have received the opportunity to prove themselves had it not been for doors opened by AA. Out of 700 African Americans who entered the top twenty-eight national colleges and universities in 1976 with the help of AA, 225 went on to get professional degrees or doctorates; 70 are doctors and 60 are lawyers; about 125 are business executives, and more than 300 are successful civic leaders (Bowen and Bok 1998). Without AA, they would not have had the opportunities.

Our society has never provided equal opportunities for everyone and has never had a true merit system. Throughout history, the system has always benefited whites, males, the powerful, and the wealthy. AA is only a small step toward correcting this injustice and achieving the true American value of equality of opportunity.

Opposing Affirmative Action

If AA provides opportunities to minorities who are *equally* qualified as white males yet do not have equal access solely because of discrimination and prejudice, there is nothing wrong with it. In reality, however, AA provides opportunities to minorities who are less qualified than white males, and this is unfair. In many colleges and professional schools, minority applicants are accepted with admission test scores and GPAs significantly lower than those generally required of whites and Asian Americans. Minorities are also hired and promoted when their test scores and performance evaluation are considerably lower than whites (Sindler 1978; Carnoy 1994; Thernstrom and Thernstrom 1997, 1998).

There is a danger in artificially elevating one's social or academic position through preferential treatment beyond and above one's actual ability or capacity. It gives people an illusion of opportunity and success that they cannot achieve in reality. For instance, many African American and Hispanic college students who are admitted under AA are being forced to drop out. The six-year college graduation rate of African Americans is 59 percent and that of Hispanics is 64 percent, compared with 84 percent for whites and 88 percent for Asian Americans (Becker 1995; Samuelson 1996; Kinsley 1995; Steele 1994). Many minority students who were perfectly capable of graduating from a good college have been channeled into attending high-pressure, competitive colleges and universities thanks to AA, and ended up dropping out. Equal opportunity does not mean regardless of merit. Under the name of equal opportunity, AA has actually been a "disservice" to many minorities who had been pushed to schools and positions that they were not prepared for (Sowell 1997).

Most of all, AA violates our most cherished value of equality by unequally treating people based on the color of their skin, not merit. It undermines our belief that hard work and merit should be rewarded regardless of race, gender, religion, or birthright. It sends a wrong message to minorities as well as whites that hard work and educational achievement are pointless.

Affirmative Action Helps Create Minority Role Models

Supporting Affirmative Action

One of the causes of the present lack of success among minorities is the sense of hopelessness and despair that is widespread among minorities. Discouraged by the long and endless battle against prejudice and discrimination, many minorities believe that no matter how hard they try, they will not be given an equal chance to succeed or prove themselves because of discrimination and prejudice. Dispirited by the improbability of attaining success, they often give up even before trying. AA allows some minorities to become successful, and these successful minorities will become role models for the following generation. Minority children will be inspired by successful minorities they see; they will realize that it is possible for them to become successful, also. This sense of hope will encourage them to work hard, earn an education, and improve their lives and community. By giving one generation a chance, hopefully, we can break the cycle of hopelessness and despair many minorities share and, eventually, the cycle of poverty. As the number of minority leaders and professionals increases in our society, the negative stereotypes often associated with them will also decline, and our society will become less prejudiced as a result.

Opposing Affirmative Action

What we need to teach our children of all races is that the only way to achieve success in our society is through education and hard work, not preferential treatments or government handouts. Instead of teaching the value of education, hard work, and responsibility, AA teaches minority children an attitude that they are always entitled to special treatment and preference because of past victimization (Justice Thomas in Reiland 1996; Steele 1994). Instead of reducing negative stereotypes of minorities, AA helps to increase negative images of minorities by reinforcing the belief that minorities are in fact so inferior that they have to rely on government handouts to uplift their situation (Steele 1994; Sowell 1997).

Affirmative Action Promotes Diversity and Pluralism

Supporting Affirmative Action

A culturally diverse society is ideal in two ways. First, diversity allows people to interact with others from culturally and historically diverse backgrounds and experiences. This exposure to diversity enhances multicultural awareness and understanding, which encourages people to become more tolerant and less rigid in their perspectives. Second, political, economic, legal, and educational systems of a society operate based on values and norms, which is often shaped by the fundamental belief system of the society, called an ideology. The ideology in a society may reside in its historical processes, but it is always shaped and constantly reshaped by social, political, and economic leaders and intellectuals of the society. A lack of minority leaders in a society thus will inevitably lead to a lack of minority viewpoints and minority voices, and subsequently to a lack of minority interests represented in the political and economic systems. This will eventually affect the formation of ideology and distribution of wealth and power among different groups. Cultural diversity is necessary to increase power and wealth for the minority communities in economic markets and political systems. Without minority leaders who can influence the formation of ideology that reflects their interests, minority communities cannot compete effectively for their equal share of wealth and power (Kennedy 1995).

Diversity also has business appeals. A diverse workforce creates a competitive corporate edge with consumers of different races and backgrounds. This is one of the reasons why many business organizations in California, such as California Business Roundtable and the Los Angeles Business Alliance, opposed the 1996 public referendum to end AA in California (ACLU 1997). When the state of Washington had an antiracial preference bill on the ballot in 1998, the opposition groups were fueled and supported by large corporations, such as Boeing Co., Microsoft Corp., Eddie Bauer Inc., Starbucks Corp., and many other local businesses (Broder 1998). About half the U.S. corporations voluntarily adopt AA, because they know diverse workplaces are better positioned to tailor their goods and services to a diverse national and global market (ACLU 1997).

Establishing a racially and ethnically diverse public-sector workforce improves its effectiveness and legitimacy. Sending a poor white man to patrol Watts or Harlem, for instance, is neither the same nor as effective as sending an African American officer. Having only white judges in courtrooms dealing mainly with minority criminal defendants is no way to persuade the community that the legal system is fair, even if some of the white judges came from poor neighborhoods (Schrag 1997).

In education, many public university officials say they are trying to promote diversity not just on ethical grounds, but because a racially and ethnically diverse class provides a richer base of knowledge and culture (Wood 1998). The Association of American Universities officially stated that students benefit significantly from education that takes place within a diverse setting. Diversity creates an environment in which students from diverse backgrounds can contribute to the education of their fellow students in a great variety of ways (ACLU 1997). In a survey of 45,000 students who graduated from twenty-eight nationally competitive colleges and universities, the majority of white students expressed appreciation for the diversity they found on campuses (Bowen and Bok 1998).

Opposing Affirmative Action

Diversity cannot and should not be the goal; it should be a natural byproduct of a genuinely open community that hires, promotes, and admits minorities based on merit and talent (Leo 1997). When diversity becomes the goal, that means there is only one reason to hire or admit minorities—"institutions simply must have African Americans and Hispanics." Racial representation is not the same concept as racial development. Representation can be manufactured, but development is always hard-earned. It is naive to believe that racial representation can and will automatically bring about racial development (Steele 1994, 212).

Affirmative Action Is Unfair; It Is Reverse Discrimination

Opposing Affirmative Action

AA is unfair and undemocratic; it is reverse discrimination, because the rights of the majority are denied at the expense of the rights of the minority. It is a self-contradictory policy. In an attempt to end one form of discrimination, it creates another form of discrimination; to promote equality, it violates equality by treating people of different races unequally. It is simply not fair to give preferential treatment for less-qualified minorities to obtain employment or admission to higher education over better-qualified whites. There is a substantial and apparent difference between African Americans as a group and whites as a group in academic ability as measured by standard aptitude and achievement tests. Preferentially admitted African American students in higher educational institutions are significantly less qualified than their white counterparts (Graglia 1995, 145; Jaschik 1992; Graham 1993; Caplan et al. 1996). African American students admitted to Berkeley under AA in 1996, for instance, had average SAT scores 288 points below the Berkeley average (Krauthammer 1998). A white honors' graduate of the University of Washington, who had struggled to become the first in her family to earn a college degree, was rejected by the University of Washington Law School in 1997. In the same year, 90 percent of the African American students who were accepted had qualifications lower than she did (Broder 1998).

One year after California and Texas dropped AA, minority enrollment declined significantly. The number of African American freshmen at Berkeley declined 57 percent; the number of Hispanics, 40 percent. The drop at UCLA was 43 percent for African Americans, 33 percent for Hispanics (Krauthammer 1998). The University of Texas Law School enrolled only four new African American students in 1997, compared with twenty-nine the year before, and the University of California's three law schools enrolled only sixteen African American students compared with forty-three the year before (Reibstein 1997).

These numbers clearly indicate that minority students did not have the same qualifications as white students did when they were admitted to colleges and professional schools.

Supporting Affirmative Action

AA is not reverse discrimination against anyone, but an effort to *include* those who had been excluded in the past. Those who believe AA is reverse discrimination do not realize that minorities suffered from greater subordination and discrimination for hundreds of years (Fish 1993). A system is fair when everybody has an equal chance or opportunity. When a group of people do not have an equal chance because of past discrimination and present socioeconomic disadvantages, the system cannot be equal. The only way to make it equal is by giving them some degree of leverage that can compensate for their disadvantages (Fish 1996, 40).

Opponents of AA are obsessed with test scores and ignore other factors that influence admission to higher education institutions, such as leadership qualities, community service, work experience, personal statements from the applicants, letters of recommendation, the applicants' prior success in overcoming personal disadvantages, and their potential contribution to the community after graduation (Graglia 1995, 148). To claim that AA is reverse discrimination simply based on test scores is to ignore these important factors. A test score is only one of many factors that predicts one's potential achievement. A lower test score does not always mean lower potential as a student. For instance, more than 90 percent of all minority medical students, including those who received preferential admittance, graduate from medical schools (Petersdorf et al. 1990; Lee 1992).

Those who argue that AA is unfair assume that there has been a standard for fairness in U.S. history. Our society has never been fair, egalitarian, or based on merit as opponents of AA assume. Many higher education institutions have provided preferential treatment to athletes and in-state residents as well as to children of alumni, major financial contributors, and prominent politicians. Why should skin color be considered a different factor in admissions than geography, alumni parentage, or sports ability (Bowen and Bok 1998; ACLU 1997)? Favoritism has always existed and influenced a person's chances of employment and success. Many jobs are filled informally based on family connections or through knowing the right people. Minorities are less represented in the professional and business world, and therefore, they have fewer informal connections, and have more limited chances of employment and success compared with the majority.

Race should not be the sole criterion in hiring or admitting minorities; AA has never taken race as the sole criterion. Race, however, certainly deserves to be one of the many factors that can be taken into account (ACLU 1997). AA would be reverse discrimination if it provided chances to unqualified minorities. However, so far as it is used as a plus factor to those who meet the basic criteria or minimum qualification level, although it may be slightly lower than whites' level, taking race into consideration is not reverse discrimination (Slambrouck 1998).

Affirmative Action Outlived Its Usefulness: It Is Time to Put an End to It

Opposing Affirmative Action

AA had served its purpose; the goal of extending formal equality to all Americans regardless of race has been achieved. African Americans as a group are much better off than they were before the adoption of AA. In the fifty years since World War II, the economic position of African Americans has improved faster than that of any other groups in America (Lipset 1995). The size of the African American middle class rose from 13 percent of the African American population in 1960 to 38 percent in 1990. The Federal Reserve reports that the real income among African American families from 1983 to 1989 rose by 35 percent and 54 percent for Hispanic families, compared with only 24 percent among white families (Reiland 1996). The individual income gap between minorities and whites declined substantially, especially among college graduates. According to the 1990 Census, the median income of African American male college graduates between 25 and 34 years of age was 96 percent of white male college graduates in the same age group; the median income of African American females of the same category was actually higher than that of white females, 125 percent (Conti in Reiland 1996).

The proportion of African Americans aged 25 and over who are high school graduates increased from 51 percent in 1980 to 85 percent in 1993, which is similar to the proportion of whites (Lipset 1995). In 1990, 11.3 percent of college students were African Americans, a figure that comes close to the percentage of African Americans in the United States (ACLU 1997).

The number of African American–owned businesses in the United States increased 46 percent between 1987 and 1992, according to the Commerce Department's report (U.S. Bureau of Census 1995). The number of elected African American public officials increased from 1,300 in 1970 to about 6,000 in 1995. We had 286 African American mayors and 372 state legislators in 1993 (Farley 1995, 240–2). The number of African American police officers nationwide rose from 24,000 in 1970 to 43,500 in 1980 (Schwartz 1994, 216). Between 1970 and 1990, the number of African American college and university professors more than doubled; the number of physicians tripled; the number of engineers almost quadrupled; and the number of attorneys increased more than sixfold (Thernstrom and Thernstrom 1998).

Clearly, AA has achieved its goal; it is time to put an end to it. The ending of AA, however, does not mean the end of economic fairness and group equity. Instead, it can open new doors that would lead to different options to solve the problem of inequality, such as improving inner-city schools, reducing teen pregnancy, and providing job training for inner-city youths (Reiland 1996).

Despite large and obvious gains made by many successful African Americans, African Americans' *average* household income has not improved much. This is mainly due to the large and growing number of single-parent households among African Americans. The out-of-wedlock birthrate among African Americans in 1995 was 68 percent, up from 26 percent in 1965. The majority of these teenage mothers live in poverty as single parents, thereby bringing the average household income down (Reiland 1996; Fuch in Lipset 1995). In fact, since the 1970s, young African Americans who manage to stay married have had family incomes almost identical of those of young white couples (Taylor in Reiland 1996). Unfortunately, however, there are not too many intact families among African Americans. Half of all African American women in the United States are heads of households, and half of them live in poverty with children. As a result, the number of African American children born into poverty increased from 43 percent in 1968 to 46 percent in 1987 and has remained about the same in the 1990s (PBS Frontline 1995; Kirsanow 1995), compared with 14 percent of white children who live in poverty (White House 1995). AA is not going to help these young teenage mothers who drop out of high school and do not have many employment prospects; we need a different approach to help this group of people.

Supporting Affirmative Action

AA is still necessary because its original goal of ending discrimination has not been fully accomplished. A centuries-long legacy of racist and discriminatory habits, customs, and attitudes has not dissipated since the Civil Rights era (ACLU 1997). Despite the undeniable improvement, minorities are still considerably disadvantaged; their economic and political situations still lag behind the majority's (Wilkins 1996; Kuran 1996; Yates 1996). In 1996, the median income for full-time working African American and Hispanic *men* (individual income) was 80 percent of the income of non-Hispanic white men (Holmes 1997; ACLU 1997). The median African American *family* income in 1971 was 61 percent of the median of white families' income; in 1995, it was only 54 percent of white families' income (Kirsanow 1995). Minority workers are still concentrated in the low-paying, unskilled labor sector (ACLU 1997). African Americans account for 10.7 percent of the workforce but only 6.9 percent of executive or managerial positions; Hispanics account for 9.2 percent of the labor force but only 4.8 percent of executive or managerial positions (PNIS 1998). Despite government set-aside programs, African American–owned firms represented only 1 percent of all business sales in 1987 (Samuelson 1996). *Business Week*'s 1991 listing of the chief executives of America's 1,000 largest corporations had only one African American chairman, and there is no African American–owned firm in *Fortune*'s list of the 500 largest corporations (Hacker 1996). Although white males make up only 43 percent of the workforce, they occupy 97 percent of the top executive positions at America's 1,500 largest corporations (ACLU 1997). Only 0.6 percent of senior management personnel are African American, 0.3 percent are Asian American, and 0.4 percent are Hispanic (White House 1995).

Statistics show an improved status only among better-educated minorities. The *average* economic situation of non-Asian minorities still remains substantially lower than whites'; the situation of less-educated, inner-city minorities (the underclass) is actually getting worse, especially since the 1970s (Kuran 1996). The poorest 20 percent of African American households' income decreased between 1968 and 1995 (in 1995 dollars) (PNIS 1998). According to the 1990 Census, 33 percent of African Americans and 29 percent of Hispanics lived below the poverty level compared with 12 percent of whites. About 50 percent of African American children and 44 percent of Hispanic children lived under the poverty level, while only 14 percent of white children did (White House 1995). The unemployment rates for African Americans were twice the national level in 1996—11.2 percent for African American males and 10 percent for African American females (Bernstein in PNIS 1998)—and this rate has not changed much since the 1970s (Kirsanow 1995). The unemployment rate of inner-city African American males is approximately 40 percent (Wilson 1991). Overall, since 1980 the population of the black underclass has tripled according to The Urban Institute report, which defines people in underclass as those who are: 1) single, female head of the household with dependents; 2) welfare dependent; 3) high school dropout or less; 4) chronically unemployed; and 5) in and out of jail (PBS Frontline 1995). Clearly, the goals of AA have not been achieved. Until they are, we may mend AA, but certainly not end it (Clinton 1996).

Affirmative Action Undermines the Quality of the Workforce

Opposing Affirmative Action

AA undermines the quality of the workforce by giving positions to people other than the most qualified. In many professional schools, minority applicants are accepted with standardized test scores and undergraduate GPAs significantly lower than those generally required of whites (Sindler 1978; Krauthammer 1998; Graglia 1995; Jaschik 1992; Caplan et al. 1996). Minorities are also hired when their test scores are considerably lower than whites. The average hired African American worker tests more than one-half standard deviation lower than his white counterpart. A number of studies show that the achievement score differences for African Americans hired under AA represents anywhere from 2 to 10 percent less productivity on the job for each standard deviation of test score difference (for details, see Carnoy 1994, 186–7). Such practice is not only unfair and less productive but could also be hazardous in some areas of work, which deal with emergency situations and require high levels of skill and ability.

Supporting Affirmative Action

The standardized tests for professional schools and employment tests are not very convincing or accurate measures of achievement or productivity. Lower test scores, irrespective of race, do not always reflect lower achievement or productivity. Moreover, the productivity rate is usually based on supervisors' ratings, which tend to be subjective, biased, and inaccurate (for discussion of this, see Carnoy 1994, 187).

Minorities who receive preferential admission to colleges or professional schools are not unqualified students. Their test scores may be somewhat lower than the whites' average, but still they are qualified to attend colleges by many standards, and have high enough scores compared with all applicants. Moreover, once admitted, these minority students are just as likely as their white classmates to go on to earn advanced degrees in law, business, or medicine. Out of 700 African Americans who entered the twenty-eight most competitive colleges and universities in the nation under AA in 1976, 225 went on to get professional degrees or doctorates; 70 are doctors and 60 are lawyers; 125 are business executives, and more than 300 are civic leaders. After they enter the workforce, African American graduates have strengthened their community by actively engaging in civic life (Bowen and Bok 1998).

Affirmative Action Stigmatizes Minorities

Opposing Affirmative Action

Rather than helping minorities, AA stigmatizes minorities and creates an environment in which minorities' contribution is not appreciated (Thernstrom and Thernstrom 1997). Affirmative Action program "stamps minorities with a badge of inferiority," no matter how competent they are or how hard they work (Justice Thomas in Reiland 1996). AA encourages people to believe that minorities are truly inferior, and that they have to depend on government handouts and be uplifted by whites. Minority members' merit and worth are diminished and not appreciated in workplaces or in educational systems, because many believe that they are there only because of AA preference. Moreover, such stigmatization and stereotyping have a tendency to work as self-fulfilling prophecies. Affirmative Action reinforces negative stereotypes about minorities among the dominant group and also creates self-doubt among minority-group members who constantly find their abilities being questioned. Minorities, especially African Americans, have struggled to overcome this implication of inferiority and self-doubt for a long time. Affirmative Action, instead of helping them to overcome these feelings, tends to reinforce them. Preferential treatment rewards minorities for being underdogs rather than for moving beyond that status. Affirmative Action provides an incentive to be reliant on the government when minorities need to be reliant on themselves the most (Steele 1994; Sowell 1997, 1995; Reynolds 1992). Beneficiaries of special treatment too often develop dependency and adopt an attitude that they are entitled to preferences regardless of their merit and effort (Justice Thomas in Reiland 1996).

Supporting Affirmative Action

There is no evidence that minorities who became successful as a result of AA are mistreated or stigmatized. On the contrary, an overwhelming majority of African American graduates from the nation's top twenty-eight colleges and universities say that they had very good experiences and were very satisfied with their undergraduate schooling. Equally important, white graduates of these schools expressed appreciation for the diversity they found on campus (Bowen and Bok 1998). Once given a chance, minorities often work hard to prove their abilities, and therefore, they are eventually recognized for their achievements, and not by race (Reno 1998). Even if minorities are stigmatized by some, that is a small price minorities have to pay to achieve true equality in the future. Potential benefits from AA outweigh the cost of being stigmatized temporarily.

Affirmative Action Increases Racial Tension

Opposing Affirmative Action

One of the unintended byproducts of AA is an increase of interracial tension, conflict, and animosity. Instead of promoting a color-blind and racially harmonious society, AA creates an extremely color-conscious and racially divided society. Already AA has led to damaging forms of resegregation, social discrimination, and prejudice among people of all socioeconomic levels. Many colleges now have racially separate dormitories, social centers, activities, even newspapers and yearbooks (Steele 1994). Racial segregation has increased in workplaces because whites, particularly white males, feel threatened by upwardly mobile African Americans. According to a survey, many whites see AA as so unfair that "they have come to dislike African Americans" (Samuelson 1996). It has caused whites to blame and scapegoat minorities for their economic troubles and even engage in minority bashing. These feelings of anger, resentment, and frustration among whites, if left to escalate, can have a harmful effect on racial and ethnic relations in the United States (Yates 1996; Samuelson 1996; Graglia 1995, 151).

In many state elections, whites' fury over AA emerged as a top voter concern; quotas and minority preferences were a primary source of antigovernment or anti-Democratic anger among many white working- and middle-class voters (Lipset 1995). The growing number of hate group activities and attacks on minorities should be seen as a reflection of anger and frustration felt by many whites. Even President Clinton acknowledged that he feels "the pain of white men," and "it is a difficult time for a lot of white males" (Clinton in Reiland 1996).

Whites are not angry over minority advancement or racial equality. What bothers them is the obvious unfairness of AA as a policy—AA provides preference to those who do not have any disadvantage, such as children of the affluent minorities, at the expense of better-qualified or disadvantaged whites.

Supporting Affirmative Action

The temporary racial tension is another price minorities must pay to achieve equality. Throughout history, no social change has been possible without conflict and struggle, because those with power and privilege do not want to give them up. The only way to demand the fair share of the benefit for the underdogs is through conflict and struggle. If we abandon AA for fear of increased racial tension, minorities will never achieve equality, and our society will return to the old-white-boy network again.

The fear of racial tension and conflict has been exaggerated by media sensationalism and political manipulation. In fact, an actual survey of many college students revealed just the opposite; the majority of minority students were very satisfied with their undergraduate experience, and the majority of white students expressed appreciation for the diversity they found on campus (Bowen and Bok 1998).

Affirmative Action Does Not Solve the Real Source of the Problem

Opposing Affirmative Action

If minority underrepresentation is a result of present discrimination only, then preferential treatment and quotas are appropriate remedies. However, if the minority's underrepresentation is the result of lack of proper qualification, then the appropriate remedy, even if it is due to past discrimination, should be to upgrade their qualification through education and training (Graglia 1995, 150). The fundamental sources of racial inequality in our society are the lack of education opportunities and poverty among minorities. Instead of forcing employers to hire and schools to admit less-qualified and underprepared minorities, we should invest in improving their educational opportunities, providing job training programs, special education benefits, and financial assistance that will enable them to catch up with the majority (Lipset 1995; Clegg 1998). AA is not and can never be a substitute for education reform. While racial preferences may offer an illusory way out for a few students, the vast majority of minorities are held back by poor public school systems, rather than racial biases (Connerly and Gingrich in PNIS 1998).

In education, for instance, the problem is not that African Americans do not get into college; it is that many do not graduate, because they are not academically prepared for college education. The six-year college graduation rate of African Americans is 59 percent and that of Hispanics is 64 percent, compared with 84 percent for whites and 88 percent for Asian Americans (Becker 1995; Samuelson 1996; Kinsley 1995; Steele 1994). Some African American students who were perfectly capable of graduating from a good college have been artificially turned into failures by being admitted to high-pressure colleges and universities, in which only students with exceptional academic backgrounds can survive. Elevating one's social or academic position artificially through a preference system is harmful to everyone, including the individual. Without AA, African American students will be held at the same standard as their peers, and that will significantly increase their chances of succeeding academically (Sowell 1997).

When industries do not hire minorities, it is not because of the color of their skin, but because they lack the basic requirements, such as reading, writing, and computing skills. According to the National Assessment of Educational Progress report, African American students, on average, are alarmingly far behind whites in all subject areas. Graduating African American seniors are almost four years behind white students in reading and math (Thernstrom and Thernstrom 1998). As a result of technological development, a growing number of jobs now require much higher levels of skill and education than before—the minimum of ninth-grade level reading, writing, and math. However, in 1992 only 22 percent of African American high school seniors, compared with 58 percent of their white classmates, had ninth-grade level math skills; 18 percent of African American seniors, compared with 47 percent of whites, had ninth-grade English skills. Even more surprising is the fact that this racial gap has been widening since the late 1980s (Thernstrom and Thernstrom 1998; Reiland 1996). If minorities have a higher unemployment rate, it is not because of discrimination, but because many minorities lack basic skills and education. If minorities are equally qualified, businesses will hire them. Instead of forcing the industry to hire these unqualified minorities, the government should try to provide higher-quality education and training for them.

In African American communities, progress in lowering the high dropout rates in schools and reducing teen pregnancy would produce far greater upward mobility than all of the government's AA programs combined. The out-of-wedlock birthrates among African Americans in 1995 was 68 percent, up from 26 percent in 1965. About half of all African American women in the United States are heads of the household, and half of them live in poverty with children. As a result, about 50 percent of African American children live under the poverty level, compared with 14 percent of white children (White House 1995; PBS Frontline 1995). Children from single-parent families are nearly twice as likely to be expelled from schools and 40 percent more likely to repeat a grade. The collapse of families and poor-quality education are more serious problems among African Americans than discrimination in the battle against poverty (Reiland 1996). The program that would work most effectively for the advancement of African Americans is encouraging intact families. In fact, since the 1970s, young African Americans who managed to stay married have had family incomes almost identical of those of young white couples (Taylor in Reiland 1996). Encouraging two-parent families would eliminate socioeconomic differences between African Americans and whites much more effectively than AA can (Kirsanow 1995).

In addition to family and education, increased violence and disorder of inner-city lives combined with drug-related gang activities certainly have a negative impact on urban youths' chances of education and success. Chaos in the street, without a doubt, will affect learning in the classroom (Thernstrom and Thernstrom 1997).

Supporting Affirmative Action

Education and training alone will not bring about racial equality. Studies have shown that, when everything else is equal, minorities still have less chance than whites due to discrimination and prejudice. A study by The Urban Institute shows that, upon sending equally qualified minorities and whites into job interviews, the young white male testers received 45 percent more job offers than their African American cotesters; 52 percent more often than Hispanic cotesters (ACLU 1997). A similar test, conducted by the Fair Employment Council of Greater Washington, Inc., revealed that African Americans were treated significantly worse than equally qualified whites 24 percent of the time, and Hispanics were treated worse than whites 22 percent of the time. In 1993 alone, the federal government received more than 90,000 complaints of employment discrimination. Moreover, 64,423 complaints were filed with state and local Fair Employment Practices Commissions, bringing the total to 154,000 (White House 1995).

Regardless of how important they are, education and job training alone cannot eliminate the pervasive effects of prejudice and discrimination; they cannot create equal opportunities. What is the purpose of education and job training when there is no chance of getting the job in the first place? Education and training and all the other reform options must be provided in conjunction with the legal and ethical efforts to bring about equal opportunities to minorities.

Affirmative Action Helps Those Who Do Not Need Help, and Does Not Help Those Who Do

Opposing Affirmative Action

While there have been impressive minority gains since the 1960s, there has also been significant regression among minorities, especially among the inner-city, underclass minorities. The economic situation of underclass minorities has not improved, in fact, in many areas it is getting worse, and the size of the minority underclass is growing (Kirsanow 1995; PBS Frontline 1995). Why is this happening? It is because AA helps children of middle- and upper-class minorities in their effort to seek higher education and pursue better-paying careers, but it does not help the underclass minorities who truly need help. The primary beneficiaries of AA have been not the disadvantaged and discriminated against but the middle- and upper-class minorities with no disadvantage at all. African Americans who are preferentially admitted to higher education institutions are frequently the children of successful professionals and have social, economic, and educational backgrounds virtually indistinguishable from those of the average middle-class white applicants (Graglia 1995, 149). Why should a son of a wealthy, well-educated African American businessman have a slot reserved for him when a son of a white assembly-line worker is excluded? (Graglia 1995, 149; Reynolds 1992; Goldman 1979; Kuran 1996; Fishkin in Lipset 1995).

Affirmative Action has had almost no effect on the low-income, poorly educated, chronically unemployed underclass minorities (Wilson 1991; Lipset 1995). Most of the dead-end, low-paying jobs are already identified as minority jobs, and minorities do not need AA to get those jobs. The living standard of underclass African Americans has deteriorated since the 1970s relative to wealthy African Americans, and even in absolute number to poor whites (Kuran 1996). From 1973 to 1987, families in the bottom quintile of the African American income distribution became 18 percent poorer in constant dollars, compared with a smaller loss of 7 percent for families in the bottom quintile of the white distribution. During the same period, families in the top quintile of the African American distribution gained 33 percent. While African Americans least in need of special help have reaped visible gains, those with the greatest need have suffered an unmistakable loss (Kuran 1996, 33). The unemployment rate among African American youths rose from 25 percent in 1971 to 40 percent in 1980. Since 1980, the population of the black underclass—welfare-dependent, single-parent, with less than high school education, who are chronically unemployed, or in and out of jail—has tripled according to The Urban Institute report (PBS Frontline 1995). There is a grave sense of frustration, anger, hopelessness, resentment, and injustice among these underclass minorities, and their feelings are often expressed in crime and other deviant or violent behaviors (Wilson 1991).

One of the latent consequences of AA is the so-called black bifurcation or black polarization, that is, a class division among African Americans. Affirmative Action created a large number of successful middle-class African Americans who quickly left the African American ghetto area to seek better housing and schools in the suburbs. The African American suburban population grew by 70 percent during the 1970s; between 1986 and 1990, 73 percent of African American population growth occurred in the suburbs (Lipset 1995). Their exodus from the ghetto weakened African Americans' sense of unity and the spirit of activism; the inner-city is left without role models, social and cultural leaders, and business contacts. The underclass African Americans in the inner-city area feel abandoned and turned against, not only by whites but also by the successful middle-class African Americans (Wilson 1991).

Clearly, AA does not help the poorly educated and unskilled to secure good jobs. We need a different approach to help these people, an approach that would include overall improvement of the urban economy and employment prospects. To succeed in a postindustrial society requires good education. Extending educational and employment opportunities and improving the quality of education in the inner cities, and expanding apprenticeship programs that combine classroom instruction and on-the-job training, are the directions to be followed, not AA. Such programs should be offered to all less-privileged people, regardless of racial and ethnic origin (Lipset 1995). Policy measures that are conceived not in terms of the actual disadvantage suffered by individuals but rather in terms of race or ethnic group membership, such as AA, will further enhance opportunities of the more advantaged without addressing the problems of the truly disadvantaged (Lipset 1995).

Supporting Affirmative Action

The reason underclass minorities do not benefit from AA is because AA is not fully implemented, yet. As more minorities receive education and obtain jobs, the effects of AA will spread to the underclass as well. Unlike what many believe, the overlap between minority groups and the poor is so large that any policy designed to help minorities will also benefit the poor. According to Lamar Alexander, the former Secretary of Education, 98 percent of the cases of race-specific scholarships were also scholarships to the economically disadvantaged, the poor (Fish 1996, 40). Programs that target specifically the urban underclass, such as educational reform, financial aid, and better employment opportunities in the inner cities are important but cannot substitute AA. While these programs help minorities achieve educational and economic development on the individual level, AA expands opportunities available for them on a societal level. These programs must be provided in conjunction with AA, not in place of AA.

Class-Based Affirmative Action Should Replace Race-Based Affirmative Action

Supporting Class-Based Affirmative Action

A growing number of scholars and politicians propose a color-blind, socioeconomic class-based AA, which will benefit anyone with a socioeconomic disadvantage regardless of race. Higher education institutions should continue to provide policies of preferential treatment but alter the criteria of admission from race to a socioeconomic disadvantage (Wilson 1991; for discussion of this, see Fish 1996). This policy will continue to help minorities but only those who need and deserve preferential treatment.

Opposing Class-Based Affirmative Action

Experience in many colleges has shown that class-based AA replaces Hispanics and African Americans of every economic level with whites and Asian Americans (Wildavsky 1999, Schrag 1997). The University of California at Berkeley has gradually switched to a class *and* race-based AA from a solely race-based admission policy since 1989. With only a partially race-blind policy in 1994, the share of admitted Hispanics dropped from 21 to 17 percent, African Americans' share fell from 11 to 7 percent, whites' share fell modestly from 37 to 33 percent, and Asian Americans' share soared from 24 to 36 percent. A completely race-blind policy using financial status alone will lead to about a 50 percent drop in African Americans' and Hispanics' enrollment in California (Caplan et al. 1996). According to Bowen and Bok's estimation, a class-based AA policy would eliminate 73 percent of African American students in the twenty-eight most prestigious colleges and universities in the nation (Bowen and Bok 1998). In fact, many institutions have already been providing preferences to low-income students for many years, either by using straight income or welfare criteria, or through programs that give preference to children from families in which no one has ever gone to college (Schrag 1997).

Affirmative Action Should Be Voluntary, Not Forced

Supporting Voluntary Affirmative Action

AA should be employed on a voluntary basis allowing private industries to gradually adjust to society's demands depending on their needs and situation. In our free market system, free competition will eventually eliminate discrimination, and businesses will hire the best-qualified employees at the lowest possible cost, regardless of race (Yates 1996). Many U.S. corporations voluntarily adopt AA because they know that a diverse workforce is better positioned to tailor their goods and services to a diverse national and global market (ACLU 1997). About 20 percent of the U.S. workforce is employed in private firms that voluntarily use AA. These firms use race as "a plus factor" for qualified applicants in job categories with histories of racial segregation (Slambrouck 1998).

Opposing Voluntary Affirmative Action

The existing AA policy is far from "forced." It only "calls for plans"; it is a "good-faith effort" to recruit and hire minorities. There are no sanctions against employers as long as they can demonstrate a "good-faith effort" to meet the regulation. If they can prove that they have looked, but "could not find anyone qualified," they can go out and hire the white male they wanted to hire in the first place (Wilkins 1996, 103). The government-mandated AA program applies only to firms that contract with the federal government, which represent about 20 percent of the nation's workforce, or those employers found guilty of discrimination, although this remains relatively rare. Studies have shown that minorities make faster employment gains at firms with government contracts than at firms without contracts, which indicates that the mandated AA is more effective than a voluntary one. All in all, fewer than half of all U.S. firms are engaged in AA (Reskin in Slambrouch 1998). We relied on the free market system to provide equal opportunity for over a century, but it did not work because of the deep-seated racism and prejudice. A completely voluntary AA will take too long to achieve racial equality, if ever.

REFERENCES

American Civil Liberties Union (ACLU). 1997. "Affirmative action." *ACLU Briefing Paper.* 1 December. (http://www.aclu.org/library/pbp17.html).

Becker, Gary S. 1995. "End affirmative action as we know it." *Business Week.* No. 3438. 21 August, 16.

Bowen, William G., and Derek Bok. 1998. *The shape of the river: Long-term consequences of considering race in college and university admissions.* Princeton, N.J.: Princeton University Press.

Broder, David S. 1998. "Affirmative action gets key test in Washington." *Washington Post.* 24 October, A1.

Caplan, Lincoln, Dorian Friedman, and Julian E. Barnes. 1996. "The Hopwood effect kicks in on campus." *U.S. News & World Report.* 23 December, 26–8.

Carnoy, Martin. 1994. *Faded dreams: The politics and economics of race in America.* Cambridge, Mass.: Cambridge University Press, 172–94.

Clegg, Roger. 1998. "Beyond quotas." *Policy Review.* May.

Clinton, William J. 1996. *Between hope and history: Meeting America's challenges for the 21st century.* New York: Times Books.

Cloud, John. 1997. "What does SAT stand for?" *Time.* 10 November.

Farley, John E. 1995. *Majority-minority relations*. 3d ed. Englewood Cliffs, N.J.: Prentice Hall.

Fish, Stanley. 1996. "Opposition to affirmative action among whites is racist." Pp. 36–42 in *Race relations: Opposing viewpoints*, edited by Paul A. Winters. San Diego, Calif.: Greenhaven Press.

———. 1993. "Reprise racism or how the pot got to call the kettle black." *Atlantic Monthly* 272:128–36.

Goldman, Alan. 1979. *Justice and reverse discrimination*. Princeton, N.J.: University of Princeton Press.

Graglia, Lino A. 1995. "Affirmative discrimination." Pp. 144–52 in *Campus wars: Multiculturalism and the politics of difference*, edited by John Arthur and Amy Shapiro. Boulder, Colo.: Westview.

Graham, James. 1993. *The affirmative action debate*. New York: Macmillan.

Hacker, Andrew. 1996. "Racial discrimination limits opportunities for blacks." In *Race relations: Opposing viewpoints*, edited by Paul A. Winters. San Diego, Calif.: Greenhaven Press.

Holmes, Steven A. 1997. "New reports say minorities benefit in fiscal recovery." *New York Times*. 30 September.

Jaschik, Scott. 1992. "Education department says affirmative action policy of Berkeley's Law School violated federal anti-bias laws." *Chronicle of Higher Education*. 7 October, A21–5.

Kennedy, Duncan. 1995. "A cultural pluralist case for affirmative action." Pp. 144–52 in *Campus wars*, edited by John Arthur and Amy Shapiro. Boulder, Colo.: Westview.

Kinsley, Michael. 1995. "Generous old lady, or reverse racist." *Time*. Vol. 146. 28 August.

Kirsanow, Peter. 1995. "The affirmative action experiment has been a colossal failure." *National Policy Analysis*, no. 134. May. National Center for Public Policy Research.

Krauthammer, Charles. 1998. "Lies, damn lies, and racial statistics." Time-webmaster@pathfinder.com.

Kuran, Timur. 1996. "A backlash against affirmative action is growing among whites." Pp. 29–35 in *Race relations: Opposing viewpoints*, edited by Paul A. Winters. San Diego, Calif.: Greenhaven Press.

Lee, Min-Wei. 1992. "Programming minorities for medicine." *Journal of the American Medical Association* 267(17):2391–94.

Leo, John. 1998. "Don't get hysterical." *U.S. News & World Report*. 27 April, 12.

———. 1997. "Jelly bean: The sequel." *U.S. News & World Report*. 10 February, 20.

Lipset, Seymore M. 1995. "Two Americas, two systems: Whites, blacks, and debate over affirmative action." *The New Democrat*. May/June.

———. 1992. "The politics of race: The meaning of equality." *Current* (June):10–15

Monk, Richard C., ed. 1994. *Taking sides: Clashing views on controversial issues in race and ethnicity*. Guilford, Conn.: The Dushkin Publishing Group.

PBS Frontline. 1995. "The two nations of black America: Viewing the class divide." (http://www.pbs.org/wgbh/pages/frontline/shows/race/economics/sam.html).

Petersdorf, Robert G., K. S. Turner, Herbert W. Nickens, and Timothy Ready. 1990. "Minorities in medicine: Past, present, and future." *Academic Medicine* 65:663–70.

Policy News and Information Service (The) (PNIS). 1998. "Race in America." (http://www.policy.com/issuewk/98/0713/071398f.html).

Reibstein, Larry. 1997. "What color is an A?" *Newsweek*. 29 December.

Reiland, Ralph R. 1996. "Affirmative action an equal opportunity?" *The Cato Review of Business and Government*. 1 November. (http://www.cato.org/pubs/regulation/reg18n3-x.html).

Reno, Janet. 1998. Commencement Address at Temple University, 18 June.

Reynolds, Wm. Bradford. 1992. "Affirmative action and its negative repercussions." *Annals AAPSS* 523:38–49.

Samuelson, Robert J. 1996. "The debate engages politics more than social policy." *Newsweek*. 28 February.

Schrag, Peter. 1997. "When preferences disappear." *The American Prospect*, no. 30 (January–February):38–41.

Schwartz, Herman. 1994. "In defense of affirmative action." Pp. 215–20 in *Taking sides: Clashing views on controversial issues in race and ethnicity*, edited by Richard C. Monk. Guilford, Conn.: The Dushkin Publishing Group.

Sindler, Allan P. 1978. *Bakke, DeFunis, and minority admissions: The quest for equal opportunity.* New York: Longman.

Slambrouck, Paul Van. 1998. "New evidence of affirmative action's effectiveness." *Christian Science Monitor*. 24 August.

Sowell, Thomas. 1997. "Body count versus education." *AEI On the Issues*. 1 August. American Enterprise Institute.

———.1995. "The Q word." *Forbes*. Vol. 155. 10 April.

Steele, Shelby. 1994. "Affirmative action: The price of preference." Pp. 210–14 in *Taking sides: Clashing views on controversial issues in race and ethnicity*, edited by Richard C. Monk. Guilford, Conn.: The Dushkin Publishing Group.

Thernstrom, Abigail, and Stephen Thernstrom. 1998. "Black progress." *The Brookings Review* 16:2 (Spring 1998):12–16.

———. 1997. *America in black and white: One nation, indivisible*. New York: Simon & Schuster.

U.S. Bureau of Census. 1995. "1992 black-owned businesses." (MB91-1). Washington, D.C.: Government Printing Office.

White House. 1995. "Affirmative action review: Report to the President." (http://www.whitehouse.gov/WH/EOP/OP/html/aa/aa03.html).

Wildavsky, Ben. 1999. "Whatever happened to minority students?" *U.S. News & World Report*. 22 March, 28–32.

Wilkins, Roger. 1996. "Affirmative action is still necessary to fight discrimination." Pp. 102–109 in *Race relations: Opposing viewpoints*, edited by Paul A. Winters. San Diego, Calif.: Greenhaven Press.

Wilson, William J. 1991. "Public policy research and the truly disadvantaged." In *The urban underclass*, edited by C. Jencks and P. Peterson. Washington, D.C.: Brookings Institute.

Wood, Daniel B. 1998. "Creativity replaces racial quotas at colleges." *Christian Science Monitor*. 15 September.

Yates, Steven. 1996. "Affirmative action is unnecessary and divisive." Pp. 110–15 in *Race relations: Opposing viewpoints*, edited by Paul A. Winters. San Diego, Calif.: Greenhaven Press.

CHAPTER

3

The Death Penalty

More than 13,000 people have been legally executed in the United States since Colonial times, most of them in the early twentieth century. By the 1930s, as many as 150 people were executed each year. Since the early twentieth century up until the 1930s, legal execution in the United States met with little public disapproval. However, as public outrage and the number of legal challenges to death sentences grew, the practice waned. After 1950, the number of executions consistently declined from 105 in 1951 to 2 in 1967, and to 0 from 1968 through 1976, primarily due to legal challenges to the death penalty (ACLU 1996a, 1998b; Blackmun 1997).

The challenges against capital punishment culminated in 1972 when the Supreme Court, in the case of *Furman v. Georgia*, ruled that the death penalty was unconstitutional as practiced at the time. The Court found that the inconsistent and arbitrary application of the sentence violated the Eighth Amendment's ban on cruel and unusual punishment. In response, thirty-five states quickly wrote new capital punishment laws that attempted to meet the requirements for fairness and consistency established by the Court. In the case of *Gregg v. Georgia* in 1976, the Supreme Court reversed its course and ruled that "the punishment of death does not invariably violate the Constitution." The Court ruled that the new statutes contained an adequate guard against arbitrariness and discrimination in capital punishment cases.

The nearly ten-year moratorium on executions ended in 1977 when Utah executed convicted murderer Gary Gilmore by firing squad. Since then, more than 350 people have been put to death, most of them in the South. As of 1998, thirty-eight states have laws providing for the death penalty: Eighteen of these states permit execution by lethal injection, fourteen by electrocution, seven by gas, two by hanging, and two by firing squad. In 1997, there were seventy-four executions in the United States, which pushed the twenty-year total to 432. As of November 1998, 3,517 convicts await execution across the nation, an all-time high since 1982 (Shapiro 1998; ACLU 1996a; Bedau 1992; Schonebaum 1998, 6).

In 1989, the Supreme Court upheld the constitutionality of executing 16- and 17-year-old juvenile murderers (ACLU 1996b). Of the thirty-eight states that allow the death penalty, thirteen set the age at 18, four set it at age 17, and twenty-one have a minimum of 16 years of age or no minimum at all. The United States has executed six juvenile offenders this decade, more than any other country. In 1998, there were sixty-three juvenile offenders on death row in prisons around the nation (Farley and Willwerth 1998). The Supreme Court also upheld the constitutionality of executing mentally retarded people, although juries would be permitted to consider retardation as a mitigating factor (ACLU 1996b).

In February 1997, the American Bar Association (ABA), the nation's largest and most influential organization of lawyers, voted to seek a moratorium on executions. Although the lawyers do not oppose capital punishment, they agreed that the imposition of the death penalty is "a haphazard maze of unfair practices," and that "efforts to forge a fair capital punishment jurisprudence have failed." They proposed that no execution should occur "unless and until greater fairness and due process prevail" (Teepen 1997).

American Public Opinion About the Death Penalty

Historically, the American public's feeling about capital punishment has run long cycles, with each reformist (abolitionist) wave breaking up during an era of increased violence. In the 1840s, anti-gallows societies inspired abolition of the death penalty in three states, but disappeared after the outbreak of the Mexican War. A second major reform era ended with World War I. The most recent reform wave, which peaked in the mid-1960s when a slight majority of Americans opposed the death penalty (52 percent in 1966), was halted by the high rise in the violent crime rate, which had begun to grow since the late 1960s (Nygaard 1997).

In the 1960s and early 1970s, a bare majority of Americans favored capital punishment. However, the mounting fear of violent crimes and the public's feeling that too many vicious criminals were getting away with murder led to an upward shift in public opinion polls (ACLU 1995a). Most major opinion surveys of the last decade show that more than 70 percent of Americans support the death penalty, and the figure has remained consistent for at least the past decade (Sowell and DiIulio, Jr. 1997; Brownlee et al. 1997; Moore 1995, 23).

The Death Penalty in Other Countries

More than half the countries in the world have abolished the death penalty in law or practice. As of 1997, ninety-nine countries abolished the death penalty in law or practice, while ninety-five countries retain it. In Europe, twenty-eight (of thirty-three) countries have abolished the death penalty either in law or in practice (Amnesty International 1997).

In 1996, more than 5,300 prisoners were executed and 7,107 were sentenced to death around the world. The highest recorded numbers of executions in 1996 are China, 4,367; Ukraine, 167; Russia, 140; Turkmenistan, 123; Iran, 110; Saudi Arabia, 69; United States, 45; Singapore, 38; Belarus, 24; and Taiwan, 21 (Amnesty International 1997).

In 1996, when China launched a crackdown on crime, people were sentenced to death at a rate of nearly seventeen a day. At least 4,367 were executed, compared with 772 people known to have been executed in thirty-eight other countries in the same year. Through the 1990s, more people have been executed or sentenced to death in China than in the rest of the world combined. Many are executed for nonviolent crimes such as corruption and theft (Amnesty International 1997).

The following sections summarize the supporting and opposing views on the death penalty.

Punishment Should Fit the Crime; Capital Crimes Justify Capital Punishment

Supporting the Death Penalty

Justice requires that punishment should fit the crime, and capital crimes justify nothing less than capital punishment. Historically, the law of retribution has been the universal punishment rationale. Anyone who inflicts undeserved evil on another deserves to suffer in the same way, or at least as much as that which he or she has caused. The issue here is the just desert. In order to maintain society's sense of justice, it is necessary to punish perpetrators of the worst crimes with the death penalty, and it is necessary that the criminals pay their debt to society. For the crime of premeditated murder, there is no possible substitute that can satisfy justice other than the death of the offender. Anything less than death would indicate that we regard the victim's life as less valuable than that of the offender (Pojman 1998a, 10-31; Colson 1997; Hoyler 1994, 488; van den Haag 1997, 168).

Opposing the Death Penalty

The retribution rationale, which takes its cue from *lex talionis* (an eye for an eye, a tooth for a tooth), holds that the offender deserves harm equivalent to the harm he or she intentionally imposed on the victim. This, however, does not mean that the punishment should duplicate the harm the criminal imposed, because that is often impractical or impossible. For example, we cannot duplicate the harm caused by a check forger or a spy. We do not rape the rapist, torture the torturer, or burn down the arsonist's property because it is morally wrong. By the same reason, it is wrong to kill the killer, even if it were his or her just desert. Instead, we need to impose an alternative punishment that produces an equivalent amount of suffering, most appropriately some number of years in prison that might add up to the harm caused by the criminals (Reiman 1998a).

The retributive principle of *lex talionis* cannot be applied in modern civilized societies. If we do employ it, we will find ourselves descending to the cruelties and savagery of the past and of the criminals. There is no punishment that can measure up for someone who committed several murders in cold blood. Although there are ways to torture the person before the killing, we should not do it because this is a degree of cruelty that is beyond the moral boundaries of a civilized society. What retribution requires in modern society is not equivalence of harm between crime and punishment, but proportionality. The worst crime will be punished by the worst punishment available, even if less in harm than the crime, the second worst crime by the second worst punishment, and so on (Reiman 1998a, 72).

The death penalty might be considered a justifiable retribution for a murderer if we can assume that the murderer is wholly responsible for her crime. However, the causes of crime, in most cases, are far more complicated. Most crimes, including murder, are consequences of many different factors in life, such as deprived environment, disruptive family background, abused childhood, personality factors, biological or psychological problems, and other limited opportunities of education and employment. The retribution rationale will hold only if neither the state nor society bears any responsibility for what the murderer has done (Reiman 1998a, 121).

The Death Penalty Is a Necessary Restitution for the Victim and Victim's Family

Supporting the Death Penalty

The victim's family has a right to seek justice and to gain peace of mind through the death of the offender. For some victims' family members, only the death penalty can assuage their sorrow. It gives the victims' families some satisfaction to know that justice has been served and that the offender could never enjoy life and see anybody he or she cares about. Sometimes, even death by lethal injection seems too easy for the victim's loved ones, as compared with the pain and agony that the victims had gone through (Brownlee et al. 1997; Kozinski and Gallagher 1995).

Fueled by the public's frustration with violent crimes and the way violent criminals are treated in our criminal justice system, the victim's rights movement is gaining unprecedented support in the United States. Victim's rights activists, in their quest for justice, have pushed for the right of victims' survivors to make personal impact statements at sentencing for murder cases, and for the right of families of murder victims to witness executions (which sixteen states now allow) (Gabrels 1997; Brownlee et al. 1997).

Opposing the Death Penalty

The death penalty does no more than sanctify the victim's desire to hurt the offender back, simply for the satisfaction that the victim derives from seeing the offender suffer. Deriving satisfaction from the suffering of others, and the policy of imposing suffering on the offender for no other purpose than giving satisfaction to her victim, is a form of vengeance, not retributive justice (Reiman 1998a, 88; U.S. Attorney General Janet Reno in Dieter 1998, 22).

Revenge is an illegitimate justification for the death penalty. Seeking revenge violates a central tenet of Western law, that criminals should be punished on behalf of society as a whole, not the victim. For better or worse, U.S. judges and juries are supposed to mete out punishment whether or not the victim's family condones or condemns it (Brownlee et al. 1997; Pojman 1998a).

Killing the offender may bring about a temporary gratification for the victim's families. However, families of murder victims usually do not experience the relief they expected to feel at the execution. Taking the offender's life does not fill the void, but it is generally not until after the execution that the families realize this (Lula Redmond, a Florida therapist who works with victims' families, in Brownlee et al. 1997). What the families of murder victims really need is financial and emotional support to help them recover their loss and resume their lives, not vengeance (ACLU 1996b).

Not every family member of the murder victim wishes the murderer of his loved one to be executed. For example, the Kennedy family has lost two of its sons (John F. and Robert) to assassination, yet has remained opposed to capital punishment, as has the family of Martin Luther King, Jr. (Hanks 1997, 92–3).

The Death Penalty Is "Cruel and Unusual"; It Violates Human Dignity and the Criminal's Right to Life

Opposing the Death Penalty

The severity of punishment has its limits—imposed by our moral principle and respect for human dignity. We do not rape the rapist, torture the torturer, or burn the arsonist's house for moral reasons. If insisting on a pound of flesh seems barbaric, why not insisting on a life barbaric? The government that respects these limits does not use premeditated, violent homicide as an instrument of social policy.

The death penalty violates the wrongdoer's essential dignity as a human being. No matter how bad a person may be, no matter how terrible one's deed, we must never cease to regard a person as an end in himself, as someone with inherent dignity. Capital punishment violates that dignity (Justice Thurgood Marshall in Pojman 1998a, 60).

Unlike other punishment options, capital punishment denies due process of the law because its imposition is irrevocable. It forever deprives an individual of the benefits of new evidence or a new law that might warrant the reversal of a conviction or the setting aside of a death sentence (Bedau 1992).

Capital punishment violates the Eighth Amendment's prohibition against "cruel and unusual" punishment (ACLU 1995a). The history of capital punishment is replete with examples of botched executions. Even with the most advanced method of lethal injection, executions are always painful, cruel, and degrading (ACLU 1996b). Progress in civilization is characterized by a lower tolerance for one's own pain and that suffered by others. Civilization brings increased power to prevent or reduce pain, and increased public repugnance for harmful acts done to others. Modern states have a duty to act in a civilized way. Capital punishment is a barbaric remnant of an uncivilized society. We need not respond to violence with violence. Killing, whether carried out by an individual or the state, is cruel and unusual in modern societies (Norman Siegel, the executive director of the New York Civil Liberties Union, in Reiman 1998a, 108–9).

Supporting the Death Penalty

The death penalty does not violate the criminal's right to life, for the right to life is not an absolute right that can never be overridden. Our right to life, liberty, and property is connected with our duty to respect the right of others to life, liberty, and property. By violating the right of another to property, we thereby forfeit our property right. Similarly, by violating the right of another to life, we forfeit our right to life. Those who show utter contempt for human life by committing remorseless, premeditated murder justly forfeit the right to their own life (Mario Cuomo's Speech in Nygaard 1997; Pojman 1998a, 30).

Rather than violating the wrongdoer's dignity, capital punishment recognizes and respects the worth and dignity of the victim by calling for an equal punishment to be extracted from the offender, and it respects the dignity of the offender by treating her as a free agent who must bear the cost of her act as a responsible agent (Pojman 1998a, 26, 61).

Is the sanctity of human life too great for others to make a decision as to whether criminals should live or die? We send thousands of good, gallant, and upright men to die in war. Compared to that, it seems ironic to contend that brutal murderers' lives are too precious to be destroyed (Theodore Roosevelt in

Kronenwetter 1993, 31). There is no necessary connection between eliminating the death penalty and civilization. In modern societies, we still have wars to which innocent people are sent to die, and we still have brutal crimes involving unimaginable pain and suffering inflicted on the victims.

We could meet the abolitionists' requirement for less pain while retaining the death penalty, for we can execute the criminals by lethal injection, which is virtually painless. Even if they suffer some pain, the murderers deserve some pain (Pojman 1998b, 141–2; van den Haag 1990).

The Death Penalty Does Not Deter Crime

Opposing the Death Penalty

The argument most often cited in support of capital punishment is that the threat of execution deters capital crimes more effectively than the threat of imprisonment. This claim, although plausible, is not supported by evidence. There is no credible evidence that the death penalty deters homicide. The states that impose the death penalty do not have lower rates of criminal homicide than non–death penalty states. States that abolished the death penalty do not show an increased rate of criminal homicide after abolition. States that have reinstituted the death penalty after abolishing it have not shown a decreased criminal homicide rate. The United States is the only Western democratic society that allows executions, yet the U.S. homicide rate is by far the highest in the industrialized world (Lawes 1969; Sellin 1959; Reiman 1998b, 156).

The death penalty has no deterrent effect on most murders because people commit murders largely in the heat of passion or under the influence of alcohol or drugs, giving little thought to the possible consequences of their acts. When their crime is not premeditated, it is impossible to imagine how the threat of any punishment could deter it. It is an impulsive behavior by those who are heedless of the consequences of their behavior to themselves as well as to others. If the crime is premeditated, such as in cases of professional criminals, kidnappers, and gang-related murderers, the criminals ordinarily concentrate on escaping detection, arrest, and conviction. The threat of even the severest punishment will not deter those who expect to escape detection and arrest. Political terrorism is usually committed in the name of an ideology that honors its martyrs; trying to cope with it by threatening death is futile (Bedau 1992; Lawes 1969; Nathanson 1987).

The death penalty does guarantee that the condemned person will commit no further crimes. This, however, is an "incapacitative," not a deterrent, effect of execution. The incapacitative component of punishment can be satisfied with life in prison or some lengthy prison term. The convicted murderers will no longer be a threat to the public so long as they remain in prison (Reiman 1998a, 118).

Supporting the Death Penalty

It is extremely difficult, if not impossible, to demonstrate a relationship between executions and homicide rates nationwide because there are too many variables to be controlled for, including demographic factors (e.g., age and racial distribution), law enforcement factors (e.g., severity of the crime, knowledge of the consequences of getting caught), social conditions, and opportunity factors, just to name a few. For this reason, social science has been unable to either conclusively support or disprove the theory that capital punishment deters crime (Schonebaum 1998, 7; Pojman 1998b, 139).

Nevertheless, there is well-documented evidence in support of the deterrent effect of capital punishment. Isaac Ehrlich's study (1975) takes into account the problems of complex sociological backgrounds, such as race, heredity, regional lines, standards of housing, education, opportunities, cultural patterns, intelligence, and so forth, and concludes that the death penalty does deter. His simultaneous equation regression model suggests that over the period of 1933 and 1969, "an additional execution per year may have resulted on the average in seven or eight fewer murders." Stephen Layson's study in 1985 corroborates Ehrlich's conclusion. His work indicates that each time the death penalty is applied, the murder rate is reduced by about eighteen murders (Layson 1985). From 1972 to 1976, when capital punishment was struck down by the Supreme Court because of *Furman v. Georgia*, the number of murders soared to twice the average number of murders that happened per year while capital punishment was allowed (Draper 1985, 97). Delaware, which executes more murderers per capita than any other state in the United States, has low homicide rates. When Texas resumed executions in 1982, Houston (Harris County) executed more murderers than any other city or state (except Texas) and has seen the greatest reduction in murder, 701 in 1981 down to 261 in 1996 (Justice For All 1997).

The lack of statistical evidence supporting the deterrent effect of capital punishment could be the result of the so-called lighthouse effect—we see cases in which deterrence fails, but not those in which it succeeds. We will never know how many potential murderers are deterred by the threat of the death penalty, or how many lives may be saved by it (Colson 1997; Pojman 1998a). If we don't have hard evidence that the death penalty deters, we should at least bet on saving potential murder victims rather than bet on saving the lives of the convicted murderers (van den Haag in Schonebaum 1998, 9).

Even though we cannot prove conclusively that the death penalty deters, commonsense evidence provides insight into the psychology of human motivation. The possibility of long-term imprisonment plus the possibility of the death penalty is likely to be a greater deterrent than the possibility of long-term imprisonment alone (Pojman 1998b, 46, 140). Once in prison, virtually all convicted murderers seek to avoid execution by appealing to reduce their sentence to life in prison. This is evidence that the death penalty is feared more, and therefore deters more than a life sentence (van den Haag in Schonebaum 1998, 8).

Swifter Execution of Death Penalty Would Increase Deterrence Effect

Supporting the Death Penalty

One of the reasons why the death penalty often fails to deter is because, as presently applied, it is not carried out swiftly. Under the current system, convicted killers who have been duly tried and sentenced to death by state courts are endlessly delaying their executions with federal appeals, based on legal technicalities, at the taxpayers' expense. The delay eliminates the cause-and-effect relationship between crime and punishment that is necessary if punishment is to deter future crimes (Sowell and DiIulio, Jr. 1997). On average, death row inmates spend about ten years appealing their conviction and sentence before being executed. The average elapsed time from sentence to execution has been increased from four years and three months in 1983 to nine years and five months in 1993 (Specter 1997, 117), and to eleven years and two months in 1995 (Justice For All 1997). Too many death row inmates are abusing the writ of habeas corpus (which allows for federal appeals of state court convictions) in order to delay their executions, or to simply go judge shopping (running the same marginal arguments past multiple sets of judges) until they find a judge who would agree with the defendant (Scheidegger 1997).

The delays leave victims' families in a difficult state of suspended anger and frustration. Families of the victim often have to endure a number of retrials, evidentiary hearings, and last-minute stays of execution for years after the crime. Sometimes their rage may go on for more than a decade without the families reaching a sense of resolution or obtaining peace of mind. This delay denies justice to the victim, the victim's family, and to society (Brownlee et al. 1997; Kozinski and Gallagher 1995; Specter 1997, 115).

Opposing the Death Penalty

Punishment can be more effective if it is employed consistently and promptly. However, the death penalty cannot be administered promptly. Delays in execution are a necessary cost of fairness, a safeguard against executing the innocent (Kaminer 1997, 125). Delays in carrying out the death sentence are unavoidable, given the procedural safeguards required by the courts in capital cases. Murder trials take far longer when the death penalty is involved. Postconviction appeals in death penalty cases are far more frequent as well. The Habeas Corpus petition, often blamed for the delays in executions, is a necessary safeguard of a fair trial process. All these factors increase the time of administering criminal justice. If we reduce such delay by abandoning the procedural safeguards and constitutional rights of suspects, defendants, and convicts, there will be a greater risk of convicting the wrong person and executing the innocent (Kaminer 1997, 121; Bedau 1992). Even with the current system, many innocent people have been found guilty. Between 1973 and 1993, at least forty-eight people on death row were released after they were found to be innocent (Gabrels 1997): Since 1993, twenty-one convicted murderers were found to be innocent after new evidence developed (Teepen 1997).

Greater Certainty of Execution Would Increase Deterrence Effect

Supporting the Death Penalty

Both criminologists and law enforcement officers agree that it is the fear of apprehension and the likely prospect of swift and certain punishment that provides the greatest deterrent to crime (Frank Friel in Dieter 1998, 22). Under the current system, however, only a tiny fraction of even the most vicious killers ever get executed. Between 1977 and 1993, a third of a million Americans were murdered, yet only 2,716 convicted murderers were on death row in 1993 for all those lives stolen since 1977, and only 226 were actually executed (Sowell and DiIulio, Jr. 1997; Kaplan 1997). Although death sentences have increased in number to about 250 per year since 1980, this is still only 1 to 2 percent (on average) of all homicides known to the police. From 1967 to 1977, a convicted murderer's chance of escaping execution was about 100 to 1. In 1993 and 1994, however, the ratio increased to 750 to 1 in favor of the criminal (Pojman 1998a, 49). From 1973 through 1996, approximately 5,900 people have been sentenced to death and 358 executed: An average of 0.02 percent of those sentenced to death were executed every year during that time (Justice For All 1997). The average sentence of someone in state prison for murder is twenty years, convicted murderers spend about 8.5 years in prison (Sowell and DiIulio, Jr. 1997).

If the crime's pay-off is likely to be high and the chances of getting caught are low, the attractiveness of the crime is heightened. If the penalty for the crime is lowered, in addition to the low certainty of punishment, crime increases in attractiveness even more. This is exactly what is happening in our criminal justice system. Neither deterrence nor justice can be achieved in this way.

Opposing the Death Penalty

In theory, it would be possible to make the death penalty swift and certain, but that would involve the specter of about fifty executions every day of the year, something without parallel or precedent in a modern civilized society. The American public would not tolerate such large-scale cruelty and waste of human life; other Western democratic societies would see it as a human rights violation (Robertson 1989, 131).

A high certainty of arrest, conviction, and punishment will certainly increase the deterrent effect of any crime. If the certainty of getting arrested and punished is high, life-term imprisonment would have a higher deterrent effect than the death penalty with low certainty. In order to increase the certainty, however, we need to look at different areas of law enforcement, such as more police officers on the street, neighborhood crime watch programs, community policing, and controlling illegal drugs. Instead of wasting resources on the complicated legal processes of capital cases, we could spend more on these law enforcement strategies that are known to be effective in controlling crime (Ross 1997a; Dieter 1998).

The Death Penalty Is Applied Unfairly to African Americans

Opposing the Death Penalty

The death penalty cannot be employed so far as racial bias continues to occur in our criminal justice system. Numerous studies have shown that African Americans are more likely to be arrested, charged, convicted, and receive the death penalty than whites (Baldus et al. 1990; Paternoster 1983; Radelet and Pierce 1985). From 1930 to 1975, 3,859 people have been executed in the United States. Of these 54 percent were African Americans. For the crime of murder, 3,334 have been executed; 49 percent were African Americans. African American offenders, as compared with whites, were more likely to be executed for crimes less often receiving the death penalty, such as rape and burglary. For rape, which was punishable by death until 1972 in sixteen states and by the federal government, a total of 455 have been executed, and 405 of them (90 percent) were African Americans (Bender 1974; Bowers 1994; in Bedau 1992).

Racial bias continued to occur even after the system was reformed in 1976 (Reiman 1998b, 162). As of January 1994, 40 percent, or 1,117 of the prisoners under the death sentence were African American, despite the fact that African Americans comprise only about 12 percent of the national population (Ross 1997b, 149).

Studies have also presented evidence for discrimination among convicted murderers on the basis of the race of their victims, with killers of white victims standing a considerably greater chance of being sentenced to death than killers of African American victims (Gross and Mauro 1984; Paternoster 1984, 1983). Roughly 80 percent of those put to death in the past two decades had killed whites, though only about half of the murder victims were white (Brownlee et al. 1997). The 227 prisoners executed between 1976 and 1994 were convicted of killing 302 victims. Of these victims, 255 (84 percent) were white and only 47 were African American or of another minority group. While 86 African American or minority prisoners have been executed for murdering white victims, only two white murderers have been executed for the death of a nonwhite, one for the murder of an African American man and one for the murder of an Asian woman (Ross 1997b, 150). Studies of racial discrimination in capital cases in Georgia, Florida, Illinois, Mississippi, North Carolina, Oklahoma, and Virginia all showed that "the average odds of receiving a death sentence among all indicted cases were about four times higher in cases with white victims than with African American victims" (Baldus et al. 1990; ACLU 1996a).

Supporting the Death Penalty

Indeed, numerous studies of the late 1800s and early 1900s have found that African Americans were executed in disproportionate number, particularly when the victims of their crimes were white. While there is a jurisdiction for the claim that discriminatory capital sentencing and execution occurred in the past, the charge that they persist today lacks support. There are more African Americans on death row than whites simply because proportionately more African Americans than whites commit violent crimes including murder (Rothman and Powers 1994; Brownlee et al. 1997). In 1994, 1,864,168 violent crimes occurred, and 25,052 offenders were convicted. Of those offenders, 56 percent were African American, 42 percent white, and the remainder were people of other races (Pojman 1998a, 3). Historically, African American homicide rates have never been less than five times white homicide rates, and in many years since the 1950s, the rates have been more than ten times higher (Sowell and DiIulio, Jr. 1997).

Many states have made significant changes in sentencing procedures since the *Furman* decision, and as a result, contrary to what many believe, whites convicted of first-degree murder are sentenced to death at a higher rate than African Americans (Pojman 1998a, 58; Rothman and Powers 1994). In 1994, of the thirty-one prisoners executed, twenty were white and eleven were African American, although 41 percent of those arrested for murder were white, and 56 percent, African American. Of those sentenced to death in 1994 (total of 323), 50 percent were white and 42 percent were African American, despite the fact that relatively more African Americans (72 percent) than whites (65 percent) or Hispanics (60 percent) had prior felony records (Department of Justice 1994). The imposition of the death penalty no longer discriminates against African Americans.

There is a legitimate explanation why offenders, regardless of their race, are more likely to receive the death penalty when the victims are white. When a murder involves people of different race, it is more likely that the victim and the killer are strangers. Whites are significantly more likely to be murdered by strangers and by someone of a different race. The African American–offender–white–victim murders, in particular, tend to be the most aggravated of all, and frequently involve armed robbery, kidnapping, rape, torture, and beating, which are more likely to receive the death penalty. In Georgia, for instance, 67 percent of the black-on-white cases, compared with only 7 percent of the black-on-black cases, involved armed robbery. By contrast, black-on-black homicides were most likely to occur during altercations between people who knew one another. Seventy-three percent of the African American–victim homicides were precipitated by a dispute or a fight, circumstances viewed by the courts as mitigating. Also, 95 percent of African American–victim homicides were committed by African American offenders, and there were so few white-on-black cases that no distinctive homicide pattern could even be ascertained (Rothman and Powers 1994). Overall, evidence shows that African Americans convicted of killing whites are more likely to be executed not because of the racial identity of the victims but because of the qualitative differences in the nature of their crimes.

The Death Penalty Is Applied Unfairly to the Poor

Opposing the Death Penalty

In addition to race, studies have shown that the defendant's socioeconomic status influences one's chance of getting the death penalty. There are more than 3,000 people on death row today, and virtually all are poor, and a significant number are mentally retarded or people with disabilities (ACLU 1996b). Approximately 90 percent of those on death row could not afford to hire a lawyer when they were tried (Tabak in Bedau 1992).

The rich defendants usually post bail, retain competent attorneys of choice for a fee, and hire investigators, expert witnesses, and even a team of juror consultants. On the other hand, the indigent defendant is often unable to post bond, more likely to remain in jail, and to proceed to trial with a court-appointed attorney or a public defender who is generally inexperienced, incompetent, uncaring, undercompensated, or overburdened with a staggering caseload, especially in southern states where most death sentences and executions take place (DiSpoldo 1997, 164; Bright 1997). The Southern Rights Center reports that Alabama limits expenses for indigent counsel to $2,000 a case; Mississippi, $1,000; and Kentucky, $2,500. There have been reports that these public defenders show up in court drunk, late, unprepared, and even fall asleep during trials. Texas courts have found no fault with attorneys who sleep through parts of death penalty trials (Teepen 1997; Pacifica News 3-28-97).

Supporting the Death Penalty

There is a reason why the poor are more likely to receive the death penalty than the rich. Most capital case murders are committed by poor people, often during robberies. The wealthy rarely murder, just as they rarely commit burglaries for obvious reasons. They are more likely to commit white-collar crimes, which are never punished by the death penalty (van den Haag 1997, 168).

If guilty whites or wealthy people escape the death penalty and guilty poor or African American people do not, the poor or African Americans do not become less guilty because the others escaped their deserved punishment. All premeditated murderers, whether rich or poor, deserve to be executed. The death penalty's only injustice is in society's failure to execute some wealthy murderers as well as the poor (van den Haag 1997, 167).

No criminal justice system can totally avoid inequality, despite all the efforts to minimize it. Defendants are tried by different juries, judges, and lawyers—and even if they had the same amount of money to spend, these variables would make a difference. All we can do is to make sure (as much as we can) that the defense attorneys are reasonably competent and that the judges and juries are impartial. Equal punishment for equal guilt is an ideal to strive for, but we should realize that it is sometimes difficult to achieve. That does not mean that we should abolish the whole system of capital punishment. Instead, we should try to minimize any systematic discrimination that might exist within the system (van den Haag 1997, 168).

Innocent People Can Be Executed

Opposing the Death Penalty

Our criminal justice system cannot be made fail-safe because it is run by human beings, who are fallible. The execution of innocent people is bound to occur. Bedau and Radelet, in their study published in 1987 in the *Stanford Law Review*, identified "350 cases in which defendants convicted of capital or potentially capital crimes since 1900, and in many cases sentenced to death, have later been found to be innocent." Of those, twenty-five convicts were executed while others spent decades of their lives in prison. Fifty-five of the 350 cases took place in the 1970s, and another twenty of them between 1980 and 1985 (Radelet et al. 1992; ACLU 1996b). Between 1973 and 1993, at least forty-eight people on death row were released after they were found innocent, according to a congressional subcommittee on civil and constitutional rights (Gabrels 1997): Since 1993, twenty-one convicted murderers were found innocent after new evidence developed (Teepen 1997). From 1993 through 1995, states placed 4,945 men and women on death row. Among those, 1,530 have had their convictions overturned or sentences reduced through appeals. This represents 31 percent of the total number originally sentenced to death (Hanks 1997, 125–6). For every seven executions—486 since 1976—one other prisoner on death row has been found innocent. Those found innocent are still the lucky ones; most of them were found innocent because the real murderers were arrested and confessed to the crimes that they were convicted of committing (Shapiro 1998). Who knows how many unlucky ones have been already executed or are still on death row waiting to be executed?

There are many reasons why wrongful convictions in capital cases are possible. They include false information given by witnesses, faulty eyewitness identification, prejudice against defendants, faulty police work, overzealous prosecution, coerced confessions, incompetent defense counsels, perjured testimony, seemingly conclusive circumstantial evidence, and the community's pressure for a conviction (Radelet et al. 1992; Bedau 1992; Shapiro 1999).

In Chicago, in 1999, three former assistant state's attorneys and four DuPage County detectives were convicted of hiding and falsifying evidence, and of conspiring to frame an African American man for the 1983 murder of a ten-year-old girl (Sugar 1999).

The execution of an innocent person is the most hideous crime we can think of. The fact that the government, which is supposed to protect its citizens, is killing an innocent person as a legitimate policy is abhorrent. If an innocent person can be executed, that means anybody could be executed for being in the wrong place at the wrong time (Hanks 1997, 111). With capital punishment, our society risks being as guilty of premeditated and unwarranted murder as any man or woman on death row (122).

Supporting the Death Penalty

The most frequently cited source in support of the claim that innocent people have been executed is Bedau and Radelet's study published in 1987 in the *Stanford Law Review*. Their claim that the "350 defendants convicted of capital or potentially capital crimes" were later "found" to be innocent is misleading and inaccurate. The figure of "350 cases" does not refer to 350 Americans wrongfully executed. The number includes cases of people who were charged with capital crimes but convicted of lesser offenses, such as second-degree murder or manslaughter; people who were convicted of capital crimes but sentenced to imprisonment rather than death; and people who were convicted of capital crimes but who had their conviction overturned on appeals. Only 200 of the allegedly wrongful convictions in their study involved first-degree murderers in which capital punishment was an option. Out of those 200 cases, only in 139 cases were the defendants actually sentenced to death, and in only twenty-three of these 139 cases was the death sentence actually carried out. So, if there were wrongful executions, it is with regard to these twenty-three cases, not 350. Even with these twenty-three cases, twelve of those cases had no evidence of innocence and substantial evidence of guilt. The remaining eleven cases represent 0.14 percent of the 7,800 executions which have taken place since 1900. In fact, there is no proof that even those eleven executed were innocent; in each of those cases, there were eyewitnesses, confessions, physical evidence, and circumstantial evidence in support of the defendant's guilt. In addition, most of the erroneous cases ending in execution occurred in the early 1900s. Since 1976, there is very little likelihood of an innocent person being executed (Markman 1994). The use of the death penalty has been limited by the courts and legislature to apply only to the most outrageous cases with undeniable evidence; prosecutors customarily refrain from asking for the death penalty in all but the most heinous crimes (Specter 1997, 116). Great effort has been made in pretrial, trial, appeals, writ, and clemency procedures to minimize the chance of an innocent being convicted or executed.

Society has a right to protect its members from capital offenses even if this means taking a finite chance of executing innocent people. The fact that this occasional error may be made, regrettable though this is, is not a sufficient reason for us to refuse the use of the death penalty, if on balance it serves a just and useful function (Pojman 1998a, 54).

At present, the chance of an innocent person being murdered by exconvicts is greater than the chance of an innocent person being executed. In 1978, 6 percent of the convicted murderers who were paroled committed another murder within six years of release. Of the roughly 52,000 state prison inmates serving time for murder, an estimated 810 had previously been convicted of murder and had killed 821 people following their previous murder convictions. Executing these inmates would have saved 821 lives (Justice For All 1997).

The Death Penalty Costs More Than Life Imprisonment

Opposing the Death Penalty

Many judges, prosecutors, and other law enforcement officials oppose the death penalty on the grounds of cost. They worry that the enormous concentration of judicial services on a handful of capital cases (many of which will ultimately result in life imprisonment) needlessly diverts increasingly scarce resources from other areas of law enforcement (Ross 1997a, 137). Under the current system, it costs more to maintain capital punishment than life imprisonment. The costs of capital punishment come largely from the increased expenses of capital trials and appeals. Because a mistake in a death penalty trial could cost an innocent person's life, extraordinary procedures are used to try to assure fairness. Capital cases have to be investigated more thoroughly by both the prosecution and defense. Pretrial proceedings in capital cases are more numerous and complicated than in life-imprisonment cases. The process of jury selection is also more complex and time-consuming to reduce potential juror biases. Adding to the high cost of capital punishment is the appeals process, which was created as a result of the *Furman* decision in 1972 to help make sure capital sentences were applied with a reasonable level of competence and fairness. The government usually pays the costs of both the prosecution and the defense, along with all the court costs because most of the defendants in capital cases are indigent (Hanks 1997, 124).

Studies in North Carolina, California, Florida, Texas, Georgia, and Maryland all show that each death penalty case costs about two to six times (depending on states) more than the cost of imprisoning one inmate in a single cell at the highest security level for forty years (Ross 1997a, 136–7). The high cost of maintaining the death penalty is the major reason why some state legislatures continue to vote against reinstating the death penalty despite public support for it (Bedau 1992).

In deciding to maintain the death penalty, our society has chosen to keep an ineffective crime-fighting method at a huge cost. The extra funds needed to investigate, prosecute, and appeal capital cases would be better spent on other crime reduction efforts that are known to be effective, such as increasing the number of police officers and neighborhood watch programs, building more prisons, punishing criminals more swiftly and surely, controlling illegal drugs, gun control, and expanding other educational or job training programs for young people to give them alternatives to a life of crime (Dieter 1998, 22–23; Ross 1997a, 138; Hanks 1997, 127; ACLU 1995b).

Supporting the Death Penalty

The death penalty can be practiced more cost-effectively than it is. Instead of expanding the list of crimes for which the death penalty is applied, the state legislature could narrow the statutes to reserve the death penalty for only the most heinous criminals. This is better and more cost-effective than loading our death rows with many more than we can possibly execute, and then picking those who will die essentially at random (Kozinski and Gallagher1995). On average, less than 1 percent of the death row inmates have been executed since 1980. Since 1973, legal protections have been so extraordinary that 37 percent of all death row cases have been overturned for due process reasons or commuted (Justice For All 1997). Why do we waste so much money on death penalty cases if we are not going to execute those convicted?

In a way, the death penalty does save money indirectly. It does by encouraging defendants to enter a guilty plea and also to confess to crimes. Because of the fear of receiving the death penalty, the accused are more likely to enter a guilty plea and avoid the death penalty in return. This saves money because it hastens the court process and also eliminates the appeal process once someone is found guilty (Fitzpatrick 1995, 1070).

The death penalty could be more cost-effective than life imprisonment if it is carried out efficiently and swiftly. It costs about $34,000 per year to keep an inmate in prison; $75,000 per year in a maximum security cell (Justice For All 1997). Why should hardworking taxpayers pay to support convicted murderers for the rest of their lives to live comfortably in prison? It is better to execute those who deserve to die and save society the cost of their keep in prison.

Criminals Are the Victims of Circumstances

Opposing the Death Penalty

Many criminologists have shown that the vast majority of crimes are a predictable response to frustrations that result from deprived social circumstances. What seems to be linked to crime is the general breakdown of stable communities, institutions, and families that has occurred in our cities in recent decades as a result of economic and demographic trends that are largely out of an individual's control. Most notably, they include poverty, unemployment, lack of education, and other opportunities for a decent living. Poverty especially leaves few defenses against the breakdown and few avenues of escape from it. It is this general breakdown that spawns crime. Every time a crime is committed, society bears some of the responsibility for the crime, and thus has no right to extract the full cost of the crime from the criminal until society does everything possible to rectify the conditions that produce their crimes (Reiman 1998a, 127).

Many offenders of violent crime had rough childhoods, including physical, sexual, and mental abuse by family members as well as by other children, which resulted in permanent emotional and psychological damage. The juvenile offenders on death row are especially the victims of recent, horrible child abuses. A recent study of fourteen condemned juvenile offenders found that all of them had suffered serious head injuries as children, all had serious psychiatric problems, all but two had been severely beaten or physically abused as children, and five had been sexually abused by relatives. Only two had IQ scores above 90 (Farley and Willwerth 1998).

Criminals are the victims of a troubled or deprived environment and need help. Society has a moral responsibility to provide them with appropriate therapy, treatment, education, job training, and moral reinforcement in an effort to resocialize and rehabilitate them. So far as we tolerate the existence of remediable, unjust social conditions that foster crime, we are accomplices in the crime that predictably results. As such, we lose the right to extract the full price from the criminal, and this means we lose the right to take the murderer's life in return for the life he has taken (Reiman 1998a, 128).

Infliction of the death penalty extinguishes all possibilities for reform and rehabilitation for the person executed, as well as the opportunity to make some compensation for the evils he has done. It also cuts off the possibility of moral growth in a human life that has been seriously deformed by adverse conditions (U.S. Catholic Bishops' Statement on Capital Punishment in Hanks 1997, 165). People can change, and many do change. Even the most vicious criminals have been reformed and rehabilitated in the past. The goal of punishment should involve penance, not just retribution. The punishment must give the criminal a chance to recognize what he has done, repent of the crime, and possibly start a new life. The death penalty precludes the opportunity for repentance and restoration to the community altogether (Duff 1995, 169–198; Falls 1986).

Supporting the Death Penalty

Those who oppose capital punishment tend to oppose punishment in general and favor rehabilitation, which repeatedly has failed in the past. Many death row criminals are incorrigible, hard-core criminals who cannot be reformed or rehabilitated given our present means for rehabilitation. If people kill others in cold blood, they must bear the responsibility for that murder. Rehabilitation theories reduce moral responsibility to medical problems and blame society, not the individual, who chose to commit the hideous crime. There are limits to what socialization and medical technology can do. Socialization can be relatively effective in early childhood, less so in late childhood, while even less effective in adulthood (Pojman 1998a, 26). As a result of these unsuccessful rehabilitation and resocialization attempts, unfortunately, innocent people pay the price. What could you say to the families of people murdered by those who had murdered before and had been turned loose or paroled? (Sowell and DiIulio, Jr. 1997).

Many liberals blame poverty and believe that poverty is the root cause of crime. Poverty is a terrible condition and surely contributes to crime, but it is not a necessary or sufficient condition for violent crimes. The majority of the people in India are poorer than most of the American poor, yet the violent crime rate is significantly lower in India than in the inner cities of the United States (Pojman 1998a, 3).

The death penalty ultimately confronts us with the issue of moral accountability in our society. Contemporary society seems unwilling to assign moral responsibility to anyone. Everything imaginable is due to a dysfunctional family, economic trouble, or some unpleasant childhood experiences. Instead of blaming others and society, we need to be responsible for our own actions, and we demand the same from criminals (Colson 1997).

There is no incompatibility between penance and just desert. One may repent of one's immoral deed and still acknowledge that she deserves to be punished for it. In fact, the very nature of repenting includes a sense of deserving to suffer for the wrongdoing. Even if one does repent, the heinousness of the deed remains, hence deserves just punishment. The truly repentant murderer would agree that he deserves to die and request an execution (Pojman 1998a, 34).

The Death Penalty Promotes Violence by Sending a Message to the Public That Killing Is Acceptable

Opposing the Death Penalty

By executing murderers, the government sends a message to the public that "violence is a justifiable mean in solving violence," and that "killing is all right when deemed justified" (Schonebaum 1998; Bedau 1992). Capital punishment, as a state-authorized killing, demonstrates a lack of respect for human life, and thereby, instead of deterring murder, fosters a climate of violence. The so-called brutalization effect (murders increase in the period following executions), which was demonstrated in California, where the homicide rate increased in the months immediately following executions in 1992 and 1993, is an example of this. The state-sanctioned executions "brutalize the sensibilities of society, making potential murderers less inhibited" (Godfry and Schiraldi 1998, 47; Bowers and Pierce 1980; Schonebaum 1998, 8). By refraining from executing murderers, the state contributes to the general repugnance of murder, sends a message that we can break the cycle of violence, and that we can envisage more humane and effective responses to the growth of violent crime. Two wrongs do not make a right (Schonebaum 1998, 8; Reiman 1998b, 161; Hanks 1997, 161–7).

Supporting the Death Penalty

Capital punishment, instead of demonstrating a lack of respect for human life, sends a message that human life is so valuable that you do not dare take away another person's life without risking your own. If you do, you have to pay for it with your own life. It demonstrates respect for the victim's life and also treats the offender as a respectable human being who has to take responsibility for his own action. Capital punishment teaches the public the Golden Rule, which mandates, "Do unto others as you would have others do unto you," that is, to treat others as you would have them treat you (Reiman 1998a, 89). Capital punishment is a justified killing as a punitive act, and any rational person can distinguish the murder as a punitive act from the criminal act. The American public is clearly aware of the difference, and thus reacts differently—with anger and frustration to the criminal homicide and a sigh of relief to the capital punishment.

The Majority of Americans Support the Death Penalty

Supporting the Death Penalty

Every major opinion survey of the last decade shows that the majority of Americans (between 70 and 80 percent)—whites, blacks, young and old alike—support the execution of murderers (Sowell and DiIulio, Jr. 1997; Moore 1995; Gabrels 1997; Colson 1997). Americans are tired of seeing too many violent crimes, and feel that too many vicious criminals get away with murder. As a democratic society, Americans have a right to have their opinion and belief expressed in a policy. The elected officials have an obligation to implement and help enforce the policy most Americans want (Gabrels 1997).

Opposing the Death Penalty

The media commonly reports that the American public overwhelmingly supports the death penalty. More careful analysis of public attitudes, however, reveals that most Americans would oppose the death penalty if convicted murderers were sentenced to life without parole and were required to make some form of restitution to the victims. The support for the death penalty drops to below 50 percent when people are given a choice between the death penalty and life without parole plus restitution (Brownlee et al. 1997; Bedau 1992). Studies also reveal that when Americans are asked whether they think vengeance is a legitimate reason to execute a murderer, 60 percent do not. Additionally, a slight majority (52 percent) do not believe that the death penalty deters crime (Schonebaum 1998, 6–7). These indicate that the majority of those who support the death penalty do so with reluctance and as a last resort, only when other alternatives fail to work. Before we resort to this last option of the death penalty, we should at least try alternatives, such as life imprisonment and restitution.

The public's support for capital punishment is a response to the high rate of violent crimes. The fear of violent crime is, however, out of proportion with reality. Murder victims are actually less likely to be killed in cold blood by strangers than they are in the heat of an argument by family members or other close associates. Most children are abducted or abused not by strangers but by relatives or friends (Brownlee et al. 1997). Most Americans are not aware of the fact that capital punishment actually makes the fight against crime more difficult by wasting valuable resources that could be applied to more promising efforts to protect the public (Morgenthau 1998, 14).

The United States Is the Only Western Industrialized Society That Allows the Death Penalty

Opposing the Death Penalty

Among the Western industrialized societies, the United States is the only country which retains and uses the death penalty for ordinary crimes. The United States is ranked seventh in the world in terms of the number of prisoners executed, following China, Ukraine, Russia, Turkmenistan, Iran, and Saudi Arabia (Amnesty International 1997). The United States is one of six countries in the world that are known to have executed juvenile offenders in the 1990s, along with Pakistan, Saudi Arabia, Iran, Nigeria, and Yemen (Farley and Willwerth 1998). Americans ought to be embarrassed to find themselves linked with governments of such nations in retaining execution as a method of crime control (Bedau 1992).

Supporting the Death Penalty

The violent crime rate is much higher in the United States than in other Western societies, and Americans are much more likely to experience violent crimes than the citizens of other Western countries (Brownlee et al. 1997). Fear of crime is one of the major concerns of most Americans (Specter 1997). The National Center of Health Statistics has reported that the homicide rate for young men in the United States is 4 to 73 times the rate of other industrialized societies. Killings per 100,000 by men 15 through 24 years old in 1987 was 0.3 in Austria and 0.5 in Japan, whereas the figure was 21.9 in the United States, and as high as 232 per 100,000 for African Americans in some states. The nearest nation to the United States was Scotland, with a 5.0 homicide rate. In 1994, 23,330 murders were committed in the United States, and the homicide rate was 37 per 100,000 men between the ages of 15 and 24 (Pojman 1998a, 2).

Americans support capital punishment not because they are less civilized or undemocratic, but because Americans are faced with higher rates of violent crimes than citizens of other Western industrialized societies.

Life Imprisonment Is a Better Option Than the Death Penalty

Opposing the Death Penalty

If deterrence is the goal, we do not need capital punishment. Life imprisonment without parole can deter and incapacitate the murderer as equally as the death penalty can. Convicted murderers will no longer be a threat to the public so far as they remain in prison. Anyone who would be deterred by the death penalty would equally be deterred by life imprisonment (Reiman 1998a; Bender 1974).

Unlike capital punishment, life imprisonment gives the guilty person time to regret, a chance to start a reformed life, or even a chance to make some restitution to society as well as to the victim's family. It also gives the wrongfully convicted person a chance to appeal.

Life imprisonment can be carried out much more swiftly than capital cases because its issues are not as pressing as in death penalty cases, and hearings and appeal attempts are reduced. It saves taxpayers' money by reducing legal processes, and it increases the deterrent effect by punishing criminals promptly. Swifter justice also helps bring closure more quickly to the victims' families compared with death sentences, which usually take about a decade to be carried out (Hanks 1997, 92–3; Brownlee et al. 1997).

Supporting the Death Penalty

The death penalty, if carried out swiftly and with certainty, will have a greater deterrent effect than long-term imprisonment. The possibility of long-term imprisonment plus the possibility of the death penalty is likely to be a greater deterrent than the possibility of long-term imprisonment alone (Pojman 1998b, 140).

Life imprisonment without parole sounds like a good alternative. In reality, however, there is nothing to prevent people under such a sentence from being paroled under later laws or later court rulings, as happens very frequently. There are many cases in which those who have murdered before and had been turned loose by judges or parole boards, or allowed weekend furloughs by progressive prison authorities, murdered again. More than 40 percent of the people on death row in 1992 were on probation, parole, or pretrial release at the time they murdered (Sowell and DiIulio, Jr. 1997; Markman 1994). Of roughly 52,000 inmates serving time for murder in 1984, an estimated 810 had been previously convicted of murder and had killed 821 people following their previous murder convictions (Justice For All 1997). Moreover, there is nothing to stop them from escaping or from killing again while in prison. Indeed, there is greater incentive to murder if criminals have committed a life-term offense, because their punishment cannot be increased for the offenses they commit in prison.

For some violent repeat offenders, capital punishment is the only deterrence that will guarantee that they won't commit similar violent crimes in and out of prison. There are some brutal, heinous crimes in which victims suffered unbearable pain. In those cases, even death by lethal injection seems too lenient compared with the brutal death victims suffered, let alone a comfortable life in prison for the rest of the murderer's life (Scalia 1997).

REFERENCES

American Civil Liberties Union (ACLU). 1996a. "Double justice: Race and the death penalty." (Http://www.aclu.org/issues/death/death5.html).

———. 1996b. "The death penalty." *ACLU Briefing Paper 8.* (http://www.aclu.org/library/pbp8.html).

———. 1995a. "New York Civil Liberties Union says no to death penalty." *ACLU Press Release.* 16 February.

———. 1995b. "Governor Weld perpetrating fraud by advocating death penalty." *ACLU Press Release.* 10 March.

Amnesty International. 1997. "The death penalty: List of abolitionist and retentionist countries." (http://www.amnesty.org/ailib/intcam/dp/abrelist.htm).

Baldus, D., C. Pulaski, and G. Woodworth. 1990. *Equal justice and the death penalty.* Boston, Mass.: Northeastern University Press.

Bedau, Hugo Adam. 1992. "The case against the death penalty." *ACLU Issues.* (http://www.aclu.org/issues/death/death1.html).

Bender, David L. 1974. *Problems of death.* Anoka, Minn.: Greenhaven Press.

Blackmun, Harry A. 1997. "The death penalty is legally unjust." Pp. 66–71 in *The death penalty: Opposing viewpoints,* edited by Paul A. Winters. San Diego, Calif.: Greenhaven Press.

Bowers, William J., and Glenn L. Pierce. 1980. "Deterrence or brutalization: What is the effect of execution?" *Crime and Delinquency* 26(4):453–84.

Bright, Stephen B. 1997. "Counsel for the poor: The death sentence not for the worst crime but for the worst lawyer." Pp. 275–309 in *The death penalty in America: Current controversies*, edited by Hugo A. Bedau. New York: Oxford University Press.

Brownlee, Shannon, Dan McGraw, and Jason Vest. 1997. "The place for vengeance." *U.S. News & World Report*. 16 June.

Colson, Charles W. 1997. "The death penalty is morally just." Pp. 60–65 in *The death penalty: Opposing viewpoints*, edited by Paul A. Winters. San Diego, Calif.: Greenhaven Press.

Department of Justice. 1994. *Bureau of Justice Statistics Bulletin*. Washington, D.C.: Government Printing Office.

Dieter, Richard C. 1998. "The death penalty is not an effective law enforcement tool." Pp. 22–38 in *Does capital punishment deter crime?* edited by Stephen E. Schonebaum. San Diego, Calif.: Greenhaven Press.

DiSpoldo, Nick. 1997. "The death penalty is applied unfairly to the poor." Pp. 162–66 in *The death penalty: Opposing viewpoints*, edited by Paul A. Winters. San Diego, Calif.: Greenhaven Press.

Draper, Thomas, ed. 1985. *Capital punishment*. New York: Wilson.

Duff, Anthony. 1995. "Expression, penance, and reform." Pp. 169–98 in *Punishment and rehabilitation*. 3d ed. Edited by Jeffrie Murphy. Belmont, Calif.: Wadsworth Publishers.

Ehrlich, Isaac. 1975. "The deterrent effect of capital punishment: A question of life and death." *American Economic Review* 65(June):397–417.

Falls, Margaret. 1986. "Against the death penalty: A Christian stance in a secular world." *Christian Century*. 10 December, 1118–19.

Farley, Christopher J., and James Willwerth. 1998. "Dead teen walking." *Time*. January.

Fitzpatrick, Tracy B. 1995. "Justice Thurgood Marshall and capital punishment: Social justice and the rule of law." *American Criminal Law Review* 32(4):1065–86.

Gabrels, Sara Terry. 1997. "New fervor for death penalty." *Christian Science Monitor*. 4 November.

Godfrey, Michael J., and Vincent Schiraldi. 1998. "The death penalty may increase homicide rates." Pp. 47–52 in *Does capital punishment deter crime?* edited by Stephen E. Schonebaum. San Diego, Calif.: Greenhaven Press.

Gross, S., and R. Mauro. 1984. "Patterns of death: An analysis of racial disparities in capital sentencing and homicide victimization." *Stanford Law Review* 37:27–120.

Hanks, Gardner C. 1997. *Against the death penalty: Christian and secular arguments against capital punishment*. Scottdale, Penn.: Herald Press.

Hoyler, Robert. 1994. "Capital punishment and the sanctity of life." *International Philosophical Quarterly*. 34(4):485–97.

Justice For All. 1997. "Death penalty and sentencing information in the United States." 1 October. (http://www2.jfa.net/jfa/dp.html#innocent).

Kaminer, Wendy. 1997. "A swifter death penalty would not be an effective deterrent." Pp. 120–25 in *The death penalty: Opposing viewpoints*, edited by Paul A. Winters. San Diego, Calif.: Greenhaven Press.

Kaplan, David A. 1997. "Life and death decisions." *Newsweek*. 16 June.

Kozinski, Alex, and Sean Gallagher. 1995. "For an honest death penalty." *New York Times*. 8 March.

Kronenwetter, Michael. 1993. *Capital punishment*. Santa Barbara, Calif.: ABC-CLIO.

Lawes, Lewis E. 1969. *Man's judgment of death*. Montclair, N.J.: Patterson Smith.

Layson, Stephen. 1985. "Homicide and deterrence: A re-examination of the U.S. Time-series evidence." *Southern Economic Journal*, 68–80.

Markman, Stephen. 1994. "Innocents on death row?" *National Review*. September.

Moore, David W. 1995. "Americans firmly support death penalty." *Gallup Poll Monthly* 357(June):23–25.

Morgenthau, Robert M. 1998. "The death penalty hinders the fight against crime." Pp. 14–16 in *Does capital punishment deter crime?* edited by Stephen E. Schonebaum. San Diego, Calif.: Greenhaven Press.

Nathanson, Stephen. 1987. *An eye for an eye?* Lanham, Md.: Rowman & Littlefield.

Nygaard, Richard. 1997. "The death penalty is not a deterrent." Pp. 108–13 in *The death penalty: Opposing viewpoints*, edited by Paul A. Winters. San Diego, Calif.: Greenhaven Press.

Paternoster, R. 1983. "Prosecutorial discrimination in requesting the death penalty: A case of victim-based racial discrimination." *Law and Society Review* 18:437–78.

———. 1984. "Race of victim and location of crime: The decision to seek the death penalty in South Carolina." *Journal of Criminal Law and Criminology* 74(3):754–88.

Pojman, Louis P. 1998a. "For the death penalty." Pp. 1–66 in *The death penalty: For and against*, edited by Louis P. Pojman and Jeffrey Reiman. Lanham, Md.: Rowman & Littlefield.

———. 1998b. "Reply to Jeffrey Reiman." Pp. 133–49 in *The death penalty: For and against*, edited by Louis P. Pojman and Jeffrey Reiman. Lanham, Md.: Rowman & Littlefield.

Radelet, Michael L., and Glenn L. Pierce. 1985. "Race and prosecutorial discretion in homicide cases." *Law and Society Review* 19:615–19.

———, Hugo A. Bedau, and Constance E. Putnam. 1992. *In spite of innocence: Erroneous conviction in capital cases*. Boston, Mass.: Northeastern University Press.

Reiman, Jeffrey. 1998a. "Why the death penalty should be abolished in America." Pp. 67–132 in *The death penalty: For and against*, edited by Louis P. Pojman and Jeffrey Reiman. Lanham, Md.: Rowman & Littlefield.

———. 1998b. "Reply to Louis P. Pojman." Pp. 151–63 in *The death penalty: For and against*, edited by Louis P. Pojman and Jeffrey Reiman. Lanham, Md.: Rowman & Littlefield.

Robertson, Ian. 1989. *Society: A brief introduction*. New York: Worth Publishers, 130–31.

Ross, Michael. 1997a. "The death penalty is too expensive." Pp. 134–38 in *The death penalty: Opposing viewpoints*, edited by Paul A. Winters. San Diego, Calif.: Greenhaven Press.

———. 1997b. "The death penalty is applied unfairly to blacks." Pp. 148–54 in *The death penalty: Opposing viewpoints*, edited by Paul A. Winters. San Diego, Calif.: Greenhaven Press.

Rothman, Stanley, and Stephen Powers. 1994. "Execution by quota?" *Public Interest* 116(Summer).

Scalia, Antonin. 1997. "The death penalty is legally just." Pp. 72–75 in *The death penalty: Opposing viewpoints*, edited by Paul A. Winters. San Diego, Calif.: Greenhaven Press.

Scheidegger, Kent. 1997. "Habeas corpus is abused by convicts." Pp. 126–29 in *The death penalty: Opposing viewpoints*, edited by Paul A. Winters. San Diego, Calif.: Greenhaven Press.

Schonebaum, Stephen E., ed. 1998. *Does capital punishment deter crime?* San Diego, Calif.: Greenhaven Press.

Sellin, Thorstein. 1959. *The death penalty*. Reprinted in *The death penalty in America*, edited by Hugo Bedau. New York: Anchor Books, 1967.

Shapiro, Joseph P. 1998. "The wrong men on death row." *U.S. News & World Report*. 9 November, 22–26.

Sowell, Thomas, and John J. DiIulio, Jr. 1997. "The death penalty is a deterrent." Pp. 103–107 in *The death penalty: Opposing viewpoints*, edited by Paul A. Winters. San Diego, Calif.: Greenhaven Press.

Specter, Arlen. 1997. "A swifter death penalty would be an effective deterrent." Pp. 114–19 in *The death penalty: Opposing viewpoints*, edited by Paul A. Winters. San Diego, Calif.: Greenhaven Press.

Sugar, Yehuda. 1999. "Fixing a broken frame: Why did the wrong man go to death row?" *U.S. News & World Report*. 15 March, 28.

Teepen, Tom. 1997. "Death by indifference." *Dayton Daily News*. 29 July.

van den Haag, Ernest. 1997. "The death penalty is not unfair to the guilty." Pp. 167–70 in *The death penalty: Opposing viewpoints*, edited by Paul A. Winters. San Diego, Calif.: Greenhaven Press.

———. 1990. "Why capital punishment?" *Albany Law Review* 54.

4 Gun Control

Gun Ownership in the United States

According to the 1994 National Survey of Private Ownership of Firearms, conducted by the National Institute of Justice, 44 million Americans (35 percent of the population) owned 192 million firearms, and 65 million of them were handguns. Gun ownership is concentrated; 74 percent of the gun owners possessed two or more guns. Gun owners are largely small-town and rural residents of above-average income (Cook and Ludwig 1997; Wright 1988); 72 percent of the rural and small-town residents reported owning guns, compared to 31 percent in large cities (Spitzer 1995, 69). The most common reason for owning firearms was recreation, followed by protection against crime. Most gun ownership is culturally patterned, linked with a rural hunting subculture. The culture is transmitted across generations; gun owners are socialized by their parents into gun ownership and use from childhood. Defensive handgun owners, on the other hand, are more likely to be urban dwellers who seek ownership in response to high crime rate (Cook and Ludwig 1997; Kleck 1997, 94).

Extent of Gun Violence in the United States

Each year, approximately 35,000 to 40,000 people in the United States are killed with firearms. Suicides claim about 15,000 to 18,000 lives, homicides account for about 12,000 to 15,000 lives, and gun accidents about 2,000. Moreover, there are about 60,000 to 100,000 nonfatal shootings and up to one million crimes committed with guns each year (Nisbet 1990, 12; Pilcher 1999). The cost of treating gunshot victims is estimated to be $20 billion a year, about 80 percent of which is covered by taxpayers, because victims usually do not have health insurance (McClurg in Washburn and Pallasch 1998).

From 1985 to 1993, firearm murder rate increased 45 percent, and the handgun murder rate increased 65 percent (CSGV 1997b). However, since 1993, the number of firearm-related fatalities dropped from 39,959 (15.4 per 100,000 people) in 1993 to 32,436 (12.1 per 100,000) in 1997. The number of nonfatal shootings also fell from 104,390 (40.5 per 100,000) in 1993 to 64,207 (24.0 per 100,000) in 1997 (Pilcher 1999).

Types of Gun Control

Gun control refers to laws aimed at limiting possession of firearms and the way firearms are used. Roughly they fall into two major categories. First, under a permissive licensing policy (targeted gun control), anyone may obtain a firearm except certain high-risk people, such as convicted criminals, minors, and the mentally incompetent. This is usually achieved through licensing of gun owners or requiring permits to purchase guns. Second, restrictive licensing policy (general gun control), such as New York's Sullivan law, permits only certain categories of people with a legitimate purpose to own a firearm, such as law enforcement officers, military personnel, and licensed security guards. Typically, home defense is not considered a legitimate purpose for obtaining a license (Bruce-Briggs 1990, 67; Bogus 1997).

Most federal and state gun regulations in the United States are moderate interventions intended to reduce criminal use while preserving the majority's access to guns for legitimate use (permissive licensing). Washington, D.C., and New York have adopted a much broader attack on the handgun problem, with a ban on sales to all but a few people (Cook 1990, 131).

History of Federal Gun Control Laws

The first congressional action pertaining to guns was the enactment of a 10 percent federal excise tax, as part of the War Revenue Act in 1919. It was more significant as a revenue-raising measure than as a tool of firearm regulation. In 1927, Congress passed a bill to prohibit the sale of handguns to private individuals through the mails. By the early 1930s, the Roosevelt administration won passage of more comprehensive gun control, including registration of machine guns, submachine guns, handguns, silencers, cane guns, and sawed-off shotguns. At the urging of the National Rifle Association and other gun groups, however, handguns were removed from the bill. The Federal Firearms Act of 1938 gave the Treasury Department control over a national licensing system incorporating gun dealers, manufacturers, and importers. The Gun Control Act of 1968 banned the interstate shipment of firearms and ammunition to private individuals (in 1986, rifles and shotguns were removed from the prohibited items) and prohibited the sale of guns to minors, drug addicts, mental incompetents, and convicted felons. Title IV of the Omnibus Crime Control Safe Streets Act of 1968 banned the shipment of pistols and revolvers across state lines to individuals, and forbade the purchase of handguns in stores in a state where the buyer did not reside (Spitzer 1995). An amendment to the Firearms Owner's Protection Act of 1986 generally outlawed the sale, transfer, and possession of new machine guns and armor-piercing ammunitions (CSGV 1997a).

The Brady law was passed in 1993 after seven years of bitter congressional battles. As enacted, the Brady law codified a five business-day waiting period for handgun purchases during which time police can make a "reasonable effort" to check the backgrounds of gun buyers. It also authorized $200 million per year to help states improve and upgrade their computerization of criminal records; increased federal firearm dealers' license fees from $30 to $200 for the first three years, and $90 for renewals. The Supreme Court in June 1997, however, decided that the federal government cannot make local police decide whether people are fit to buy handguns. After this decision, mandatory background checks were no longer imposed on the state or local governments; it was voluntary. A national system of instant background checks for gun buyers began in November 1998, as a part of the Brady Act. Twenty-seven states have decided to do some or all of the checks themselves; the FBI will do the checks for the rest. This instant check, however, replaced the five-day waiting period.

The Violent Crime Control and Law Enforcement Act of 1994 prohibits the future manufacture, transfer, and sale of nineteen specific assault weapons and their copycats, as well as ammunition magazines with more than ten rounds. Weapons manufactured before the ban were excluded, and they are still legal for sale and ownership (CSGV 1997a). After a series of school-related killings, President Clinton, in July 1998, pushed for mandatory sentences for adults whose negligence lets children under age 18 get access to guns. Fifteen states, as of July 1998, have laws making it a parental responsibility to keep guns away from children (*New York Times* 7-9-98). Many U.S. handgun manufacturers in 1997 agreed to voluntarily include safety locks in new weapons they sell by 1999. However, in July 1998, the Senate rejected the Democratic party's plan that requires all handguns sold in the United States to include safety locks to prevent accidents (*New York Times* 7-22-98).

In the 1990s, encouraged by the successful lawsuits against cigarette makers, a growing number of cities, gun-violence victims' families, and antigun organizations have started to sue the firearm manufacturers, dealers, and distributors, seeking millions of dollars to defray the cost of violence. In 1998, the city of New Orleans filed a product liability suit against gun manufacturers, accusing them of failing to incorporate safety features to prevent their guns from being fired by unauthorized people, curious children, despondent teenagers, and criminals who obtain the guns through theft. In the same year, the city of Chicago and Cook County filed a $433 million lawsuit against thirty-eight firearm dealers, manufacturers, and distributors, accusing them of illegally flooding the city, which banned the possession and sale of handguns in 1983, with guns that they know will be used in crimes. A number of other cities, such as Miami, Florida, and Bridgeport, Connecticut, are taking similar legal actions against the firearm industries (Levin 1998).

Since the deadliest school shooting incident, in April 1999, when two high school students in Littleton, Colorado, killed twelve classmates and one teacher, and wounded twenty-five others before killing themselves, lawmakers have proposed tougher federal gun control laws. Some of these proposals include making it more difficult for teens to buy weapons, raising the legal age for possession of handguns from 18 to 21, mandatory child safety locks on all guns, background checks on buyers at gun shows, lifetime ban on gun ownership for juveniles convicted of violent crimes, making parents liable for children committing crimes with parents' guns, limiting handgun purchases to one per month, mandatory three-day waiting period before purchasing a handgun, and tougher penalties for firearm offenses by juveniles.

State and Local Gun Control Laws

There are reportedly some 20,000 gun control ordinances in the various jurisdictions of the United States. Most are trivial, reasonable, and uncontroversial, such as prohibitions against discharging a weapon in urban areas or against children carrying weapons. As of 1999, twenty-two states and many large cities have laws against carrying concealed weapons. In a few large cities and states, particularly in the Northeast, a license is required to buy or possess a handgun, and in a very few but growing number of Northeastern cities and states, a permit or license is required to possess any sort of firearm (Bruce-Griggs 1990, 68). Maryland passed a measure in 1988 barring the sale of cheap handguns. California became the first state in the nation to enact an assault weapons ban in 1989, followed by New Jersey in 1990 and Connecticut in 1993. Virginia, Maryland, and South Carolina passed a measure limiting handgun purchases to one a month (Spitzer 1995, 183).

Public Opinion about Gun Control

Public opinion about gun control seems to vary depending on the polls. In 1993, a Time/CNN Poll found that 23 percent of adult Americans favored a handgun ban. According to the Gallup Poll in the same year, 39 percent supported handgun ban; 66 to 77 percent favored banning the manufacture, sale, and possession of semi-automatic assault guns such as AK-47 (Kleck 1997, 322). According to the Harris Poll in the same year, 52 percent supported a ban on the sale of handguns; 62 percent supported a special tax on handguns; 81 percent favored the registration of all handguns; 70 percent of gun owners supported stricter gun control; 73 percent favored bans on cheap, poor-quality handguns, such as Saturday Night Specials; and 73 percent of the public and 72 percent of gun owners supported a ban on semi-automatic assault weapons (Harris 1993).

The following sections summarize the supporting and opposing views on gun control.

The Right to Bear Arms Is Protected by the Second Amendment

Opposing Gun Control

The Second Amendment of the Constitution says, "A well regulated militia being necessary to the security of a free state, the right of the people to keep and bear arms shall not be infringed." This amendment guarantees all U.S. citizens the right to own a firearm (Aitkens 1992; Silver 1997). Gun control laws that take away this right from the law-abiding people who have done nothing wrong is a violation of the Constitution. Should there be any control of firearms, it must be formulated in such a way that would decrease the misuse of guns while still protecting this constitutional right (Lund 1987).

Proponents of gun control argue that the Second Amendment only guarantees the states the right to create militia and use guns for military purposes, and that the National Guard is the only modern-day equivalent of the militia. Their argument is wrong, because "people" and "militia" both mean all citizens of the United States as individuals. The "right of the people" in all amendments has been viewed as the right of individuals, and the Second Amendment should not be an exception (Aitkins 1992). Historically, and under the current law, militias consisted of "citizen-soldiers," which means all able-bodied citizens who are expected to muster, bearing their own arms, during times of threat (Silver 1997). The need for a militia to protect our freedom is probably not as great as it was in 1792, but there are other purposes of firearms in modern societies, such as hunting, sports, recreation, and self-protection. Hunting is an American tradition older than the Constitution; self-protection is both longer and more deeply protected in common law than in the Constitution (Spitzer 1995, 49).

Supporting Gun Control

The framers of the Second Amendment intended only to grant states the right to maintain militias and to allow citizens to own guns for use in their militia. Private, nonmilitia use of firearms is not protected by the Second Amendment. The National Guard is the modern-day equivalent of the militia. The Second Amendment arose from the colonists' fear of a standing army in the hands of a powerful central government. As they created that new central government— the United States of America—many drafters were unsure whether the states would retain the authority to maintain militias. The Amendment responded to that concern and that concern only (*Los Angeles Times* 1993; Silver 1997). There is no constitutional barrier to stricter gun laws, even including a ban on the possession of handguns (Spitzer 1995, 185). The modern purposes for which the Second Amendment is often cited—hunting, sports, self-protection—bear no relation to that amendment (Spitzer 1995, 48–9). All federal decisions consistently have held that federal statutes regulating firearms do not violate the Second Amendment unless they interfere with maintenance of an organized state militia, and the court referred to the militia as "a body of citizens enrolled for military discipline," not as an armed citizenry at large (*Los Angeles Times* 1993).

Guns Are No Longer Needed in Modern Societies

Supporting Gun Control

In the past, especially for the settlers, hunting game was a vital source of food, and protecting oneself from animal predators and hostile Native Americans was a matter of survival. Guns were thus a necessity of everyday life for reasons of subsistence and for self-protection. The United States, however, no longer has a frontier, and, in fact, it is now primarily urban and industrial rather than rural and agricultural. Consequently, the large number of firearms that have gotten and continue to get into civilian hands no longer serve any useful purpose and are more trouble than they are worth. They no longer contribute to the establishment of law and order but instead undermine efforts to establish order, as the high rate of firearm-related crime shows. The primary and unique purpose of firearms in modern America, especially handguns, is to provide an efficient means of destroying human lives (Tonso 1990).

Opposing Gun Control

People own guns not to kill others but for recreation, self-protection, or for collection. The hunting tradition still exists, especially in rural areas. So, too, did the element of competitive sport shooting, a form of recreation. Today, about 14 million people identify themselves as hunters, which represent about 7 percent of the population. The second most frequently cited reason is self-protection (Spitzer 1995). Also, a great many Americans own and collect firearms for purely aesthetic reasons and as a hobby (Nisbet 1990, 14). Guns are an important part of our culture. The early frontier experience, the role of the citizen-soldier in the Revolutionary War, the continued wars against Native American tribes and bandits while settling the nation's frontier, together with

America's hunting tradition made the gun an important part of our culture that cannot and should not be eliminated (Hofstadter 1990).

Guns Don't Kill; People Kill

Opposing Gun Control

Gun violence is a problem in the United States. Guns themselves, however, are not the cause of the violence, and gun control will do nothing to decrease violent crimes. People who decide to kill will find a way to kill even if they do not have access to guns. Guns cannot be singled out and blamed for all the evil crimes in our society. Killers can use knives, clubs, or even cars.

We need crime control instead of gun control. Instead of taking guns away from law-abiding citizens, we should take guns away from the criminals, and take criminals off the street. If crime measures are to be effective, they must deal with the root causes of crime and violence, such as poverty, inequality, injustice, discrimination, unemployment, educational opportunities, and family dissolution. Guns are not the real cause of the problem (Kleck 1990a, 162; Amo 1989; Zimring and Hawkins 1987).

Supporting Gun Control

The reason we need to focus on guns is because guns make it easier for people to kill. Unlike other common weapons, a gun gives an offender the capacity to threaten deadly harm from a distance, thus allowing the offender to maintain a buffer zone between himself and the victim and to control several victims at once. A decision to kill is easier and safer to implement with a gun than with other weapons; there is less danger of victim resistance during the attack, and the killing can be accomplished more quickly and impersonally, with less sustained effort than is usually required with a knife or blunt objects (Cook 1990, 133–5).

The use of a gun also increases the severity of any resulting injuries and the probability of the victim's death, compared with what would have occurred with other weapons. When a gun is used, the chance of death is about five times as great as when a knife is used (Kleck 1990, 151) and sixteen times greater than when a blunt object is used (Yeager et al. 1990, 230; Block 1977; Zimring and Hawkins 1987). A gun has the greatest value against relatively invulnerable victims (e.g., physically strong, guarded, or armed). It is because of their capacity to kill instantly and from a distance that firearms are virtually the only weapon used in killing police officers (Zimring and Hawkins 1987; Cook 1990, 133). Guns facilitate some crimes that would not occur if guns were absent, such as robberies of the well-defended, lucrative business establishments, mass murders, drive-by shootings, random shootings, and killing of innocent bystanders.

Easy Access to and Availability of Guns Increase Violence

Opposing Gun Control

From 1964 to 1994, the gun ownership rate in the United States increased by 100 percent, and the handgun ownership rate increased by 188 percent (Kleck 1997, 64; Spitzer 1995, 69). During this time, the violent crime rate increased sharply, particularly the firearm-related crimes. From 1985 to 1994, the nation's murder rate increased 23 percent, the firearm murder rate increased over 46 percent, and the handgun murder rate increased 65 percent (CSGV 1997b).

There are significant links between general handgun availability and the use of handguns in violent crimes (Zimring and Hawkins 1987). About a 10 percent increase in the fraction of households that own guns is associated with approximately a 5 percent increase in the rate of gun robbery. If guns were less readily available, the criminal homicide rate would fall, especially in crimes involving less vulnerable victims. A reduction in gun availability would reduce armed robberies, especially of well-defended commercial places. It will also reduce violence perpetrated not for economic gain, but rather in the heat of the moment that turns injurious or lethal not so much because anyone intended it to, but because in a moment of rage, a firearm was at hand. The immediate availability of a gun makes these circumstances more dangerous than would a less lethal weapon (Cook 1990, 138–9; Spitzer 1995, 186).

Easy access to guns is the major cause of violence in schools. In just one school year (1997–1998), in several different incidences, seventy students were gunned down, twenty-two of them killed by young teenagers who brought guns to school and randomly killed students and teachers. In April 1999, the deadliest school shooting occurred in Littleton, Colorado, when two high school students killed twelve classmates and a teacher, and wounded twenty-five others, before killing themselves. A national survey in 1990 by the Centers for Disease Control and Prevention revealed that one in twenty high school students reported carrying a firearm, usually a handgun, during the past month (of the survey). School security experts and law enforcement officials estimate that 80 percent of firearms students bring to school come from home (CSGV 1997b).

Opposing Gun Control

There is no evidence that the prevalence of guns in an area leads to a higher violence rate. It is not just the availability of guns that threatens our society, but the availability of guns in the wrong hands. The vast majority of gun owners never commits a serious crime of violence with their guns (Spitzer 1995; Kleck 1997, 383–4). A cross-sectional analysis of robbery in fifty cities found that the density of gun ownership was statistically unrelated to the overall robbery rate when other causal factors were taken into account. The two cities with the highest robbery rates, Detroit and Boston, differed markedly in gun ownership. Boston was one of the lowest, and Detroit was above average (Cook 1990, 144). Kleck's study indicated that general gun availability has no measurable net positive effect on rates of homicide, suicide, robbery, assault, rape, or burglary in the United States (Kleck in Kates 1995, 43).

Guns are even more readily available in Switzerland and Israel than in the United States, but their gun-related crime rate is much lower than in the United States. Gun ownership is much more widespread in small towns and rural areas than in big cities. Violent crime, in contrast, is disproportionately a big-city problem (Wright 1998).

The positive association often found between aggregate levels of violence and handgun ownership appears to be primarily due to the fact that more law-abiding citizens buy handguns to defend themselves as the rate of violent crime rises (Kleck 1990a; Kates 1995; Kleck 1997, 94).

Rather than reducing crime, bans on gun ownership make criminals feel safer because they know that their potential victims are unarmed and less able to defend themselves (Kates 1995, 43; Polsby 1997, 32; Wright and Rossi in Polsby 1997, 31).

Reduction in gun availability would not reduce violence in general, but would change the distribution of violent crimes. The reduction would be concentrated among the least vulnerable victims, such as physically strong, male, and well-guarded people (e.g., police officers). The most vulnerable, such as the old, infirm, women, and handicapped, on the other hand, would be more likely to be victimized (Cook 1990, 138).

Easy Access to and Availability of Guns Increase Suicide Rates

Supporting Gun Control

Gun availability is significantly associated with total suicide rates (Lester 1989). Between 1972 and 1994, U.S. civilian gun ownership increased by 54 percent. During this time, the percentage of suicides committed with guns increased from 53.3 to 60.3 (per 100,000) (Kleck 1997, 265). Each year, approximately 17,000 people die from firearm suicide. More Americans die from firearm suicide than firearm homicide. From 1988 to 1992, 60 percent of suicide fatalities involved firearms, and 64 percent of firearm suicides involved handguns. Suicidal adolescents are seventy-five times more likely to commit suicide when a gun is kept in their home. From 1980 to 1992, the suicide rate for 10- to 14-year-olds increased 120 percent, for 15- to 19-year-olds it increased 28 percent. Firearm-related suicides accounted for 81 percent of the increase in this group (CSGV 1997b). Suicide rate would decrease without guns, especially among teens, because guns are more lethal and easier to execute than other suicide forms. About 90 percent of gun suicide attempts are successful, compared with about 80 percent for hanging, 77 percent for death from carbon monoxide, 70 percent from drowning, and 23 percent from poisoning (Spitzer 1995).

Most suicides, especially teenage suicides, are impulsive acts related to depression. The greater the difficulty of obtaining a means to commit suicide, the less likely it is that an attempt will occur and less likely that the attempts will be fatal.

Opposing Gun Control

Between 1972 and 1994, U.S. civilian gun ownership increased by 54 percent. The suicide rate, however, was virtually constant, fluctuating only slightly within the narrow range from 11.8 to 13.0 (per 100,000), although there was a mild increase in the percentage of suicides committed with guns as opposed to other methods (53.3 to 60.3 percent). This indicates that the gun availability might affect the method of choice but not frequency of total suicide (Lester in Kleck 1997, 265). The prospective suicide attempters merely substituted other lethal means of suicide when guns were not available (Lester in Kleck 1997; Kleck and Patterson 1993). The use of a gun seems to be more lethal than other forms of suicide. However, the choice of a gun may simply reflect the seriousness of the person's intent. If suicides involving firearms are more a product of the strength of intent rather than easy availability of weapons, limiting access to firearms will not reduce the rate of suicide. Japan has a suicide rate that is twice as high as America's despite strict gun control. Cultural and social factors appear to affect the suicide rate far more than the availability of firearms (Zimring in Kopel 1992; Carlson 1997).

Easy Access to and Availability of Guns Increase Gun-Related Accidents

Supporting Gun Control

People who keep guns in the home for self-protection place themselves and their families at risk. Accidents account for about 40 percent of all gun-related injuries. More than half of all gun accidents occur in and around the home (Spitzer 1995, 74). In 1991, there were 1,441 unintentional shooting fatalities. Of these, 551 fatalities were children 19 years of age and younger (NCHS 1994). For every accidental death involving firearms, there are about seven nonfatal injuries. Each year, an estimated 1,500 children ages 14 or younger are treated in hospital emergency rooms for unintentional firearm injuries (Bennet 1997). According to a study of unintentional firearm deaths of eighty-eight California children (14 or younger) during the years 1977 through 1983, easy access to firearms was the chief cause of the accidents. In at least 48 percent of the cases, children gained access to firearms that were stored loaded in the house in which the shooting occurred (Wintemute et al. 1989). In 1996, of the 1,134 people killed by firearms, 135 were children under age 14 (Meier 1999).

Opposing Gun Control

General gun ownership levels do not appear to be related to rates of fatal gun accidents. Such acts are very rare and largely confined to a small, unusually reckless segment of the population, often involving heavy drinking (Kleck 1997, 384). Guns become unsafe only when people use them carelessly. Virtually every accident involving a gun can be prevented if a person understands gun safety rules and follows them correctly (NRA 1992). For the average gun owner, the risk of a gun accident could counterbalance the benefits of keeping a gun in the home for protection (Kleck 1997a, 322).

Children's deaths from gun accidents are relatively rare, compared with other accidents, particularly those involving swimming pools and motor vehicles. We cannot demand confiscating about 70 million handguns to save a few hundred children a year, whose lives can be saved by a few simple safety measures (Kates 1990a, 301).

Gun accidents involving both children and adults have actually fallen dramatically since the 1970s, thanks to private safety efforts. In 1988, 277 children under the age of 15 were killed by accidental firearm discharges. That number represents a 48 percent drop from 1974, even as the number of guns per capita increased. From 1968 to 1988, the annual rate of fatal gun accidents fell from 1.2 to 0.6 per 100,000 population (Kopel 1993, 70).

Handguns are simple mechanisms that are entirely safe for any owner who is responsible enough to observe elementary precautions. Safety education is therefore the best way to continue reducing gun accidents (Kopel 1993). We can also require the gun industry to make guns safer and childproof, by incorporating safety locks, load indicators, and trigger locks (Witkin 1998). In addition, parents should take more responsibility for their children's actions and safety.

Guns Are Not an Effective Means of Self-Defense

Supporting Gun Control

A gun kept in the home for self-protection is far more likely to cause serious injury or death to family and friends than to an intruder. Firearm-associated risks at home include injury or death from unintentional gunshot wounds, homicide during domestic quarrels, and the ready availability of an immediate, highly lethal means of suicide (Kellerman and Reay 1986; Yeager et al. 1990, 235; Drinan 1990, 55; Spitzer 1995, 77). An FBI report in 1973 reveals that a firearm kept in the home for self-defense is six times more likely to be used in a deliberate or accidental homicide involving a relative or a friend than against a burglar or unlawful intruder. Only 3.6 percent of those owning guns even had the opportunity to use their firearms when they were assaulted or robbed either at home or on the street (National Crime Panel Survey of 1973 in Drinan 1990, 58).

According to the study in King County, Washington, between 1978 and 1983, for every time a gun in the home was used in a self-defensive homicide against an intruder, there were 1.3 accidental gunshot deaths, 4.6 criminal homicides involving family members, relatives, or friends, and 37 firearm-related suicides. Over 80 percent of the homicides in the same study (1986) occurred during arguments or altercations. Easy access to firearms may therefore be particularly dangerous in households prone to domestic violence. Suicide was the most common form of firearm-related death in the home. Easy access to guns increases the probability that an impulsive suicide attempt will end in death (Kellerman and Reay 1986; Patterson in Kellerman and Reay 1986).

For the majority of the population, the rate of victimization is low enough to question the usefulness of firearms as a means of self-protection. The majority of burglaries (90 percent) are committed while no one is at home, and very few individuals are killed during the course of a burglary (Yeager et al. 1990). Most assaults, if they occur, take place outside the home. About 12 percent of robberies take place inside a home, motel, or hotel room, while 60 percent take place on a street or in a park or field (Hindelang et al. in Yeager et al. 1990). Unless a person is prepared to carry a loaded handgun in her possession at all times, the chance of preventing a robbery that occurs outside the home is negligible (Yeager et al. 1990, 221).

Even if one has a weapon, the chance for the victim to actually deploy the gun is very slim. An assault, robbery, or rape attack almost always occurs so quickly that the victim is taken by surprise. Even if a gun were available, there is not enough time to retrieve, load, and draw a handgun on an assailant (Yeager et al. 1990, 235). In only about 1.2 percent of incidents of home robberies, people who have guns were able to thwart the crime. Home defense can be more effective by using locks, alarm systems, safes, improved lighting, window bars, dogs, and neighborhood watch groups than the use of firearms (Spitzer 1995, 81).

The use of a weapon in resistance to a criminal attack usually results in a greater probability of bodily injury or death to the victim. A study in Chicago revealed that robbery victims who make some attempts at resistance are three times more likely to be injured and eight times more likely to be killed than those who put up no defense (Yeager et al. 1990, 215–35). Often, the gun one has for self-defense is used against the victim by the criminal. Among all police officers killed in the line of duty from 1984 to 1988, about 20 percent were killed with their own weapons (Spitzer 1995, 77). From 1988 to 1997, sixty-two police officers nationwide were killed with their own weapons, according to the FBI (Meier 1999).

Opposing Gun Control

The armed citizen or the threat of the armed citizen is probably the most effective crime deterrent in the nation. According to a survey of felons, most criminals are more worried about meeting an armed victim than they are about running into the police (Polsby 1997, 31). Many report that they had been scared off, shot at, wounded, or captured by an armed victim (Kleck 1988; McGrath in Kates 1997, 45). The presence of guns in the home is a major reason why the high-crime United States has a lower burglary rate than low-crime societies, such as England, Canada, and the Netherlands, where guns are largely forbidden and intruders do not have to worry about the possibility of victim resistance with guns (Chapman in Kates 1997, 48). Burglars in these countries are also more likely to invade occupied homes than burglars in the United States (Mayhew et al. in Kleck 1988). An interview with convicted juveniles who frequently victimized foreign tourists in Florida revealed that they prey on foreign tourists because they know that the tourists do not have guns.

There is no way of knowing how many private citizens' lives were saved because the intruder or attacker was scared off by a gun. Studies using homicide data exclude as much as 96 percent of all defensive gun uses which *did not* result in the death of criminals but only scaring them off (Carlson 1997, 60). Kleck and Gertz contend that defensive gun use is much more common than a widely quoted survey by the federal government indicates. According to their anonymous survey, each year in the United States there are about 2.2 to 2.5 million defensive gun uses of all types by civilians. The frequency of defensive gun uses roughly equals the total number of U.S. arrests for violent crime and burglary (Kleck and Gertz 1995). According to Wright and Rossi's analysis, gun-armed civilians capture or scare off thirty times more criminals than they kill (Wright and Rossi in Kates 1990, 254).

The firearm equalizes the means of physical terror between the strong and the weak. The weak must resort to firearms to defend themselves against the physically strong (Wright 1998). The gun is the greatest equalizer. Only the gun gives the weaker, older, less aggressive victims equal or better chances against a stronger attacker. Without the help of a gun, women, the old, and the weak would be in greater danger of victimization (Cook 1990, 132; Kates 1990c, 262). Women comprise the fastest-growing group of gun owners in the United States. The proliferation of single-parent, female heads of households and particularly professional and single women working and living in high-crime areas, accounts for this trend (Kates 1990c).

Proponents claim that victims who resist are often seriously hurt or killed, and therefore it is better to submit to attackers' demands and give them what they want. When assailants demand material belongings, you may give them what they want, but what if they are going to rape you? Being raped has totally different psychological and emotional consequences from losing belongings (Kates 1990c, 263). According to Cook's study, those who submitted to the felons' demands were twice as likely to be injured than those who resisted with guns. Those who resisted without guns were three times as likely to be injured as those with guns (Cook 1990).

Twenty out of thirty victims killed in gun robberies in Dade County (Florida) between 1974 and 1976 did not resist the robber. At least in half of the robbery cases the killing was deliberate; for example, the victim was tied and then executed, or shot several times from close range. There is a growing number of nonprofessional (nonutilitarian), so-called joy robbers, who view robbery as a form of recreation and the gratuitous violence against the victim may be just part of the fun (Cook 1990, 142–3). Self-defense is the only and absolute right of individuals in these situations. No one should have to surrender one's dignity, safety, property, or life to a criminal. We have a right to defend ourselves and protect our family with whatever means available.

Even if there is no immediate danger of crime, guns can give you a "feeling of safety" and "security." A 1990 survey of gun owners found that 42 percent reported feeling safer with guns. This is one of the benefits of gun ownership—having peace of mind and feeling safer and more secure (Wright and Daly in Spitzer 1995, 80). Especially for people who live in remote, rural areas or in high-crime areas of central cities, guns provide the most effective means of self-defense and security (Drinan 1990, 59).

Police cannot realistically be expected to provide personal protection for every citizen and, indeed, are not even legally obliged to do so (Kleck 1997, 184). Even police officers, according to a survey of police officers, believe that their departments are understaffed and unable to adequately protect individuals, and that law-abiding, responsible adults should have the right to own firearms for self-defense (Kates 1995).

Gun Control Takes Guns Away from Law-Abiding Citizens Only, Not Criminals

Opposing Gun Control

Any form of gun control measures, such as buyer screening, owner registration, licensing, purchase permit with background checks, or total prohibition (general gun control) would take away guns from law-abiding citizens or make it difficult for law-abiding citizens to purchase guns, while having no effect on the criminals' ability to obtain guns. Criminals, regardless of the law, will find ways to get guns if they want them. According to the Bureau of Alcohol, Tobacco, and Firearms's study, which traced guns used in 76,260 crimes in twenty-seven cities, 51 percent of the traced guns were purchased from licensed dealers by people acting as straw intermediaries for the real owners, and 35 percent were stolen. The remainder came from private sellers or black-market dealers without background checks (Ross 1999).

That is why the existing gun laws in the United States have been ineffective in curtailing gun-related crimes, deaths, and injuries. Regardless of the gun laws, the number of armed criminals and the amount of armed crime have tended to increase, not abate (Wright and Rossi 1986). Cook's study (1976) found that cities in states with gun-purchase permit laws had as much robbery and gun robbery as cities not subject to such laws. Since 1976, the District of Columbia has had the country's most extreme gun laws; no civilian may buy or carry a handgun, nor may any gun be kept loaded or assembled in the home for self-defense. Nevertheless, Washington has one of the highest homicide rates in the country (Kates 1995). New York enacted one of the nation's toughest gun laws, the Sullivan law, in 1911, which imposed strict requirements on the sale, possession, and carrying of concealable weapons. Even so, handgun violence in New York City continued to rise (Nisbet 1990, 23; Spitzer 1995, 182).

Supporting Gun Control

Gun control measures, if enforced properly on the national level, can be effective in keeping guns away from criminals. Since the Brady law was enacted in 1994, for about a three-year-period until December 1997, the background checks had blocked an estimated 242,000 handgun sales: 61.7 percent of the cases were disapproved because the buyers were convicted or indicted felons (Sniffen 1998).

According to Kleck's comprehensive study of the effectiveness of gun control laws, gun buyer screening measures, such as owner licensing and purchase permit with background checks, could reduce homicides and suicides. Local licensing of gun dealers may reduce robbery, aggravated assault, and suicide (Kleck 1997, 387). Studies have shown that laws prohibiting gun possession by mentally ill people reduce suicides (Lommers 1984 in Kleck 1997, 364). The Bartley-Fox Amendment in Massachusetts (an anticarrying law) was quite effective. The gun assault rate went down substantially following its implementation. Gun control is not "the solution" to America's violent crime problem, but it is one aspect of the effort to find a solution (Cook 1990, 144–6).

Gun Control Measures Are Effective in Other Countries

Supporting Gun Control

Those nations that tightly restrict gun ownership are the nations where people live free from the fear of drive-by shootings, mass murder-suicides, and domestic quarrels that escalate into homicides (Bogus 1997, 39). In Canada, handgun ownership by private citizens is restricted. The average U.S. handgun murder rate (4.05 per 100,000) is significantly greater than the average Canadian homicide rate for all methods of killing (2.73 per 100,000). Guns are tightly regulated in the United Kingdom (even the police are unarmed), and violent crime is trivial compared with that in the United States (Sproule and Kennett 1989). In Japan, other than the police and the military, no one may purchase or own a handgun or a rifle. Japan has 1.2 homicides per 100,000 citizens, compared with 8.4 in the United States; Japan's robbery rate is 1.4, compared with 220.9 in the United States (Kopel 1992).

Epidemiologists studied crime in Seattle and Vancouver, two cities with remarkably similar geographies, histories, population sizes, demographics, cultures, and overall crime rates. The burglary rates were nearly identical in both cities, as were rates of assault and murder with knives and clubs. But the risk of being shot to death was nearly five times higher in Seattle, and the chance of being assaulted at gunpoint in Seattle was eight times greater than in Vancouver. The only plausible explanation is that guns are reasonably restricted in Vancouver, Canada, but they are widely available in Seattle, Washington (Sloan et al. 1988; Safran 1997, 18–21).

Opposing Gun Control

Both Canada and Great Britain had lower violence rates than the United States before the strict controls were implemented. Before 1920, gun control was at least as lenient in Great Britain as in the United States. In 1919, the homicide rate in England was 0.8 per 100,000, compared with 9.5 in the United States. Canada had a national handgun registration system since the early 1920s, and tightened the restriction further in 1976. In 1919, Canada's homicide rate was 0.69 compared with 9.5 in the United States. The current difference in violence rates, therefore, cannot be a result of gun control laws (Kleck 1997, 360; Wright 1988). In Canada, there was a marginal tendency for nonshooting homicides to increase subsequent to gun control implementation in 1976, suggesting that gun control may encourage murderers to use other methods than firearms to kill (Sproule and Kennet 1989). In Great Britain, although firearm homicide rate is lower than in the United States, nonfirearm burglary rate is higher than in the United States (Chapman in Kates 1995, 48).

Japan's low crime rate has more to do with culture than gun control. Traditionally, Japanese government and police are much more oppressive and effective in controlling crime than U.S. law enforcers. Japan has a tight social control system, formal and informal, and a conformist culture that helps keep citizens out of crime. In addition, Japan is the world's most homogeneous and unified society in terms of ethnicity, race, and culture, which reduces chances of conflict and tension (Kopel 1992).

Switzerland has a militia system: Government supplies assault rifles to all adult males, and those are required by law to be stored at home. Yet,

Switzerland's murder rate is 15 percent of ours (Bruce-Briggs 1990, 79–80). Israeli citizens are, for political and defensive reasons, required to arm themselves. Every settlement has an arsenal, and almost every individual is armed. Israelis have accumulated a huge number of privately owned military weapons, including automatics, yet the crime rate in Israel is much lower than in the United States (Bruce-Briggs 1990, 80).

In Australia, gun licensing, gun registration, and gun prohibition measures taken by six states and a territory have had no success in reducing crimes (Kelly 1992). "Gun-controlled" Mexico and South Africa have murder rates more than twice as high as in the United States (Polsby 1994).

Nations differ in so many respects, including history, culture, racial problems, ethnicity, crime rate, and political situations, that it is impossible to draw valid conclusions linking gun control measures and gun violence (Wright and Rossi 1986; Wright 1988).

Targeted Gun Control versus General Gun Control

Targeted Gun Control (Permissive Licensing)

Gun control laws should be aimed at restricting gun possession among narrowly targeted high-risk people, such as convicted criminals, alcoholics, mentally ill, illegal aliens, drug addicts, fugitives from justice, and people under the age of 18, rather than banning guns in the general population. Such gun control measures like gun owner licensing and purchase-to-permit systems are more effective in deterring crime and do not violate ordinary citizens' right to own firearms and to defend themselves (Wright and Rossi 1986; Cook 1990; Kleck 1989, 1997).

Most gun ownership is for legal purposes. Less than 2 percent of handguns and handgun owners will ever be involved in violent crime (Kleck 1989, 1997, 94). People who kill family members and acquaintances are not representative of the gun-owning public. Such people typically have criminal records and violent histories (Kates 1990b). Some proponents' claim that murderers are good law-abiding people committing impulsive gun murders while engaged in arguments with family members or acquaintances is exaggerated. About 75 percent of offenders arrested for murder had at least one prior arrest for violent felony or burglary. Most serious crimes are concentrated in the relatively small number of people who have been arrested for many other crimes (Wright and Rossi 1986; Chaiken in Kates 1990b, 271). Most family murders are preceded by a long history of assaults and domestic violence (Straus in Kates 1990b, 272). About 70 to 75 percent of domestic homicide offenders have been previously arrested and about half previously convicted (Kates 1990b, 272).

We cannot take guns away from the 98 to 99 percent of the law-abiding citizens who have not done anything wrong, in order to take guns away from the 1 or 2 percent of the population who criminally misuse firearms. Such gun control measures not only violate law-abiding citizens' right to bear arms but also are ineffective in reducing crime. Felons in various surveys have said that banning handguns would make their lives safer and easier by disarming victims without affecting their own ability to obtain weapons (Polsby 1997).

If there were no or few firearms already in circulation, a general ban would be possible. The number of firearms presently available in the United States is so great that the general control measures would not work. At present, prohibition would require buying, collecting, or confiscating some 200 million privately owned firearms and preventing future production or smuggling of existing weapons, which is not likely to be realized (Bruce-Briggs 1990, 68; Zimring and Hawkins 1987; Polsby 1997, 32). Proponents of general gun control are naive to believe that we can somehow return to some imaginary square one stage where nobody had a gun or a reason to use one (Polsby 1997, 33).

If guns are outlawed, only outlaws will have guns. Laws are most likely to be obeyed by law-abiding people, and the gun laws are not an exception. Any control measure that applies equally to criminals and noncriminals is most certain to reduce gun possession more among the noncriminals than the criminals (Kleck 1988). Only the law-abiding gun owners would turn theirs in, not the criminals. Criminals usually get their weapons through informal, off-the-record transactions, mostly involving friends and associates, family members, and various black-market sources (Wright and Rossi 1986; Aitkens 1992; Polsby 1997). General gun control measures will only increase black-market guns, often run by organized crime (Wright 1988).

General Gun Control (Restrictive Licensing)

If we are going to control guns as a means of controlling crime, then we have to deal with the guns already in private hands; controls over new purchases alone will not suffice (Wright 1988). Most guns used in crime come from family members and friends or are stolen. About 69 percent of the adult inmates surveyed (by the Criminal Justice Research Center) reported that they acquired their handguns from family, friends, and other private owners. Between 1985 and 1994, an average of 274,000 guns were reported stolen to the FBI each year (CSGV 1997b). The Bureau of Alcohol, Tobacco, and Firearms traced guns used in 76,260 crimes in twenty-seven cities for three years since 1996 and found that 51 percent of the traced guns were purchased from licensed dealers by people acting as straw intermediaries for the real owners, and 35 percent were stolen (Ross 1999). Targeted gun control would only increase the purchase of weapons by strawmen, who buy them on behalf of felons or others who are prohibited by federal law from purchasing weapons.

It is easy to identify criminals after they have been convicted, but identifying the people who should not be allowed to own a gun *before* they commit a crime is an impossible job. About 71 percent of the people who commit handgun murders are not convicted felons (Bogus 1997, 40). Targeted measures cannot prevent legal access to guns among some violent people without criminal convictions (Wright and Rossi 1986). The so-called good guy–bad guy distinction may apply to robbery and theft situations. Most homicides, however, are impulsive acts taken by individuals who have little or no criminal background and who are often known to the victim, the typical good guys. The majority of murders typically involve people who loved, or hated, each other—spouses, relatives, or close acquaintances (Spitzer 1995, 186). It is impossible to distinguish between the low-risk and high-risk candidates for gun ownership; everyone is a potential killer.

The question of mental competence is even more difficult to handle. There are no clearly defined and universally accepted medical or psychiatric definitions of mental illness, drug addiction, or alcoholism. Existing definitions are too vague and arbitrary to be useful for legal purposes, making prohibitions based on them unconstitutional. Besides, most mentally ill people are not violent: Normal people with violent tempers are more dangerous to the public than most mentally ill people (Kleck 1990b, 155). To make matters worse, there are laws that protect the confidentiality of medical records, which makes it difficult to screen potential aggressors. Whether or not gun shop owners will check their customers' backgrounds is another issue to deal with. Why would they make this effort and take the chance of losing a customer, when they could make a quick and easy sale (Lacayo 1995, 47)?

Overall, there is no feasible way to identify people with criminal intentions, violent propensities, psychoses, uncontrollable tempers, suicidal depressions, or those who become dangerous when drunk or are irresponsible enough to leave a loaded gun where a child may find it (Bogus 1997, 40). The only way to prevent gun-related crime, violence, suicide, and accidents is to remove guns from everyone except the authorized categories of people.

Assault Weapon Ban

Supporting Assault Weapon Ban

High-capacity, semi-automatic assault weapons are designed primarily for military use and have no sporting purpose. The increasing number of assault weapons in private hands poses a public safety risk (Sugarmann 1997, 53; Lyons 1997). Many forms of assault weapons can be concealed easily, can be converted to automatic weapons easily, and can be used to spray areas with large quantities of bullets in a short amount of time. For these reasons, assault weapons are frequently used by gangs, drug dealers, and mass murderers. They represent about 1.5 to 3 percent of the guns in the country, but make up 7 to 10 percent of the guns used in crime (Lyons 1997). The so-called sporterized assault weapons (changed slightly to be imported legally) were used in almost 1,200 crimes in 1995 and 1996 (Spitzer 1998).

Police officers are in a particularly dangerous position with the increase of assault weapons. In 1995, assault weapons were used in one out of ten homicides of police officers (CSGV 1997b). Many police departments are upgrading their service weapons from .38 caliber revolvers to 9 mm semi-automatics because they are unable to keep up with the firepower of many criminals (Lyons 1997). California governor Pete Wilson, in September 1997, announced that the Los Angeles police will be armed with assault rifles to match the firepower of the criminals they face. Six hundred army surplus M16s have been supplied to Los Angeles police officers (*New York Times* 9-16-98).

We cannot allow such an escalation of military arms competition in our city streets. Lives of innocent bystanders would be in great danger if we do. We need to outlaw all clip-fed weapons, weapons capable of shooting automatically or semi-automatically, and weapons that can be converted easily to automatic or semi-automatic weapons. Their import, manufacture, and sale to civilians should also be prohibited on a national level (Briskin 1998).

State and community level bans on assault weapons have achieved considerable success in deterring gun violence. According to the Oakland, California, Police Department, since California banned assault weapons in 1989, instances in which an assault weapon was used in commission of a crime have decreased by half (CSGV 1997b).

Opposing Assault Weapon Ban

Assault weapons are just ordinary semi-automatic firearms like those that have existed in this country for over a century (LaPierre 1994, 37). Despite the scary looking, military-style features and notoriety they gained over the years, assault weapons are no more lethal than hundreds of firearms that remain legal. They fire at the same rate as any other semi-automatic gun, no faster than a revolver. Their ammunition is of intermediate caliber, less formidable than the cartridges fired by many hunting rifles (Sullum 1997). The semi-automatic AK-47 and UZI are in some respects no more lethal than other conventional and low-tech weapons such as the shotgun (Austerman 1989).

Compared with other weapons, assault guns are responsible for very few deaths in the United States. Assault rifle firearms figured in less than 1 percent of all homicides committed in the United States, while the handguns favored by many petty criminals were used in between 30 and 50 percent of such killings. Banning them will not reduce crime and will only lead to the erosion of the right to bear arms (Austerman 1989).

Handgun Ban

Supporting Handgun Ban

The primary function of a handgun is to kill a human being. Unlike rifles or shotguns, they serve no practical sporting purpose. The particular public policy concern with handguns arises from the fact that they are far more likely to be used to intimidate, injure, and kill people than long guns. Handguns can be concealed easily, making it the most favored weapon of criminals. Even though handguns account for only about a third of all guns owned in the country, they were used in 75 percent of homicides committed with guns, about 50 percent of all homicides, and 80 percent of robberies involving firearms (Spitzer 1995, 69). If we cannot ban all firearms, the only sensible solution, in the interest of civil liberties as well as public safety, is to ban the private possession of handguns (Drinan 1990, 62; Sugarmann 1997, 53).

Opposing Handgun Ban

Control aimed solely at handguns is a mistake because it encourages substitution of more lethal types of guns. An offender who has been blocked only from getting a handgun is likely to use a long gun or a sawed-off shotgun, which generally provides sufficient concealability. Long guns are actually more deadly than handguns because they usually propel larger-caliber bullets at a higher rate of speed. In general, long guns are about three to four times more lethal than handguns currently used in assaults (Kleck 1990b, 156–7; Spitzer 1995, 70; Cook 1990, 140; Wright and Rossi 1986).

Handguns are used about as often for defensive purposes as for criminal purposes because handguns are more convenient and effective for self-protection than long guns. The small size of handguns makes it possible for noncriminals to carry one in public for self-protection or to store one in a bedside table for protection against night-time intruders (Kleck 1997, 140).

Brady Law

Supporting the Brady Law

As a part of the Brady law, passed in February 1994, the five-day waiting period and voluntary background check on handgun purchasers went into effect nationwide. A background check identifies those people prohibited by law from purchasing a handgun, such as convicted felons, fugitives from justice, drug addicts, illegal aliens, juveniles, and those adjudicated mentally ill. People under a domestic violence restraining order were added in September 1994. A national system of instant background checks for gun buyers, operated by the FBI and state governments, began in November 1998, as a part of the Brady Act, and replaced the five-day waiting period law. The Justice Department's Bureau of Justice Statistics reported that in less than three years since the Brady law took effect (until December 31, 1997), 242,000 purchases were stopped because of the checks, out of 10,356,000 purchase applications; 61.7 percent of the cases were disapproved because the buyer was a convicted or indicted felon. More than three out of five sales that were rejected were because the buyer had a felony conviction or was under felony indictment (*New York Times* 6-22-98).

Being national in scope, this regulatory strategy avoids the leakage problem of gun seekers traveling to less strict areas to acquire guns (Kleck 1997, 388). The Brady law is not the solution to crime and violence, but a small step in the right direction toward the goal of reducing crime and violence in our society.

Opposing the Brady Law

The effectiveness of the Brady law is limited because the state and local criminal records are inaccurate and incomplete. In 1992, only 18 percent of state criminal records were accessible by computer; by 1995, only 33 percent of the fifty million state criminal history records were accessible (*Dayton Daily News* 6-30-97). Furthermore, it is not certain how accurate the states' histories are regarding deposition of arrests and trials. The wide variations in states' record-keeping practices will result in differential application, at least until there is a significant improvement in record-keeping (Spitzer 1995, 161).

The Brady law does not actually require local police to conduct background checks; the federal government cannot prosecute those who fail to do so. In states where the check is required, local law enforcement officers report that it requires too much paperwork and is too time-consuming for them to do the background checks. They are already understaffed and overburdened with other more urgent law-enforcement-related duties than a background check of potential gun owners. Without substantial federal funding, local law enforcement agencies do not have enough resources or staff to handle all the background checks.

We Need Stricter Gun Control Measures

Supporting Gun Control

The existing laws are insufficient and ineffective in reducing gun-related violence. We need stricter gun control measures as well as stricter enforcement of existing laws. A nationwide licensing program would be an effective first step. Such a program already exists for sellers, manufacturers, and importers of firearms, but it does not extend to private citizens who buy and use the guns. In addition, we need a firearms registration program that would require the registration of all privately owned firearms on a national level, as in automobiles. Federal law already requires firearm manufacturers, importers, and makers to register each firearm they make or import. However, unless the registration is followed up by the current owner, it is impossible to trace who owns which guns (Udulutch 1992, 200; Drinan 1990, 55; Tonso 1990, 38).

We need to tighten federal licensing requirements for gun dealers and control over their records of sales. The Bureau of Alcohol, Tobacco, and Firearms (ATF) must be given greater authority to control sales of firearms and ammunition (Sugarmann 1997, 53; Knickerbocker 1998). We need to control the private transfers of firearms that account for the overwhelming majority of gun acquisitions by violence-prone people. There were about 2.4 million nondealer transfers in 1990. A critical element of an effective system for regulating gun acquisition would be a requirement that the numerous nondealer transfers of guns be routed through licensed gun dealers and thereby subjected to the same background check as dealer transfers (Kleck 1997, 388).

A stricter check of residency requirements would help prevent interstate gunrunning. Limitations on the number of guns an individual can buy as in the state of Virginia (e.g., one per person a month) is also an option. Implementing a gun return program would reduce the number of guns now in circulation. The government can appropriate sufficient funds to buy back guns for the purpose of destroying them. Prospective gun owners can be required to take official gun safety courses and then pass a test that covers maintenance and safety, and attend target practice. Increasing tax on firearms and ammunition might discourage sales, thus decreasing availability (Bogus 1997, 36–9).

Opposing Gun Control

Licensing and registration are a screen not against criminals but against honest citizens. They are an inefficient system that creates inconvenience to the law-abiding owners without affecting criminals' ability to obtain guns (Bruce-Briggs 1990, 69). Increased tax or any other price increase measures may affect criminal gun acquisition only when they reach very high levels (Wright and Rossi 1986). The price is not a very important consideration for most felons. It is their income-producing tool; they are willing to pay the going rate. High price will burden millions of legitimate handgun users, and it might drive them into the black markets. A sharp rise in handgun prices would increase the attractiveness of gun theft and, therefore, might draw some criminals into the market as producers of stolen handguns (Wright and Rossi 1986). Furthermore, imposing high taxes on guns and ammunition would ensure that only the wealthy and privileged few would be allowed gun ownership.

Currently, we have about 20,000 gun regulations, mostly at the state and local levels. The problem is not that we do not have enough laws, but the existing laws are not enforced strictly. Existing gun laws have not been given a fair chance to work because in many places they are not adequately enforced (Kates 1990d, 63).

Federal Gun Control Laws versus State and Local Laws

Supporting Federal Laws

The gun control laws we have often fail to work because there are too many of them, they are indifferently enforced, and because they vary widely from one jurisdiction to the next. The purchase and possession of guns in the United States are controlled by a chaotic jumble of 20,000 state and local laws that operate in such a way that areas with poor controls undermine those with better ones. State laws are often ineffective because they are easily evaded if bordering states do not have equally restrictive controls. Efforts at state and local regulation have consistently been frustrated by the flow of firearms from one state to another. What we need are federal firearms regulations that are strictly enforced all across the nation (Hofstadter 1990, 33–4; Wright 1988; Kleck 1990b, 157; Drinan 1990, 62; Spitzer 1995, 182; Udulutch 1992).

New York enacted the nation's first tough gun law in 1911. Known as the Sullivan law, the measure imposed strict requirements on the sale, possession, and carrying of concealed weapons. Even so, guns continue to pose a major problem, especially in New York City, because guns are readily available in neighboring states. New York City confiscated about 20,000 illegal guns in 1994, and about 90 percent of them came from easy-to-purchase states with no registration requirements (Spitzer 1995, 182; Nisbet 1990, 23).

Opposing Federal Laws

The concept of federalism implies that the states should have as much autonomy as possible in drafting their criminal law and other statutes. Federal controls are less satisfactory because traditionally there has been a very limited federal law enforcement apparatus in the area of ordinary crimes. The FBI regards itself more as an investigatory than a law enforcement agency. Nothing at the federal level corresponds to a street police force and local police agencies. Furthermore, the need for gun control differs sharply from one state to another. Some states have almost no violent crime, with or without guns, while others have a great deal (Kleck 1990b, 158).

We Need to Regulate the Gun Manufacturing Industries

Supporting Gun Control

Guns are the second most deadly consumer product (after cars) on the market. In Texas and Louisiana, the firearms-related death rate already exceeds that for motor vehicles (Sugarmann 1997, 51–2). Unlike other consumer products, such as automobiles, prescription drugs, pesticides, or toasters, however, firearms have not been subjected to rigorous safety standard regulations and consumer protection laws (Knickerbocker 1998). Gun industries must carry the same burden of responsibility as car manufacturers, which have incorporated seat belts, air bags, and child-safety locks and keys in an effort to make their products safer, to prevent unauthorized use, and, not coincidentally, to ward off lawsuits (Witkin 1998). Most gun firms have exhibited a "callous disregard for safety, and watched kids die year after year and done nothing about it," even though "some safety improvements would involve simple mechanical devices" (Henigan in Witkin 1998). For instance, for decades, Smith and Wesson, one of the nation's biggest gun makers, has been selling guns with a magazine safety, made of a few strings and a lever that cost from $0.09 to $2, because it prevents accidental shootings. However, none of the other gun makers do (Meier 1999). Without governmental regulation or the threat of lawsuits, these industries will not voluntarily regulate themselves to produce safer products. Instead, gun manufacturers have made guns that are more dangerous and attractive to criminals. For example, when a glut in the market caused handgun production to plummet in 1982, the industry, to stimulate sales, produced assault weapons (Sugarmann 1997, 51). One manufacturer even proudly advertised an oil-resistant gun handle that evades fingerprints. Another company sidestepped laws by selling an assault weapon through the mail in an easily assembled kit, with the frame sold separately (S. W. Daniel Co.) (Bai 1998).

Guns can be made safer and child-resistant. If we can send a motorized computer to Mars, certainly we can advance our technology to make guns safer and childproof. The technology is available, like key-operated internal locks or loaded-chamber indicators, and guns can be made childproof by installing child-resistant triggers, which show whether a gun is loaded. Firearms can be personalized, like the Smart Guns, which use radio signals to prevent anyone other than the authorized users from operating them (Witkin 1998).

After years of sparring with the National Rifle Association, gun control proponents have begun to target the gun industry with lawsuits, whereby the manufacturer is held liable, just like the tobacco and automobile industries. A growing number of cities, like Chicago and Miami, and victims of gun violence are suing the gun manufacturers who illegally flooded the cities with cheap handguns. In February 1999, a federal jury found several gun makers liable in three New York City shootings because of negligent marketing practice. Law-yers at Sarah Brady's Center to Prevent Handgun Violence, which now has six-teen cases pending against the industry, say they won't let up until gun makers perfect Smart Gun technology that would keep anyone but the owner from fir-ing the weapon (Bai 1998). The Centers for Disease Control and Prevention estimated that the annual national cost of intentional and unintentional gun in-juries was more than $20 billion per year, with 80 percent of the cost covered by taxpayers' money (Sugarmann 1997, 52; Spitzer 1995, 69; CSGV 1997b). The gun makers, like cigarette makers liable for smoking-related diseases, must be held liable for the cost of treating gun-related injuries.

Opposing Gun Control

Holding a manufacturer responsible for misuse of a product that works exactly as intended would stand the civil liability system on its head. You cannot sue the manufacturers of lawful, nondefective products for criminal acts of people beyond their control. Gun manufacturers also supply firearms to police and law-abiding citizens to protect themselves (Sanetti in Levin 1998). Gun manu-facturers' responsibility ends when they sell the guns to licensed distributors. Responsibility in accidental death of children lies with the parents who leave a loaded gun in a child's reach. In accidents involving an adult, the person who ignored the basic rules of gun safety is liable for the accident, not the gun mak-ers (Witkin 1998).

R E F E R E N C E S

Aitkins, Maggi. 1992. *Should we have gun control?* Minneapolis: Lerner Publications.
Amo, Gary. 1989. "Gun control: Myth and reality." *Los Angeles Lawyer*. June.
Austerman, Wayne R. 1989. "These deadly, depressing, syncopated, semiautomatic assault rifle blues." *Chronicles*. November.
Bai, Matt. 1998. "Targeting gun makers." *Newsweek*. 13 April.
Bennet, James. 1997. "Gun makers to offer child safety locks." *San Jose Mercury News*. 9 Octo-ber.
Block, Richard. 1977. *Violent crime*. Lexington, Mass.: Lexington Books.
Bogus, Carl T. 1997. "Private ownership of handguns should be banned." Pp. 34–42 in *Gun control: Opposing viewpoints*, edited by Tamara L. Roleff. San Diego, Calif.: Greenhaven Press.
Briskin, Lawrence. 1998. "Gun control essential to nation." *Dayton Daily News*. 5 June.
Bruce-Briggs. B. 1990. "The great American gun war." Pp. 63–85 in *The gun control debate*, ed-ited by Lee Nisbet. Buffalo, N.Y.: Prometheus Books.
Carlson, Tucker. 1997. "Private ownership of handguns is not a public-health hazard." Pp. 55–61 in *Gun control: Opposing viewpoints*, edited by Tamara L. Roleff. San Diego, Calif.: Greenhaven Press.
Center for Study of Gun Violence (CSGV). 1997a. "Partial summary of federal regulations ap-plicable to firearms and ammunition." (http://www.gunfree.internet/csgv/fedregs.htm).

————. 1997b. "The basic facts of guns in our schools." (http://www.gunfree.internet/csgv/bsc_sch.htm).

Cook, Philip J., and Jens Ludwig. 1997. "Guns in America: National survey on private ownership and use of firearms." *National Institute of Justice Research in Brief*, May (http://www.ncjrs.org/textfiles/165476.txt).

Cook, Philip J. 1990. "The effect of gun availability on violent crime patterns." Pp. 130–47 in *The gun control debate*, edited by Lee Nisbet. Buffalo, N.Y.: Prometheus Books.

————. 1976. "The effect of gun availability on robbery and robbery murder." Pp. 743–81 in *Policy studies review annual*, edited by Robert Haveman and B. Bruce Zellner. Beverly Hills, Calif.: Sage Publishers.

Drinan, Robert F. 1990. "The good outweighs the evil." Pp. 54-62 in *The gun control debate*, edited by Lee Nisbet. Buffalo, N.Y.: Prometheus Books.

Harris, Louis. 1993. *A survey of the American people on guns as a children's health issue*, a study conducted by L. H. Research, Inc., for the Harvard School of Public Health, June.

Hofstadter, Richard. 1990. "America as a gun culture." Pp. 25–34 in *The gun control debate*, edited by Lee Nisbet. Buffalo, N.Y.: Prometheus Books.

Kates, Don B. 1990a. "Gun accidents." Pp. 300–303 in *The gun control debate*, edited by Lee Nisbet. Buffalo, N.Y.: Prometheus Books.

————. 1990b. "The law-abiding gun owner as domestic and acquaintance murderer." Pp. 270–74 in *The gun control debate*, edited by Lee Nisbet. Buffalo, N.Y.: Prometheus Books.

————. 1990c. "Defensive gun ownership as a response to crime." Pp. 251–69 in *The gun control debate*, edited by Lee Nisbet. Buffalo, N.Y.: Prometheus Books.

————. 1995. "Shot down." *National Review*. 6 March.

Kates Don B., Jr. 1990d. *Guns, murders, and the constitution: Policy briefing*. San Francisco: Pacific Research Institute for Public Policy.

Kellermann, Arthur, and Donald T. Reay. 1986. "Protection or peril?: An analysis of firearm-related deaths in the home." *New England Journal of Medicine* 314(24):1557–60.

Kelly, Ned. 1992. "Australian gun control measures are ineffective." Pp. 260–68 in *Gun control: Current controversies*, edited by Charles Cozic. San Diego, Calif.: Greenhaven Press.

Kleck, Gary. 1997. *Targeting guns: Firearms and their control*. New York: Aldine de Gruyter.

————. 1990a. "The relationship between gun ownership levels and rates of violence in the U.S." Pp. 123–29 in *The gun control debate*, edited by Lee Nisbet. Buffalo, N.Y.: Prometheus Books.

————. 1990b. "Policy lessons from recent gun control research." Pp.148–64 in *The gun control debate*, edited by Lee Nisbet. Buffalo, N.Y.: Prometheus Books.

————. 1989. "The relationship between gun ownership levels and rates of violence in the United States." In *Firearms and violence: Issues of public policy*, edited by Don B. Kates, Jr. San Francisco: Pacific Research Institute for Public Policy.

————. 1988. "Crime control through the private use of armed forces." *Social Problems* 35(1):1–19.

————, and Marc Gertz. 1995. "Armed resistance to crime: The prevalence and nature of self-defense with a gun." *Journal of Criminal Law and Criminology* 86(1):153–84.

————, and E. Britt Patterson. 1993. "The impact of gun control and gun ownership level on violence rates." *Journal of Quantitative Criminology* 9:247–88.

Knickerbocker, Brad. 1998. "Child-safety activists target American gun-makers." *Christian Science Monitor*. 28 April.

Kopel, David B. 1993. "Gun play." *Reason*. July.

————. 1992. "Japanese gun control laws are oppressive." Pp. 252–59 in *Gun control: Current controversies*, edited by Charles Cozic. San Diego, Calif.: Greenhaven Press.

Lacayo, Richard. 1995. "A small-bore success." *Time*. 20 February, 47–48.

LaPierre, Wayne. 1994. *Guns, crime, freedom*. Washington, D.C.: Regnery Publishing.

Lester, David. 1989. "Gun ownership and suicide in the U.S." *Psychological Medicine* 19:512–21.

Levin, Myron. 1998. "Chicago sues gun makers and sellers." *Los Angeles Times*. 13 November.

Los Angeles Times. 1993. "Taming the gun monster: Is it constitutional?" Editorial. 1 November.

Lund, Nelson. 1987. "The Second Amendment, political liberty, and the right to self-preservation." *Alabama Law Review* 39:103–30.

Lyons, Kenneth T. 1997. "Banning assault weapons will reduce gun violence." (Testimony before the Senate Committee on the Judiciary, 3 August). Pp. 167–70 in *Gun control: Opposing viewpoints*, edited by Tamara L. Roleff. San Diego, Calif.: Greenhaven Press.

Meier, Barry. 1999. "Gun makers' approach to basic safety." *New York Times*. 19 March.

National Center for Health Statistics (NCHS). 1994. "Advance data from vital and health statistics," No. 242. Hyattsville, Md.

National Rifle Association of America (NRA). 1992. "Practicing gun safety can reduce gun-related accidents." Pp. 226–29 in *Gun control: Current controversies*, edited by Charles Cozic. San Diego, Calif.: Greenhaven Press.

Nisbet, Lee, ed. 1990. *The gun control debate*. Buffalo, N.Y.: Prometheus Books.

Pilcher, James (Associated Press). 1999. "Gun-related injuries lowest in 30 years." *Dayton Daily News*. 19 November.

Polsby, Daniel D. 1997. "Private ownership of handguns lead to lower rates of handgun violence." Pp. 26–33 in *Gun control: Opposing viewpoints*, edited by Tamara L. Roleff. San Diego, Calif.: Greenhaven Press.

———. 1994. "The false promise: Gun control and crime." *Current*. June.

Ross, Sonya (Associated Press). 1999. "Clinton seeks to expand gun tracing." *Yahoo News*. 21 February.

Safran, Claire. 1997. "Private ownership of handguns lead to higher rates of gun violence." Pp. 17–25 in *Gun control: Opposing viewpoints*, edited by Tamara L. Roleff. San Diego, Calif.: Greenhaven Press.

Silver, Steven. 1997. "Private gun ownership is protected by the Second Amendment." Pp. 75–81 in *Gun control: Opposing viewpoints*, edited by Tamara L. Roleff. San Diego, Calif.: Greenhaven Press.

Sloan, John Henry, Arthur L. Kellerman, Donald T. Reay, James A. Ferris, Thomas Koepsell, Frederick P. Rivara, Charles Rice, Raurel Gray, and James LoGerfo. 1988. "Handgun regulations, crime, assaults, and homicide: A tale of two cities." *New England Journal of Medicine* 319(19):1256–62.

Sniffen, Michael J. (Associated Press). 1998. "Gun buyers to face instant checks." *Yahoo News*. 29 October.

Spitzer, Robert. 1998. "Assault weapon ban." *Christian Science Monitor*. 16 April.

———. 1995. *The politics of gun control*. Chatham N.J.: Chatham House Publishers.

Sproule, Catherine F., and Deborah J. Kennett. 1989. "Canada's low gun homicide rate proves the effectiveness of gun control." *Canadian Journal of Criminology* 31(3):245–51.

Sugarmann, Josh. 1997. "Private ownership of handguns is a public-health hazard." Pp. 50–54 in *Gun control: Opposing viewpoints*, edited by Tamara L. Roleff. San Diego, Calif.: Greenhaven Press.

Sullum, Jacob. 1997. "Banning assault weapons will not reduce gun violence." Pp. 167–70 in *Gun control: Opposing viewpoints*, edited by Tamara L. Roleff. San Diego, Calif.: Greenhaven Press.

Tonso, William R. 1990. "Social problems and stagecraft: Gun control as a cause in point." Pp. 35–53 in *The gun control debate*, edited by Lee Nisbet. Buffalo, N.Y.: Prometheus Books.

Udulutch, Mark. 1992. "The constitutional implications of gun control and several realistic gun control proposals." *American Journal of Criminal Law* 17(1):19–54.

Washburn, Gary, and Abdon Pallasch. 1998. "City takes on gun industry." *Chicago Tribune*. 13 November.

Wintemute, Garen J., Stephen P. Teret, Jess F. Kraus, Mona A. Wright, and Gretchen Bradfield. 1989. "When children shoot children." *Journal of American Medical Association* 257(22):3107–09.

Witkin, Gordon. 1998. "Childproofing guns." *U.S. News & World Report.* 22 June, 24–26.

Wright, James D. 1988. "Second thoughts about gun control." *The Public Interest* 91(Spring): 23–39.

Wright, James D., and Peter H. Rossi. 1986. *Armed and considered dangerous: A survey of felons and their firearms.* New York: Aldine de Gruyter.

Yeager, Matthew G., Joseph D. Alviani, and Nancy Loving. 1990. "How well does the handgun protect you and your family?" Pp. 213–38 in *The gun control debate,* edited by Lee Nisbet. Buffalo, N.Y.: Prometheus Books.

Zimring, Franklin E., and Gordon Hawkins. 1987. *The citizen's guide to gun control.* New York: Macmillan.

CHAPTER
5

Health Care Reform

For most Americans, health care is financed through private insurance that is usually provided by employers. Publicly financed Medicaid is available to the poor, and Medicare provides limited coverage for the elderly and people with disabilities. Health care services are provided by private, fee-for-service physicians or managed care providers. In 1995, employer-provided insurance covered about 64 percent of the population, and about 80 percent (86 percent in 1998) of their health care was provided by private managed care firms, such as health maintenance organizations (HMOs) or preferred provider organizations (PPOs) (Shapiro 1998). Approximately 12 percent of the population was covered by Medicaid in 1995, and 15 percent (16 percent in 1997) had no insurance coverage, most of them being lower-income workers or employees of small businesses (Meckler 1998; PNIS 1998).

Many Americans believe that our health care system has serious problems and requires a major overhaul. Our health care costs are too high and growing too rapidly; too many people are uninsured or underinsured; the administrative process of health care is too complex and wasteful; and health care is not distributed equally to everyone (Lemco 1994, 2).

The health care reform debates began in the 1950s when President Truman advanced a proposal for national health insurance without success. Many people regarded the enactment of Medicare and Medicaid in 1965 as the first step toward achieving national health insurance. However, both President Nixon's and President Carter's proposals to extend universal coverage to the non-aged failed, and nothing happened for two decades until the early 1990s (Aaron 1996, 1–3). The major concern that brought the health care reform issue back on the frontline in the early 1990s was the high cost of health care. Between 1980 and 1992, U.S. health care spending rose from 9 percent of the gross domestic product (GDP) to 14 percent (Clinton 1993, 7). In 1993, President Clinton proposed to provide all Americans with health insurance and to slow the growth of health care spending. This effort also failed in the Republican-dominated Congress, eliminating any realistic possibility of government-led health care reform for the foreseeable future (Aaron 1996, 3).

The following sections summarize the arguments over whether our health care system should be reformed.

Our Health Care Costs Too Much

Supporting Reform

The single most urgent problem regarding health care in the United States is high and rising costs. In 1965, 6 percent of the GDP was spent on health care. In 1980, the figure rose to 9 percent; and in 1994, to 14 percent (Glenn 1994). Health care spending is rising much faster than wages, business receipts, or government revenues. Between 1980 and 1991, the average cost of health insurance for an employee and his or her family rose from $1,018 (in 1991 dollars) to $4,464, while employee out-of-pocket expenses for health care rose from $248 to $1,300 (Rasell 1994). In 1997, average family coverage purchased through the workplace cost $5,472; bought by an individual family, it was $6,840 (Lief 1997).

The United States spends far more on health care than do other industrialized countries that have universal health care, despite having so many people uninsured. In 1993, the United States spent about 12.4 percent of the GDP on health care ($2,566 per capita) compared with 8.1 percent in Germany ($1,287 per capita), 6.5 percent in Japan ($1,145 per capita), 6.2 percent in the United Kingdom ($932 per capita), and 9.0 percent in Canada ($1,795 per capita) (Rasell 1994).

Opposing Reform

The cost of health care is not the only cost that increased. Since the 1960s, Social Security taxes increased from 2 percent to 12.4 percent (Mitchell 1997); the cost of welfare spending increased 8.4 times (Rector 1996); the per-pupil cost of public school education increased three times (Carter 1999). The share of income spent by consumers on housing, automobile, and children's college education rose substantially also. The share of income spent on airline travel increased about three times, yet no one is concerned that consumers are spending more of their income on air travel, nor should we be. In fact, in an affluent society as in the United States, it is not surprising that consumers prefer to spend large amounts of money on good-quality health care and the ability to travel (Reischauer in Glenn 1994).

In advanced societies, medical costs are likely to grow more quickly than other expenses because the development of medical technology increased the life expectancy of many people. A longer life expectancy means greater consumption of health care by the elderly population (White 1995, 3; Cutler 1996,

260; Schwartz 1992). In addition, the United States plays a leadership role and spends a lot more money in medical research and development than in other advanced societies, and that cost is included in our health care budget (Ayres 1996, 168).

There is no definite answer to how much a nation should spend on health care. How do we decide what constitutes a reasonable level of expenditure on health care, as compared with defense or education? Is there some magic number—7 or 10 or 15 percent of the GDP—that is reasonable or fair? What is more important than the percent of the GDP spent on health care is the quality of care, the way money is spent, and the way health care is distributed (Daniels et al. 1996, 60).

The Third-Party Indemnity Insurance System Is Responsible for High Health Care Costs

Supporting Reform

Many analysts conclude that the third-party payment system of indemnity insurance is one of the reasons for spiraling health care costs. This type of insurance eliminates price constraints and incentive to cut costs on the part of the consumer as well as the providers. Most Americans have insurance bought by employers, and they do not pay for health care directly. When consumers are removed from the buying process, they have less incentive to be frugal, to shop around, and make cost-benefit calculations (Glassman 1998; Dentzer 1991). Doctors also feel no responsibility to control the costs to the third-party payer. In fact, with insurance available to pay the bills, physicians have powerful economic incentives to provide expensive services regardless of the medical effectiveness or necessity (Relman 1993; Cutler 1996, 253).

Opposing Reform

Unlike other commodities or services, health care demand is highly concentrated. In any given year, approximately 20 percent of the population incurs about 80 percent of the total medical expenses (Hacker 1997, 14). In order to protect themselves, people must join systems of shared savings. Either private or public, some form of pool or shared saving is necessary to spread the cost and to protect people against an unpredictable risk of health care expenses (White 1995, 25).

The health care market is very complex and difficult to understand even for health care professionals. Even if consumers are free to make health care purchase decisions, they cannot shop around or become cost-effective because most people do not have enough medical knowledge or information to know what kind of care or which policy they need (Dentzer 1991).

We Spend Too Much on Administrative Costs

Supporting Reform

One of the reasons for high health care costs is huge administrative expenses. In 1991, the administrative costs in the United States were about 24 percent of all health care spending, in contrast to 11 percent in Canada, which has Nationalized Health Insurance (Woolhandler and Himmelstein 1994b; Sperduto 1994, 210; Ayres 1996, 191). Between 1970 and 1991, the number of health care administrators in the United States increased by 697 percent, while the total number of health care personnel increased by only 129 percent (Woolhandler and Himmelstein 1994b, 137).

Most of the administrative costs stem from the inefficiency of having more than 1,500 private health insurance companies selling many different services, restricting enrollees to particular doctors, and imposing different levels of cost sharing, different deductibles, and different preexisting condition exclusions. The cost of recording, billing, reviewing, processing, auditing, and justifying medical charges is an enormous paperwork burden for hospitals, doctors, and insurance companies (Rasell 1994; Clinton 1993, 6). Also included in these expenses are the costs of insurance marketing, the profits and reserves of private insurance companies (Sperduto 1994, 210).

The Fee-for-Service System Is Responsible for High Health Care Costs

Supporting Reform

Under the traditional fee-for-service system, patients choose their doctors, and the insurance company pays a percentage of the fees, after a deductible. This system creates financial incentives for doctors to provide more tests and treatments than necessary, causing health care costs to rise (Sperduto 1994, 208; Rubin 1995). According to the Rand Corp. evaluation, roughly 30 percent of the care provided by doctors under the fee-for-service system is questionable, and another 15 percent is downright unnecessary and even dangerous (Dentzer 1991). For instance, 25 percent of all babies born in America were delivered by cesarean section in 1990, compared with 11.5 percent in England, where the health care is nationalized (Inlander 1994). To minimize physicians' abuse under the fee-for-service system, we need a standard fee schedule for each procedure, and a list of necessary procedures for each treatment. Such limits could regulate doctors' fees and prevent unnecessary care of patients.

Opposing Reform

The fee-for-service system motivates physicians to do their best to treat and satisfy their patients. They have to be efficient and medically effective to be able to compete. Under the Nationalized Health Service system (as in England) or HMOs where physicians receive a salary, there is less incentive on the part of doctors to satisfy their patients or to provide the best-quality care possible because there is no competition (Woolstein 1994; Barnes 1993).

Whether a certain procedure is needed for a specific patient is an arbitrary decision that must be made by individual doctors based on their professional judgment and evaluation of the patient. That is what doctors are trained to do, and we must have trust in our doctors and in their professional judgments. The government or other third parties, such as insurance companies, cannot make those decisions without knowing each individual patient's particular circumstance and medical condition. If we begin to undermine physicians' professional autonomy and suspect their integrity, we cannot maintain the trustful doctor-patient relationship that is fundamentally important in health care.

High Physicians' Income Is Responsible for the High Cost of Health Care

Supporting Reform

One of the causes of high health care costs in the United States is physicians' fees. U.S. physicians charge more than physicians in other industrialized societies, and their income increased faster than the average worker's income. From 1984 to 1990, the median net income of physicians rose by 12.4 percent, while the median for full-time employed women rose 6.1 percent, and the median for men fell 3.4 percent (White 1995, 153; Inlander 1994). The average physician's income in the United States is almost twice as high as in Canada or in Germany and three times as high as in Japan or in England (Rasell 1994).

Opposing Reform

U.S. doctors go through longer and more extensive training than doctors in other countries. We have many more specialists who delay their full income and incur more debt to receive years of additional training. In addition, U.S. doctors must pay much larger premiums for malpractice insurance and have much higher administrative overhead costs than doctors in other countries (White 1995, 50, 152).

It is not only the physicians' income that rose during the 1980s and 1990s. Incomes of most upper-class professionals, especially corporate executives, entertainers, finance advisers, and lawyers, rose much more than that of the average middle class, while that of the working class fell sharply. Even in the medical field, physicians are not the only ones whose income rose. Pharmaceutical, medical supply, and insurance industries also reaped high profits during the past three decades, wasted a lot on marketing and advertising, and charged consumers a lot more than they did in other countries (White 1995, 152; Woolhandler and Himmelstein 1994b). For instance, pharmaceutical companies in the United States charge three times what they charge in other nations for prescription drugs (Clinton 1993, 14). Why must doctors sacrifice their income when other professionals, such as lawyers, bankers, and corporate executives, are seeking high income without receiving any criticism (Gaylin 1994)?

We Have Too Many Specialists

Supporting Reform

Along with the expansion of health care has come a great increase in specialization and technological sophistication, which raised the price of medical services (Relman 1993; Schroeder 1992). Greater financial rewards attracted many physicians to enter specialized subareas of medicine. As a result, we have too many specialists and not enough generalists. In the 1930s, 87 percent of all physicians were general practitioners. In 1992, only 30 percent of physicians were generalists and 70 percent were specialists. Specialists charge a lot more than general physicians for their services; specialists tend to perform more medical procedures and use high-cost technologies, which result in higher overall health care costs (Schroeder 1992).

Under the British Nationalized Health Care System, 90 to 95 percent of all health care is provided by primary care physicians who receive only 14 percent of the nation's total health care costs. In the United States, 80 percent of all problems are first seen by specialists who charge considerably more for their services than primary care physicians do (Ayres 1996, 163). Basic preventive services are often neglected at the expense of high-cost treatments and high-technology equipment that are used unscrupulously by many specialists (Clinton 1993, 10).

Opposing Reform

Specialists are a vital component of the U.S. health care system. General physicians do not always have the specialized knowledge or technique to provide the care patients need as specialists do. Decreasing the number of specialists will not reduce health care costs and will only lower the quality of care Americans receive (Wassersug 1993).

Too Many Malpractice Lawsuits Drive the Cost of Health Care Up

Supporting Reform

The increase of malpractice litigation has forced the cost of health care to rise. The American Medical Association reported that an average of 3.2 claims per 100 physicians were made each year prior to 1981. The rate rose to over 10 per 100 physicians in 1985, although it fell to 7.4 in 1989. The average award has increased from $229,000 in 1975 to over one million dollars in 1985, excluding out-of-court settlements. Malpractice insurance costs represented about 5 percent of physicians' gross revenues in 1986 (Ayres 1996, 192).

Physicians are only humans and will make mistakes. It is unfair for patients to expect perfection from their physicians. Not every adverse outcome is the result of malpractice; not every medical treatment or surgical operation can or will be successful. Physicians may arrive at the proper diagnosis and provide excellent medical care and still obtain results that are less than perfect (Lozano 1992).

Defensive medicine is a direct result of the malpractice system. Doctors are forced to provide numerous tests and procedures, some of which may be unnecessary, to protect themselves against the very remote possibility of misdiagnosis, which might lead to lawsuits. It is estimated that the cost of defensive medicine is approximately $20 billion per year (Lozano 1992).

There is little evidence that the malpractice system does anything to improve the quality of medical care. Guilty physicians who settle suits before trial undergo no professional sanction and can keep their lawsuits secret. Studies have found no link between adverse malpractice experience and changes in patterns of practice (White 1995, 57).

Opposing Reform

The malpractice system is necessary to provide a remedy or at least redress for a tort, by compensating an injured individual, and to benefit society as a whole by encouraging physicians and hospitals to practice high-quality medical care (White 1995, 57; Ayres 1996, 192). Imposing liability is a powerful deterrent to negligence (Corboy 1993). Physicians are not eager to regulate themselves. The incidence of mistakes due to negligence is much greater than the number of internal disciplinary actions or malpractice suits. Studies show that the amount of negligent error was eight to ten times the number of malpractice suits, and sixteen to twenty-five times the number of successful suits (White 1995, 57).

The practices doctors consider defensive medicine—spending more time with patients, more thorough explanations of risks, more frequent consultations with other doctors, more follow-up visits, and additional testing—strongly resemble good medical practice. Implicit in the argument concerning defensive medicine is the acknowledgment that the fear of malpractice suits makes doctors and hospitals more careful (Corboy 1993; White 1995, 57).

Malpractice awards cannot be blamed for rising health care costs. Capping malpractice awards will not significantly reduce claims payments. According to the American Medical Association's own figures, premiums for medical malpractice insurance for hospitals and doctors totaled less than one percent of the total health care cost. If insured malpractice suits were abolished entirely, the savings would represent less than one percent of the health care bill (Corboy 1993).

Too Many People Are Uninsured

Supporting Reform

The Census Bureau report found that 16.1 percent of Americans—43.4 million people—had no health insurance for all of 1997, up from 15.6 percent in 1996. It was the steepest increase in five years and came despite a booming economy that created millions of new jobs (Meckler 1998). Most of the uninsured were lower-income workers and their families, especially employees of small companies (Quinn 1998). About 85 percent of those who lacked insurance belonged to families that included an employed adult (Clinton 1993, 3). As health care premiums rose, many employers dropped coverage, and that boosted the ranks of the uninsured. The Congressional Budget Office estimates that about 200,000 additional Americans lose their insurance every time insurance premiums rise 1 percent (Glassman 1998). While nearly all of the uninsured are poor, they are not poor enough to qualify for Medicaid, the state and federal program for the poor. In 1994, Medicaid covered only 45 percent of those below the poverty line, compared with 66 percent in 1984 (Lemco 1994, 9).

Opposing Reform

Having no health insurance is not the same as having no health care. Everyone gets health care in the United States, including the poor, the uninsured, and even illegal immigrants. When the poor and uninsured show up, hospitals, morally or legally, cannot turn them away. Being uninsured means "one is more likely to use emergency-room care and less likely to use office, clinic, or regular inpatient care." Once admitted, the uninsured receives the same high-quality care as the insured, one of the best in the world (Barnes 1993; White 1995, 142; Dentzer 1991).

Supporting Reform

There is substantial evidence that lack of insurance coverage has a negative effect on health outcomes for the uninsured (Daniels et al. 1996, 8). The uninsured are twice as likely to be hospitalized for conditions that are treatable through appropriate ambulatory care and are more likely than the insured to delay needed care until they become acutely ill and more costly to treat. As a result, they have higher mortality and morbidity rates (White 1995, 55). For instance, the death rate for breast cancer is 50 percent greater among uninsured women compared with those with insurance (Ayres 1996, 142).

Health Care Costs Rose Because of Cost-Shifting

Supporting Reform

As the number of uninsured people increases, doctors and hospitals must charge inflated fees to those who have insurance to make up for the loss created by the uninsured, a practice widely known as cost-shifting (Dentzer 1991; Clinton 1993, 15). With the indemnity insurance system, no one insisted that bills must reflect the actual care given. Hospitals can send out bills that cover the overall costs, cost of treating the uninsured as well as the insured. In 1991, the American Hospital Association estimated that hospitals cost-shift about $10 billion for uncompensated care annually. Another study found that the uninsured accounted for 11 percent of the nation's personal health care expenditures in 1988 (Barnes 1993).

The uninsured are the free-riders of our society, who have chosen not to insure themselves and their family members because they know their basic health care needs will be met when they need them, even without insurance. The cost of health care has risen because of these free-riders who do not pay for the services they receive.

We need to mandate all employers to provide insurance to their workers and every self-employed individual to be insured. Such plans will greatly reduce the need for cost-shifting. It is not fair for hard-working Americans to pay higher premiums to cover for the health care bills of the free-riders who take advantage of the generosity of our health care system.

Opposing Reform

Cost-shifting is part of the function of insurance, that is, spreading the cost of health care and providing help for the unfortunate and sick. Those who are fortunate enough not to need health care help pay for the sick; and those who are able to pay for their health care help pay for those who cannot (White 1995; Feder and Levitt 1996, 228).

The majority of the uninsured is not uninsured by choice; they simply cannot afford to insure themselves because of the high cost of insurance (Quinn 1998). As health care premiums rose, many small businesses could not afford to buy coverage for their workers. Individual workers, when they purchase insurance on their own, must pay about 20 to 50 percent higher premiums compared with when it is bought by the employers. In addition, individual purchasers do not have the same tax benefits as employers are entitled to for providing insurance to their employees (Glassman 1998; Ayres 1996, 128, 184; Clinton 1993, 4; Daniels et al. 1996, 10). Unless the insurance policies and tax laws are changed, cost-shifting is necessary to help the poor and less fortunate.

The Development of Medical Technology Justifies the High Costs

Opposing Reform

The high cost of health care is largely caused by the development of medical research that led to the proliferation of expensive new medical technology (Schwartz 1992; Cutler 1996, 260). Many economists argue that new medical technology accounts for as much as 50 percent of the growth in health care costs beyond overall inflation (Patel and Rushefsky 1995, 167). New and better ways of discovering and treating diseases and better and more efficient devices and drugs have a price. For instance, new treatment for a severe anemia, a new kind of pacemaker that prevents sudden death, safer and better quality of X-rays, expensive procedures such as coronary-bypass surgery, hip replacement operations, and organ transplants have improved the quality of health care and kept people alive longer (Collins 1993). Development in neonatology can now save babies with low birth weights at extremely high cost (Patel and Rushefsky 1995, 167).

U.S. consumers demand the best quality and the newest technology when it comes to health care, regardless of cost. Any effort to contain health care costs at the expense of costly but effective treatments and procedures will run counter to the wishes of many Americans and to the ethics of the medical profession (Schwartz 1992).

Supporting Reform

Not every type of medical technology is beneficial; some are unsafe, ineffective, or not cost-effective (Patel and Rushefsky 1995, 169). Some technologies sustain people with chronic illnesses at a great expense; they extend the life of patients without actually curing their diseases. Too often, expensive new technologies and invasive treatments are used to keep people alive longer, often in a vegetative and unproductive state (White 1995).

Much of the technology has been disseminated without adequate evaluation (Sperduto 1994, 206). Some technologies may decrease costs by allowing care to be given in a lower-cost setting, by replacing expensive procedures, keeping people healthier, reducing hospital stay and recovery time, and returning people to work sooner. Such technologies may be both low cost and high benefit. In contrast, some technologies may be very costly but produce only marginal benefits. It is these technologies—high cost and low benefit—that raise serious concerns on the part of critics of our health care system. It is clear that we need a systematic cost-benefit analysis of medical technologies. That would help us weed out wasteful technologies—those that are unsafe, ineffective, or not cost-effective—while encouraging the development of cost-reducing, high-benefit technologies (Patel and Rushefsky 1995, 169; Cutler 1996, 261; Schwartz 1992).

Good Quality Care Justifies High Cost

Opposing Reform

While many are complaining about the high cost of health care, the reality is that Americans have the best-quality health care in the world (Barnes 1993). The rise in health care costs is a product of the expanding capabilities of medicine. Our unbridled appetite for better care and our continuing expansion of the definition of what constitutes health care caused the high and rising costs (Gaylin 1994). Modern medicine continues to discover new diseases as well as treatments for the diseases. New and better medical technology prolongs our lives and keeps us healthier. Health care providers are trained longer and better. Patients are better diagnosed, treated, and rehabilitated than in the past. If something improves in quality and quantity, its increase in cost is not inflationary and is justifiable (Riggs 1992; Gaylin 1994; Barnes 1993).

Our concept of health care has changed; health care today does not mean what it did a hundred years ago. For instance, the idea of mental illness has been greatly expanded, and we now treat many more patients with mental problems than years ago. Infertility was not considered a disease until this generation. Many orthopedic operations are performed not to cure illnesses but to enhance people's performances or to help people continue to play golf or ski (Gaylin 1994).

Supporting Reform

Judging by the two most common measures of health—life expectancy at birth and the infant mortality rate—U.S. health care is not the best or even among the best. In 1990, the life expectancy in America was 72 years for men and 78 years for women. That is behind Canada, France, Germany, Italy, Japan, and Great Britain, ranking sixteenth in the world. On infant mortality rate, the

United States fared worse, ranking nineteenth in 1989 with a rate of 9.7 (Barnes 1993; Sperduto 1994, 206; White 1995, 133).

The United States could save a substantial amount of health care costs without sacrificing quality of care. Much of the health care waste has nothing to do with the quality of care; it comes from high administrative costs, profits by private insurance, pharmaceutical, and other medical supply industries, malpractice lawsuits, and unnecessary procedures and tests.

Opposing Reform

Life expectancy and infant mortality rates are a reflection of lifestyles and other social factors, not just the type of health care system. Exacerbated social problems, such as high homicide rate, gun violence, and high AIDS infection rates adversely affect the U.S. life expectancy (Barnes 1993). The United States has much higher gun-related violence and homicide rates than any other industrialized society. The United States also has four times as many AIDS cases per capita as Canada (White 1995, 150).

More than two-thirds of the infant mortality rate in the United States is attributable to a greater prevalence of low-weight births. Low birth weight is largely a result of poor social conditions, not lack of medical care (Cutler 1996, 262). Most other countries make no effort to save low birth weight infants. They are not recorded as live born and are not counted in infant mortality statistics. In contrast, U.S. hospitals make heroic efforts in neonatal intensive care, saving some infants, losing others, and driving the infant mortality rates up (Barnes 1993).

In the 1990s, managed care has become the most popular option of health care for many employers who provide health insurance for their workers. The following sections present supporting and opposing views on the managed care system, and discuss whether managed care should be reformed.

Managed Care: Is It a Good Option?

During the early 1970s, the federal government tried a competitive market strategy to contain health care costs through prepaid group plans (PGPs), commonly known as health maintenance organizations (HMOs). The concept of PGPs was not new; such plans had existed in the 1920s. During the early 1970s, however, the number of HMOs grew as a result of favorable market conditions and the support provided by the Nixon administration (Patel and Rushefsky 1995, 139).

HMOs are a system in which enrollees pay a fixed fee in advance, and in return receive a comprehensive set of health services. HMOs have networks of primary care physicians who refer patients to selected specialists when necessary (Patel and Rushefsky 1995, 41). HMOs usually require that patients choose doctors only from those in a network of physicians who have agreed to accept lower fees (Galewitz 1999). Physicians are usually given a fixed amount of money annually for each patient under their care (Ayres 1996, 131–2).

The 1990s brought an unprecedented growth of managed care. By 1995, there were more than five hundred HMOs in operation. HMOs' share of consumers increased from 19 percent (of the employees whose coverage is provided by employers) in 1993 to 29 percent in 1998. Proliferating even more rapidly were more loosely organized systems of managed care, such as preferred provider organizations (PPOs) and point-of-service (POS) plans (Hacker 1997, 15; Galewitz 1999). PPOs are a less restrictive form of managed care than HMOs. A PPO has a limited set of health care providers that contract with an employer or an insurer to provide a comprehensive set of services on a fee-for-service basis. The contract usually involves a negotiated, discounted set of fees (Conklin 1994, 176; Galewitz 1999). PPOs have effectively increased price competition among providers not only among the physicians but also among hospitals (Feldstein in Conklin 1994, 177). The PPOs have become the dominant form of health insurance since 1993, rising from 27 percent of employees in 1993 to 40 percent in 1998 according to the Mercer study. Point-of-service (POS) plans, a variation on the HMO concept that gives consumers some out-of-network coverage, have risen from 7 percent in 1993 to 18 percent in 1998 (Galewitz 1999). Overall, the managed care system has become a fact of life for American health care, covering 86 percent of employees (whose health care coverage is provided by their employers) and their families in 1998, up from 55 percent in 1993 (Shapiro 1998).

The Managed Care System Cuts Health Care Costs

Supporting Managed Care

Managed care's biggest success has been its ability to control costs (Sunshine 1996, 209). Growth in national health expenditures has slowed significantly since 1990 as a result of substantial increases in managed care enrollments. The increase in health care premiums has slowed considerably: They rose just 2.5 percent in 1996 and 3.3 percent in 1997, compared with as much as 18.6 percent a year in the last half of the 1980s (Brink and Shute 1997, Shapiro 1998). Overall health care costs rose an inflation-adjusted 1.9 percent in 1996, the lowest increase in nearly 40 years (PNIS 1998, Brink 1998).

Managed care created competition among doctors and hospitals, and therefore, effectively reduced health care fees. Managed care saves money by eliminating economic incentives for doctors to over-treat patients and over-provide services to make money, which happens under the fee-for-service system. Studies indicate that total costs for managed care enrollees are about 10 to 40 percent lower than those of comparable people with the traditional fee-for-service system (Dentzer 1991).

Opposing Managed Care

Managed care (abbreviated MC) contains costs by putting customers at risk, encouraging providers to limit care that is judged by the insurance plan to be worth less than its cost (Pauly and Goodman 1996, 284). MC is operated based on the monthly premium paid by subscribers. Those premiums constitute the total budget for the MC plans. Providing more services does not produce more revenues. In fact, the more they provide, the less the profit (Patel and Rushefsky 1995, 188). HMOs carefully limit hospitalization and the length of hospital stay, and encourage their physicians to provide as little care as possible. Various incentives are offered to encourage doctors to limit services and referrals to specialists (Patel and Rushefsky 1995, 142).

Many economists agree that MC plans are reaching the limit in their ability to save health care costs. They have exhausted resources in reaching employers as customers, in squeezing physicians' pay, and in rationing treatments (Sherrid 1997; Charski 1998; Goldstein 1998). About 85 percent of Americans who get their medical insurance through their employer are already in some form of MC (Charski 1998). Patients demand newer medical technology, better coverage of treatments, and greater freedom to select doctors and visit specialists when they want (Goldstein 1998). All of these options cost money. Already, there is evidence that MC premiums, which had been relatively stable in the early 1990s, started to climb. According to the Mercer survey of 4,200 employers, MC premiums rose 6.1 percent in 1998, the biggest increase in seven years, and is expected to rise 9 percent in 1999 (Galewitz 1999). The Office of Personnel Management announced that premiums for the federal health insurance program for workers and retirees will increase an average of 10.2 percent in 1999, the biggest jump since 1989 (Goldstein 1998).

In 1998, many HMO companies reported significant loss in incomes and substantial loss in the value of their stocks. Many are forced to raise their premiums as a result (Sherrid 1997; Brink 1998). To deal with the rising costs, employers are continuing to drop coverage for retirees; reducing drug benefits for some active workers; or asking workers to pick up a higher share of the health care costs. In 1998, the percentage of companies with 500 or more workers providing health benefits to retirees over age 65 fell to 36 percent, down from 46 percent in 1993 (Galewitz 1999).

Quality of Care Suffers under Managed Care

Opposing Managed Care

Under the MC system, the fewer procedures done, consults requested, or patient days in the hospital, the more money saved from the per-member payment pool. The physicians and the managers of the plan have a faulty financial incentive to provide less care (Sperduto 1994, 209). Some MC organizations reward physicians for deferring or withholding care that is deemed too expensive, pitting the financial interest of the doctor against the medical needs of the patient (PNIS 1998). They try to contain costs by further reducing hospital stays, restricting patients' access to specialists and expensive medical tests, and limiting patients' choice of physicians (Froomkin 1998).

Many MC firms place a major burden on physicians by closely scrutinizing their practice patterns and patient care decisions (Ayres 1996, 187). Physicians are given various forms of incentives to lower costs, such as cash bonuses for withholding care or for seeing more patients (Sherrid 1997; O'Reilly 1998). Many HMOs pay physicians a fixed fee per registered member, regardless of how much treatment each patient needs. Under this practice, called capitation, the less care doctors provide, the greater the reimbursement they receive (in Easterbook 1997). Some plans have gag clauses that prohibit doctors from speaking freely about the range of treatments available to their patients (Brink and Shute 1997). These practices undermine the trust patients must have in their doctors that is crucial in the practice of medicine (O'Reilly 1998).

MC has no hope of substantially slowing the health care cost spiral unless it can ration administering expensive high-technology treatments (Schwartz 1992). In any health care system, some decisions about how to allocate funds and how much money to spend on what types of treatments and services are being made all the time. Under MC, most of these decisions are made by employers, benefit administrators, and MC officers behind closed doors. Policies are canceled or changed; procedures are denied; providers are dropped with little or no accountability (Daniels et al. 1996, 57). Patients face uncertainty about whether their costs will be reimbursed. According to a survey conducted jointly by the Kaiser Family Foundation and Harvard University, about 24 percent of the MC subscribers had difficulty getting permission to see a specialist, 19 percent had problems getting their plans to pay an emergency room bill, and 17 percent were unable to file an appeal to an independent agency for a denied claim (PNIS 1998).

A study has shown that HMO patients are less likely than fee-for-service patients to undergo cardiac catheterization and angioplasty after an acute infarct (Casale in PNIS 1998). HMO enrollees have a 20 to 40 percent lower hospitalization rate compared with fee-for-service patients at least in part because of the incentives to reduce hospital utilization (Patel and Rushefsky 1995, 142).

Supporting Managed Care

Despite well-publicized anecdotal reports of denied treatments by MC plans, studies show that the quality of care does not suffer under MC. On the contrary, most studies suggest that MC has improved the general quality of care and made health care more affordable to many consumers (Easterbrook 1997). MC eliminates only the unnecessary treatments and procedures that were widespread under the fee-for-service system. It does not eliminate necessary care based on the criteria determined by medical professionals (Easterbrook 1997; Brink 1998; Hellinger in PNIS 1998). According to the American Association of Health Plans' review, MC physicians spend more, not less, time with patients; MC plans offer a wide selection of providers and rarely deny physician-ordered treatments (PNIS 1998). According to the National Center for Policy Analysis's policy brief, MC patients were less likely to suffer ruptured appendices and had earlier diagnoses for four types of cancer (breast, cervical, colon, and melanoma) than did fee-for-service patients (PNIS 1998; Brink 1998). Thanks to MC, fewer people are dying of unnecessary surgery (Millenson in Brink 1998); older patients suffer fewer episodes of potentially ineffective care, hospital jargon for care that prolongs an inevitable death (Brink 1998).

The majority of the MC subscribers are satisfied with the service they receive and with the doctors they see under their plans (Armey 1998; Rubin 1995). An ABC News and *Washington Post* poll conducted in 1998 found that 80 percent of HMO members are satisfied with the quality of care they receive (Hartman 1998).

Studies have shown that with experience managed care services are getting better at caring for the sick. They are coming up with innovative and efficient ways of providing service and satisfying customers while saving money (Miller in Shapiro 1998). Eventually, the quality of MC's service will be controlled by the competition in the market. Inefficient MC plans with poor performance records will lose their customers to the ones with good-quality performances unless they improve their service and become more efficient. Market force is the best regulator of quality and performance (Sunshine 1996; Enthoven and Singer 1996).

Managed Care Creates Competition

Supporting Managed Care

MC motivates consumers, insurers, and providers to be more cost-conscious, and it encourages the health care system to be efficient, flexible, innovative, and competitive. The idea is to create a market-driven health care system based on informed, cost-conscious consumer choices (Enthoven 1992). HMOs create competitive pressures on the fee-for-service system so that all providers and insurers would begin to look at costs. As MC organizations become larger buyers of services, they can use tough bargaining powers in dealing with doctors and hospitals (Patel and Rushefsky 1995; Daniels et al. 1996, 155). MC plans compete among themselves, too. Those that provide better combinations of cost and service would be rewarded in the market with more consumers (White 1995, 8).

Opposing Managed Care

Competition's ability to control costs depends on having enough competitors. At least two MC setups must be present in a community if there is to be competition, and each of them needs a potential market of roughly 250,000 people to achieve economies of scale. Only about half of all Americans live in places densely populated enough to support two or more such programs (Randal 1993). The growing number of HMO mergers and consolidations during the late 1990s have created a few large companies, dominant in certain geographic areas. These large firms have greater market power over the premiums charged, the payments made to doctors and hospitals, and the services offered, while reducing choices to customers and competition in the market (Davis in Quinn 1998; Randal 1993).

In order for MC plans to be competitive, consumers must have a reliable and accurate source of information about the performance of different MC plans such as treatment coverage, cost of treatments, treatment outcomes, waiting time for appointments and treatments, and other aspects of individual group care, so that sponsors and consumers can select the best of several programs (Ayres 1996, 177). Unfortunately, consumers are often unaware of the quality of services of different MC providers. There is not enough standardized information (i.e., report card) available to consumers to compare different types of services and quality of care. Moreover, making this information truly comparable and in a language understandable for laypeople is very difficult (White 1995, 167–78). Often, consumers are not in a position to shop around or bargain because they do not have enough knowledge about medicine, and they cannot predict what kind of illness they might get in the future. Health care insurance contracts are extremely complex, ambiguous, and hard to understand even for medical professionals. Very few people read and understand their coverage contracts. When they do, it is typically after they become ill and need treatment (Enthoven and Singer 1996, 195; White 1995, 174).

Most purchasers of MC are employers with a large number of employees. Individual consumers are not in a situation where they can shop around or change plans for the better or cheaper. Even when employers want to change plans, it would require persuading a whole group of people to switch from one plan to another. Changing health plans means changing doctors, and thus, many employees are reluctant to change plans (Enthoven and Singer 1996, 196). In addition, throughout the private sector, preexisting condition restrictions limit the ability of insured people to change plans. Up to two-thirds of conventional insurance policies have restrictions on preexisting conditions, as do most MC plans (Cutler 1996, 255).

Managed Care Exacerbates Problems of Inequality in Health Care

Opposing Managed Care

The basic logic of managed competition exacerbates the problems of inequalities in the demand for health care and ability to pay for insurance. MC plans cut costs by practicing what is known as biased self-selection. They select only young and healthy people who use less medical care and avoid enrolling elderly or high-risk people (Patel and Rushefsky 1995, 142; Brink 1998; White 1995, 8). This policy places greater burden on public health care facilities that must pick up an unfairly high share of caring for the chronically ill, old, and poor.

The traditional insurance system covered poor people through what is known as cost-shifting. Hospitals and doctors sent out bills higher than the actual care given to cover for people who showed up with no money or insurance. MC, on the other hand, pays only for the actual care provided to their insured patients, thus it creates greater burdens on public health care facilities which cannot, legally or morally, refuse treatment of the poor and uninsured (Brink 1998). The purpose of health insurance is to spread risks so that the healthy and wealthy can help pay for the cost of treating the sick and the poor. MC's biased self-selection and cost-shifting to community hospitals undermine the fundamental principle of insurance as well as the idea of health care as a community service.

The bulk of the savings achieved by HMOs in the early 1990s has been achieved by cutting back on expensive and unprofitable facilities such as burn centers, neonatal intensive care units, and emergency rooms. They did so knowing that municipal and university hospitals are still around to pick up the slack (Gaylin 1994). This type of cost-shifting between private and public sectors or from one part of the private sector to another cannot be accepted (Daniels et al. 1996, 57). Many of the nation's teaching hospitals are already in financial crisis and are having a very difficult time maintaining the academic mission of training new doctors and investing in research and development, as well as treating the sickest and poorest patients (Goldberg 1999).

Supporting Managed Care

As competition among MC increases, MC plans will be forced to include a broader range of subscribers including the old and the sick. Already about 85 percent of Americans who got their medical insurance through employers in 1998 are in some form of MC (Charski 1998). In order to maintain their competitive edge, MC firms will also have to expand their services to include high-cost, low-profit areas as well.

Instead of blaming MC firms for not sharing the burden of cost-shifting, we need to come up with better economic plans that would allow more people to purchase insurance. That will eliminate the need for cost-shifting altogether and, as a result, will lower MC premiums to many others. It is not fair for many hardworking and money-saving individuals to have to pay for the health problems of free-riders who take advantage of the generosity of our health care system and get free health care.

Doctors Are Not Happy with the Managed Care System

Opposing Managed Care

The rush to MC has not pleased many physicians who are frustrated with the intrusion of insurance company managers into their practices (Ayres 1996, 187). Under the MC system, physician autonomy in clinical decision making is often limited. The MC system has shifted the decision-making process and power from doctors to MC administrators. Health care rules and regulations are being made and changed by businesspeople who are not aware of the medical aspects of what they are doing, and whose immediate goal is making profits (Kodner 1998; Brink and Shute 1997; Sperduto 1994, 209).

HMO plans monitor the prescribing and treatment patterns of doctors closely. They develop standard procedures that doctors are expected to follow for specific diseases. They have utilization review panels, committees that review patient records and decide what treatments the health plan will cover (Brink and Shute 1997). Such policies put too much pressure on the doctors, who must constantly worry about cutting cost in providing care for the patients. Many doctors believe that their ability to provide good-quality care is often undermined by the pressure to cut costs (Donelan et al. 1997).

Frustrated by the MC abuses, in June 1999, the American Medical Association members voted to form a doctors' union to battle against the growing power of health insurance companies and MC firms.

Supporting Managed Care

Without the intrusion of insurance companies and their incentive to cut costs, doctors will not be cost-conscious, and we cannot contain the rising cost of health care. One of the reasons health care costs soared was because there was no regulation that would monitor doctors' practice patterns and limit doctors' fees. Managed care plans have helped to bring the inflated fees of treatment, which existed under the fee-for-service system, down to where they should be. Managed care firms do not report having any problems recruiting physicians. If doctors are not happy with the system, they would not stay with the plans, as many do (Easterbrook 1997; Sunshine 1996, 209; Brink and Shute 1997).

Managed Care Provides Preventive Care

Supporting Managed Care

MC emphasizes prevention, early diagnosis and treatment, and effective management of chronic conditions to prevent them from becoming serious, acute problems. Its service includes regular visits to the doctor before one develops major symptoms, follow-up services after major surgery, and immunization for children. Under the fee-for-service system, patients often postpone visits to doctors until their symptoms become severe, because most insurance plans do not cover regular visits to doctors (Enthoven 1992; Froomkin 1998; Weiner in Daniels et al. 1996, 151). Hospitalization rates among HMO members are about 40 percent lower than among people with traditional insurance coverage because of effective preventive care (Conklin 1994, 176).

Opposing Managed Care

Prevention is not always better or more cost-effective than the traditional curative medicine. Many mass screening programs will identify vast numbers of false positives for each illness detected, driving up the cost per case to an undesirable level (Russel in Deber 1994, 59). Even if it saves money in the long run, prevention often requires more spending in the short run. Spending on children's nutrition, for example, can reduce later illnesses related to malnutrition, but it will do little or nothing to reduce the incidence of disease in the first year the money is spent. Therefore, spending on such prevention cannot replace spending on care, and it should not help with budget deficits. There is no good budgetary argument for prevention as a replacement for the cure (White 1995, 22). The hospitalization rate among HMO members is lower than those with traditional insurance not because of effective preventive medicine but because HMOs select young and healthy subscribers who usually need less medical care than the old and sick, and because HMOs effectively discourage and limit hospital utilization by their enrollees (Patel and Rushefsky 1995, 142; Brink 1998; Froomkin 1998).

Managed Care Plans Provide Limited Choices for Their Members

Opposing Managed Care

People who move from fee-for-service care with indemnity insurance into MC have significantly fewer choices (Daniels et al. 1996, 162). Managed care organizations decide which doctors their enrollees can see, which hospitals to use, when they can use them, and for how long. It is almost impossible for the enrollees to choose medical options not approved by the primary physician.

Patients can see specialists only if the insurance plan and the primary care physician agree that the referral is necessary, and they can see only the specialists belonging to the network (Ayres 1996, 187; Froomkin 1998). According to a survey conducted by Kaiser Family Foundation and Harvard University, 24 percent of those with MC plans reported experiencing difficulty getting permission to see a medical specialist (PNIS 1998).

Supporting Managed Care

The growth of MC is affecting different people differently. Medicaid recipients, who usually have difficulty finding doctors willing to treat them, generally experience greater choices under MC. Previously uninsured people also have greater choice of primary care providers under MC (Daniels et al. 1996, 161).

In order to counter employers' and patients' dissatisfaction with limited networks of providers, HMOs have had to enlist more and more doctors and hospitals. In 1997, more than 80 percent of HMOs offered an option that lets patients opt out of networks altogether (usually for an additional price), up from 36 percent in 1990, and that number is growing (Sherrid 1997).

Managed Care Reform: Is It Necessary?

Since Congress rejected President Clinton's Health Care Reform Bill in 1994, the number of people who have been nudged into MC has increased to 60 percent of the population in 1996 (from 36 percent in 1992) (Froomkin 1998; Dickerson 1997). As MC participation rates climbed, so did complaints from MC subscribers over denied claims and limited choice of doctors (Dickerson 1997). Managed care, which once was hailed as a cost-cutting solution to rising medical costs, has become a target of intense criticism, accused of irresponsible and potentially dangerous penny-pinching at the expense of patients' health. Public furor against MC is so intense that the idea of establishing certain patients' rights in the new MC environment became one of the hottest issues in the 1998 elections (Froomkin 1998). As people's mistrust of MC increased, the proportion of people who favor federal regulation of MC increased also. According to surveys by the Kaiser Family Foundation and Harvard University, 65 percent of the American public favor government regulation of MC (Goldstein and Dewar 1998).

Patients' Bill of Rights Act

In 1998, both Democratic and Republican parties proposed a Patients' Bill of Rights Act. This proposal, which received the endorsement of the American Medical Association and numerous consumer groups, sought to protect patients from abuses by MC firms and medical insurance groups. The proposed

Patients' Bill of Rights Act would make all MC plans: 1) pay for emergency room care in any situation a prudent person would consider a crisis; 2) let women see an obstetrician or gynecologist without prior authorization, or designate one as their main doctor; 3) allow patients willing to pick up extra costs to see doctors who do not have contracts with the plan; 4) provide care from specialists when medically necessary at no extra cost to patients; 5) end blocks or financial incentives that discourage doctors from discussing all treatment options; 6) collect and disclose statistics on consumer satisfaction and the quality of care, such as success rates for specific operations; and 7) assure a speedy internal review of disputed coverage decisions or external appeals process in cases of denied treatment. The Democrats' proposal added patients' right to sue their MC providers for damages if they have been improperly denied care. This legislation was designed to lift the 1974 federal law (Employee Retirement Income Security Act) that blocks most people who receive health care through their employer from suing their MC providers for denying treatment (Borger 1998; Froomkin 1998; Quinn 1998; Lord 1998; Marquis 1999). In July 1999, the Senate approved the Republican-sponsored bill, but President Clinton vetoed it because it does not allow patients to sue their MC providers. In October 1999, however, the House of Representatives passed the Patients' Bill of Rights that includes the right of patients to sue their HMOs.

Do we really need MC reform? Or has the need for MC reform been exaggerated by the media? The following sections provide an overview of supporting and opposing arguments regarding MC reform.

Supporting MC Reform

A market-based health care system operated by for-profit corporations is bound to cut costs at the expense of quality of care unless there are federally enforceable guidelines and regulations to prevent such abuse (Waxman in *Online Newshour* 7-21-98). Polls consistently show that about 70 percent of Americans support the Patients' Rights legislation, and twenty-seven states have already passed it in some form (Shapiro 1998). Those who oppose this bill fear that such reform measures will increase health care costs and that will increase the number of people without insurance. A report by the independent Congressional Budget Office estimates that this legislation, if enacted, would increase consumer costs by only $2.00 a month and business costs by $5.00 a month for each covered employee. There is little evidence that such a small additional cost would significantly increase the number of uninsured (Waxman in *Online Newshour* 7-21-98).

Since 1974, most consumers with employer-based insurance were unable to sue their insurers or MC providers for denying treatment as a result of the federal employment law, known as the Employment Retirement Income Security Act (ERISA). This law unfairly protects the MC industry while hurting many consumers' rights to decent health care. This law makes it easier for MC providers to deny costly treatments, to provide lower-quality service to make profits, and to get away with mistakes they make. Lawsuits—or the threat of them—are the most effective way to keep profit-seeking insurers from denying patients' necessary care to increase profits (Marquis 1999). Going to court when one feels he or she has been harmed, especially about something as fundamental as medical care, is not something the government or politicians can deny consumers. Managed care industries are not so special that they are entitled to live under a different set of rules than other industries. If they mistreat consumers to make more profit, or if they make negligent mistakes, they deserve to be tried (Borger 1998).

Opposing MC Reform

The overall achievements of MC—restraining costs, avoiding unnecessary operations, promoting prevention—are largely taken for granted in the controversy over MC reform. Had health care inflation not slowed, that would be considered a far greater national problem than MC firms' alleged mistreatment of a few patients. This Patients' Bill of Rights Act is a "legislation by anecdote." It is a concerted effort by the misinformed public and politicians to overhaul the only cost-effective and efficient health care system ever invented so far, based on unsupported anecdotal evidence, exaggerated and sensationalized by the media, ignoring all the achievements MC has brought about so far (Easterbrook 1997).

The Congressional Budget Office estimated that the provisions in the Patients' Bill of Rights Act would raise health insurance costs by 4 percent across the board (Gradison, President of Health Insurance Association of America, in *Online Newshour* 7-21-98). Every 1 percent increase in the cost of insurance causes 200,000 Americans to lose their coverage and leads to a 2.6 percent drop in small-business coverage. If enacted, this legislation will drive up prices and liability costs, force many employers to drop or reduce coverage, and swell the ranks of the uninsured (Armey 1998).

Thanks to market forces, MC has evolved and improved. It is repairing its problems faster than Washington can even identify them. Many employers have shifted out of old-fashioned, restrictive HMOs into more flexible plans, like PPOs, that allow members to go out of network for a slight fee. The customer satisfaction rate is extremely high (Armey 1998). Almost 80 percent of the MC enrollees are satisfied with the quality of health care they receive (Shapiro 1998; Hartman 1998). This proves that the market is the toughest regulator of all. Managed care's ability to provide innovative services to consumers will be hampered if additional federal regulations are imposed (Gradison in *Online Newshour* 7-21-98).

The tort system is extremely expensive and inefficient when it comes to aiding people injured by negligence. If we allow enrollees to sue MC firms, there will be an avalanche of lawsuits, and that will raise the premiums and overall health care costs to consumers (Hartman 1998; Marquis 199; Enthoven in Borger 1998). What we need instead is to make it easier for patients to appeal MC decisions of treatments and coverage by mandating MC plans to provide some kind of out-of-network utilization review process to guarantee that no one is unfairly denied necessary care (Hartman 1998; PNIS 1998). The experience in nineteen states shows that when doctors and HMOs bicker over proper treatments, a neutral expert's opinion is the best way to resolve disputes, not a legal battle (Pollitz in Shapiro 1999).

Prior to examining the major health care reform options on the national level, supporting and opposing views on three insurance policies that are directly related to health care—underwriting, cost-sharing, and rationing—are discussed in the following section.

Underwriting and Preexisting Condition Exclusions

There has been an increasing tendency for insurance companies and MC plans to use policies of "underwriting" or "experience (risk) rating" (Patel and Rushefsky 1995, 114). Underwriting is the process through which insurers determine applicants' levels of risks in order to exclude those at high risk or to charge them higher rates (Daniels et al. 1996, 45–6). Premiums are adjusted based on the likely risk of needing health care. Underwriting also occurs when insurance companies or MC plans refuse to insure workers in an entire firm (a practice known as redlining) whose workers have hazardous working conditions, such as mining and construction industries (Patel and Rushefsky 1995, 115).

Insurance companies and MC firms often deny coverage for people with preexisting conditions—an insurance term for medical conditions or diseases diagnosed before people apply for coverage—or require much higher premiums (Clinton 1993, 3). Up to two-thirds of conventional insurance policies have restrictions on preexisting conditions, as do most MC organizations (Cutler 1996, 255).

Opposing Underwriting

Health care costs are not evenly distributed across the population. In any given year, approximately 20 percent of the population incur about 80 percent of total medical expenses (Hacker 1997, 14). One percent of the population is so sick it consumes 30 percent of medical expenditures, and the sickest 5 percent consume 58 percent (Berk and Monheit in Daniels et al. 1996, 48). The object of medical underwriting is thus to maximize profits by screening out individuals likely to need health care and seeking healthy individuals who could pay premiums but not require much health care (Ayres 1996; Hacker 1997, 14).

Insurance was originally intended as a means to spread the risk of individual misfortune among the larger community. To make insurance accessible and affordable, the sick should be pooled with the healthy, the old with the young, those with high risks with those with low risks. The more factors are eliminated, the more risks would be shared, and the more affordable the insurance becomes. Selecting those who have low health risks and placing more burden of financing care on those who have high risks undermine the purpose of insurance and the idea of community (Patel and Rushefsky 1995, 105–6; Feder and Levitt 1996, 228). Most countries prohibit medical underwriting or risk rating. The United States is unique among nations in having allowed this actuarial fairness principle rather than social fairness to be used for years in medical insurance (Daniels et al. 1996, 46; Hacker 1997, 13).

Instead of underwriting or experience rating, we need a policy of community rating. In community rating, insurance rates are set on the same terms to all purchasers, regardless of factors such as lifestyle risks, health status, preexisting conditions, claims experience, or demographic characteristics. With this system, the risk of using the insurance is spread over a larger population (Seidman 1994, 197; Patel and Rushefsky 1995, 113; Daniels et al. 1996, 46).

Supporting Underwriting

Medical expenses are distributed very unevenly. As a result, an insurer must seek to cover good risks, who are less likely to need much care, and to avoid bad risks, who are more likely to need care. That is the only way to survive in an unregulated market and to protect those who buy insurance from escalating costs. If an insurer cannot avoid covering bad risks, the insurer must charge them higher premiums proportionate to the expected costs of providing the health care services that they will require (Enthoven and Singer 1996, 196).

It is unfair to force people who are at low risk to cross-subsidize the security bought by people at high risk when they purchase insurance. Many health risks are the results of choices we make, such as driving styles, lifestyles, smoking habits, and diet patterns. It seems only fair that those who make safer and healthier lifestyle choices are entitled to benefit from the savings in lower premiums (Daniels et al. 1996, 46).

Opposing Preexisting Condition Exclusions

Throughout the private sector, the preexisting condition restriction limits the ability of insured people to change MC plans. People with a history of health problems (or whose family members have health problems) often find it very difficult to change jobs because of this preexisting condition limitation (Hacker 1997, 14). We need to limit preexisting condition exclusions for people newly purchasing coverage and eliminate preexisting condition exclusions for people who change insurance (Feder and Levitt 1996, 228).

Supporting Preexisting Condition Exclusions

Preexisting condition exclusions are necessary to deter healthy people from deferring insurance purchase. If anyone could step up anytime and buy coverage without such exclusions, people would have an incentive to wait to buy coverage until they become sick, thus driving premiums up to an unaffordable level (Enthoven and Singer 1996, 187; Patel and Rushefsky 1995, 121; Feder and Levitt 1996, 228). When New York state mandated a community rating of insurance, numerous low-risk insurees dropped their coverage, causing insurance premiums to escalate (Daniels et al. 1996, 149).

Cost-Sharing

In most insurance and MC policies, patients share in the direct cost of health care services for their own coverage or that of dependents out of pocket. Cost-sharing can include deductibles, coinsurance, or copayments. A deductible is the fixed amount that must be paid by the patient before the insurance benefits begin. Coinsurance is the percentage contribution patients pay once the deductible is exceeded. Copayments are generally a fixed contribution, rather than a percentage contribution, toward each unit of service (Patel and Rushefsky 1995, 151).

Since the early 1990s, out-of-pocket expenditures in the form of medical copayment have escalated. This trend is evident in both public and private sectors. For example, Medicare premiums, copayments, and deductibles are steadily going up. The elderly in 1996 paid about 28 percent of the cost of their health care out of pocket. This represents a 50 percent increase, as a share of their income, compared with when Medicare started (Binstock in Daniels et al. 1996, 141). In the private sector, workers are paying more for their health care out of pocket. Between 1980 and 1991, the average employee's out-of-pocket payment for health care rose from $248 a year to $1,300 (Rasell 1994). Many state employees are being asked to pay part of their premiums also (Daniels et al. 1996, 141).

Supporting Cost-Sharing

Cost-sharing is necessary because it reduces insurance premiums, encourages customers to be more cost-conscious about health care, and, most importantly, because it discourages frivolous use of medical services (Seidman 1994, 197). Studies have demonstrated that cost-sharing in the form of deductibles or coinsurance reduces unnecessary use of health care services by the consumers (Newhouse et al. in Patel and Rushefsky 1995, 152). Cost-sharing is used in other countries, such as in France and Japan, and it is limited to ambulatory services in Australia (White 1995, 273).

Opposing Cost-Sharing

With insurance cost-sharing, many will minimize their visits to doctors or post-pone the first visit for nonurgent problems. Those who cannot afford to pay the charges will forgo nonemergency services until the symptoms become acute. This means that early detection and preventive services will be decreased. When the care is provided at a later stage, it often results in more suffering for the patient and higher costs for all. Moreover, unless cost-sharing is adjusted to subscribers' income, it will place too much of a burden on lower-income families (Seidman 1994, 197–8; White 1995, 273; Daniels et al. 1996, 48).

Cost-sharing does not necessarily save health care costs. Canada and Germany spend much less in health care than the United States does with hardly any cost-sharing (White 1995, 156). Financial benefits from cost-sharing are often offset by the administrative costs that come from collecting the fees (198).

Health Care Rationing

The rationing of health care means restricting certain treatments to a certain group of people (e.g., depending on person's health status, age, medical history, or ability to pay) or limiting certain procedures that are not considered effective or cost-efficient.

Support Rationing

The major problem we face in the U.S. health care system is that we want to cut the cost of health care while maintaining the same high standard of health care services we are used to (Randal 1993). We want the latest and the most sophisticated medical technology, and we want to apply it indiscriminately to the very young, the very old, and the hopelessly ill. We want physicians to do everything possible for patients even when there is little or no hope for a cure or survival. We want the best, yet we want to pay the least (Patel and Rushefsky 1995, 165).

We cannot do everything for everybody. Limited resources will inevitably force us to make choices among competing health care needs (Gaylin 1994). We must make a choice between investing in expensive technologies that deliver a significant benefit to only a few people or ones that deliver a more modest benefit to a larger number of people. Sometimes we must make a choice between investing in a service that helps the sickest, most impaired patients or one that helps those whose functioning is less impaired. In any health care system, some choices will have to be made by a fair, publicly accountable decision-making process. Our rights are not violated if the choices that are made in this way turn out to be ones that do not happen to meet our personal needs but instead meet the needs of many others (Daniels et al. 1996, 27).

The first step is to admit to the cruel necessity of rationing health care. Then the second is to set limits on health care according to principles of equity and justice (Gaylin 1994). Two generally acceptable reasons for excluding services are that they are not needed for the treatment or prevention of disease or disability (called medical necessity) and that they are ineffective. To provide a scientific basis for these judgments, much research on outcomes and on the development of clinical guidelines must be done (Daniels et al. 1996, 42; Enthoven 1992).

Health care costs are less in many other countries because expensive treatments are prescribed only when there is evidence that the intervention is appropriate and useful (Ayres 1996, 175). In Great Britain, patients over the age of sixty are generally not considered suitable for kidney transplants. Limited resources and age are two factors that act as a basis for a great deal of rationing in Britain (Patel and Rushefsky 1995, 175).

In 1989, the state of Oregon sought to guarantee a basic health care package to everyone by rationing. The state legislature, based on statewide public debate, decided where on the list the state could afford to draw the necessary cutoff line. For example, it would pay for hip replacement and neonatal care, but not liver transplants or in vitro fertilization. The Oregon plan is by no means perfect. However, at least the state has addressed the uncomfortable truth that they cannot have equity in their health care system without making choices (Gaylin 1994).

Opposing Rationing

The notion of medical need is subjective and can be interpreted or defined in different ways, or changed depending on technological development and value judgment. It is impossible to specify a purely scientific standard of medical need, the basic concept that lies behind the idea of rationing (Daniels et al. 1996, 42; Callahan 1992). Furthermore, arriving at any societal consensus about the definition of medical need would be very complex and problematic, if not impossible (Patel and Rushefsky 1995, 176; Daniels et al. 1996, 42).

Medical care decisions should be made based on individual cases. The expected value or payoff from any procedure depends on the particular characteristics, physical condition, and severity of an illness in a particular patient. Every individual case is different, and every patient reacts differently to treatments (Schwartz in Hentoff 1994). Even aging affects people differently; some are extremely healthy relative to their age, while others seem much older for their age. The government, or any other professional body or group, cannot arbitrarily decide which treatment should be provided to which group of people. Any attempt to justify rationing using principles such as social worth, ability to pay, or age would create enormous potential for mischief (Patel and Rushefsky 1995, 176). For instance, under the name of rationing society decides who gets a heart and who can go on dialysis; who can live and who should die. Physicians have the duty to care for all patients who desire treatment, regardless of the seriousness of their illness, the expense of a procedure, or the chance of recovery. Rationing goes against the medical ethics the physicians are obligated to follow (Hentoff 1994).

Rationing should not and cannot be a choice unless we have exhausted our effort to reduce the waste from inefficient systems, such as overpayment by insurance companies, profits by corporations, and administrative costs that are estimated to be about a third of all health care expenditures. It would be a violation of our rights to health care if medically effective services are prohibited because waste and inefficiency consume valuable resources (Daniels et al. 1996, 27).

Rationing would hurt poor people the most; mainly women, children, and people with disabilities who must rely on some form of public assistance and cannot purchase private insurance that would cover a wide variety of choices and options. The Oregon plan rationed health care only for the poor people enrolled in Medicaid. Under the name of rationing, poor women and children were required to bear the burden of controlling health care costs in Oregon (Pear in Hentoff 1994; Patel and Rushefsky 1995, 150).

Health Care Reform: What Are the Options?

In the following sections, six national-level health care reform options are discussed.

Universal Equal Care versus Tiered System

Supporting Universal Equal Care

Any effort to reform our health care system must be aimed at achieving universal care, that is, it must provide equal quality care for everyone in society. Our health care system offers state-of-the-art technology and world-class care for those who can afford it, yet mediocre or below-average care for those who cannot afford it (Lemco 1994, 1). There is discrimination based on income; those with private insurance plans, especially very generous ones, tend to get better service than those on public plans (such as Medicaid) or those without health insurance at all (Patel and Rushefsky 1995, 105). Fifteen percent of the population are below the federally determined poverty level, and only about half of them receive Medicaid. One-fifth of this group has insurance of some sort, but close to one-third is completely uninsured. The rate of hospitalization for bacterial pneumonia in 1989 was 2.78 per 1,000 children under age five in high-income children compared with 11.21 in low-income children; asthma was 2.55 and 11.12; and intestinal disorders 1.20 and 5.67. Lack of screening and preventive care among the poor have serious consequences. Fourteen percent of all cervical cancer in poor women are already far advanced when discovered, compared with only 5 percent in higher-income women (Ayres 1996, 145).

Universal access to equal quality care is a compelling goal in any industrial society. It is morally wrong to let the sick or injured suffer, die, or be disabled for their inability to pay for medical care (Enthoven and Singer 1996, 187). The majority of the public supports mandated universal coverage of health care. In thirteen different national polls, an average of 72 percent said that they supported universal health insurance (Yankelovich 1996, 79; Aaron 1996, 4).

The United States is unique among its industrialized neighbors in not supporting universal access to health care. All of the advanced countries provide universal coverage in a system of shared savings for health care, supported either by taxes paid to the government or premiums paid to separate health insurance funds (White 1995, 6; Lemco 1994, 4).

Supporting Tiered System

Universal care is neither feasible nor plausible without rationing. Each of the countries that provide so-called universal coverage limits costs through a system of regulating fees and rationing treatments (White 1995, 7). They may provide a decent level of care, yet none provides all the care that people desire (Callahan 1992).

Even in those countries with universal care, inequality in health care has become inevitable. People with enough money started to purchase private supplementary insurance that allows them to receive better services without waiting or treatments that are not provided under universal coverage (White 1995, 77). In Germany, 20 percent of the population has alternative private insurance; in Great Britain, about 10 percent. In Australia, nearly 40 percent have private insurance that provides both supplementary coverage and greater choice (272).

In a society that permits significant income and wealth inequalities, some people will want to pay more for better-quality care and additional services. Why not let them? After all, we allow people to use their after-tax income and wealth as they see fit to pursue better quality of life and opportunities they prefer. The rich can buy special security systems for their homes, safer cars, and private schooling for their children. Why not allow them to buy supplementary health care for their families? (in Daniels et al. 1996, 28). Not allowing the rich to seek better-quality health care violates their liberty to use their resources to improve their lives as they see fit (in Daniels et al. 1996, 28).

Supporting Universal Coverage

The tiering of health care in other countries is different from the pattern in the United States. In the United States, most people have fairly decent coverage but a large segment has much less. In other countries, everybody is guaranteed decent standard coverage, and a few have more. One approach creates a very weak safety net for the poor; the other creates an escape valve for the well-to-do (White 1995, 6). There is nothing wrong in allowing better care for some who can afford to pay, so far as decent coverage for the underprivileged minorities is guaranteed. In the United States, we provide explicitly inferior coverage for a minority of the population while providing the majority high-quality care (White 1995, 272).

One objection to allowing a supplementary tier is that its existence could undermine the basic tier either economically or politically. It might attract better-quality providers away from the basic tier, or raise costs in the basic tier, reducing the ability of society to meet its social obligations. The supplementary tier might weaken political support for the basic tier by undercutting the social solidarity needed if people are to remain committed to ensuring equal quality care for all (Daniels et al. 1996, 28).

Private, Competition-Based Systems versus Public, Government-Controlled Systems

Since the 1973 Health Maintenance Organization (HMO) Act and the 1975 Supreme Court decision that medicine was not exempt from antitrust laws, health care in the United States has been found increasingly in the marketplace. While there has been some enthusiasm for government-controlled, regulation-based reform in the 1970s, the overall health care policies in the United States are moving toward more and more competition-based private systems.

Supporting Competition-Based Systems

The private-sector market force regulates itself through competition over price and quality. Competition is the best way to ensure innovation and efficiency in any economic activity, and health care is not an exception (Sunshine 1996, 216–7). The market force in health care motivates innovation in products, services, technology, quality improvement, and cost reduction. Market-based systems are flexible and motivate continuous adaptation to changes in technology and demands. Government programs, on the other hand, are often associated with waste, pork barrel, complexity, rigidity, and coercion (Enthoven and Singer 1996, 185). Any government legislation to protect health care providers from market forces and to block the cost-reducing effects of competition could stifle marketplace innovation (Sunshine 1996, 216).

Opposing Competition-Based Systems

Health care is not like other commodities; there cannot be a free market in health care. The typical supply-and-demand market theory does not always apply to health care. Patients do not know enough about medical care, about whether or not they are going to need the care, and about how much they need to save to buy the service ahead of time (White 1995, 24).

Mismatches between individual desires to consume and ability to pay are not a problem in the normal market. People get around the constraints of limited income by delaying a purchase, or saving for it. However, that is not the case in the health care market. When you need medical treatment, in most cases, the need is urgent. In a normal market, the volume and variety of goods and services are determined by individual choices. Getting sick, however, is often beyond one's control (White 1995, 24–5).

For consumer choice to be an effective check on quality and value in health insurance, consumers must be able to switch policies even if their health deteriorates. Most consumers (about 61 percent) receive health insurance through work, and their employers offer little or no choice of health plans. These consumers cannot "vote with their feet" and change insurance plans if they encounter problems. Moreover, under the current system of widespread underwriting and preexisting condition exclusions, switching policies is not an easy option. The necessary conditions for a free market simply do not exist in the area of health care (Butler 1996, 245; Waxman in *Online Newshour* 7-21-98).

Supporting Government-Regulated Systems

Making profits in health care can be a serious source of trouble, because denying adequate care can be an easy option to make profits. Very few other national systems allow profits to be made by directly treating the sick (Light in Daniels et al. 1996, 55). The frequent assertion that for-profit delivery systems are more efficient has not been supported by comparative research on the subject. Competition in health care, including managed care competition, has not been found to reduce overall expenditures after taking into account cost-shifting and biased self-selection (Daniels et al. 1996, 55).

A pure market in health care is unattainable; the health care market suffers from too many shortcomings. Government regulation is thus necessary to help improve the performance of the market and to protect consumers (Patel and Rushefsky 1995, 132). The belief that health care is a right is deeply ingrained in the American consciousness. This belief includes the government's obligation to ensure health care for everyone, including those who are too poor to pay for it. When any benefit is regarded as a right, Americans automatically assume it is the government's responsibility to honor it (Yankelovich 1996, 75). Such issues as underwriting, risk selection, uncompensated care, and rationing all have a tendency to work against the poor and the sick, those who need health care most (Sunshine 1996, 209). When the spreading of risk is not done by insurance providers voluntarily, it should be enforced by the government (Enthoven and Singer 1996, 201).

One of the causes of high health care costs has been the lack of governmental regulation regarding cost control. One effective plan would be for the government to set standard treatments and price schedules for all physicians and hospitals (Dentzer 1991). This would reduce undercare by the MC plans and overcare by the fee-for-service doctors (Seidman 1994, 199). In addition, there should be government control over capital expenditures for new hospitals and equipments, to make sure that there is not too much wasteful duplication of equipment and facilities (Lemco 1994, 3).

National Health Insurance (NHI) (Single-Payer Plan)

Many advocates support a government-provided universal insurance, the National Health Insurance. This system is often called the single-payer plan because the single payer would be the government, which would pay physicians, hospitals, and other health care providers directly with tax revenues collected from citizens. This approach eliminates private insurance, Medicare, and Medicaid and replaces them with a single, government-sponsored insurance plan. This system can be described as a publicly funded and privately provided system. Health care is financed publicly through payroll taxes but is delivered by private hospitals and doctors. Services are free at the point of delivery; doctors are paid fee-for-service by the government. The government uses the national and state global budget with fee schedules and institutional budgets to hold down costs. Canada's National Health Insurance is an example of this system: Germany, Japan, France, and Holland exhibit variants of this model (Patel and Rushefsky 1995, 25; Daniels et al. 1996, 73; Woolhandler and Himmelstein 1994a, 1994b).

Supporting NHI

The NHI (single-payer plan) would eliminate the need for private insurance companies, thereby saving money. The administrative cost would be much less under NHI than it is in the current U.S. health care system, because there would be only one insurer, the government. This means that billing would be straightforward, reimbursement would be quick, and paperwork would be kept to a minimum. With no competition among private insurers, there would be no advertising costs to pass on to consumers (Woolhandler and Himmelstein 1994b; Lemco 1994, 18).

Canada's NHI is comprehensive; it covers all medically necessary services provided by physicians. It is universal; it provides equal-quality coverage to all legal residents of a province. It is portable; it allows beneficiaries to have coverage when they are away from their home province, or, if they move, until they become vested in their new province's plan. Health care itself is privately provided, and thus patients have freedom to choose doctors and hospitals (Bernard 1992; White 1995, 63).

Unlike the private insurance or MC premiums, NHI is a means-tested system, because it is financed through payroll taxes. People pay according to their ability, usually proportional to their income. Health care burdens are not greater for low-income families (Bernard 1992).

Overall, Canada's NHI is more efficient and cost-effective than the U.S. health care system. They spend 40 percent less per person on health care than the United States, yet Canadians visit their doctors more often than Americans (Lemco 1994, 24).

Opposing NHI

If the goal of achieving NHI is to contain the cost of health care, the quality of care must suffer. Universal coverage under NHI is unachievable without rationing or sacrificing quality. The countries with universal coverage provide a decent level of health care; none provides all the health care that people might want. They limit care because they came to recognize the economic iron law of universal health care plans; to be affordable to everyone, they must be limited (Callahan 1992).

If we want to achieve NHI with the same quality of care we receive now, significant tax increases would clearly be needed. If funded solely at the federal level, it would require a 46 percent increase in income tax receipts or a 59 percent increase in FICA (Social Security and Medicare) payroll tax rates (Neuschler 1994).

In Canada, to control costs, the provincial governments dictate hospital operating budgets, set doctors' fees through bargaining with medical associations, limit the number of specialists, allocate the purchase of expensive equipment, and restrict costly procedures such as open heart surgery to a few hospitals in major population centers (Lemco 1994, 19).

Under the NHI system, anything new represents an additional cost. Such a system discourages innovation, perpetuates existing inefficiencies, and leads to creeping obsolescence and service rationing (Neuschler 1994, 145). Canada has had a single-payer system for twenty years, and its system is loaded with problems of deteriorating services, overburdened doctors, and long hospital waiting lists. A quarter of a million Canadians are on waiting lists for surgery. The average waiting period for elective surgery is four years. Sophisticated diagnostic equipment is scarce in Canada and growing scarcer. There are more MRIs (magnetic resonance imagers) in Washington state, which has a population of 4.6 million, than in all of Canada, which has a population of 26 million (Woolstein 1994).

Even with rationing and limited high-tech equipment, many Canadians now believe that their health care costs are out of control, that the country can no longer afford such a universal system. Canada has the second most expensive health care system in the world following the United States and faces serious pressure to reduce spending (Lemco 1994, 14; Barnes 1993; Haislmaier 1992).

For the majority of Americans, the pluralistic, multipayer system has been and will continue to be the preferred policy. Most Americans prefer having the highest-quality care and choice of health care and insurance options (Fortin in Kong 1999).

Supporting NHI

Canada's health care system has its share of problems. Nevertheless, the vast majority of Canadians are fundamentally satisfied with their medical services. There is a widespread sense of security that comes from knowing that an illness, however catastrophic, never results in financial disaster (Lemco 1994, 15).

Every country in the world rations health care. The question is how, and how much. The United States limits services by ability to pay. By contrast, Canada, under NHI, provides uniform access to equal-quality care to the entire population. All Canadians, rich and poor, regardless of the state of their health, age, or employment status, are covered by the same comprehensive system (Bernard 1992; Marmor and Mashaw 1994, 77).

In Canada, patients with immediate or life-threatening needs rarely wait for services. Overall, rates of hospital use per capita are considerably higher in Canada than in the United States. There are indeed waiting lists for a few specialized, nonurgent operations in major Canadian cities (Bernard 1992). However, the United States also has long waits for nonurgent care for some people. Many people wait months before they can afford to pay high copayments and deductibles. Many HMOs require substantial waiting periods for medical appointments, partly to discourage frivolous use of services (Lemco 1994, 22–3).

Canadians' overall health status is better than that of Americans. The infant mortality rate per 1,000 live births is 7.9 in Canada compared with 10.4 in the United States; deaths from heart disease per 100,000 is 348 in Canada compared with 434 in the United States. The overall life expectancy is 77 in Canada, compared with 75 in the United States (Bernard 1992).

National Health Service (NHS) (Socialized Medicine)

Another health care option is National Health Service (NHS). Under this system, the government controls and operates health care services and industries related to health care, including hospitals, doctors, and pharmaceutical and other medical supply industries. This is a publicly financed and publicly provided system of health care; it is financed by general taxation or through payroll taxes, and the service is provided by doctors and other health care providers who are government employees. Great Britain, Sweden, and Italy have a health care system similar to this. In Britain, the NHS owns most hospitals, pays physicians on a salaried or capitation basis, and has no insurance overhead (Patel and Rushefsky 1995, 25; Woolhandler and Himmelstein 1994b).

Supporting NHS

This system eliminates the insurance industry, and much of doctors' offices and hospitals' administrative expenses, and even billing for services. Administrative costs are considerably lower under this system than in private insurance systems. In Great Britain, administrative costs amount to 6 percent of total health spending, compared with 26 percent in the United States. This system also eliminates advertising costs and corporate profits by other health care–related industries (Woolhandler and Himmelstein 1994b).

The British system does contain costs. Their system spends about a third as much per capita as does the United States' system, and costs over the past decade have risen at a rate only about 2 percent above inflation. The British system is built around primary care physicians: 90 to 95 percent of all health care is provided by these family physicians who receive only 14 percent of the NHS's total costs. In the United States, 80 percent of all problems are first seen by specialists. The health status of the British is no worse than that of Americans, and actually better according to some statistics. Their life expectancy averages 76 compared with 75 in the United States; infant and maternal mortality is 9 (per 1,000) and 7 (per 100,000) compared with 10 and 8 in the United States (Ayres 1996, 163).

Opposing NHS

NHS will not work in the United States. Government-run NHS means creation of a huge government bureaucracy, which will inevitably become inefficient and expensive. Any form of government-controlled and guaranteed health care service would raise costs, taxes, and result in massive waste. Medicaid and Medicare are examples of government-run health care programs gone out of control. Their costs have already skyrocketed (Woolstein 1994).

When health care is free, there is little incentive for either patients or doctors to minimize costs, resulting in massive waste and inefficiency. Great Britain created NHS in 1948. The first problem with NHS was the skyrocketing demand for medical services. With health care paid for entirely by the government, there was no reason not to go to a doctor. NHS soon found itself in direct competition for funds with national defense, pensions, and all other governmental functions. Budget cuts for NHS caused a steady deterioration in the quality of British medical care. The waiting time for routine, nonemergency surgery had increased to years; On average, British doctors have more than 3,000 patients compared with 500–600 for the average U.S. doctors. NHS doctors spend an average of less than five minutes with their patients, who usually wait hours to see them (Woolstein 1994).

In Great Britain and in many other countries with socialized medicine, quasi-legal clinics have developed to care for patients who can no longer tolerate the abysmal medical services provided by NHS. About 10 percent of the British population have supplementary private insurance to gain quicker access to or to receive better-quality care (Daniels et al. 1996, 27; White 1995, 5, 272). As a result of widespread dissatisfaction, in 1989, the British government began to modify its NHS, and reintroduced market-based health care competition (Woolstein 1994; Barnes 1993).

Mandated Employer-Based Health Insurance

Another alternative plan is the government-mandated employer-based health insurance system. This system is often called a play-or-pay plan, because employers would be required by law to either provide health insurance to their workers or pay a tax to fund a public health insurance plan that would finance health care for uncovered workers (Hacker 1997, 5). This is the method used to fund health care in countries like Germany and Japan instead of a broad tax on all citizens (Ayres 1996, 183).

Supporting Employer-Based Health Insurance

In 1993, nine out of ten Americans who received health coverage had it through their employers. It is a system that has been working for the majority of Americans (Clinton 1993, 81). Mandating an employer-based system would only be an expansion of the existing system, which does not require a major overhaul of our health care system. About 85 percent of the uninsured are full-time employees and their dependents (Clinton 1993, 3). If all the employers agreed to insure their employees and their dependents, the ranks of the uninsured would shrink dramatically (Ayres 1996, 183; Rochefort 1993; Wekesser 1994, 198).

Opposing Employer-Based Health Insurance

Employer-based insurance inevitably creates problems of inequality. Insurance companies or MC plans view each individual firm or individual buyer as a self-contained unit, instead of pooling all those covered under the insurance company's policies. Therefore, smaller firms have more difficulty in negotiating favorable rates for their workers than do larger companies. Smaller employers (at least those with less than fifty employees) are too small to spread risks, too small to achieve economies of scale in administration, and usually too small to offer multiple choices of plans. A small risk pool also makes it difficult to negotiate reasonable premium rates; their rates could dramatically increase if only a few of their employees or their family members developed a serious illness. As a result, their costs per worker are much higher than in larger firms (Patel and Rushefsky 1995, 109; Enthoven and Singer 1996, 194; Ayres 1996, 184). Administrative costs are 40 percent of premiums for self-employed people or companies with fewer than five employees; 25 percent of premiums for companies with less than 50 workers, compared with 8 percent for those with more than 1,000 workers (Ayres 1996, 184; Clinton 1993, 6). For many small businesses, providing health insurance for their workers has become almost impossible. In 1996, 97 percent of firms with 1,000 or more workers offered health insurance to their employees compared with only 36 percent of those with less than 25 workers (Ayres 1996, 128; Clinton, 1993, 4; Daniels et al. 1996, 10).

Health care insurance is not a contract between each employee and each insurer, and therefore, employer-based insurance is not portable. Private plans have vesting periods before a new employee is covered and normally lapse when a person changes jobs, and many exclude preexisting conditions (White 1995, 43). As a result, many workers feel locked into their current jobs because of preexisting condition exclusions or other insurance restrictions that may come with a new job. As health care costs rise, the problems of job locks will increase (Cutler 1996, 251; Clinton 1993, 3). In addition, this system can be unfair to many women and their dependent children who lose their health care coverage when their spouses die or they divorce (Clinton 1993, 3).

Another flaw in this system is that employers—not the employees—have the power to choose health plans, doctors, hospitals, the type of care employees receive, and the type of payments. Employees do not have many choices under this system. When their employers switch health care plans, employees usually have to change their doctors and hospitals (Brink and Shute 1997). If individuals were allowed to purchase their own care—rather than being forced to purchase through their employers—individual buyers would have greater choices and become more cost-conscious, and the market would regulate itself more effectively (Jecker 1993; Pauly and Goodman 1996, 278).

Employer-based insurance can become susceptible to abuse by the employers. Already, prompted by rising health care costs, employers of all sizes have reduced health coverage benefits to their workers and retirees or raised deductibles and other copayments. Between 1987 and 1995, the percentage of the nonelderly population with employer-based health insurance declined from 69.2 to 63.8 percent, while the percentage covered by Medicaid increased from 8.6 to 12.5 percent (PNIS 1998). Sometimes, workers have to sacrifice wage increases for health benefits (Clinton 1993; White 1995, 43). When workers become too expensive to keep on the payroll, employers are more likely to lay off their employees or not hire them in the first place (Wekesser 1994, 198; Bernard 1992). This plan also encourages employers to hire part-time workers, temporary workers, and contract service workers to avoid providing health care benefits. As health care costs rise, this problem will become even more acute (Cutler 1996, 251; Jecker 1993).

Employer-based insurance is not means-tested, that is, coverage payment is not proportional to the ability to pay. The share of the health care burden for lower-income families is much greater than it is for high-income families (Daniels et al. 1996, 50–74). For instance, in a company that offers a health insurance plan covering dependents with a $200 a month premium, a general manager who makes $100,000 a year pays the same $200 as the janitor who makes $15,000 a year. The premium is only 2.4 percent of the general manager's income, but 16 percent of the janitor's income (Patel and Rushefsky 1995, 113). Whether the money for health care is gathered through taxes, premiums, or other related means, it should be based on the ability to pay as in progressive tax rates (Rochefort 1993; Daniels et al. 1996, 50).

Mandated Individual (Consumer)-Based Health Insurance with Medical Savings Account

Supporting Individual-Based Insurance

Instead of employer-based insurance, we can require all families to join a health plan with a basic package of benefits. This plan would be an individual mandate, rather than an employer mandate. We can provide refundable tax credit for individuals who purchase insurance, instead of employer tax deduction for health care (Patel and Rushefsky 1995, 117–8; Butler 1996, 238; Pauly and Goodman 1996, 276). The current system gives employers and their workers a tax break to buy health insurance, yet those who pay for insurance out of their own pocket get no such break. This is particularly unfair to many self-employed U.S. workers.

Under the individual-based system, each household would own its own health plan and determine how much of its compensation would be devoted to coverage and what that coverage would include. Consumers would have more control over their coverage, have more choices, and become more cost-conscious. Health insurers, on the other hand, would have to compete by satisfying the consumer, not the employer, regarding quality and price (Butler 1996, 237).

This plan severs the tie between work and health insurance. Employees can carry their insurance from job to job without worrying about coverage or preexisting condition exclusions and would not have to provide sensitive health information to their employers (Glassman 1998; Patel and Rushefsky 1995, 118).

This plan gives those who are not covered by employer-based insurance—the unemployed, self-employed, and those whose employers do not provide coverage—the same tax break enjoyed by corporations, and the same option to shop in the marketplace for the highest-quality care at the lowest price (Armey 1998; Love 1998).

In order for each family or individual to be adequately covered, this reform plan requires the creation of medical savings accounts (MSAs) that would cover routine medical expenses not covered by catastrophic insurance coverage. MSAs would let people set aside money, tax free, to pay routine medical bills and the premium for a high-deductible insurance policy—cheaper than a regular health plan—to protect them in the event of expensive illness not covered by catastrophic coverage (Love 1998). This would allow people to buy insurance that covers only large medical expenses and to pay out of pocket for smaller ones. Paying small medical bills from one's own resources would encourage wise purchase decisions (Pauly and Goodman 1996, 276–7; Glassman 1998).

With MSAs, even a family of moderate income could tolerate insurance with a substantial deductible, thus holding down the insurance premium they have to pay. Individual families would be able to withdraw unused funds for other purposes at the end of each insurance year. This program brings consumers directly into the health care market, thus making them more cost-conscious and giving them more choices (Glassman 1997; Love 1998).

Opposing Individual-Based Health Insurance

If families are free to choose the health benefits they want, that will lead to a "death spiral" of adverse selection by the insurance companies and MC plans, which would undermine the risk-spreading function of insurance. Insurance companies would "cherry-pick" good risks and avoid bad risks, leaving sicker families unable to afford coverage (Enthoven in Butler 1996, 244–5). People would buy coverage mainly for treatments they know they will need; healthy and wealthy individuals might choose high deductible options to pay lower premiums, forcing high-risk people to pay higher premiums (Enthoven and Singer 1996, 194).

Some forms of insurance pools are not only ideal but also necessary to spread risks and economize administrative costs. Group purchases can hold down the administrative cost of insurance, provide a form of risk-spreading that is not possible with individual insurance purchases, and can inhibit adverse selection by insurance companies (Pauly and Goodman 1996, 282). For people who are not employed, who work for small companies, or who change jobs frequently, an insurance pool could be based on groups other than employment, such as a union, a church, or a local farm bureau—organizations with which they might have a more permanent affiliation (Butler 1996, 246). We need some form of social institution that would motivate pooling and hold together in the face of heterogeneous risks to ensure that insurance remains affordable to high-risk people (Enthoven and Singer 1996, 192).

MSAs could lure healthy people and their money out of the insurance pool, and thereby raise insurance premiums for the sick (Love 1998). With the security coverage of MSAs, those who need the insurance the least—the young and healthy—are likely to choose high deductibles, thereby paying less premiums. If families must rely on MSAs, lower-income families might stint on health care and damage their health, because the less they spend on health care, the more money they get to keep (Pauly and Goodman 1996, 285).

MSAs are likely to aid the healthy and wealthy more than the poor and sick. The healthy and wealthy can take advantage of the tax benefit without having to spend much (proportionate to their income) on their health care, while the sick, poor, and old must spend a lot more out of pocket without much tax benefit, because their tax rate is lower (Glassman 1997).

REFERENCES

Aaron, Henry J., ed. 1996. *The problem that won't go away*. Washington, D.C.: Brookings Institute.

Armey, Dick. 1998. "Health care quality: Bureaucracy or consumer choice?" Freedom Works. (http://freedom.gov/library/healthcare/healthcare.asp) (visited 10-7-98).

Ayres, Stephen M., M.D. 1996. *Health care in the United States: The facts and the choices*. Chicago: American Liberty Association.

Barnes, Fred. 1993. "What health care crisis?" *American Spectator*. May.

Bernard, Elaine. 1992. "The politics of Canada's health care system: Lessons for the U.S." *New Politics*. Winter.

Borger, Gloria. 1998. "Dangerous liaisons." *U.S. News & World Report*. 3 August, 24.

Brink, Susan. 1998. "HMOs were the right Rx." *U.S. News & World Report*. 6 March, 47–50.

———, and Nancy Shute. 1997. "Managed care is pushing aside the private-practice doctors typified by TV's Marcus Welby or Dr. Kildare." *U.S. News & World Report*. 13 October, 60–64.

Butler, Stuart M. 1996. "The conservative agenda." Pp. 236–49 in *The problem that won't go away*, edited by Henry J. Aaron. Washington, D.C.: Brookings Institute.

Callahan, Daniel. 1992. "Symbols, rationality, and justice: Rationing health care." *American Journal of Law and Medicine* 18:1&2.

Carter, Casey. 1999. "A question of capacity." *Policy Review* 93:(January–February).

Charski, Mindy. 1998. "A healthy trend ends." *U.S. News & World Report*. 28 September, 60.

Clinton, Bill J. 1993. *Health security: The president's report to the American people*. White House Domestic Policy Council (forwarded by Hilary R. Clinton).

Collins, Sara. 1993. "How advances raise health care costs." *U.S. News & World Report*. 7 June.

Conklin, David. 1994. "Health care: What can the U.S. and Canada learn from each other?" Pp. 169–84 in *National health care: Lessons for the United States and Canada*, edited by Jonathan Lemco. Ann Arbor, Mich.: University of Michigan Press.

Corboy, Philip H. 1993. "Medical malpractice insurance and defensive medicine." *National Forum: The Phi Kappa Phi Journal* 73:3(Summer).

Cutler, David M. 1996. "Cutting costs and improving health." Pp. 250–65 in *The problem that won't go away*, edited by Henry J. Aaron. Washington, D.C.: Brookings Institute.

Daniels, Norman, Donald W. Light, and Ronald L. Caplan. 1996. *Benchmarks of fairness for health care reform*. New York: Oxford University Press.

Deber, Raisa B. 1994. "Philosophical underpinnings of Canada's health care systems." Pp. 43–68 in *National health care: Lessons for the United States and Canada*, edited by Jonathan Lemco. Ann Arbor, Mich.: University of Michigan Press.

Dentzer, Susan. 1991. "How to fight killer health costs." *U.S. News & World Report*. 23 September, 50–58.

Dickerson, John F. 1997. "A non-surgical fix for health care." *U.S. News & World Report*. 5 May, 50.

Donelan, K., R. J. Blendon, G. D. Lundberg, and D. R. Calkins. 1997. "The new medical marketplace: Physicians' views." *Health Affairs* 16(5):139–48.

Easterbrook, Gregg. 1997. "Healing the great divide: How come doctors and patients ended up on opposite sides?" *U.S. News & World Report*. 13 October, 64–68.

Enthoven. Alain C. 1992. "A cure for health costs." *World Monitor*. April.

———, and Sara J. Singer. 1996. "Market-based reform: What to regulate and by whom?" Pp. 185–206 in *The problem that won't go away*, edited by Henry J. Aaron. Washington, D.C.: Brookings Institute.

Feder, Judith, and Larry Levitt. 1996. "Steps toward universal coverage." Pp. 225–35 in *The problem that won't go away*, edited by Henry J. Aaron. Washington, D.C.: Brookings Institute.

Froomkin, Dan. 1998. "Backlash builds over managed care." *Washington Post*. 16 October.

Galewitz, Phil. 1999. "Health costs seen rising 9 percent." *Yahoo News*. 25 January.

Gaylin, Willard. 1994. "Moral and ethical decisions must be made for regulations to work." Pp. 231–43 in *Health care in America: Opposing viewpoints*, edited by Carol Wekesser. San Diego, Calif.: Greenhaven Press.

Glassman, James K. 1998. "Treating the symptoms." *U.S. News and World Report*. 9 February, 54.

Glenn, Kelly V. 1994. "Government intervention has hurt America's health care." Pp. 22–25 in *Health care in America: Opposing viewpoints*, edited by Carol Wekesser. San Diego, Calif.: Greenhaven Press.

Goldberg, Carey. 1999. "Teaching hospitals say Medicare cuts have them bleeding red ink." *New York Times*. 6 May.

Goldstein, Amy. 1998. "U.S. health care costs to double, report says." *Washington Post*. 15 September, A01.

———, and Helen Dewar. 1998. "Senate kills patients' rights' bill." *Washington Post*. 10 October, A01.

Hacker, Jacob S. 1997. *The road to nowhere: The genesis of President Clinton's plan for health security*. Princeton, N.J.: Princeton University Press.

Haislmaier, Edmund. 1992. "Problems in paradise: Canadians complain about their health care system." *Backgrounder* (Heritage Foundation). 19 February.

Hartman, Brian. 1998. "Distracted by impeachment and elections, Congress bails on health care." (ABCNews.com). 12 October.

Hentoff, Nat. 1994. "Rationing health care is inhumane and unethical." Pp. 191–95 in *Health care in America: Opposing viewpoints*, edited by Carol Wekesser. San Diego, Calif.: Greenhaven Press.

Inlander, Charles B. 1994. "Physicians are too greedy." Pp.75–80 in *Health care in America: Opposing viewpoints*, edited by Carol Wekesser. San Diego, Calif.: Greenhaven Press.

Jecker, Nancy S. 1993. "Can an employer-based health insurance system be just?" *Journal of Health Politics, Policy, and Law*. Fall.

Kodner, I. 1998. "The patient–physician relationship: Can we reclaim medicine?" *Vital Speeches of the Day*. September, 64(22):696–698.

Kong, Dolores. 1999. "Single-payer health plan saves money, reports show." *Boston Globe*. 28 April.

Lemco, Jonathan, ed. 1994. *National health care: Lessons for the United States and Canada*. Ann Arbor, Mich.: University of Michigan Press.

Lief, Louise. 1997. "Kids at risk: Uninsured children increasingly come from middle-class families." *U.S. News & World Report*. 28 April, 66–70.

Lord, Mary. 1998. "Patience for a bill of rights." *U.S. News & World Report*. 5 October.

Love, Alice A. (Associated Press). 1998. "Few opened medical savings accounts." *Yahoo News*. 30 September.

Lozano, Jose. 1992. "Malpractice and the health care crisis." *American Medical News*. August, 24–31.

Marmor, Theodore R., and Jerry L. Mashaw. 1994. "Canada's health insurance and ours: The real lesson, the big choices." Pp. 69–84 in *National health care: Lessons for the United States and Canada*, edited by Jonathan Lemco. Ann Arbor, Mich.: University of Michigan Press.

Marquis, Julie. 1999. "Jury's huge award in HMO case renews debate on patients' rights." *Los Angeles Times*. 22 January.

Meckler, Laura. 1998. "Lack of health insurance a problem." *Yahoo News*. 19 October.

Mitchell, Daniel J. 1997. "A brief guide to Social Security reform." *Talking Points*. The Heritage Foundation, no. 22. 7 August.

Neuschler, Edward. 1994. "Is Canadian-style government health insurance the answer for the United States' health care cost and access woes?" Pp. 121–46 in *National health care: Lessons for the United States and Canada*, edited by Jonathan Lemco. Ann Arbor, Mich.: University of Michigan Press.

O'Reilly, B. 1998. "What really goes on in your doctor's office." *Fortune* 138(4):164–74.

Online Newshour. 1998. "Bill of health?: Should the government pass legislation regulating managed care?" 21 July. (http://www.pbs.org/newshour/forum/july98/hmo.html).

Patel, Kant, and Mark E. Rushefsky. 1995. *Health care politics and policy in America*. Armonk, N.Y.: M. E. Sharpe.

Pauly, Mark V., and John C. Goodman. 1996. "Using tax credit for health insurance and medical savings accounts." Pp. 274–90 in *The problem that won't go away*, edited by Henry J. Aaron. Washington, D.C.: Brookings Institute.

Policy News and Information Service (PNIS). 1998. "Issue of the week: Can managed care be managed?" (http://www.policy.com/issuewk/98/0608/index.html).

Quinn, Jane B. 1998. "Fighting for health care." *Newsweek*. 30 March.

Randal, Judith. 1993. "Managed competition would not improve America's health care system." *The Progressive*. May.

Rasell, Edie. 1994. "Overuse of medical services hurt the health care system." Pp. 38–43 in *Health care in America: Opposing viewpoints*, edited by Carol Wekesser. San Diego, Calif.: Greenhaven Press.

Rector, Robert. 1996. "Welfare reform." In *Issue '96: The candidate's briefing book*, edited by Stuart M. Butler and Kim R. Holmes. Washington, D.C.: The Heritage Foundation.

Relman, Arnolds S. 1993. "What market values are doing to medicine." *National Forum: The Phi Kappa Phi Journal* 73:3(Summer).

Riggs, Jr., Webster. 1992. "Better care, higher costs." *American Medical News*. 10 February.

Rochefort, David A. 1993. "The pragmatic appeal of employment-based health care reform." *Journal of Health Politics, Policy, and Law*. Fall.

Rubin, Rita. 1995. "Time to switch to an HMO?" *U.S. News & World Report*. 12 June, 83–85.

Schroeder, Steven A. 1992. "The glut of specialist physicians hurt the health care system." *Los Angeles Times*. 4 March.

Schwartz, William B. 1992. "Do advancing medical technologies drive up the cost of health care?" *Priorities*. Fall.

Seidman, Bert. 1994. "Proposals for health care reform." Pp. 185–200 in *National health care: Lessons for the United States and Canada*, edited by Jonathan Lemco. Ann Arbor, Mich.: University of Michigan Press.

Shapiro, Joseph P. 1999. "Seeking a second opinion: A new law for patients when an HMO says no to care." *U.S. News & World Report*. 8 March.

———. 1998. "There when you need it." *U.S. News & World Report*. 5 October.

Sherrid, Pamela. 1997. "Mismanaged care?: Wall Street takes the scalpel to HMO companies." *U.S. News & World Report*. 24 November, 57–62.

Sperduto, Paul W. 1994. "How to access national health policy proposals and create the single best plan." Pp. 201–23 in *National health care: Lessons for the United States and Canada*, edited by Jonathan Lemco. Ann Arbor, Mich.: University of Michigan Press.

Sunshine, Steven C. 1996. "How does antitrust enforcement fit in?" Pp. 207–22 in *The problem that won't go away*, edited by Henry J. Aaron. Washington, D.C.: Brookings Institute.

Wassersug, Josesph D. 1993. "Don't deify the role of gatekeeper." *American Medical News*. May, 24–31.

Wekesser, Carol, ed. 1994. *Health care in America: Opposing viewpoints*. San Diego, Calif.: Greenhaven Press.

White, Joseph. 1995. *Competing solutions: American health care proposals and international experience*. Washington, D.C.: Brookings Institute.

Woolstein, Jarret. 1994. "National health care would be disasterous." Pp. 142–50 in *Health care in America: Opposing viewpoints*, edited by Carol Wekesser. San Diego, Calif.: Greenhaven Press.

Woolhandler, Steffie, and David U. Himmelstein. 1994a. "Resolving the cost-access conflict: The case for a national health program." Pp. 85–98 in *National health care: Lessons for the United States and Canada*, edited by Jonathan Lemco. Ann Arbor, Mich.: University of Michigan Press.

———. 1994b. "The U.S. should nationalize health care." Pp. 134–41 in *Health care in America: Opposing viewpoints*, edited by Carol Wekesser. San Diego, Calif.: Greenhaven Press.

Yankelovich, Daniel. 1996. "The debate that wasn't: The public and the Clinton health care plan." Pp. 70–109 in *The problem that won't go away*, edited by Henry J. Aaron. Washington, D.C.: Brookings Institute.

6 Human Cloning

Cloning involves manipulating an animal cell so that it grows into an exact duplicate of that animal. The idea of cloning is not new; scientists have been cloning sheep and cows from embryos, though not from adults' cells. During the 1980s and early 1990s, research on human embryos was banned due to the pressure by pro-life groups on the Reagan and Bush administrations. The Clinton administration, however, was more pro-choice and thus regulations on cloning have been relaxed to an extent.

In 1993, Robert J. Stillman, an embryologist at George Washington University, and his colleagues cloned human embryos. They took cells from seventeen human embryos (defective ones that an infertility clinic was going to discard), grew each one in a lab dish, and obtained a few thirty-two-cell embryos, a size that could be implanted in a woman, though they did not (Begley 1997a). Up to this point, the process of cloning involved splitting a single embryo into a certain number of embryos, which then would all have the same genetic make up.

The debate over human cloning boiled up since February 1997 when Scottish scientist Ian Wilmut and his colleagues at the Roslin Institute in Edinburgh first cloned a sheep named Dolly from a single adult cell, raising the possibility of human cloning in the future. Instead of normal development of a new individual through the merger of sperm and egg cells, Wilmut created Dolly by taking genetic material from mammary tissue of an adult female sheep and grafting that material into the ewe's egg cell. The result was a carbon copy of the mother.

Just a few weeks after Dolly was created, Don Wolf, a senior scientist at the Oregon Regional Primate Research Center, used one of the techniques employed by Wilmut, called nuclear transfer, to produce a pair of rhesus monkeys named Neti and Ditto. In nuclear transfer, scientists take an egg cell and remove its nucleus, which contains the genetic code. They then place another nucleus in its place. In the case of Neti and Ditto, the nuclei came from monkey embryos developed through in vitro fertilization, whereas in Dolly's case, the nuclei came from a mammary cell. Although they were not clones of a single monkey but a brother-sister pair with both a mother and father, Neti and Ditto are proof that nuclear transfer can work in species closely related to humans.

In October 1997, Jonathan Slack, a leading British embryologist at Bath University in England, raised the possibility of using a single cell to grow human organs and tissues for transplant surgery. Slack has created headless frog embryos by manipulating certain genes. If the technique is ever developed, it would provide perfectly matching organs and tissues to patients who need them, and it would relieve the shortage of donated organs. In 1998, the first human embryonic stem cells were isolated, making the cultivation of human organs one step closer to reality. Researchers predict that within five years they will be able to culture different kinds of human tissue in the lab for testing drugs (Brownlee 1998).

Also in 1998, using cloning techniques similar to those that created the sheep Dolly, researchers produced six genetically identical calves, in an experiment that could possibly lead to producing cows that give human milk or protein to make drugs, and another team of researchers created more than fifty female mice of three generations. In April 1999, a Canadian biotechnology company cloned goat triplets with exactly the same genetic make up. The company plans to create goats that carry a spider gene in its chromosomes. Spider silk proteins will be recovered from the goats' milk and processed into Biosteel, the strongest and toughest fiber known (White 1999).

In January 1998, U.S. physicist G. Richard Seed announced that he would open a human cloning clinic in the Chicago area, using the cloning techniques used by Ian Wilmut. Seed's announcement prompted President Clinton to impose a five-year moratorium on human cloning research funded by the federal government and to request a voluntary ban on similar research in private labs. By imposing a cloning moratorium, President Clinton hopes that the scientific, medical ethics, and religious communities would have a chance to explore legal, scientific, and ethical ramifications of human cloning.

Following President Clinton's moratorium, both Republican and Democratic parties are trying to introduce legislation regarding human cloning. The Republican legislation (First-Bond Proposal) seeks banning of all cloning in human embryo research, and the Democratic legislation (Feinstein-Kennedy Proposal) places a ten-year ban on human cloning but allows the cloning of human cells and tissues for research, up to the point of transferring the cloned cells to a woman's uterus. The Republican and Democratic plans have stalled in the Senate due to the lack of common ground between the two proposed bills (*CNN* 3-26-98).

Many scientists are concerned that the Republican legislation to ban human embryo research can terminate potentially vital medical research before it even begins. The National Bioethics Advisory Commission recommended that scientists be allowed to continue research into cloning techniques but be prohibited from cloning humans (Gorman 1997, 66). The World Health Organization (WHO) looked at the technical and ethical aspects of human cloning and decided that human cloning was an extreme form of experimentation that must be universally opposed. The Vatican called for a worldwide ban on human cloning. As of 1999, nineteen European nations have signed an anticloning treaty; Australia, Spain, Germany, Denmark, and the United Kingdom ban cloning of humans (Nash 1998).

Religious Groups' Views on Human Cloning

The Catholic church prohibits most kinds of tampering with human reproduction. A 1987 Vatican document, *Donum Vitae*, condemns cloning because it violates "the dignity both of human procreation and of the conjugal union" (Woodward 1997; Herbert et al. 1997). Although Protestant theology generally supports using technology to fix flaws in nature, most Protestant theologians agree that cloning humans crosses the line. It places too much power in the "hands of sinful humans, who are subject to committing horrific abuses" (David Fletcher, philosophy professor, in Herbert et al. 1997). Judaism also tends to favor the use of technology to improve on nature's shortcomings. However, many rabbis agree that cloning is an area where we cannot go, because it violates the mystery of what it means to be human (Rabbi Richard Address in Herbert et al. 1997).

Dr. Maher Hathout, a cardiologist and a spokesman for the Islamic Center of Southern California, on the other hand, says that, from a Muslim perspective, there are no limits on scientific research. "Knowledge is bestowed on us by God. We believe that God gave us creativity, that He is the best of all creators, according to the Koran. The only problem will come with how we are going to use it, for good or for bad" (*Dayton Daily News* 3-19-97).

Cloning Methods: How Is It Done?

Cloning is a process of producing genetically identical organisms. It may involve the division of a single embryo, in which case both the nuclear genes and the small number of mitochondrial genes would be identical, or it may involve nuclear transfer, in which case only the nuclear genes would be identical (Elshtain 1998). The nuclear transfer technique requires a fertilized egg cell and a somatic cell of the donor. A somatic cell is one that comes from another area of the body such as skin or a segment of muscle. The information center in both cells is called the nucleus. The fertilized egg cell is already programmed to develop into an adult organism, and the actual cloning takes place when the somatic cell is brought in. A technician uses an ultra-thin needle to remove the somatic cell's nucleus, which contains the genetic instruction for producing an exact copy of the animal from which the cell came. The nucleus is then injected into an ovum whose own nucleus has been removed. The new nucleus has the genetic information needed from the donor, and the egg cell has already been programmed to develop into an adult. Just like a fertilized egg, the ovum will develop into a complete animal after it gestates in the uterus of a surrogate mother, and the animal created in this way will be a genetic copy of the donor (Begley 1997b).

Use of Human Cloning Technology in Four Areas

If human cloning technique is fully developed, it could be used for whole or partial human cloning, genetic engineering, or transgenics. Each of these topics is discussed next.

Whole Human Cloning

Whole human cloning is the creation of an entire person who has the same genetic, nuclear gene set as his or her donor. This is also called reproductive cloning because it aims at the birth of identical individuals. Parents might want to clone an existing child with a disease to obtain perfectly matching body parts for transplant, or to replace a dying child. Single women or gay couples might want to have children with their genetic gene set rather than using donated sperm.

Tissue and Organ Reproduction (or Regeneration): Partial Human Cloning

This is a method of growing specialized cells in a culture dish to create tissues and organs for transplant, without creating a whole human. Experiments with animals suggest that by turning on and off the right genes, specific tissues may be grown. If similar experiments in human cells become successful, it could lead to dramatic new treatments for many diseases. For instance, they could grow new pancreas cells for those with diabetes, blood cells for leukemia patients, new skin for burn victims, and other body parts and organs for the needy (Kassirer and Rosenthal in CNN.com 3-26-98). Much of the cloning research at universities and in the biotech industry centers on growing tissues for transplants or duplicating human proteins such as telomerase to make it possible to manipulate cell functions (Coale 1997).

Genetic Engineering

Cloning is the technology that will make it possible to apply genetic engineering to humans. Genetic engineering is a manipulation of DNA in such a way that a child can be born free of certain genetic diseases or unfavorable predisposition, such as obesity and alcoholism, or to be born with desirable attributes, such as high intelligence and athletic ability. If cloning humans becomes possible, scientists believe that it would also be possible to alter genetic make up of newborn babies or to select certain traits in babies (Barr 1997).

Transgenics

Lastly, transgenics is the altering of animal embryos with human genes so that animals can produce proteins or drugs humans need. One step further from this technique is the creation of chimera, a human-animal hybrid that can be used to study tissue growth and produce organs, among other possibilities (Hager and Rogers 1998). In May 1998, using techniques similar to those that created the sheep Dolly, researchers produced six genetically identical calves in an important step toward building herds of designer cattle. This research proves that it will be economically possible to mass produce cows that give human milk or make drugs, or even create pigs that grow human organs (Steve L. Stice, chief scientist at Advanced Cell Technology Inc. in Worcester, Mass.).

In the following sections, supporting and opposing views of these four cloning-related techniques are discussed.

Whole Human Cloning

Supporting View

There is nothing wrong with creating a twin of a child to save the child's life. What can be wrong with the idea of parents who love their child so much that they will happily raise another, identical to the first, so that one of his or her kidneys or a bit of bone marrow might allow the first to live (John Fletcher, former ethicist for the National Institute of Health, in Kluger 1997)? Not only can we save one person from death but also can give another person a new life. What is wrong with creating a twin of a child who died in an accident? It would be a consolation to the parents who lost their child that they loved so much.

The nuclear transfer technique could also help infertile couples, gay couples, singles, or anyone who wants a biological descendent without using donated sperm. The nucleus of a donor's egg could be replaced with the nucleus from the mother to be, thus allowing the offspring to include genetic contributions from the parents who would raise the child. Human cloning could be a more effective and less expensive method for infertile couples to have children, because it increases the odds of becoming pregnant. Cloning would allow multiple embryos to be produced—some could be implanted, and others frozen in case the first attempt failed, or in case the couple desired more children. Cloning embryos could make it so a woman would not have to repeatedly go through the procedure of expensive hormone treatments, egg retrieval, and laboratory fertilization (Begley 1997b; Rae 1998).

Cloning could also help older women become pregnant. If an older woman has a low chance of a successful pregnancy but wishes to become pregnant, she can obtain a donor's egg from a younger woman and have a technician replace the egg's nucleus with a nucleus from her own egg. This would allow the offspring to include genetic contributions from both her and her husband (ABCNEWS.com 10-27-97).

Opposing View

What is wrong with duplicating a sibling whose bone marrow could save a sick child? It is wrong because you are using another human being merely "as a source for replaceable organs" (Father Richard McCormic, a Jesuit priest, in Woodward 1997). Naturally occurring identical twins are perfectly ethical, because there is no intention to clone. Scientifically engineered human cloning is a different issue. Unlike animals, humans have sense of identity, individuality, and autonomy. It would be unfair to the cloned person to know that he was created for a certain purpose; it would be psychologically harmful if the person sensed that she had been brought into the world for a purpose of saving another person's life, and that could affect her sense of individuality and autonomy. We need to think about what kinds of psychological and social problems the cloned person might go through (Peters 1997; Shapiro 1997; Herbert et al. 1997).

Infertility is not an absolute evil that justifies doing anything and everything to overcome it (Father Richard McCormick in Woodward 1997). There are other options, such as adoption.

Once we allow human cloning for medical reasons, it will be difficult to prevent cloning for other purposes. Some megalomaniacs might want to clone themselves purely for egotistic self-recreation. In such cases, we would have adults raising children who would also be their twins. Cloning an adult's twin is narcissistic and ethically wrong under any circumstances (Herbert et al. 1997; Father Richard McCormick in Kluger 1997).

If human cloning is allowed, it will be difficult to prevent someone from cloning you without your knowledge or permission. Everyone gives off cells all the time. Whenever we give a blood sample or visit the dentist, for instance, we give off cells, and those cells all contain one's full complement of DNA. What if a woman were obsessed with having a child of an apathetic man? Or think of the commercial value of a super-athlete or musical virtuoso. Even though experience and effort certainly shape these talents as much as genetic gifts, the unscrupulous would not likely be deterred (Philip Bereano in Herbert et al. 1997).

Tissue and Organ Reproduction

Supporting View

If obtaining human organs is the goal, you don't have to create a whole human being. Instead, scientists could match the genetic code of the recipient and create the exact organ the person needs. Genetically engineered plant and animal products are already being tested, and scientists believe that it would be possible to produce human organs from a single cell in the future. The idea is to turn back the cell's internal clock to when they were newly formed and malleable—and then reprogram their genes to regrow tissues and organs. First, healthy cells are obtained from a patient with, for example, leukemia. The DNA is removed from these cells, then inserted into an unfertilized egg cell. These clones then begin to divide. At this point, growth hormones are added to the clones, which force them to develop only into specialized cells and tissues. In the case of a leukemia patient, these cells would be forced to develop into bone marrow cells (Macklin 1997; Nash 1998; Dr. Roger Pedersen in ABCNEWS.com 2-9-98). Progress in this type of research could very well teach us how to regrow skin for burn victims, cartilage and bones for accident victims, repair damages to the brain and nervous system, produce bone marrow for cancer patients, human insulin for diabetics, retinal tissue for the blind, Activase to dissolve blood clots, and Epogen to treat anemia caused by kidney disease (Kestenbaum 1998; Macklin 1997; Nash 1998; Kolata 1998; Marwick 1997; Walz 1997). Unlike cells from an unrelated donor, these cloned cells would incur no danger of rejection; patients would be spared the need to take powerful drugs to suppress the immune system (Nash 1998).

This type of cloning research could also help scientists better understand the rapid growth of cancer cells. Cancer cells create tumors because the mutated cells grow and divide too rapidly. By studying embryonic stem cell growth, scientists could find out how to stop the growth of cancer cells (Kassirer and Rosenthal in CNN.com 3-26-98; Walz 1997). Considering all these potential benefits, it would be unethical not to continue this line of research (Dr. Robert Winston, a fertility expert, in Nash 1998).

Opposing View

If this cloning practice is strictly limited to creating substitute organs, it would be within moral boundaries. However, if this is legally allowed, we have to worry about the "slide down" effect, which could lead to the creation of "headless humans." In October 1997, Jonathan Slack, professor of developmental biology at the University of Bath in southwestern England, produced headless frog embryos by manipulating genes in frog eggs. According to Slack, scientists can reprogram a human egg in such a way that, instead of the whole embryo, it would just form the desired organs and the heart and circulatory systems necessary to maintain the body (Barr 1997). What if one desires to clone a headless body of himself to make sure he could have access to perfectly matching body parts whenever he needs them? If you create bodies without heads (or certain brain parts), are they human? What will be their status and rights in our society (Jeffrey Reiman, professor of philosophy at American University, in Barr 1997)?

Another question that needs to be answered before any human cloning method can be declared legal is when does human life start, that is, where do we draw the line as to what is considered human life? Do embryonic cells deserve the same moral standing as a human being? Pro-life supporters argue that human life starts at the point of conception, whereas some pro-choice supporters believe that life does not start until birth. Opponents of human cloning, like pro-life advocates, argue that developing embryos are a form of human life that need to be treated with the same respect as other human beings, and therefore any experiment involving human embryos would be morally wrong (Senator Kit Bond in ABCNEWS.com 2-9-98).

Genetic Engineering

Supporting View

Cloning techniques can help eliminate genetically inherited diseases. There are countless numbers of diseases that are caused by genetic disorders. Through cloning techniques, scientists could learn to turn off the genes that cause genetic disorders, and they could replace flawed genes with normal DNA. Cloning could prevent many hereditary diseases, such as sickle-cell anemia, Tay-sachs disease, cystic fibrosis, muscular dystrophy, epilepsy, and a host of others including some mental disorders (Gorman 1997; Kolata 1998).

At present, introducing genes into chromosomes is very much a hit-or-miss operation. Scientists might achieve the result they intend once in about twenty tries, making the procedure far too risky to perform on a human embryo. Through cloning, however, scientists could make twenty copies of the embryo they wished to modify, greatly boosting their chance of success (Nash 1998).

Opposing View

The risk of abuse is greater than the benefit when it comes to genetic engineering. One of the gravest concerns about the misuse of genetic engineering is the deliberate manipulation of genes to enhance human talents and creation of human beings according to certain specifications (Herbert et al. 1997). Once we allow the manipulation of genes to eliminate genetic disorders, some overzealous parents might want to insert or delete certain genes so that their children can be modified according to their preference. They might try to eliminate predisposition to some unfavorable tendency, such as alcoholism and obesity: they might even want to add desired qualities for a fee, such as hair and eye color, intelligence, and athletic ability, and create "super humans" (Lee Silver, a molecular biologist, in Nash 1998). Choosing personal characteristics of one's children as if they were options on a car is an invitation to misadventure (John Paris, bioethics professor, in Kluger 1997). We cannot apply the principles of industrial design and quality control to human beings (Jeremy Rifkin in Kluger 1997). Nature should be the only thing that determines the outcome of a human being, and that should never be changed.

Once you program for producing superior beings, you are into eugenics, and eugenics of any kind is unethical and inherently discriminatory (Father Richard McCormick in Woodward 1997). Those with financial resources could manufacture perfect children by using genetic alteration. What concerns most ethicists is the commodification of human beings and their genes. What will prevent the transfer of a dollop of DNA to a wealthy bidder who wants an especially beautiful, swift, or smart child (Lisa Cahill in Woodward 1997)?

In the long run, large-scale cloning of this type (made-to-order babies) could deplete genetic diversity in humans. It is in the diversity of our population that we find interest and enthusiasm; it is the diversity that drives the human evolution process (John Paris, bioethics professor, in Kluger 1997). Genetic engineering should be banned because it could transform procreation into production, where human children become the customized products (Gary Bauer, president of the Family Research Council, in Hansen 1998). If it is allowed, science will be driven by the demands of the commercial market for human genes (Hager and Rogers 1998). The process of human evolution should be left alone: humans must resist the temptation to interfere with or manipulate the evolutionary process (Rifkin, head of the Foundation on Economic Trends, in Kluger 1997).

Transgenics (Cloning of Animals with Human Genes)

Supporting View

Instead of using human clones for organ transplant, scientists could use animals as organ donors. Pigs, for example, have organs similar in size to human organs. However, the human immune system attacks and destroys tissues from other species. In order to avoid that problem, scientists could alter the pig's genetic code by using human genes. This would allow efficient and cost-effective mass production of organs for transplants (Herbert et al. 1997).

Transgenic technology has been available for at least a decade, and cloning is actually the latest enhancement of transgenics. For years, a handful of transgenics companies have been altering the embryos of goats, pigs, and mice with human genes so they can produce human proteins. The most advanced company in this area, Genzyme Transgenics Corp., has grown goats whose milk contained a human anticlotting protein that could be used in heart-surgery patients. The PPL Therapeutics Company has already bred cows that can produce milk containing a protein beneficial for premature infants who cannot nurse. Other companies, like Alexion Pharmaceutical, are working on ways to create pigs with hearts and kidneys that would not be rejected in human transplants.

The latest cloning technology could make transgenics more efficient and cost-effective. It could engineer the desired animal with the new drug-producing genes and replicate it hundreds of times at once. PPL Therapeutics hopes to clone genetically engineered animals that will produce a type of tissue glue for use in surgery and also produce a human protein, MAT, that is being tested for treating cystic fibrosis (Reibstein and Beals 1997; Begley 1997b).

Opposing View

Under the name of transgenics, what scientists are doing is creating human-animal chimeras. In Greek mythology, the chimera was a part lion, part goat, and part dragon creature that terrorized the country of Lycia. In real life, it is an animal customized with genes from different species. Cloning researchers are hoping that human-animal chimeras could potentially be used to study tissue growth and organ production, among other possibilities (Hager and Rogers 1998).

Creating human-animal chimeras for medical purposes is scientifically feasible and viable according to scientists. A decade ago, biologists created a goat-sheep cross called a geep. If we allow the creation of human-animal hybrids, however, down the road it could be a disaster for human culture and civilization (Jeremy Rifkin and Stuart Newman in Hager and Rogers 1998). Although the human-animal hybrids could be useful in medical research and organ production, the mixing of human embryo cells with that of other animals is unethical and can bring about unpredictable, potentially dangerous consequences. How do we decide how much human qualities and what kinds of human qualities are acceptable in animals to achieve the medical goals? What would be the legal and moral status of the part-human and part-animal creatures in our society? How should we treat these creatures? We need to consider these issues before we allow transgenics technology to be used with human embryos.

Stuart A. Newman, a cellular biologist at New York Medical College, applied for a patent on a method for making creatures that are part human and part animal. Despite the potential medical benefits these hybrids might bring about, Newman does not intend to create one, nor does he want any other scientists to do it. He hopes that a patent would give him legal means to block scientists from creating the human-animal hybrids (Weiss 1998b; Hager and Rogers 1998).

The following sections summarize the supporting and opposing views on human cloning in general.

It Is Too Early to Allow Human Cloning

Opposing Cloning

Science often moves faster than our ability to understand its implications. Human cloning is one of the areas that requires a careful examination of the legal, ethical, and religious ramifications. We need time to study the potential consequences of cloning and whether cloning is something our society truly needs. We need to think about what, if any, circumstances might warrant cloning, as well as the circumstances under which it should never be allowed. We haven't even worked out the issues related to surrogate motherhood, and now we have technology racing ahead into a whole new category of cloning (White 1998; Kassirer in CNN.com 3-26-98). Most Americans feel uneasy about human cloning for these reasons. According to a poll taken in March 1997, 87 percent of the U.S. public opposes human cloning (Watson 1997).

Supporting Cloning

The fear of human cloning comes from a paranoia and a false image of clones being robotic monsters or other freaks of nature. In the 1960s, there was a serious debate regarding the morality of transplanting a human heart. In the 1980s, there was a controversy over the morality of producing test-tube babies. Both have become widely accepted and practiced now. Twenty years after it was introduced, the in vitro fertilization technique has become a common procedure in helping infertile couples. Human cloning is not that different from in vitro fertilization. Both are reproductive interventions that create life, and both reproduction processes occur in a laboratory setting (Rae 1998). The only difference is that cloning creates time-delayed identical twins, whereas in vitro fertilization creates a genetically unique human being. Clones, like identical twins, are two separate and distinct individuals, each with her own mind and soul. In reality, the clone and the donor would differ more than identical twins, because the clone would be brought up in a different time and environment from her donor.

If we ban human cloning now, it will harm valuable research advances in the future. It will stifle any genetic research that could help scientists learn how to manipulate genes to fight diseases. Human cloning can be desirable in certain situations and under certain conditions. Any legislative provision on human cloning must not jeopardize the biomedical research that involves cloning of human genes, cells, or tissues (Alan Holmer, president of Pharmaceutical Research and Manufacturer of America, in Marwick 1997; Harold Varmus, NIH Director, in Weiss 1998a; Lundberg 1997).

Human Cloning Is Too Risky

Opposing Cloning

Human cloning is too dangerous to be allowed and should at least be heavily regulated, if not banned. As of now, there is no guarantee that cloning is safe and effective for humans. Scientists have not studied the potential side effects of cloning on humans: The process that works with sheep may not work the same way with humans.

If adult cells were used as nuclear donors, scientists speculate that there might be some risks involved. For instance, scientists are not sure whether the cloned individual would experience an accelerated aging process and therefore have a shorter life-span. They do not know whether clones may become more susceptible to cancer, whether they would be fertile, and if so, whether they or their offspring would suffer from a higher rate of genetic abnormalities (Kestenbaum 1998; Begley 1997a; White 1998).

Another danger of cloning is the possibility of genetic mutation and defective births as a result. Ian Wilmut, the creator of Dolly, opposes human cloning because horrible and even fatal birth defects could result from cloning experiments in humans. Mutation is always a problem with every cell, and scientists don't even know where to check for them. The cloned cell may undergo a series of mutations, caused by radiation, chemicals, or just by chance (Ralph Brinster, reproductive biologists, in Begley 1997a).

In France, a calf cloned from a single skin cell of another cow's ear mysteriously died at seven weeks. Scientists have already noted that cloned animals are at least ten times more likely to be unhealthy than their naturally conceived counterparts. One possible culprit is genetic imprinting, a process in which maternal and paternal genes ensure that neither predominates the offspring. With only one parent, the cloned fetus could be left without a balance of genes necessary to thrive. The disorders they see in clones might be triggered when the imprinting process goes wrong (Couzin 1999).

Any attempt to develop methods of whole human cloning would require large-scale human experimentation. To create Dolly, it took 277 failed attempts, including the deaths of several defective clones. Ryuzo Yanagimachi, who cloned fifty mice, had about 1 percent success rate, which he calls "a rather encouraging figure" (Couzin 1999). One percent success, coupled with many more disastrous outcomes, is too risky when it comes to human cloning. What happens to the products of unsuccessful attempts at cloning humans? Who will take responsibility for the births of deformed babies? Is this human sacrifice worth the benefit?

Supporting Cloning

There has always been potential danger in every major scientific or medical breakthrough in history. These are the obstacles scientists must overcome for a better future. Scientific progress begins with taking risks and overcoming barriers. Scientists will study the potential risks involving human cloning and eventually come up with a safe, sound method of cloning humans. No human cloning will take place until a safer method is developed through animal experimentation. It took 277 attempts to create Dolly because it was the first time. With experience and better technology, cloning methods will become safer and more effective, thereby avoiding birth defects.

Human Cloning Is Morally Wrong

Opposing Cloning

The deliberate creation of human beings for experimental purposes, for spare parts, or to satisfy someone's vanity is morally wrong. There is no ethical objection to genetically identical human beings existing, because naturally created identical twins are not discriminated against. However, deliberately creating genetically identical human beings raises serious ethical concerns regarding human responsibility and instrumentalization of human beings. Creating humans cannot be equated to manufacturing drugs. Human embryos, however they are created, are human beings. To assert that we need only regulate the practice of human cloning as if it were a drug, and not a process of creating life, is morally obtuse (Bailey 1998; Senator Kid Bond in CNN.com 3-26-98). Unlike other animals, human clones would have minds of their own as well as feelings. We cannot produce them simply to use them for organ transplants. Manufacturing a made-to-order person undermines human dignity and individuality, and it encourages people to treat children like commodities to satisfy their desires (Annas 1997).

Every human being is unique, born of a miracle that reaches beyond laboratory science. We must respect this profound gift and resist the temptation to replicate ourselves (President Clinton). Cloning is a form of replication, not reproduction. It goes against the natural order of reproduction; it destroys the uniqueness of each human, which is a gift from God; and it violates human dignity and individuality.

Supporting Cloning

Identical twins are a natural form of cloning, yet there are no ethical or identity problems involved with them. Why is it unethical to create identical twins using a different method? Why is it unethical to have another child in order to save an existing one? Is it more ethical to let your sick child die when you know that there is a way to save that child's life? Some parents have already conceived a second child with nonfatal bone marrow transplant in mind, and many ethicists do not oppose this. Cloning would increase the chances for a biological match from 25 percent to nearly 100 percent (Herbert et al. 1997).

People Should Not Play God

Opposing Cloning

Many object to human cloning with the argument that people should not play God. The playing-God objection is based on the idea that creating human life in an unnatural way is defying God. Only God gives human lives. Cloning is "tampering with God's work of creation"; it is a usurpation of God's role as a creator of humans. In cloning, the scientists, rather than God or nature, determine the outcome of human life, and that is wrong. The creation and destruction of human life is one area humans cannot be in control of (Kevin Wildes, philosophy professor, in Herbert et al. 1997).

Supporting Cloning

Those who support cloning, including some theologians, argue that cloning is not the same as creating life from scratch. The ingredients used in cloning are already alive or contain the elements of life. It is still only God who creates life in the process of human cloning (Fletcher in Herbert et al. 1997). The status of a cloned person before God would not be any different from anyone born the old-fashioned way (Ted Peters, professor of Pacific Lutheran Theological Seminary in Berkeley). Religious ethicists should focus their attention on what we should do to prevent the human cloning technique from being abused rather than totally banning it.

The Identity Right and Individuality of the Clone Will Be Violated

Opposing Cloning

If a child is cloned after a parent, what rights would she have? How about her identity and individuality (Herbert et al. 1997)? Each individual is created to be unique and special. God gave each person unique talent, appearance, and personality to be used in a special way (Peters 1997). Clones would not have a unique identity and they would lack individuality because they would be a carbon copy of another person (Roberts 1996, 547).

If you deliberately set out to copy a parent, you cannot treat that cloned child as a unique individual. If clones are created to provide organ parts, they might be treated as property or commodity. Once the purpose is achieved, the clone may no longer be useful for the creator and could be mistreated. If the cloned person realizes that she was created for a specific purpose, it would have a devastating psychological impact, and it would not be fair for the clone.

Supporting Cloning

Creating a clone does not necessarily violate the dignity of the original or of the genetic copy (Lisa Cahill, a moral theologian, in Woodward 1997). A clone would be an individual with her own identity; the clones would have the same status and legal rights as other people. A clone would not belong to the original, would not be disposed of as if it were a commodity, and would not be less of a person just because he has the same genetic make up as the donor. A cloned person would be an individual with his own separate mind, personality, and soul (Woodward 1997). Identical twins, which are "clones by nature," do not suffer from identity crises or feel like "less of a person" because there is another individual with the same gene complement. Identical twins often show different qualities and characteristics. Although a human clone might superficially resemble the individual from whom she was made, she would differ dramatically in the traits that define an individual—personality, character, intelligence, and talent. Clones would actually be more different than identical twins, who share the same egg, uterus, and early home environment, because they would be raised in a different time, different environment, and most likely by different people (Jerome Kagan, a psychologist, in Begley 1997a; Elshtain 1998).

Cloning Is a Form of Asexual Reproduction That Can Take Males Out of the Reproductive Process

Opposing Cloning

Natural reproduction among mammals involves the joining of sperm from the male and an egg from the female, which produces a genetically unique individual. In cloning, on the other hand, the embryo can get all the necessary genes from one individual. A woman who wanted to clone herself would not need a man. Besides her DNA, she would only need an egg and a womb, her own or another woman's. A man who wanted to clone himself, on the other hand, would need to buy the egg and rent the womb (Herbert et al. 1997).

When human cloning duplicates only female cells, it takes males out of the reproductive process. Dolly was conceived using an ewe's egg and a cell from another ewe's body. No semen from a ram was involved. If human cloning is allowed, descendants could be born without male's genetic background. If this cloning is allowed and widely practiced, it could affect our concept of descendants, marriage, family, and it could affect the genetic make up of humans in the future.

Supporting Cloning

Human cloning, even if it becomes legal and widely available, will be practiced only in critically necessary cases, such as to save the life of a dying child or to solve serious infertility problems. Most people would agree that saving a dying child's life justifies this form of asexual reproduction. If a sterile second-generation Holocaust survivor wanted a male heir to continue an otherwise doomed family line, then Rabbi Tendler said that he might advise the man to clone rather than use donor's sperm (Woodward 1997). Most people under normal circumstances would want to have their offspring in the traditional way, with genetic backgrounds from both parents.

REFERENCES

ABCNEWS.com. 1997. "Monkeying around with cloning." 27 October. (http://www.abcnews.com/sections/scitech/cloning908/index.html).
ABCNEWS.com. 1998. "Congressional clone war: Researchers, politicians clash." 9 February. (http://www.abcnews.com/sections/living/dailynews/congress clone 0209.html).
Annas, George. 1997. "Should the U.S. ban human cloning?" *CQ Researcher* 7:423.
Bailey, Ronald. 1998. "Seeds of trouble." *National Review* 50:19–24.
Barr, Robert. 1997. "Cloned human organs may exist soon." *Washington Post*. 21 October.
Begley, Sharen. 1997a. "Little lamb, who made thee?" *Newsweek*. 10 March, 53–59.
———. 1997b. "Spring cloning." *Newsweek*. 30 June.
Brownlee, Shannon. 1998. "Heartbeats in a dish: Researchers grow cells that form the basis of human life." *U.S. News & World Report*. 16 November.
CNN.com. 1998. "Journal says human cloning research ban would be 'misguided.'" 26 March. (http://www.cnn.com/health/cloning.controversy/index.html).
Coale, Kristi. 1997. "California takes on human cloning." *Wired News*. 10 September. (http://www.wired.com/news/politics/story/6737.html).
Couzin, Jennifer. 1999. "What's killing clones?" *U.S. News & World Report*. 24 May.
Dayton Daily News. 1997. "Cloning science outpaces ethics." 19 March.
Elshtain, Jean. 1998. "Bad seed." *The New Republic* 218.
Gorman, Christin. 1997. "To ban or not to ban." *Time* 149.
Hager, Mary, and Adam Rogers. 1998. "A biotech roadblock." *Newsweek*. 13 April.
Hansen, Kristin. 1998. "Bauer says human cloning should be banned." 10 April. (http://www.townhall.com/cloning.html).
Herbert, Wary, Jeffery L. Sheler, and Traci Watson. 1997. "The world after cloning." *U.S. News & World Report*. 10 March.
Kolata, Gina. 1998. *Clone: The road to Dolly, and the path ahead*. New York: William Morrow.
Kestenbaum, David. 1998. "Cloning plan spawns ethical debate." *Science* 279:315.
Kluger, Jeffrey. 1997. "Will we follow the sheep?" *Time*. 10 March, 69–72.
Lundberg, George D. 1997. "Threatened bans on human cloning research could hamper advances." *The Journal of American Medical Association* 277:13.
Macklin, Ruth. 1997. "Human cloning? Don't just say no." *U.S. News & World Report*. 199:64.

Marwick, Charles. 1997. "Put human cloning on hold, says bioethicists." *Journal of American Medical Association* 278(1):13–14.

Nash, Madeleine. 1998. "The case for cloning." *Time*. 9 February, 81.

Peters, Ted. 1997. *Playing God*. New York: Routledge.

Rae, Scott. 1994. *The ethics of commercial surrogate motherhood: Brave new families?* Westport, Conn.: Praeger.

Reibstein, Larry, and Gregory Beals. 1997. "A cloned chop, anyone?" *Newsweek*. 10 March.

Roberts, Melinda. 1996. "Human cloning: A case of no harm done?" *Journal of Medicine and Philosophy* 21:537–54.

Shapiro, Harold H. 1997. "Ethics and policy issues of human cloning." *Science* 277:195–96.

Walz, Richard. 1997. "The gains of human cloning." *The Medical Institution of Bioethics*. Issue 89. 13 March, 13.

Watson, Traci. 1997. "Cloning a flap over research." *U.S. News & World Report*. 17 March, 36.

Weiss, Rick. 1998a. "Human cloning research will be regulated." *Washington Post*. 20 January.

———. 1998b. "Patent sought on making of part-human creatures." *Washington Post*. 2 April, A12.

White, Gayle. 1998. "Is cloning mastermind playing God?" *The Atlanta Journal and Constitution*. 16 April. (http://www.lexis-nexis.com/universe).

White, Patrick. 1999. "Canada firm clones goat triplets to make spider silk." *Yahoo News*. 27 April.

Woodward, Kenneth L. 1997. "Today the sheep, tomorrow the shepherd?" *Newsweek*. 10 March, 60.

7 Physician-Assisted Suicide

Do terminally ill patients have the constitutional right to a doctor's aid in committing suicide? Should our society allow doctors to prescribe life-ending drugs for terminally ill but mentally competent people who no longer wish to live? The right to die issue has been simmering for some time in the United States, especially since 1976, when the parents of Karen Ann Quinlan won a legal battle to have their daughter, who was in an irreversible coma, removed from a respirator. The Supreme Court first addressed the question of the right to die in 1990, in the case of a Missouri woman thrust into a vegetative state by a car accident (*Cruzan v. Director, Missouri Department of Health*). The parents wanted permission to disconnect their daughter's feeding tube. The court ruled that a person has a constitutionally protected right to refuse unwanted life-sustaining medical treatment. This case, however, involved the passive withdrawal of artificial life support, in contrast to physician-assisted suicide (abbreviated PAS), which is an active form of euthanasia. The issue is a question of whether mentally competent, terminally ill patients should have a right to end their lives with the aid of a doctor.

As of 1999, thirty-five states have statutes prohibiting assisted suicide. An additional eight states recognize assisted suicide as a common law crime. However, these prohibitions are being challenged. In November 1994, Oregon voters narrowly (51 to 49 percent) approved an initiative legalizing PAS (Death with Dignity Act). A federal judge immediately declared the measure unconstitutional and blocked the law from being activated. The Oregon legislature, in June 1997, declined to either amend or repeal the act, and returned it to the electorate for a second vote. In October 1997, the Supreme Court justices turned down an appeal from a lower court's ruling ordering dismissal of the lawsuit that had kept the law tied up in federal court since shortly after its adoption. In November 1997, Oregon voters again decided to retain PAS law. During the first year under the nation's only assisted-suicide law, twenty-three people obtained doctor-prescribed lethal drugs; fifteen of them used these drugs to end their lives; six died from their illnesses before using the drugs; and two others were alive as of January 1999.

According to Oregon's Death with Dignity Act, a mentally competent adult suffering from a terminal illness—defined as likely to result in death within six months—may receive lethal doses of medication after consulting with two doctors and waiting fifteen days. The law includes provisions designed to ensure that the patient's decision is voluntary and not the result of depression (Greenhouse 1997).

In April 1996, two federal courts, in New York City and San Francisco, ruled in separate decisions that New York's and Washington's long-standing prohibitions against PAS were unconstitutional (*Vacco v. Quill* in New York and *Washington v. Glucksberg* in San Francisco). These two cases were brought by a Seattle patients' rights group called Compassion in Dying, along with seven physicians and six terminally ill patients. The Supreme Court rejected the constitutionality of PAS in these two cases in June 1997, but ruled that states had broad latitude in deciding such issues.

In October 1996, the Supreme Court of Michigan let stand a 1991 Michigan court order that bars Dr. Jack Kevorkian from helping people commit suicide. The Michigan order had never been enforced, however, until 1998. Dr. Kevorkian, who says he has attended more than forty suicides since 1990, has been tried and acquitted three times on assisted suicide charges. In 1998, the Michigan legislature enacted a ban on assisted suicide, passing a criminal statute designed to close the legal loophole that allowed Dr. Kevorkian to escape punishment in all three cases in which he had been tried. Dr. Kevorkian was later found guilty of second-degree murder and sentenced to ten to twenty-five years in prison for assisting in the death of a patient with Lou Gehrig's disease.

Physician-Assisted Suicide in Other Countries

The United States is not the only country trying to deal with the issue of PAS. In May 1995, the legislature of the Northern Territories State of Australia passed a voluntary euthanasia law that permits terminally ill people to ask for a medically assisted death. The Australian Senate, the federal Parliament's upper house, however, voted 38–33 to reverse the law in March 1997. As of March 25, 1997, four terminally ill people have used the law to end their lives.

PAS is still technically a crime in the Netherlands. Since the 1970s, however, the Dutch Parliament and Supreme Court have ruled that, provided certain conditions are met, physicians may assist people to die. By the early 1980s, the medical profession and courts in the Netherlands had established guidelines for physicians to perform assisted suicide and euthanasia. In 1984, the Supreme Court of the Netherlands accepted PAS and euthanasia, not only for the terminally ill but also for the chronically ill and elderly, not only for the physically ill but also for the mentally suffering (ERGO 1995).

Public's, Medical Professionals', and Religious Groups' Views on Physician-Assisted Suicide

In the United States, approximately 50 to 70 percent of the public (numbers vary depending on surveys) favor a law allowing doctors to help terminal patients end their lives (Shute 1997; Kettl 1996; Bachman et al. 1996). When actually voting in official ballot measures, 46 percent in Washington (in 1991) and 46 percent in California (in 1992) supported PAS; and in Oregon, 51 percent in 1994 and 60 percent in 1997 supported PAS (ERGO 1995, 1998).

Among the 2,761 Oregon physicians surveyed, 60 percent said PAS should be legal in some cases; 46 percent said they might prescribe a lethal dose of medication to a terminally ill patient who legally requested it; 31 percent said they would be unwilling to do so on moral grounds (Colburn 1996). Most of the Michigan physicians, among 1,119 surveyed, prefer either legalization of PAS (40 percent) or no law at all (37 percent), and only 17 percent prefer a complete ban on the practice (Bachman et al. 1996). The American Medical Association, the leading professional organization of physicians, however, remains adamantly opposed to PAS, arguing that better treatment and care should be the solution for terminal patients, not PAS.

Even among religious groups, the issue is sharply divided. The hierarchy of the Roman Catholic church and churches on the religious right oppose PAS, whereas the United Church of Christ (Congregational), the Unitarian church, and Methodist church on the West Coast support it (ERGO 1995).

How Often Is PAS Requested and Performed?

Among the national sample of 828 physicians, 12 percent reported that they had received one or more explicit requests for PAS. Of the 156 patients who requested PAS, 38 (24 percent) received a prescription, and 21 of them died as a result (Back 1996). Request for PAS appears to be more frequent among AIDS and cancer patients. In a 1995 survey of 118 doctors who treat AIDS patients, 53 percent said that they had granted at least one terminally ill AIDS patient's request to help them die (Stenson 1996). A study of cancer specialists found that 57 percent had been asked for help in suicide and 13.5 percent had written a lethal prescription (Rosenthal 1997).

The following sections summarize the supporting and opposing views on PAS.

Physician-Assisted Suicide
Is a Constitutionally Protected
Fundamental Right

Supporting PAS

Assisted suicide is a fundamental right protected by the Fourteenth Amendment's guarantee of personal liberty. A mentally competent, terminally ill, adult individual has a personal liberty interest, when facing an imminent and inevitable death, not to be forced by the government to endure unnecessary pain and suffering. The liberty interest encompasses an interest not only in avoiding severe physical pain but also the despair and distress that come from physical deterioration and the inability to control basic bodily or mental functions in the terminal stage of an illness (Tribe in Biskupic 1997; Reinhardt in Epps 1997).

When people support PAS, they are not supporting a right to kill themselves, but a right to choose. A person facing imminent death should have a choice in deciding how to die and in controlling the circumstances of his or her death (Tribe in Reibstein 1997). Their decision to hasten death peacefully flows out of the Constitution's protection of "personal autonomy" and "bodily integrity" (Tucker in Reibstein 1997). Without this choice, terminal patients die either in unnecessary pain and suffering or in a prolonged terminal sedation. Terminal patients who do not wish to die in these fashions should be given the right to decide how much pain they are willing to go through, and when and how they wish to die. Many competent, terminal patients have a strong interest in choosing a peaceful, humane, and dignified death rather than being reduced to a state of prolonged helplessness, diapered, sedated, and unconscious (Reinhardt 1996). In order to have a peaceful, humane, and dignified death, terminal patients need the assistance of their physicians.

Assisted suicide is a constitutionally protected right because it is an "intimate" and "personal" decision and a part of the "right to define one's own concept of existence" (Quill in *New York Times* 1-5-97). What can be more personal than the decision to end one's life in its final, painful days? It has to do with one's own body, one's own medical care, and suffering in the face of death. This is a private area the government may not enter (Tucker in Biskupic 1997).

Opposing PAS

There is no question that individuals have a constitutionally significant liberty interest in controlling their fate. However, because of the risks and dangers of abuse involved, the liberty interest regarding PAS can be outweighed by the state's interest in preserving and protecting the lives of its citizens, especially the lives of the most vulnerable—the elderly, poor, and infirm (*New York Times* editorial 1-5-97).

PAS is a matter that goes beyond liberty interest; it is a question of ethics, of allocation of resources, and of our commitment to treat the elderly and infirm (Justice Kennedy in Biskupic 1997). The state does not evaluate the quality of life among its citizenry; the state does not preserve and protect only those whose lives are deemed "worth living." The overriding state's interests justify its decision to ban physicians from prescribing lethal medication. The preservation and protection of the lives of its citizen is the highest constitutional value given to the state (Williams in Biskupic 1997; McCuen 1994, 37; *New York Times* editorial 1-5-97).

If a decision needs only be "personal" and "intimate" to qualify for constitutional protection, a decision to use hallucinogenic drugs for recreation, engage in a consensual dual, sell one's body into prostitution, or any number of other equally personal and intimate activities currently subject to state prohibition would be constitutionally protected. Furthermore, if the fact that a choice is "intimate and personal" is enough to guarantee its protection under the Fourteenth Amendment, the asserted right to commit suicide cannot be confined to the terminally ill. A decision to commit suicide because of a failing business or family tragedy would seem just as "intimate and personal" as a decision to commit suicide based on other reasons or no reason (U.S. Catholic Conference in *New York Times* 1-5-97).

A Refusal of Unwanted Medical Treatments to Hasten Death Is Legal, Why Not Physician-Assisted Suicide?

Supporting PAS

Under the current law, those in the final stage of terminal illness who are on life-support systems are allowed to hasten their death by directing the removal of such systems, but those who are similarly situated, except for the attachment of life-sustaining equipment, are not allowed to hasten death by self-administering prescribed lethal medication (Canady 1996). Allowing terminal patients on life-support systems to refuse treatment and die, while banning PAS for other terminal patients, is a form of discrimination; it violates the Fourteenth Amendment's equal protection guarantee to people who want to speed death through a prescription for fatal drugs (decision of the 2nd U.S. Circuit Court of Appeals in New York in Canady 1996). From the patient's point of view, there is no moral or rational difference between allowing patients on life support to have a doctor pull the plug to hasten death and requesting a doctor to provide a lethal medication to achieve the same result, except that the latter may be quicker and more humane (Reibstein and Klaidman 1997; Dworkin et al. in *New York Times* 1-5-97). The legal distinction between withdrawal of life support and PAS makes no sense to those who are suffering while dying or to the families and loved ones who watch them suffer. When it comes to the rights of the terminally ill, the state must not distinguish between unplugging a respirator and giving a lethal medication (Tribe in Biskupic 1997).

Without legalized PAS, the only alternative doctors have with terminal patients on the threshold of dying is to give them a heavy dose of sedatives, which will keep them comatose until they die. What is the difference between keeping patients comatose until they stop breathing and ending their lives directly? (Rosenthal 1997; Doyle et al. 1993).

Opposing PAS

There is a clear, legal, commonsense, moral distinction between removing artificial life-support systems and seeking PAS. It is a distinction between letting someone die and killing someone; a distinction between passively letting nature take its course so that the underlying disease causes death and requesting a third party to actively be involved in killing someone (Reibstein and Klaidman 1997). When a person on a life-support system (e.g., respirators, artificial nutrition, and hydration) wants the system discontinued, he is not committing suicide, but is allowing nature to take its course (Justice Kennedy in Biskupic 1997). Allowing patients to withdraw life-sustaining treatment, therefore, is based on the right to be free from an unwanted intrusion. On the other hand, requesting PAS involves claiming "some right to have a third party, in this instance a physician, to help kill themselves" (Vacco in Biskupic 1997). It implicates the assistance of others in committing suicide. It is not an issue of simply "choosing to die," but it is that "they want assistance from a physician to do it." It is a decision about whether one of the citizens is allowed to help another kill himself or herself. The risk of abuse and undue influence is higher in the PAS context than it is in the refusal of treatment context (Williams in Biskupic 1997).

We Need a Better Way of Dying Than Needless Pain and Suffering

Supporting PAS

Whether the request is the withdrawal of life-sustaining treatments or PAS, the wish of terminal patients is the same—a speedy death in peace and dignity, free from physical pain and emotional suffering. For many terminal patients, death comes with unrelenting pain, indignity, and senseless, life-sustaining treatment to prolong the agony. Modern medical technology can extend life beyond a functional level, and many terminal patients live in prolonged pain and suffering or in a persistent vegetative state for a long time. Patients' do-not-resuscitate requests are frequently ignored, and many are never asked about their preferences. More than half of Americans die in the hospital, often isolated and in pain, while tethered to a frightening array of high-tech equipment (Shute 1997). About 25 percent of terminal patients die in unnecessary pain (Biskupic 1997). The fear of a painful dying process changed the public's attitude toward dying and drove many chronically ill to seek out doctors who would help them die.

Most people want to die at home, at peace, and lovingly tended by family. Being in uncontrollable pain, being comatose due to heavy doses of pain medication, or being a burden to family members for an extended period, for many people, seems to be worse than death. Without PAS, the only alternative for the terminally ill is a painful and long process of self-starvation or dehydration, or dying in a medically induced sedation. In fact, many physicians administer ever-increasing doses of palliative medication until the doses reach toxic levels. For those who do not want either one of these, PAS is an ideal option. Why can't we honor terminal patients' wish to end their lives early in peace and dignity and their wish not to burden their family members either emotionally or financially? Forcing people to suffer in pain is no more moral or ethical than allowing them to die as they wish (Morgan 1996).

Opposing PAS

Many studies report that the reason for requesting PAS is usually not the physical pain. In studies done in the Netherlands, where PAS is allowed, only 5 percent of patients said it was the pain (Bindels 1997). The most common concerns patients have at the time PAS is requested are nonphysical. According to a survey of 828 physicians, the patients' concerns most often perceived by physicians are worries about loss of control, being a burden, being dependent on others for personal care, and loss of dignity (Back et al. 1996). About 59 percent of those who wish to die have a depressive syndrome and/or have a low level of support from friends or family (Muskin 1998). One study of cancer patients showed that among those most likely to request PAS, the deciding factors were their concern about the quality of life and depression (Bindels 1997).

It is unfortunate that we have a medical practice that routinely ignores the emotional problems of the terminally ill. If we have a health care system in which dying patients should worry about being a burden to others financially and emotionally, we must change the system rather than letting them die prematurely. The dying patients' quality of life can be improved a great deal by providing more comprehensive care, better insurance policies, and hospice programs. Many successful hospice programs have shown that naturally induced death does not have to be terribly painful, a burden to others, or less dignified than assisted suicide as supporters of PAS claim. Enduring pain up to the last minute, and participating in life as much as possible until the final moment is not less dignified than committing suicide (Cundiff 1992).

The Netherlands Has Successfully Allowed Physician-Assisted Suicide for More Than Twenty-Four Years; Why Can't We?

Supporting PAS

The Netherlands has openly allowed PAS (and euthanasia) for more than twenty-four years, and still the Dutch faith in PAS remains strong. Polls consistently show that about 80 percent favor PAS, up from 44 percent during the early 1970s when it started (Shapiro 1997b). More than a third of the general Dutch population decides at some point when to stop medical treatment that would otherwise prolong their lives, and about 2 percent opt for PAS (Bindels 1997).

Opposing PAS

In the Netherlands, in 1995, there were 3,200 reported cases of euthanasia. About three-fifths of all euthanasia cases go unreported; one in five of those unreported cases involve patients who did not have a recorded request; some were in a coma, and some supposedly had merely spoken with the doctor. Many involuntary killings go unpunished by the Dutch, and courts grant dubious exceptions about who can be helped to die. It appears that once a doctor has the authority to end human life, even under carefully regulated conditions, she will find it easy to do so in ambiguous situations. Judges have set up guidelines to protect patients, but in practice, the guidelines are often ignored and physicians make decisions on their own. In such circumstances, even people with disabilities or mental retardation can be at risk. Many carry anti-euthanasia "passports" to tell health care workers that they wish to live in case of an emergency. Even the severely depressed but not physically ill have received help from physicians to commit suicide (Shapiro 1997b).

The Dutch experience demonstrates the inevitable "slide down effect" that begins when a society allows PAS. The acceptance of a right to PAS for terminally ill, competent patients had led the Dutch to embrace PAS for the chronically ill, the elderly, and those who are suffering mentally. Even more alarming, the Dutch acceptance of PAS has led to voluntary and involuntary euthanasia. Once a country legitimizes the killing of those who suffer physically at their request, the country will allow killing of those who suffer mentally. When a society allows euthanasia for those who request it, involuntary euthanasia for any life the society deems not worth living is not far behind (Canady 1996).

Furthermore, the conditions that make the practice of PAS acceptable in the Netherlands are absent in the United States. In the Netherlands, patients usually stay with one family doctor for a long time. Patients who get help in dying have known their doctor for an average of eight years. When a doctor knows his patients well, there is a strong bond between a doctor and a patient, and that makes it easier for them to talk about death. In the U.S. health care system, people switch doctors often, and there is no close-knit doctor-patient relationship as in the Netherlands. Also, in the Dutch health care system, 99 percent of the Dutch have health insurance, which provides access to comprehensive care, including nursing homes. The Dutch terminal patients face virtually no out-of-pocket expenses at the end of life. On the other hand, in the United States, about 15 percent of the population have no insurance at all, and many more have only limited coverage. The hospitalization and nursing home costs especially at the end of a life can impoverish even average middle-class Americans. In the Netherlands, patients do not request PAS to avoid financial burden to their family, whereas in the United States, patients can be motivated or pressured to seek PAS by the fear of burdening their spouses and families. For PAS to even be considered, we must first have universal health care, free of charge, and equal-quality care for everyone (Shapiro 1997b).

Suicide Is Morally Wrong under Any Circumstances

Opposing PAS

Suicide is morally wrong under any circumstances. No matter what the condition of a person's life, there is still value in it. No grief, pain, misfortune, or broken heart can be an excuse for suicide. No one has a right to end one's own or another's life: No one has the right to help others kill themselves. Our country was founded on a strong moral tradition that condemns suicide and murder. No matter which way proponents of PAS try to justify it, assisted suicide comes down to killing. And killing is wrong for whatever reason. Assisted suicide, even when voluntary and done by a patient's own hands, would cross the moral border into state-sanctioned killing (Reibstein and Klaidman 1997; Cundiff 1992).

Supporting PAS

Our law and tradition against suicide derived from a time when death was rarely preceded by a long period of physiologically degenerative suffering. The time has changed, and the laws must be changed accordingly. With the development of medical technology, advanced terminal illness often causes long and unbearable suffering to the patients. Assisted suicide for the terminally ill is a "justifiable suicide." It is a rational and planned "self-deliverance" from a painful and hopeless disease which will shortly end in death (Humphry 1995; Quill in Reibstein and Klaidman 1977). The terminal patients are not asking doctors to kill them. They are asking for the right to end their lives when and if they become terminally ill and feel the suffering and pain are too much to bear, not only for themselves but also for their families. In that sense, the doctors are not taking the lives of anyone; they are giving patients an opportunity to speed up the process of dying, an opportunity to end their suffering and have peace (Rogatz in Rosenthal 1997).

Without the help of a physician, some terminal patients try to end their pain and suffering by taking their own lives. Self-inflicted suicides, however, are often unsuccessful, more painful, and can result in unwanted consequences, such as living in a vegetative state or being kept alive on life-support systems, which can be an even greater burden and emotional shock to family members. In rare instances, societies justify killing. It is accepted in war, in self-defense, and for punishment of awful crimes. PAS is a form of mercy killing, which is justifiable (Earley in *U.S. News & World Report* 1-13-97).

Christian Theology Demands Respect for Life and Recognizes That Human Life Is Sacred

Opposing PAS

Our life is a gift from God. Humans cannot take God's gift away. Only God can take it away. PAS, like suicide and homicide, is a crime that no human law can claim to legitimize. Legalizing PAS will bring about a culture of death, which, taken as a whole, will end up becoming "the freedom of the strong against the weak" (Pope John Paul II in *New York Times* 1997).

Supporting PAS

Those who believe in such a Christian theology do not have to be involved in PAS. But there are millions of atheists and agnostics as well as people of other religions and even Christians who do not agree with such a theology, and they all have rights, too (Humphry 1995). God also gave us free will, which can be exercised in obedience to God. Modern medical technology creates circumstances in which involuntarily prolonged existence becomes a less ethical alternative than a conscientiously chosen and merciful termination of life. Exercising free will in such circumstances is in obedience to God (Hager and Falkowski 1997).

Potential Risks from Allowing Physician-Assisted Suicide Are Greater Than the Benefits

Opposing PAS

PAS may sound humane, but it can lead to the deaths of many people who are not competent, not terminally ill, and not truly ready to die, but are steered toward suicide by cost-conscious doctors or family members (Dellinger in Associated Press 11-13-97; Hendin and Klerman 1993). If PAS becomes legal, doctors and family members may pressure patients to end their lives prematurely against their will. Some terminal patients might feel the pressure of not becoming a burden to the family or even consider it their duty to die. This pressure will be particularly greater for the poor and elderly. The heart of the opponents' argument is the traditional obligation to protect these vulnerable groups of our society (Reibstein and Klaidman 1997; Dellinger in *U.S. News & World Report* 1-13-97).

PAS, once legalized, will be difficult to contain. There is a risk that courts will be forced to broaden the assistance to include the chronically ill, mentally ill, mentally retarded, the depressed, and even the handicapped and disabled as happens in the Netherlands (Reibstein and Klaidman 1997; Rosenthal 1997). Furthermore, there is a danger that the decision to assistance can move from a patient's request to a surrogate's or other proxy's request as happens in the Netherlands. It is also possible that family members of the terminally ill, financially and emotionally drained from caring for the sick, might obtain the prescription and kill the patient (Rosenthal 1997; Cundiff 1992).

Without equal and universal access to health care, there is a danger that PAS will be practiced unfairly. From the ethical point of view, only those who have complete health care coverage can request PAS. Those at greatest risk to lose their lives will be the poor, those without a family, the elderly, and especially those who have no access to adequate health care (American Jewish Committee's Press Release 1997).

As health care costs continue to soar, insurance companies and hospitals tend to seek the most cost-effective means of treating patients. PAS is cheaper than long-term hospitalization or rehabilitation. The risk of abuse is especially greater in today's HMO or other managed care environment in which the quickest and cheapest answer is always preferred. Doctors may be pressured to use the most cost-efficient option of PAS to save money before they try all available treatment options (Rosenthal 1997).

Supporting PAS

The risks of PAS can be minimized by providing regulations as safeguards. If there is a danger of abuse, we should regulate against potential abuses, not shut off a constitutional right (Tribe in Reibstein and Klaidman 1997). For instance, we can require psychological therapy and counseling and evaluation by social workers for terminal patients seeking PAS to guarantee that the decision is made voluntarily and not under any pressure or stress. We can require second opinions from more than one physician, a written statement by the patient, and a waiting period to make sure the decision is not made in a fit of emotion.

One year after Oregon allowed PAS, it was used sparingly and only for the very sick in the very last days of their lives. Only fifteen people ended their lives with lethal medication: An additional six got the prescription but died of their diseases. The Oregon Health Division's report found no abuse of the law or rush to suicide (Shapiro 1999).

Physicians Should Always Be Healers, Not Killers

Opposing PAS

Unlike other occupations in our society, physicians have the capacity to injure or even cause the death of their patients. The state, therefore, has an important interest in maintaining a clear line between physicians as healers and physicians as instruments of death of their patients (Williams in Biskupic 1997). The principle that doctors should not intentionally harm their patients overrides all the other ethical considerations that support PAS. The power to assist in intentionally taking the life of a patient is antithetical to the central mission of healing that guides both medicine and nursing. Physicians should be trained and socialized to save and preserve lives and not to do any harm or cause death. This is an important professional commitment physicians must adhere to. Maintaining the integrity of the medical profession as dedicated to healing and not killing is extremely crucial. If we break down this barrier and allow physicians to assist suicide, we place on doctors the burden of choosing life or death, which is a conflict of interest. It is wrong for anyone to take on the power of deciding whether a person should live or die. It is a power that most health care professionals do not want and should not have (Foley 1997; Palermo 1997; Rosenthal 1997; position of the AMA).

If we make death a legally available choice for physicians, it will inevitably change the way doctors treat patients. Instead of trying to cure patients' illnesses or make patients' lives easier and better by providing good palliative care, doctors will tend to focus on whether continued care is "worth it," and whether a person's life is "worth living." (Senator Hatch in *New York Times* 1-5-97).

Allowing PAS will undermine not only the integrity of the medical profession but also our trust in doctors. If PAS becomes legal, some, especially the members of economically disadvantaged groups, may become reluctant to seek and receive treatment for their physical or psychological symptoms because of the fear that their physicians will hasten death. There is evidence that the legalization of assisted suicide in the Northern Territory of Australia has undermined the Aborigines' trust in the medical care system (Foley 1997).

Supporting PAS

The proper role of physicians should be to take actions that are in the best interest of their patients. If assisting a dying patient is in the patient's best interest, physicians should be able to take that action. For patients who suffer irremediable and severe pain and are confronting an imminent and unavoidable death, PAS, as a voluntary, last-resort option, may constitute not harm but the only available relief. The true harm may lie in being compelled either to continue unnecessary suffering or to end one's life in a lonely and violent manner (position of the American Medical Students Association in *New York Times* 1997; Jung 1997).

Hospice Program Is a Better Option Than Physician-Assisted Suicide

Opposing PAS

There is a perception that terminal patients must choose between a painful existence devoid of value on one hand and assisted suicide on the other. There is another, more appropriate option, that is hospice care. Hospice is an interdisciplinary team approach to the care of terminal patients, and it addresses the physical, emotional, social, and spiritual needs of the dying patients and their families. The hospice's primary responsibility to its patients and their families is to ensure that people do not die alone, in pain, and as a burden to their families (National Hospice Organization Press Release on PAS 1997). The terminal patients who reject the traditional curative treatment can go instead into a hospice program and receive pain management, comfort, and personal attention until they die. Hospice care neither prolongs life by providing patients with aggressive treatments nor hastens their death. Instead, it can provide good-quality pain control and an acceptable quality of life for terminal patients. Hospice care can take place at home, incorporating family as the unit of terminal care. It allows family members as well as the dying to prepare for the death.

Supporting PAS

The hospice program may be an option for some dying patients but cannot replace PAS. For some patients, terminal pain cannot be controlled with drugs. In such cases, in hospice care, the patients are dragged into a long, medically induced coma until they die. For those who do not wish to die in that fashion, PAS is the only option. Also, for some people, personal quality of life is vital. If one's body has been so destroyed by a disease that the person does not think it is worth living, PAS should be an option (Humphry 1995). Moreover, the hospice program is not available everywhere. Even where it is available, it requires a competent caregiver at home or nearby constantly, and that, in many cases, is not feasible. Because most of the hospice programs involve home care, it often entails emotional and physical caretaking burdens on the family.

Better Care of Terminal Patients Should Be the Answer, Not Physician-Assisted Suicide

Opposing PAS

Most terminal patients suffer from three symptoms: 1) physical pain; 2) psychological distress (e.g., anxiety, depression); and 3) existential distress (the experience of life without meaning) (Foley 1997). Uncontrolled physical pain often contributes to psychological depression; and the desire to die is most closely associated with the diagnosis of depression (Foley 1997). If physicians pay more attention to pain control and become more aggressive in keeping terminal patients comfortable, there will be little need for PAS (Rosenthal 1997). When patients request PAS because of pain, the task for the medical profession should be providing better palliative care rather than calling for the cheap and easy lethal medication (Dellinger in Biskupic 1997). If patients request PAS because of the poor quality of life they must endure, our task should be providing a better quality of life, not to end it.

Medical technology is available for managing pain and other symptoms associated with terminal illness. But these are not routinely provided. In a report by Cassel's committee (Mount Sinai Medical Center), doctors and hospitals are poorly prepared to give appropriate care to patients who are hopelessly ill and dying. Only 5 of 126 medical schools in the United States require a separate course in the care of dying; only 17 percent of the residency training programs offer a hospice rotation. In our medical system, the majority of terminal patients die in hospitals or in nursing homes (about 78 percent), and only about 10 to 14 percent of those who die at home receive hospice care (Foley 1997).

We need to better educate health care professionals and the public on the issue of death and dying. We need a better medical policy that will enhance the quality of life for the dying as well as the availability of comfort care. Health care professionals should be trained and educated to provide not just better palliative treatment but also better psychological therapy, social intervention, and a physician-patient relationship. Too often in our health care system physicians do not know enough about their patients to provide assistance with dying as a medical treatment.

Seriously ill patients by and large want to live, if they can have their pain controlled, and receive love and support from their family members and friends. When they request PAS, their major concern is not just pain but future loss of control and becoming a burden to others. The Oregon study shows that only one out of twenty-three who received lethal medication cited fear of pain as a reason for seeking suicide (Shapiro 1999). If physicians were better educated in the management of pain and suffering, and if more patients were aware of the options available to them through hospice, advanced care planning, and counseling, there would be no need to resort to PAS (AMA's position). The Oregon's Health Division report, after studying the one-year enactment of the PAS law, concluded that Americans need to know more about offering comfort, care, and social support to the terminally ill, something most of the dying people want desperately but too often go without (Shapiro 1999).

Supporting PAS

For some patients, the pain can be so overwhelming that they cannot focus on anything beyond their unremitting suffering, and life becomes nothing more than their pain. Even without pain, their life consists merely of lying inert, which some patients reject as intolerable. For those patients, the desire to end life can be a fully competent and rational choice, and PAS should be allowed as an option (The Coalition of Hospice Professionals in *New York Times* 1-5-97).

Predicting Terminal Illness Is Never Accurate

Opposing PAS

No one can decide what illness is terminal or how long a patient will live, and no one can weigh the relative severity of terminal and emotional pain (Justice Scalia in Biskupic 1997; Rosenthal 1997). Especially in the evolving field of today's medicine, we can never be sure whether a disease is terminal or that a certain result of illness will occur. The Oregon law allows patients who are expected to live less than six months to request a lethal dose of drugs. Predicting death has never been accurate, however (Morgan 1996, 45). About 60 percent of Oregon physicians surveyed worried that they cannot judge when a patient has fewer than six months to live (Shapiro 1997c). Terminal patients often live longer than expected. Hospices usually admit patients who are expected to live less than six months. About 15 percent of the hospice patients, however, live longer than six months (Shapiro 1997a). Moreover, no one can define how much pain or what kind of pain is intolerable enough to grant a suicide, or how long a patient should tolerate pain before dying. How about the terminal patients who are going to live in terrible pain for ten years? Why shouldn't they have a right to PAS? Is physical pain worse than emotional pain? Why should it be limited only to physical pain? How can any doctor decide at which point one's life has no value? How can any physician say, "You are right. I think you are better off dead."

Supporting PAS

Whether one should end one's life and when and how to terminate one's pain and suffering should be a decision made by the suffering patient only. Doctors and other health care professionals can help the patient make such decisions but cannot make the decision for them and cannot be responsible for their decision. Different people react differently to pain: Some are more tolerant than others.

Different people react differently to treatments also: Some respond better than others. Moreover, every terminal patient has a different background affecting her decision, such as family support, financial situation, and emotional strength. Each case, therefore, must be carefully examined by health care professionals. Ultimately, it should be an individual decision made by a mentally competent patient. No one can make life-or-death decisions for someone else, no doctor or law can decide at which point one should terminate his life. Only the person on the threshold of dying can and should be allowed to make that decision.

The Decision to End One's Life Is Often an Irrational One

Opposing PAS

People sometimes act without fully considering the consequences of their actions and make decisions based on emotion or inaccurate information. Everyone, once in a while, makes an irrational decision based on emotion and later regrets it. The decision to die, for some terminal patients, may be provoked by temporary pain, suffering, and depression. It is possible that a person who wished to die because of terrible agony but did not get the assistance, lives on, and says, "I am glad that I didn't do that." (Justice Ginsberg in Biskupic 1997). Suicide usually is not a well-thought-out plan but an impulse of a person suffering from depression or other mental illness. About half the people who survive a suicide attempt want to be fully resuscitated (Kettl 1996; McCuen 1994). Figuring out what a dying patient really wants is very hard. Patients often change their minds on how much care they want, based on how they feel from day to day (Shute 1997). Especially someone who is in serious pain or depression is not in a position to make a sound decision of any kind, not to mention a life-or-death decision. There is no way of ensuring that they will not regret their decisions. Unlike many other decisions people make, the decision to die is an irreversible one. A legal prevention of self-harm protects us from a decision made in a fit of emotion, which we would later regret. The law against PAS gives us our fair due by allowing us not to be overcome by emotions or biases.

People in good health often believe they would want legal means to end their lives if they become seriously ill. Clinical evidence, however, has confirmed the suspicion that when people face a dreaded disease, life becomes even more precious, and patients usually call for maximum medical efforts to continue life (American Jewish Committee Press Release 1997).

Supporting PAS

The risk of making the irrational decision of suicide can be minimized by requiring a waiting period and psychological evaluation. If doctors are trained to evaluate patients' mental state, emotional strength, and other background situations, such as family support and financial situation, we should be able to prevent any irrational decisions of suicide made in a fit of emotion.

For instance, the Death with Dignity Act in Oregon, passed in 1994, requires that a patient seeking PAS must ask a doctor orally and in writing, see another doctor for confirmation, ask the first doctor again fifteen days later, and also consider formal opportunity to change his mind before taking the final step. The physicians who comply with the request must: 1) determine if the patient is terminally ill, capable, and has voluntarily made the request; 2) inform the patient of alternative options, such as comfort care, hospice care, and pain control; 3) refer the patient for counseling if appropriate; 4) request that the patient notify next of kin; and 5) inform the patient that she has the opportunity to rescind the request at any time (ERGO 1998). With such proper protocols and safeguards to regulate its application, legalized PAS will effectively minimize decisions made in a fit of emotion.

Legalizing Physician-Assisted Suicide Will Lead to Widespread Suicide Attempts

Opposing PAS

Legalizing PAS will destigmatize suicide and make it more acceptable in our society. It will send a message to the public that suicide is all right and is an acceptable means of solving one's problems. Such a change in the public's belief and attitude can lead to a suicide spree, especially among teenagers who have low self-esteem and are often confused or depressed. By seeing that the sick are now legally allowed to commit suicide, those who are temporarily depressed or disappointed might become more likely to take their own lives (Levine 1997). Legalizing PAS could even lead to a higher homicide rate because it sends the message to the public that it is all right to kill someone if the person seems to be suffering.

Supporting PAS

The problem of teenage suicide or suicide of other kinds is a totally different issue that does not involve incurable diseases and intolerable pain. To solve such problems, we need an approach that is different from dealing with terminally ill patients. To deny the rights of terminally ill patients based solely on an unproved assumption that legalized PAS might lead to a higher suicide rate among the healthy is illogical and far-fetched. Such an argument is similar to saying that capital punishment leads to a higher murder rate, because capital punishment sends a message that killing is all right. There is a clear, legal, ethical, and commonsense difference between PAS as a last resort for terminally ill patients and other suicides committed or contemplated by those who are suffering from temporary pain and depression.

REFERENCES

American Jewish Committee. 1997. "American Jewish committee forum on physician-assisted suicide."

Associated Press. 1996. "White House urges Supreme Court to rule against euthanasia." *Dayton Daily News*. 13 November.

Bachman, Jerald G., Kirsten H. Alcser, David J. Doukas, Richard L. Lichtenstein, Amy D. Corning, and Howard Brody. 1996. "Attitude of Michigan physicians and the public toward legalizing physician-assisted suicide and voluntary euthanasia." *New England Journal of Medicine* 334, no. 5 (1 February).

Back, Anthony L., Jeffrey L. Wallace, Helene E. Starks, and Robert A. Perlman. 1996. "Physician-assisted suicide and euthanasia in Washington state: Patient requests and physician response." *Journal of the American Medical Association* 275, no. 12 (27 March):919–25.

Bindels, Patrick J. E. 1997. "Euthanasia and physician-assisted suicide in homosexual men with AIDS." (http://www.mediconsult.com).

Biskupic, Joan. 1997. "Justice skeptical of assisted suicide: Court hears arguments on establishing right." *Washington Post*. 9 January.

Canady, Charles T. 1996. "Physician-assisted suicide and euthanasia in the Netherlands." Statement of Charles T. Canady, representing Florida's 12th District on 27 September 1996. RPD 1623.

Colburn, Don. 1996. "Survey shows not all physicians are in favor of assisted suicide." *Washington Post*, 23 February.

Cundiff, David. 1992. *Euthanasia is not the answer*. Totowa, N.J.: Humana Press.

Doyle, D., G. W. C. Hanks, and N. MacDonald. 1993. *The Oxford textbook of palliative medicine*. New York: Oxford University Press.

Epps, Garrett. 1997. "Judges who support the right to die." *U.S. News & World Report*. 13 January.

Euthanasia Research and Guidance Organization (ERGO). 1998. "The physician-assisted suicide Oregon Trail." (http://www.efn.org/~ergo/Orlaw.html).

———. 1995. "Frequently asked questions about right to die." 19 November.

Foley, Kathleen M., M.D. 1997. "Competent care for the dying instead of physician-assisted suicide." *New England Journal of Medicine* 336, no. 1 (January).

Greenhouse, Linda. 1997. "Justices remove last legal barrier to Oregon suicide measure." *New York Times*. 16 October.

Hager, Mary, and Lawrence Falkowski. 1997. "Report of the task force on assisted suicide." (http://www.rights.org/~deathnet/ergo_library.html).

Hendin, Herbert, M.D., and Gerald Klerman, M.D. 1993. "Physician-assisted suicide: The dangers of legalization." *American Journal of Psychiatry* 150:143–45 (January).

Humphry, Derek. 1995. "Why I believe in voluntary euthanasia." (dhumphry@efn.org).

Jung, Paul, M.D. 1997. "Medical Students Association: Only national medical group to support PAS." AMSA release. 6 January. (http://www.amsa.org/new/release4.htm).

Kettl, Paul. 1996. "A debate over physician-assisted suicide," at the Annual Meeting of the American Psychiatric Association in New York, 6 May. (http://www.suicide.hmc).

Levine, Art. 1997. "In Oregon, a political campaign to die for: Assisted-suicide fight turns ugly." *U.S. News & World Report* 123:56–57.

McCuen, Gary. 1994. *Doctor-assisted suicide*. Wisconsin: McCuen Publications.

Morgan, Rebecca. 1996. "The issue of personal choice: The competent incurable patient and the right to commit suicide." Pp. 3–51 in *The right to die: Who decides?*, edited by Melvin Urofsky and Philip Urofsky. New York: Garland.

Muskin, Philip R. 1998. "The request to die: Role for a psychodynamic perspective on physician-assisted suicide." *Journal of American Medical Association* 279:323–28.

National Hospice Organization. 1997. "NHO press release on physician-assisted suicide." (http://www.nho.org).

New York Times. 1997. "Before the court, the sanctity of life and death." 5 January.

Palermo, Tony. 1997. "No right to die, local reps say." *Sun Herald*. 5 April.

Reibstein, Larry. 1997. "Whose right is it?" *Newsweek*. 21 January.

Reibstein, Larry, and Daniel Klaidman. 1997. "The Supreme Court will decide: Can doctors help their patients kill themselves?" *Newsweek*. 13 January.

Reinhardt, Stephen. 1996. *Compassion in dying v. state of Washington*, 79F. 3rd. 790, 9th Cir.

Rosenthal, Elisabeth. 1997. "Doctors face tough decisions on assisted suicide." *New York Times*. 13 March.

Shapiro, Joseph P. 1999. "Casting a cold eye on 'death with dignity': Oregon studies year one of a benchmark law." *U.S. News & World Report*. 1 March, 56.

———. 1997a. "Death be not swift enough." *U.S. News & World Report*. 24 March.

———. 1997b. "Euthanasia's home." *U.S. News & World Report*. 13 January.

———. 1997c. "On second thought: Oregon reconsiders its pioneering assisted suicide law." *U.S. News & World Report*. 1 September.

Shute, Nancy. 1997. "Death with more dignity." *U.S. News & World Report*. 24 February.

Stenson, Jacqueline. 1996. "Many doctors and nurses help AIDS patients die." *Medical Tribune News Service*. 11 July.

U.S. News & World Report. 1997. "Death Rights." 13 January.

8 Social Security Reform

Social Security (SS) refers to the Old-Age Insurance program initiated by the Social Security Act in 1935 that has grown into today's Old-Age, Survivors, and Disability Insurance (OASDI). After the stock market crash and the worldwide depression, which left millions of Americans destitute and without savings, the SS system was created by the Roosevelt administration to solve the problems of widespread elderly poverty. This system is a generationally transferred (pay-as-you-go) social insurance program funded by payroll taxes (FICA). The current generation of workers contribute to the system during their working careers to support retired beneficiaries and, in return, earn entitlement to family benefits on retirement, disability, or death.

Social Security is the federal government's largest spending program. In fiscal year 1997, it paid nearly $367 billion in benefits (approximately 20 percent of the total federal budget) to 44.2 million people. Sixty-two percent of them were retired workers; 11 percent disabled workers; another 11 percent dependents of retirees and disabled workers; and 16 percent survivors of deceased workers (spouses and children). The average payment for a retired worker in 1999 was $780 a month; the average for a couple was $1,310 a month (PNIS 1999). For more than 90 percent of the retirees who receive benefits, SS provides more than 40 percent of their cash income (Gramlich 1998, 1); for 18 percent of them, it is their only source of income (Clinton 1998). About 96 percent of the workforce contribute to the system: The only major excluded group of workers is state and local government employees in some states. About 92 percent of those aged 65 and over receive benefits (Gramlich 1997, 148).

With both the size and real wages of the labor force rising rapidly, the history of SS in the 1950s, 1960s, and 1970s was that of gradual expansion. Beginning in 1954, disability insurance was added to the program, and inflation protection was made explicit (Gramlich 1998). Since then, SS has been amended several times. The most recent change was the 1983 Social Security Amendment, which included payroll tax increases, raising the retirement age to 67 after 2002, and imposing an income tax on high-income beneficiaries (Quinn and Mitchell 1996; Bosworth 1997, 156).

When the program started in the 1930s, payroll tax rate to support the program was 2 percent. In 1999, payroll tax for SS was 12.4 percent of wages, divided equally between employer and employee, with a maximum salary cap of $72,600 (Mitchell 1997). Even with the tax increases, SS Trust Fund is projected to run out of money in 2034, as the baby boom generation retires. With this gloomy projection, many lawmakers have proposed major reform plans including a funded (privatized) pension system.

What Are the Problems with Our Social Security System?

As of 1999, Social Security is in surplus; it takes in about $60 to $100 billion more annually than it needs to pay benefits to current retirees because the majority of the baby boom generation is still working and paying taxes. However, the long-term problem of SS will start when 75 million baby boomers begin to retire. By 2013, payroll taxes will be less than the benefits being paid out. There will be fewer workers to support the retirees (Francis 1998b), and the baby boom retirees will receive a declining rate of return on their lifetime contributions unless the tax burden is increased substantially to the following generations (Quinn and Mitchell 1996). By 2021, it will start redeeming the Trust Funds to pay benefits until 2034. When the Trust Fund reserves are exhausted, payroll taxes will be able to pay only 75 percent of the current benefits (Francis 1998b; Jaffe 1998). This long-term financial viability of SS is what worries many Americans, especially the younger generations who fear that they may not be able to collect what they contribute to the system when they retire (Bosworth 1997, 156).

What Are the Causes of the Social Security Problems?

Aging of the Baby Boom Generation

The aging of the baby boomers, those born in the years between 1946 and 1964, will create severe financial pressures on the SS system. This is the largest generation in U.S. history, 75 million people. In general, they married late and had relatively few children. They are also expected to live longer than the previous generations, causing the ratio of workers to retirees to decrease when they retire (PNIS 1999; Gramlich 1998, 27).

Increased Life Expectancy

People live many years longer than when SS was first created in the 1930s. In 1935, the overall life expectancy at birth was 61 years. More than half of all Americans did not even live long enough to collect their SS benefits. In 1998, the average life expectancy at birth was 75 years for men, 78 for women (Gramlich 1998, 27; Mitchell 1997). People spend a significantly longer portion of their lives in retirement relative to those of their working years.

Declining Ratio of Workers to Retirees

As a result of the aging population and increased life expectancy, the ratio of SS contributors to beneficiaries has declined steadily over the years. In 1950, it was 16 to 1; in 1960, 5 to 1; in 1998, 3.3 to 1; and it is projected to be about 2 to 1 by the year 2030 (Quinn and Mitchell 1996; Gramlich 1998, 27–28; PNIS 1999).

Increased Benefit Payments

The economy performed poorly in the late 1970s and early 1980s, resulting in double-digit inflation levels. The high inflation rapidly increased SS benefits because they were automatically indexed to compensate for inflation, while slower wage growth and high unemployment depressed tax revenues (Bartlett 1997, 226). This problem was compounded by an inadvertent technical error in the 1972 legislation, which overindexed benefits (Tobin 1988, 54). As a result, the level of benefits has risen much faster than the real wages of the workers. For most of the past and current retirees, the benefit level has far exceeded what they paid in. For example, a man with average lifetime earnings who retired at age 65 in 1980 could expect to receive in SS retirement benefits 3.7 times more than his contributions would have generated, had they been invested in low-risk government securities. For a similar woman, the ratio was even higher—4.4 times—because of her longer life expectancy. The overly generous benefits, at a time when people are living longer, outstripped its means (Kotlikoff 1998; Quinn and Mitchell 1996; Editors of *The New Republic* 1-26-98).

Government Diversion of Trust Funds

Since 1969, SS has been included in the federal budget, and money from payroll taxes has been spent in other federal programs, in exchange for special Treasury bonds that will finance SS in the future (Lipman 1999). Especially since the 1983 SS reform, which allowed the government to collect far more money through payroll taxes than what is needed to pay benefits to the retirees, surplus has increased to about $60 to $100 billion a year, which is about 20 percent over the expenditure (Century Foundation 1998). A $2.3 trillion surplus was supposed to have been built up since 1983. However, the extra money has been spent by lawmakers to support other government programs and to reduce the federal budget deficit, and now it consists of IOUs from the Treasury. To convert them into cash requires the government to cut benefits, raise taxes, or borrow in amounts approximating $7 trillion in twenty years after 2013 (Zuckerman 1998; Bosworth 1997).

Is This Social Security Problem a Crisis?

Yes, It Is a Crisis

The SS system is broke. It is in much worse fiscal shape than the public thinks or government representatives acknowledge (Kotlikoff 1998). Although the crisis is not imminent, it will happen within a decade if we do not take major actions to reform the system. The deficits will begin in 2012, and by 2022, annual deficits will be $100 billion per year, skyrocketing to more than $200 billion per year by 2030 (Beard in Beard et al. 1997).

What about the Trust Funds? The argument that there will not be a crisis rests on the belief that we will have $3 trillion in the Trust Funds by 2020. However, there is no $3 trillion. These are Trust Funds in name only, consisting of IOUs the government has written to itself. We cannot pay the deficits with money that does not exist (NCPA 1996; Beard et al. 1997). To pay the $3 trillion, the government must either cut spending by $3 trillion somewhere else; add $3 trillion to the national debt; or tax every family in America $42,857 (Bartlett 1997, 229; ES2000 1999).

No, It Is Not a Crisis

The widely reported forecast that the SS system will be "bankrupt" or "insolvent" by 2034 is misleading and exaggerated. What we are facing is a projected shortfall in thirty years, not an imminent crisis (Century Foundation 1999; Marmor and Mashaw in Beard et al. 1997). News reports and commentators have exaggerated both the size and imminence of the deficit and the difficulty of restoring balance (Ball and Bethell 1997, 278).

The SS trustee's projections are based on extremely pessimistic economic assumptions: that growth will average just 1.8 percent in the next twenty years, a lower rate than in any comparable period in U.S. history; that growth will slow even further in later years; that this labor shortage will not lead to a rapid growth in wages. These projections are genuinely a worse-case scenario (Baker 1998). The trustee's projections do not take into account the increases in productivity, which will allow each retiree to be supported by an even smaller number of workers. An increase of productivity of 2 to 3 percent, still less than the average of the past several years, would generate $1 trillion more for the Trust Funds. A full 1 percent increase in GDP would put the Trust Funds in surplus for the next seventy-five years (Rosenbaum 1999; Baker 1998). While the number of beneficiaries is expected to double, the number of workers paying taxes is expected to increase as well. Women are entering the workforce in large numbers; immigration continues; and the baby boomers have produced baby boomlets (Century Foundation 1998; Mashaw and Marmor in Beard et al. 1997).

The contributions of the baby boomers have led to the buildup of significant reserves in SS. The 1983 reform, which included payroll tax increases and taxes on SS income, has brought about $60 to $100 billion of surplus per year (Quinn and Mitchell 1996; Baker 1998; Francis 1998b), approximately 20 percent as much as its expenditure (Century Foundation 1998), and it is expected to accumulate to $3.3 trillion in 2020 before it starts to go down (Ball and Bethell 1997, 271; Gramlich 1998, 30; Mashaw and Marmor 1996). This surplus will generate interest revenue to help support the system when baby boomers retire. In the worse-case scenario, that surplus will last until 2034. Even after that, payroll taxes only, if not raised, would be able to pay 75 percent of the benefits, if the economy grows only 1.6 percent a year after inflation, far below average of past decades (Francis 1998c; Century Foundation 1998). If we set aside a portion of the federal budget surplus for the Trust Funds, as President Clinton proposed, and the economy performs better than the trustees predict, we would have a manageable problem or perhaps no problem at all (Rosenbaum 1999). Even in the worse case, there is no reason to be excessively pessimistic, given that relatively modest adjustments to the program from time to time can be made to correct the problem, such as small benefit cuts and tax increases (Bartlett 1997, 227).

Do We Need a Major Overhaul or Minor Adjustments?

The current SS system is not a funded retirement plan; it is a generationally transferred, pay-as-you-go system under which taxes collected from current workers are used to pay current retirees. When we make contributions to SS, we do not have a separate account for our money as in private pension plans. Instead, we have a promise by the nation's political system that we will get the benefits during retirement. The money will come from taxing the wages of our children and grandchildren (PNIS 1999). When it comes to reforming SS, there are basically two alternatives: a drastic reform that would replace the current pay-as-you-go system with a privately funded system or making minor adjustments to the current system.

Supporting Minor Adjustments

Since its enactment in the 1930s, SS has been one of America's most successful antipoverty programs, saving millions of elderly from living out their lives in poverty. The program has also provided important protection for families after the death or disability of the family's breadwinner (Century Foundation 1998; Gramlich 1998, 43–44; Ball and Bethell 1997, 276). In 1959, the poverty rate was over 35 percent for retirees. In 1979, it had dropped to 15.2 percent; since 1996, it has been below 11 percent (Clinton 1998). Without SS payments, 56 percent of those over 65 years of age would live below the poverty line (Mashaw and Marmor 1996).

Social Security has always paid its benefits on time; it has never been subject to episodes of fraud or mismanagement; and it operates efficiently with a very low administrative cost—less than 1 percent of the total revenue (Ball and Bethell 1997, 276; Wasow and Smith 1995; Kay 1997; Quinn and Mitchell 1996; Jaffe 1998). Social Security protection is portable, following the worker from job to job, and benefits are not threatened by the failure of a business or the decline of an industry (Ball and Bethell 1997, 288; Tobin 1988, 59). Social Security benefits are also real annuities, which ensures against outliving one's assets, with an added protection for surviving spouses (Gramlich 1998, 43–44; Hurd 1997, 219). Unlike most private pension programs, SS is inflation protected, that is, the benefits automatically retain their real value as consumer prices rise (Ball and Bethell 1997, 260; Gramlich 1998, 44). It is a nearly universal program; nearly 96 percent of the working population contribute to the system (Gramlich 1997, 48). Precisely because of the universality, dependability, effectiveness in achieving the goal, and cost-effectiveness, SS has been one of the most popular and supported government programs since its inception. Why overhaul the system that has worked so well for so many years? We can be prepared for future problems while preserving the basic structure of the current system. Many times in the past, problems have been solved through modest adjustments in the existing benefits and tax structure. Some of those minor adjustment options include: tax increases, raising the retirement age, increasing wage cap subject to taxation, reducing cost-of-living adjustments, taxing of benefits, extending coverage to currently excluded state and local employees, means-testing of benefits, using the federal budget surplus, and preventing the government from using the surplus to fund other programs (Francis 1998a; Mashaw and Marmor 1996; Hage 1995; Wasow and Smith 1995; Goldstein and Hager 1998).

Supporting a Major Overhaul

Social Security has been effective and successful in reducing poverty among the elderly, yet at a very high price. Social Security taxes have been raised from 2 percent when the program started in 1935 to 12.4 percent (in 1999) (Mitchell 1997). In 1994, for example, expenditures on the elderly (SS and Medicare) amounted to roughly a third of the entire federal budget (Marmor et al. 1997,

199). The lifetime value of SS and Medicare benefits approaches one-half million dollars for an average-income couple retiring in 1997 (Steuerle 1997, 243).

The current pay-as-you-go system makes it very difficult to achieve intergenerational distribution and equity, because this system is vulnerable to demographic changes. Thus far, several generations of beneficiaries have obtained excellent returns on their contributions (Tobin 1988, 53; Steuerle 1997, 245). The younger generation, including the baby boomers, however, face unfair prospects. They will receive a substantially reduced rate of return on their contributions to SS (Marmor et al. 1997, 199; Bosworth 1997, 175; Tobin 1988, 64; Gramlich 1998, 9). It is not fair for the younger generations to support their seniors with heavy, ever-increasing payroll taxes, and to get little or nothing of value in return (Tobin 1998, 47; Glassman 1997). At the same time, the success of private retirement funds since the late 1980s has increased the public's awareness of the high benefits of private retirement programs compared with SS (Bosworth 1997, 175).

Those who dismiss the projection of SS crisis claim that we have enough surplus to finance future retirees. Although these reserves are large and growing, they are not enough to solve the problem; they represent less than eighteen months of projected pay-outs (Quinn and Mitchell 1996). Moreover, the surplus is not set aside to grow in recognition of the future liabilities it must finance. The government has been borrowing the surplus to pay for other programs and to reduce the federal budget deficit. When the surplus is needed in the future with the retirement of baby boomers, the government will have to either borrow money from somewhere else or raise taxes (Bosworth 1990, 31).

The old pay-as-you-go system worked well for sixty-one years. However, demographics are changing, and the old way of financing the system is broken (Beard in Beard et al. 1997). Some of its design features reflect yesterday's needs and respond inadequately to today's social phenomena. There is no reason to expect that SS in the twenty-first century should look exactly like its mid-twentieth-century ancestor. Adaptability of goods and services is a hallmark of economic growth. Both public and private insurance should respond to evolving demands; they should not be isolated from competition from newer goods and services that society may come to deem more valuable (Steuerle 1997, 241; Beard in Beard et al. 1997). The future popularity of SS will depend on how well and promptly the system can adjust to modern demands and changes in our society (Gramlich 1998, 38).

We can no longer rely on minor adjustments; we need a drastic reform that would solve the problem once and for all. In the mid-1970s, SS was in crisis. Based on Ball's proposal of reform, the government raised taxes some, cut benefits some, and declared that SS was safe for seventy-five years. This prescription was off by forty-four years and more than $5 trillion. In 1980, SS was in crisis again. By 1983, taxes were raised again, and the retirement age went up. Social Security was supposed to be saved for seventy-five years, but the numbers were wrong again, by fifty-three years and more than $7 trillion (Beard in Beard et al. 1997). For how long can we botch up this fundamentally flawed system of SS? We need a major overhaul of the system that would solve the problem once and for all.

Minor Adjustment Options

The following sections summarize the supporting and opposing views on various adjustment options that are either currently proposed or have been implemented in the past.

Social Security Payroll Tax Increase

Supporting Tax Increase

The SS Administration projects that over the next seventy-five years, SS will slip out of balance by an amount equal to about 2 percent of the total taxable payroll. This means that an immediate increase in the payroll tax of about 2 percent (over the current 12.4 percent) would generate adequate funds to pay full benefits through 2073—a relatively simple fix (Lieberman 1997; Century Foundation 1998).

Social Security spending in the United States, although it appears to be substantial for some, amounts to less than 5 percent of the GDP, a relatively low ratio by world standards. According to the World Bank, the U.S. ratio of public pension spending to GDP is only 70 percent of the average for Organization of Economic Cooperation and Development (OECD) countries, less than half the share in countries such as Italy and Austria (Gramlich 1998, 69).

Opposing Tax Increase

When the system was founded, payroll taxes totaled 2 percent on the first $3,000 of annual earnings. Since then, the OASDI tax rate has been increased several times, reaching the current 12.4 percent in 1990, on covered earnings that are indexed annually and are capped at $72,600 (as of 1999). If the system operates on a pay-as-you-go basis, the intermediate projection suggests that the payroll tax rate would need to increase to about 16.5 percent in 2030, and it would have to rise further to about 18 percent in 2070 (Bosworth 1997, 160). Continually raising tax rates is a mathematical impossibility (Steuerle 1997, 245). Payroll taxes are now a heavier burden than income taxes for about 75 percent of taxpayers (Mitchell 1997). The payroll taxes are not progressive as income taxes are. The regressive nature of payroll tax hurts the working poor more than high-income earners (Zuckerman 1998). Increased payroll tax could raise business costs and prices, and that could make it harder for U.S. firms to compete internationally. Any tax on current income can act as a disincentive to save. Every time the public sector tax increases, there could be less incentive for people to save to provide pensions on their own (Gramlich 1998, 148–9).

Raising (or Removing) Income Cap Subject to Social Security Tax

Supporting Income Cap Raise (or Removal)

Historically, the most significant inequality in the payroll tax has been its imposition of a substantial tax burden on the working poor. Social Security tax is more regressive than the income tax in three ways. First, instead of graduated rates, it imposes a flat rate of 6.2 percent on both employees and employers. Second, it covers only wage income and completely exempts investment income, which goes mostly to the wealthy. Third, it applies only to the first $72,600 of an individual's income. The more you earn beyond that amount, the lower your effective payroll tax rate. As a result, almost 75 percent of U.S. families pay more in payroll taxes than they do in income taxes (Mitchell 1997; Editors of *The New Republic* 1-26-98). Since the 1980s, Republicans have used the populist rhetoric of tax relief to hide what has actually been a tax shift. Progressive income taxes have been cut, while regressive payroll taxes have been raised, and this shift has been a factor in the haggling problem of income inequality. We need to reform the payroll tax to generate a little more fairness in the tax burden. We can either make payroll taxes deductible from regular income taxes (as Senators Kennedy and Ashcroft propose) or remove (or significantly raise) the cap on wages subject to SS tax. Raising the cap alone would remove two-thirds of the projected actuarial shortfalls in SS (Graetz 1998, 96–100; Editors of *The New Republic* 1-26-98).

Opposing Income Cap Raise (or Removal)

Although payroll tax is not progressive, the SS benefit structure is highly redistributive. The redistributive structure of SS justifies the regressiveness of the tax contribution (Graetz 1988, 100). The size of the SS monthly check is linked to earnings during one's working career. However, the complex formulas are arranged to give proportionately more money to low-income workers. High-wage earners receive significantly lower pensions per dollar of payroll tax contributions than do their low-wage contemporaries (Tobin 1988, 60). The average person, who earned about $27,000 in 1997, will get a benefit at age 65 equal to about 42 percent of her earnings. The worker at the current maximum wage base of $72,600, however, will get a monthly check representing only 26 percent of his wages (PNIS 1999).

Imposing too much tax burden on high-income earners could weaken the middle-class political support upon which the stability of SS depends. A major source of middle-class discontent with SS now is that they believe they are paying more into the system than they can hope to receive as retirees. Removing or increasing the income cap would compound this problem by suddenly raising the FICA taxes of every individual taxpayer with an income above $72,600, not poor, certainly, but not rich, either (Editors of *The New Republic* 1-26-98).

Beginning in 1975, Congress recognized the unfairness of subjecting poor working families to a significant payroll tax burden and enacted an Earned Income Tax Credit (EITC) to poor families with dependent children (Graetz 1988, 97). This indirect tax relief already compensates the regressiveness in payroll tax.

Reducing Social Security Benefits

Supporting Benefit Cuts

The high inflation in the late 1970s and early 1980s rapidly increased SS benefits because of the automatic CPI adjustment of SS benefits. In addition, the faulty method of indexing the benefits calculation that was introduced during the Nixon administration resulted in overly generous benefits since the mid-1970s that far exceeded what most of the retirees paid in (Quinn and Mitchell 1996; Bartlett 1997, 226; Tobin 1988, 54).

The level of benefits retirees receive has risen much faster than the real wage increase of the workers expected to pay for the benefits (Kotlikoff 1998). From 1970 to 1980, while average monthly real wages declined by 7.4 percent, average monthly SS benefits rose in real terms by 37 percent (Tobin 1988, 49–50).

SS was never designed to stand alone as an income source for retirees. Rather, it is supposed to serve as a first tier, to be supplemented by employer pension benefits and personal savings (Quadagno and Quinn 1997, 141). Continuous payment of such generous benefits would put too much burden on the following generation and would discourage personal savings for all Americans, young and old.

Opposing Benefit Cuts

Cutting benefits across the board would be too harsh on the elderly, especially for whom SS is the major source of income. For more than 90 percent of the aged who receive benefits, SS provides more than 40 percent of their cash income (Gramlich 1998, 1); for 18 percent of them, it is their only source of income (Clinton 1998). The recent erosion of private pension coverage has greatly increased the reliance on SS for the retirement income for many Americans. In the 1980s, 45 percent of the retirement income for average wage earners came from SS; in 1996, that figure was 57 percent (AFL-CIO 1995). Only 43 percent of the retirees have private pensions that could supplement SS (Ball and Bethell 1997, 259). Proposals for reduction in SS benefits seem particularly limited because the benefit in the United States is already quite modest by international standards. For the worker earning half the average wage, the couple benefit is at the poverty threshold, and for a single person it is below poverty (Bosworth 1997, 161).

Means-Tested Benefit Cuts

Supporting Means-Testing

Another approach to cutting SS benefits is means-testing, that is, reducing benefits of high-income senior citizens who do not need SS (Gramlich 1998, 55). For instance, the Concord Coalition proposes reducing benefits for all families whose total incomes exceed $40,000 a year (Ball and Bethell 1997, 280). The higher-paid are more likely to have pension coverage and have set aside substantial savings on their own; reduction in SS benefits would not affect their means of subsistence as it would affect low-wage earners. The purpose of SS should be only to ensure against poverty, not to provide widespread protection against lost wages (Phillips in Kingson and Schulz 1997, 49). Means-testing would be a simple and easy way to reduce the projected SS shortfalls without burdening anyone with increased taxes or endangering anyone to fall below the poverty level.

Opposing Means-Testing

SS is a pension program, not a welfare program. As people pay into it during their working lives, they earn a right to something in return, just as they expect interest payments when they buy government bonds. Means-testing ignores the logic behind mandating participation in an SS program. If individuals are mandated to participate in a retirement scheme, then an adequate amount of retirement benefits should be made available to them (Steuerle 1997, 256; Ball and Bethell 1997, 280).

From the beginning, individual equity has been an important part of SS: The higher one's past wages have been, the higher the benefit, because the system focuses on making up for wage loss. In welfare, on the contrary, payments ordinarily decrease as the recipients' wages rise, because the program focuses on meeting the basic needs. Means-testing would turn SS into a welfare system for the poor (Cohen in Kingson and Schulz 1997, 50; Ball and Bethell 1997, 264).

Most people approve of SS and are willing to pay SS taxes precisely because SS benefits are not means-tested. The goal of SS is not only to protect their parents and grandparents today but also to build a foundation for themselves and their families tomorrow. SS must be maintained in such a way that even the well-off should have reasonable returns on their SS investment (Kingston and Schulz 1997). If this goal is not met, political support for SS would be undermined, ultimately placing low- and moderate-income Americans at greater economic risks (Kingson and Schulz 1997, 41). The existing system is already so redistributive that any effort to further reduce benefits among high-wage workers would create widespread disaffection, and thus it would give high-income workers a very powerful incentive to get out of SS (Bosworth 1997, 161; Kingson and Schulz 1997, 42–50; Ball and Bethell 1997, 280).

Means-testing applies unfairly against those who saved a lot for their own retirement, have private pension, work part-time after retirement, and those who retire late to save more money (Gramlich 1998, 55). Workers would be encouraged to consume during their working years, because any saving for retirement would be offset by reduced SS benefits (Bosworth 1997, 161). As the SS problem increases, the nation would want to encourage people to work longer and save more. What sense does it make to penalize those who have engaged in these desirable behaviors? (Gramlich 1998, 55). Its message to young people is "If you save and prudently attain a healthy retirement income on your own, you will be penalized—your SS benefits will be cut" (Ball and Bethell 1997, 280).

Reduce Cost-of-Living Adjustments (COLA)

Supporting Reduction in COLA

One way of cutting benefits is to reduce the indexation of SS benefits for inflation. The SS reform commission suggested that the automatic cost-of-living adjustment over the years has overstated inflation and thus increased benefits substantially. There has been an upward bias in the consumer price index (CPI) of about 1.1 percentage points a year. As a result, SS benefits generally rose more than they would have if dictated by price increase alone (Gramlich 1998, 54; Century Foundation 1998; Miller 1998). Were the indexation formula immediately adjusted downward by this amount, roughly half of the actuarial deficit could be eliminated (Gramlich 1998, 53). The Bureau of Labor Statistics announced in 1996 that it is putting in place measures that are expected to decrease the CPI by 0.21 percent per year; this change will take care of an estimated 14 percent of the shortfall (Century Foundation 1998).

Opposing Reduction in COLA

Everybody agrees that there should be inflation protection for retirees, that is, the benefits should be adjusted to keep up with the growth of prices.

Eliminating or significantly paring cost-of-living adjustments would have the harshest impact on those for whom the system was built in the first place—those who are old and in need of income (Steuerle 1997, 255). The longer people live, the more likely they are to deplete whatever personal savings they may have accumulated, yet their expenses continue to rise, particularly in health care (Ball and Bethell 1997, 265–6).

SS is the nation's most important hedge against inflation. SS is virtually the only pension program in the United States with automatic inflation protection (Gramlich 1998, 2). Private pensions are rarely increased for inflation. Therefore, the longer people live, the more dependent they become on SS. There are many widows over the age of 80 who have outlived their savings and whose pensions have dwindled with time and inflation. SS is their only defense against destitution (PNIS 1999).

Increase of Retirement Age

Supporting Retirement Age Increase

Another approach to solving the SS problem is to raise the retirement age, which is 65 as of 1999 but already legislated to rise to 67 incrementally starting in 2002. Future workers would be living longer into their retirement years, and therefore it is not unreasonable to make them pay into the Trust Funds for more years (Gramlich 1998, 56). When SS was set up in 1935 with an eligibility age of 65, life expectancy was 61 years. In 1999, life expectancy is 76 years and rising. Life expectancy is expected to rise by an additional 10 to 20 percent by 2025 (Bartlett in Bosworth 1997, 161). However, most Americans are retiring at younger and younger ages. The average age for receiving benefits declined from 69 in 1950 to 64 in 1990 (Bosworth 1997, 161). In 1950, nearly half of all American men aged 65 and over were in the labor force: In 1997, fewer than one in six were (Quadagno and Quinn 1997, 128).

When people live longer, and they are healthier than previous generations, they should work longer. Working longer will allow them to save more for their retirement and depend less on SS.

Opposing Retirement Age Increase

While many workers arrive at age 65 in good health and are physically able to work a few more years, not all are. There are still coal miners and other workers in physically demanding jobs. For them, the lengthened work careers could be a real imposition. In general, much of the burden of the retirement age increase would fall on the lower-income and blue-collar workers who typically start working at an early age, work in physically strenuous occupations, and cannot afford to save much for retirement on their own (Kijakazi and Greenstein 1998; Ball and Bethell 1997, 272; Sammartino in Kingson and Schulz 1997, 58). In addition, low-income people die at an earlier age than the better-off, thus receiving less lifetime benefits. The mortality rate among the poorest 10 percent of Americans is seven times that of the top 10 percent (Smith in Dentzer 1997). Increasing the retirement age would thus be a double blow for low-income people (Dentzer 1997). Moreover, economists are not sure to what extent jobs will be available for those who want to postpone their retirement. Extending the retirement age might also create job shortage problems for the younger generation (Ball and Bethell 1997, 272).

Use of the Federal Budget Surplus

Supporting the Use of the Federal Budget Surplus

To solve the projected insolvency problem of SS, President Clinton proposed to transfer 62 percent of the projected budget surpluses (estimated to be $4.5 trillion over the next fifteen years), which would be more than $2.7 trillion, to SS (Clinton 1999). This would extend the solvency of the funds to 2055 without lowering benefits or raising taxes (Zuckerman 1999; Crutsinger 1999).

Opposing the Use of the Federal Budget Surplus

The idea of relying on the federal surplus to pay for SS has major flaws. First, this plan relies on the expected budget surplus in the next fifteen years. What if we do not continue to have the surplus after 1998, the first year with federal budget surplus in thirty years, due to unfavorable economic situations or some catastrophic political event, such as war. Already, a great deal of the surplus was used to finance the bombing in Yugoslavia in 1999. Second, $2.3 trillion of the $2.8 trillion President Clinton wants to set aside for SS is money already earmarked for SS. The excess in SS collections (the Trust Funds) would be about $2.3 trillion if the government had not diverted it to finance other government programs and to reduce federal budget deficits (Crutsinger 1999). In fact, the federal budget surplus in 1998 was created largely because the government borrowed money from the SS Trust Funds. That money rightfully belongs to SS, and it should not have been taken out of Trust Funds from the beginning. The issue is not whether this surplus should be used to support SS; the government must pay back what it owes to the SS Trust Funds.

Prevention of Social Security Surplus Diversion

Prevent Surplus Diversion

The contributions of baby boomers have led to significant build up of SS reserves, and this surplus will continue to build until baby boomers begin to retire in about 2010. According to the SS Administration, the revenue has exceeded expenditure by about $60 billion per year, and the reserves would build to $3.3 trillion by 2020 before they start to go down (Ball and Bethell 1997, 271; Quinn and Mitchell 1996). However, this Trust Fund surplus has been diverted to support various government programs and to reduce the federal budget deficit. The use of Trust Funds was an especially attractive option for the Reagan and Bush administrations, because it allowed them to increase military spending without increasing income tax (Bosworth 1997, 32–3).

In order to protect the SS Trust Funds, we need to restore a complete separation of the SS Trust Funds from the unified federal budget (AFL-CIO 1995). Preventing the surplus from being used by the government would greatly reduce the anticipated SS shortfall without raising taxes (Nordhaus 1990, 179).

Allow Surplus Diversion

There is nothing wrong with the government borrowing from the SS surplus to pay for other programs. That IOU earns interest at the same rate as real Treasury bonds sold to the public (Crutsinger 1999) and therefore brings higher returns back to the Trust Funds. In addition, reducing the national debt will help the economy grow, and a healthier economy will in turn help support government entitlement programs including SS (Republican party's position in CNN News 4-23-99). Thanks to the SS surplus, for the first time in thirty years, we achieved a federal budget surplus in 1998. If the economy continues to grow, and the government can pay the money back with interest, it would increase the reserve and benefit all Americans (Editors of *The Nation* 6-1-99).

Privatizing Social Security as a Major Reform Option

A growing number of lawmakers have proposed privatizing SS to solve the problems of the current SS system. Privatizing means transforming SS from the current pay-as-you-go scheme into a funded system of individual savings. New generation workers would start their own pension fund to finance their retirement; they would own and manage their fund; and any amount not used to pay for their retirement would be passed on to their heirs (Lilley 1999). The fund would grow during the participant's working career, not only by additional contributions but also by compound interest. At the time of retirement, this fund would be converted actuarially into an indexed annuity that would last for the life of the participant (Tobin 1988, 65).

Chile's privatized plan, which started in 1981, requires workers to put 10 percent or more of their wages into an individual retirement account, which is not taxed until withdrawal. The amount of pension due on retirement depends on the amount a worker accumulates, along with the investment returns earned by one of fourteen private pension fund companies the worker selects to manage the account. The portfolios are regulated and the returns are monitored by the government (Krauss 1998).

Before discussing whether to privatize SS, it is necessary to understand different types of privatization. The strengths and weaknesses of privatizing SS depend on whether the savings plan is intended to supplement or to substitute SS; if it is to substitute SS, whether in whole or in part; whether privatization should be mandatory or voluntary; and whether the individual accounts should be managed by individuals or the government.

Full versus Partial Privatization

Supporting Full Privatization

Under the full privatization plan, SS taxes would be eliminated and workers would instead deposit the money into private accounts earning market-rate interest. Chile has implemented this system since 1981, and it has worked successfully. There are no payroll taxes in Chile, only private retirement plans based on joint employer-employee contributions (Rotella 1998). This idea of full privatization is not new even in the United States. It is similar to the Thrift Savings Plan (TSP) available for federal employees. Federal employees can opt out of SS and invest the money in the TSP that is managed by the Federal Retirement Thrift Investment Board, a board of professional appointees. This plan has worked effectively for many federal employees (Weaver 1998; Greenstein 1999).

A partially privatized system (allowing only a portion of SS tax to be privatized) will leave us with two retirement systems—one defined-benefit, pay-as-you-go plan, and the other, a defined-contribution funded plan (individual account)—with extra administrative costs, because it will involve managing a large number of extremely small retirement accounts. The fixed transaction costs of transmitting and recording contributions to these accounts, sending annual reports to the accounts' owners and disbursing payment could wipe out much of the returns on private savings. Partial privatization will also leave the nonprivatized portion of SS vulnerable, because high-income earners who can accrue a higher rate of return in private accounts would try to opt out of SS as much as possible. For these reasons, if privatizing a dollar of the retirement portion of SS makes sense, privatizing all of it makes more sense (Kotlikoff 1998).

Supporting Partial Privatization

Social Security is not just a retirement pension program; it is a social insurance program, which supports disabled workers, survivors of deceased workers, and their spouses and dependent children, as well as an income redistribution program. The full privatization of SS will destroy the social insurance and in-come distribution elements of SS. Any effort to privatize SS must maintain an adequate level of defined benefit structure to support the social insurance func-tion while allowing a portion of the defined contribution to be invested in the private sector. The creation of personal accounts can thus be accepted only if it is added as a second tier to the current pay-as-you-go system (Beard in Beard et al. 1997). Partial privatization would create a double-deck system, with a lower deck focusing on income adequacy and income redistribution, and an upper deck generating benefits directly related to contribution (Quinn and Mitchell 1996). The SS system in the United Kingdom consists of such two tiers, a flat-rate basic state pension and an earnings-related pension based on contribution (CBPP 1999).

Substitutive versus Supplementary Personal Accounts

Under the partial privatization plan, individual pension accounts can be fi-nanced either by diverting a portion of the current payroll tax (substitutive) or by an additional payroll tax (supplementary).

Supporting Substitutive Personal Accounts

Personal accounts must be created with a portion of the existing payroll taxes. The current payroll tax of 12.4 percent is already high enough. Additional taxes would place too much burden on the lower-income workers who do not have much to save after taxes. Three plans—Senators Breaux and Gregg; Representa-tives Kolbe and Stenholm; and Senators Moynihan, Kerrey, and Simpson—propose a 2 percentage point deduction from the 12.4 percent payroll tax, which can be diverted to either mandatory or voluntary personal savings accounts (Goldstein and Hager 1998; Ball and Bethell 1997, 282; Kijakazi and Green-stein 1998; Allen 1999). Another approach, advocated by a group within the SS Advisory Council of 1994–1996 proposes a compulsory private savings account supported by 5 percentage points of the current 12.4 SS tax rate (Ball and Bethell 1997, 282; Mashaw and Marmor 1996).

Supporting Supplementary Personal Accounts

Instead of raising payroll taxes to reduce the projected SS deficit, workers can contribute the additional money to their personal accounts. This contribution would thus be on top of the existing 12.4 percent of payroll tax (Gramlich 1998, 64; 1997, 154; Orszag 1999b). The substitutive plan would significantly reduce the SS reserves that are needed to pay for the current retirees, thus it would exacerbate the future insolvency problem. With the supplementary plan, the existing social insurance function of SS would remain intact, while solving the problem of insolvency. People would be required to make new savings invested in private markets, thus increasing overall national savings and leading to a stronger economy (Gramlich 1998, 7, 66).

This plan would be particularly ideal for baby boomers, who would pay more of the costs of their retirement in their own account, instead of increasing the contribution rates for the smaller generation that follows. With supplementary accounts, the magnitude of the added burden on future workers would be greatly reduced (Bosworth 1997, 165). Even a modest contribution, if put into effect soon enough, would build a large fund that, when coupled with market rate of return, would completely eliminate the long-term deficit (Ball and Bethell 1997, 271–2).

Mandatory versus Voluntary Personal Retirement Accounts

If the privatization of SS were allowed, should it be on a voluntary basis or should it be mandated?

Supporting Voluntary Personal Accounts

In case of full privatization, participants must be given an option to opt out of privatization, that is, it must allow people to choose whether they wish to stay with the old system or switch to a personal retirement account. No one should be forced to change to private savings when he feels insecure about it, just as much as no one should be forced to remain in a pay-as-you-go system when she thinks she could do better on her own (Fargo in PNIS 1998; NCPA 1996).

Even in the case of partial privatization, participants must be given an option to divert part of SS taxes and decide how much they should invest in their pension account. It would always be possible to induce people to save voluntarily on top of SS, carefully warning them of their reduced future benefits in case they do not save (Gramlich 1998, 67), or to encourage supplementary protection through tax incentives for private pensions and individual savings (Ball and Bethell 1997, 281). In the polls, 56 percent of Americans favored voluntary SS, although 75 percent said they would participate anyway (Tobin 1988, 58).

The fraction of a person's income that is reasonable for him or her to set aside for retirement depends on that person's circumstances and lifestyle. The most obvious example is a person with AIDS who has a short life expectancy and limited financial means, yet would be required to use a significant fraction of his or her earnings to accumulate what is almost certain to prove a worthless asset. Individuals can best judge for themselves how to use their own resources (Friedman 1999).

Supporting Mandatory Personal Accounts

SS is highly redistributive; that is, high-income workers get lower returns on their contributions, and low-income earners get higher returns. If people were given the option to leave the system, the majority of the high-income workers would opt out of SS, leaving less funds to support low-income workers. Rather than being a universal program that covers all Americans, SS would gradually turn into a welfare program covering only low-wage workers, and providing higher cost of social insurance for these workers. It would also become more vulnerable politically, because high-income workers would have less reason to support it (Gramlich 1998, 21).

. A privatized system should require a mandatory contribution to ensure that those opting out of SS are actually saving money for their retirement (NCPA 1996). A voluntary system would allow the improvident to escape their share of paying for their own retirement needs, leaving the community as a whole to pay for them through some safety-net program like Supplemental Security Income (SSI) (Ball and Bethell 1997, 266). Some individuals are too shortsighted to provide for their own retirement. A voluntary system might encourage some lower-income individuals to make no provision for their old age deliberately, knowing that they would receive the means-tested amount (Friedman 1999).

Centralized versus Decentralized Management of Personal Accounts

Private pension funds, created under a privatized system, can be managed either by individuals (decentralized) or by the government (centralized).

Supporting Decentralized Management

Under the decentralized plan, individuals choose their own private financial providers and invest in a wide range of assets, like the current IRA (CBPP 1999). This approach gives individuals more control over their fund and more investment options to choose from. Depending on age, income level, and lifestyle, individuals can choose high-risk, high-return investment options to increase their fund or low-risk, low-return options for higher safety.

Supporting Centralized Management

Personal management of retirement accounts can be too risky. Most people have no experience in investing and have no time to acquire expertise in investing (Ball and Bethell 1997, 287). For the majority of people, SS must remain as the main source of old-age income that bears as little market risk as possible (Mashaw and Marmor 1996). If we allow privatization, either full or partial, the individual accounts must be centrally managed by the government to reduce risks. The centralized plan for individual accounts provides individuals with investment options that are limited to a few broadly diversified index funds that are managed either by the government or by government-appointed investors (CBPP 1999). Individuals would have constrained investment choices on how these funds were to be invested, ranging from a portfolio consisting entirely of bond index funds to equity index funds (Gramlich 1998, 83–84). This public management of the individual accounts simplifies administration costs and reduces the risk that the accounts will be misinvested (Gramlich 1998, 65; Orszag 1999b).

Privatization of Social Security: Is It a Good Idea or a Bad Idea?

The following sections discuss the supporting and opposing views of privatizing SS.

Many Other Countries Have Successfully Privatized Their Pension Systems. Why Can't We?

Supporting Privatization

Privatized pension is not a laboratory concept, it is a reality in many different countries of the world, and its results have been very positive (Bustamante in Rotella 1998). Chile was the first nation in the Western Hemisphere to adopt a state-run pension system in 1929, and the first nation in the world to completely privatize it in 1981. Its plan requires workers to pay 10 percent of their income a year into a private retirement account of their choice, which they own and control (Bishop 1998). More than 90 percent of workers participate in the system (Mitchell 1997). Since 1988, British workers have been allowed to opt out of their public pension system and invest in individual pension accounts; more than 70 percent of British workers have chosen the private system (NCPA 1996).

In addition to Chile and Great Britain, either fully or partially privatized systems exist or are being implemented in Australia, Singapore, Mexico, Peru,

Italy, Colombia, Sweden, Uruguay, Malaysia, El Salvador, Argentina, and Bo-
livia (Mitchell 1997). Twelve of the fifteen countries in the European Union
have some combination of a flat benefit and an earned-right system (Gramlich
1998, 74). The World Bank, not normally considered a hotbed of free-market
thought, endorsed a privatized pension system (Mitchell 1997).

Opposing Privatization

The situation that led to privatization in Chile and many other countries is not
comparable to that of the United States. Chile's old system, like many other
Latin state-run pension systems, was an administrative disaster. Its bureaucracies had been pillaged and mismanaged to the point of collapse; it was
underfunded and failed to provide adequate coverage to most workers. Our system, by contrast, is well managed, clean, and nearly universal; it is efficient,
cost-effective, reliable, and free of mismanagement or abuse. In the United
States, privatization is far too radical a cure for what is essentially a modest actuarial shortfall. The political and economic costs of privatizing the system would
outweigh the benefits we can expect from privatization (Rotella 1998; Kay
1997).
    Privatization in other countries, including Chile, has not been in effect
long enough to see its full impact; it is too early to judge privatization efforts in
other countries until the system has matured (PNIS 1998). Already, privatization in other countries has revealed many problems. In Chile, up to 20 percent
of workers' contributions go to middlemen as management fees; only a little
over half of Chilean workers make regular contributions, and the system provides little progressive redistribution of income. The reason why some consider
Chile's system a success is because of the fortuitous timing. Unusually high rates
of return in both stocks and bonds in the 1980s have exaggerated its long-term
success. The 12.7 percent average return between 1982 and 1994 coincided
with boom years in Chile's economy complemented by the government's high
borrowing costs (Kay 1997). The popularity of Chile's system quickly dwindled
when its average return declined to a 2.5 percent loss in 1995, followed by modest gains of 3.5 percent in 1996 and 4.7 percent in 1997 (Krauss 1998).

Privatization Provides Greater
Control over Our Retirement Plans

Supporting Privatization

One of the advantages of privatizing SS is that it gives us the option to own and
manage part (or all) of our SS tax, and in so doing, accumulate a real asset, in
our own name, that can be transmitted to our children upon our death (Weaver

1998, Smith 1998). Under the current pay-as-you-go system, there is no SS account with our name on it, accumulating contributions and adding interest to create our benefits (Wasow and Smith 1995). There is no guarantee that we will receive what we pay into the system plus interest when we retire (Longman 1998).

Many Americans do not trust the government and would prefer market risks to political risks (Mashaw and Marmor 1996). A savings account bearing our name would make us feel more secure as opposed to SS in which the rules about contributions and benefits change precariously and are all quite mysterious to average individuals (Ball and Bethell 1997, 281; Mashaw and Marmor 1996). Owning personal pension accounts would give us a fair and clear idea of our individual contributions and benefit rights. It might even improve financial literacy for many Americans, generating more serious thought about retirement planning, and thereby increasing personal saving rates (Tobin 1998, 67; Quinn and Mitchell 1996).

Watching annual savings grow in a pension fund reconnects basic American values of hard work, taking care of one's family, saving for one's retirement and having the chance to pass an inheritance on to one's children to offer them financial independence and an improved standard of living (ES2000 1999). Under the privatized system, all workers, rich and poor alike, would have the opportunity to accumulate real wealth—shielded from political manipulation—and to build estates with which to better their lives and the lives of their children (Weaver 1998).

Opposing Privatization

Ever since it was created in the 1930s, SS has maintained its principal goal—keeping elderly retirees and the disabled (and their dependents) out of poverty. It has been running for more than sixty years without ever missing a payment. Our SS avoids inflation risks, bankruptcy risks, and market risks (Mashaw and Marmor 1996; Corn 1998). No private market investment provides SS's risk-free protection against inflation or market fluctuation (Century Foundation 1999). SS provides its payout in the form of a real valued annuity, a payment that continues for the life of the worker, which is costly in the private market (Baker 1997; AARP 1999). On the contrary, benefits from private accounts could vary depending on investment behavior, stock market performance, economy, and many other factors (Kijakazi and Greenstein 1998). One may own a personal account under the privatized system, yet would not have the risk-free, inflation-adjusted, guaranteed annuity income. With corporate downsizing and the loss of corporate pensions and downward wage pressure for many people, SS is the only reliable, guaranteed retirement income. SS should be strengthened with its current structure, rather than dismantled by privatization (Corn 1998).

With Privatization, We Can Get Higher Rates of Return on Our Investment

Supporting Privatization

Another attraction of privatizing SS is the potential of greater return on stocks compared with SS. If Americans were allowed to direct their payroll taxes into safe investment accounts similar to 401(k) plans, or even super safe Treasury bills, they would accumulate far more money in savings for their retirement than they would receive from SS (Shapiro and Wildavsky 1998; Beach and Davis 1998). Under the current system, those who were born after 1960 would get an annual investment return of roughly 2 percent, adjusted for inflation, on the taxes they pay into SS (Hage 1995). Those born in the early 1970s would average about a 1 percent real rate of return, and those born after that would average essentially a zero rate of return. These internal rates of return would be even lower if tax increases or benefit cuts are added (Kotlikoff 1998).

On the other hand, even after adjusting for inflation, annual stock market returns over the past seventy years have averaged 7 percent (Mitchell 1997), and over the past forty years, more than 8 percent (Gergen 1998). Some members of the SS Advisory Council who support privatization expect a total annual return to stockholders of 7 percent over the next seventy-five years (Century Foundation 1999). It is estimated that, with compound interest for forty years, retirement income for low-income workers in the private plan will be three times greater—and for middle-income workers, five times greater—than what they would get under SS (Mitchell 1997). The Chilean funds have grown rapidly and had delivered a stunning 12 percent average annual return in the first fifteen years since privatization started in 1981 (Krauss 1998; Gramlich 1998, 80). The annual returns for private retirement accounts in Australia and Great Britain have been between 5 and 10 percent (Mitchell 1998b).

The prospect of receiving worse than market-rate return is the major reason why SS is seen as an unattractive form of investment for many young workers. They argue that they could do better making their own investment. It is not fair to mandate people to contribute their retirement savings to accounts that fare much worse than available market rates (Gramlich 1998, 38; Ball and Bethell 1997, 274).

Opposing Privatization

The private savings plan would not always generate a higher retirement income than the present SS system (Baker 1997). The projections for the stock market are plainly inconsistent and unpredictable. Over the last seventy years, the average real return for stockholders was close to 7 percent, but that reflected an economic growth rate of approximately 3.5 percent. If, as the trustees project, economic growth over the next seventy-five years averages less than 1.5 percent—a decline of more than 2 percentage points—stock price growth will also decline by roughly 2 percentage points (Baker 1997; PNIS 1998). If the market continues to yield 7 percent returns for the next seventy-five years, as some predict, the economy will have grown much faster than 1.5 percent annually, and SS will be so flush with increased FICA contribution that there will be no need to fix the system (Century Foundation 1999).

Advocates of privatization perceive SS in the context of savings plans and pension plans. It is neither. Most rate-of-return or money's worth arguments are fundamentally flawed because they fail to consider the insurance aspects of the SS program. Social Security is a system of social insurance, an intergenerational compact. Unlike pension plans or private investments, personal returns on investment are not the only consideration (PNIS 1998).

Moreover, the higher rate-of-return argument of privatization does not include the high management fees people must pay to have their account managed under the privatized system, and the cost of converting their investment to annuities on retirement, which on average, costs about 20 percent of the account balance (Francis 1998a).

Administrative Costs Are Too High under a Privatized System

Opposing Privatization

Privately managed individual accounts necessarily incur huge administrative and management fees (Baker in Francis 1998d). Under the name of privatization, a chunk of our payroll taxes would be channeled to financial middlemen who would get their hands on $150 billion of new money each year with 130 million new accounts (Lieberman 1997). Stock brokers, insurance companies, and other financial advisors usually charge their customers an average of 1 to 2 percent a year on the value of the money they hold (Baker 1998). In addition, there are substantial management fees that could be charged for overseeing millions of small accounts (Lieberman 1997). The SS Advisory Council estimates that over a forty-year working career, administrative costs would consume an average of approximately 20 percent of the funds in private accounts; including the annuity cost, an additional 5 to 10 percent (Greenstein 1999; Kijakazi and Greenstein 1998; Gramlich 1998, 62).

A study of privately managed individual retirement accounts in the United Kingdom shows that more than 40 percent of their value is consumed by administrative fees and other related costs. It involves 25 percent of accumulation costs (costs for administration and fund management); 15 percent of alteration costs (the additional costs incurred when an account holder fails to contribute consistently to a single financial provider, due to job changes or changes of financial providers); and 10 percent of annuity costs (cost of changing the fund to an annuity that would last one's lifetime) (Orszag 1999a; CBPP 1999). The administrative costs of Chile's system (not including annuity costs) are at least

15 percent—"at least" because, according to some studies, they are considerably higher (Diamond and Myers in Ball and Bethell 1997, 286). Even when Chile's private system achieved an impressive average return on investment of 12.7 percent between 1982 and 1994, after paying commissions and administrative costs, it was only 7.4 percent (Kay 1997; Lieberman 1997). Actually, Chileans have become highly critical of privatization since 1994, when returns from a poor stock market dropped significantly while charges levied by the fund-management companies have failed to come down (Bishop 1998).

In comparison, there is no doubt that the current SS program provides exceptional money's worth. Social Security administrative expenses absorb less than one percent of the total fund (Chen and Goss 1997, 87–88; Ball and Bethell 1997, 286).

In addition, private pension funds engage in costly sales campaigns to capture members from each other. They pay insurance agents and brokers to solicit business; they pay an enormous amount in advertising and marketing. Many executives and brokers in the financial industry receive huge salaries. Privatization would add these expenses, which are currently absent from the SS system (Kijakazi and Greenstein 1998; Baker 1998; Kay 1997; Rotella 1998).

The *Wall Street Journal* called privatizing SS "the biggest bonanza in the history of the mutual fund industry." By diverting only 2 percent of payroll taxes from SS into private accounts, the government could shunt $60 billion a year into the coffers of investment funds, banks, and insurance companies. That is the reason why these business and finance industries are pouring money into right-wing think tank efforts, lobbying efforts, and publicity aimed at putting privatization on the national agenda (Dreyfuss 1996).

Supporting Privatization

A privatized system can be made simple to administer. The cost of administration depends on the structure of individual accounts. Some proposals for individual accounts seek to take advantage aggressively of potential economies of scale through centralized management, that is, offering individual accounts only through the government-controlled independent board of investors and limiting the investment options to only a few choices. The Thrift Savings Plan (TSP) available for federal employees is an example of such a centralized plan (Orszag 1999a). The overhead cost of this plan is just 0.06 percent (Quinn 1998). There are other exceptional funds, such as the nonprofit Teachers Insurance and Annuity Association College Retirement Equities Fund (TIAA-CREF), whose administration expenses are considerably lower than many expect with privatization. It is possible that strict government regulation could push the administrative costs down (Baker 1997). Even with the fully decentralized private account, such as IRAs currently available to many Americans, their market-rate returns of investment, after paying management fees, have been consistently higher than Treasury bonds (Baker 1997).

The cost of annuitizing pension savings could be reduced if conversion could take place under government-established rules, which select insurance companies through competitive bidding. In being forced to bid for the right to annuitize a cohort's account balance, the insurance industry would end up providing this service at the lowest possible price (Kotlikoff 1998).

Private Management of Retirement Funds Is Too Risky

Opposing Privatization

Although private stocks, on average, have outperformed bonds in the postwar periods, there is no guarantee that the future will repeat the past (Quinn and Mitchell 1996; Baker 1998; Zuckerman 1998). The history of capitalism has shown that markets are highly volatile. Since the late 1980s, the market has performed exceptionally well. Using market performance for a period that includes these years to predict future performance may generate estimates of average return for individual accounts that prove to be too high (Kijakazi and Greenstein 1998). The long bull market, moreover, has made many forget the risks of market downturns and instead resentfully count returns they would be getting if their hefty payroll taxes were instead invested in stocks (Miller 1998). Growth of the economy could slow down in coming decades as fewer young people enter the workforce and the numerous baby boomers retire (Baker 1998; Feldmann 1998).

Although stocks have produced an average of 8 percent returns during the past forty years, that is only an average. Market averages are not the same as individual returns. In real life, average means returns are higher in some years, and lower in other years; some get less than average returns, while others get more than average; and some stocks perform higher than average, while others lower (Francis 1998d). In 1997, the average fund was down about 5 percent—not bad, compared with some other countries. In the same year, Chile's stock market has lost more than 25 percent in dollar terms, largely in response to faltering exports to Asia and falling copper prices tied to Japan's economic slowdown (Krauss 1998). Some individuals will retire at a point where the market has just taken a sharp downturn. People who retire during the downturn and finance retirement from stock sales would have a return well below the market average. Moreover, some individuals, with bad judgment or bad luck, may end up with stocks that significantly underperform in the market (Baker 1997). Even if we do not expect another Great Depression, the events of October 1987 should remind us that the stock market can make quite precipitous corrections (Mashaw and Marmor 1996).

Who must bear the ultimate risk of poor investment returns, either because an individual chose or because the economy as a whole performed poorly?

Most likely, the federal government would have to bail out millions of people at taxpayers' expense (Zuckerman 1998; Ball and Bethell 1997, 286).

Those who do well in the stock market would be mainly the ones who are already well insulated against the financial vagaries of retirement (Editors, *The Nation* 6-1-98). Market volatility might be acceptable to the well-to-do, but it is potentially catastrophic to retirement incomes of the majority of low- and middle-income people who have few financial assets other than SS (Zuckerman 1998; Ball and Bethell 1997, 287). The lower one's earnings over a lifetime and the more SS pensions matter to one's retirement security, the less likely one would prefer having that protection subject to market risks (Mashaw and Marmor 1996).

Supporting Privatization

It is possible to make the privatized system safer than opponents claim. For those who are inexperienced in investing, or who do not wish to have their retirement funds subject to market risks, we can create a centralized management system, which is made of the government-controlled independent board of investors. Under this system, investment options would be limited to choices among several diversified, conservative portfolios; investors would be guaranteed to receive at least average market-rate returns (Feldmann 1998; Mitchell 1997; NCPA 1996). The Thrift Savings Plan (TSP), available to federal employees as an alternative to SS, is an example of such a system. It is a centrally managed system run by the Federal Retirement Thrift Investment Board, a board of professional appointees nominated by the executive branch and approved by Congress (Greenstein 1999; Weaver 1998; Mitchell 1997).

The truth about stocks is that while in the short term they are risky, in the long term they are even less risky than bonds or Treasury bills. Since 1926, stock returns have been negative in twenty out of seventy-one years. However, over every fifteen-year period between 1926 and 1996, stocks produced only positive returns, and the highest average annual real return was 12.6 percent, and the lowest was 1.0 percent. In other words, never in history have U.S. stocks failed to beat inflation by at least a full point over a twenty-year stretch (Glassman 1997).

Social Security Is More Than Just Retirement Savings: It Is a Social Insurance Program

Opposing Privatization

SS is not just retirement savings: SS is also a disability and life insurance policy. It pays benefits to disabled workers and their families, and survivors' benefits to the families of workers who have died (Gramlich 1998, 38; AARP 1999; Clinton 1998). About 30 percent of beneficiaries are disabled workers, widows, and the children of deceased workers (Shapiro and Wildavsky 1998; Mashaw and Marmor 1996). This is why we have to act with care when we make needed repairs to the program (Clinton 1998).

Because of its insurance function, SS must pool risks. Families pooled together are protected by paying for only the average risk (Ball and Bethell 1997, 276; AARP 1999). This binding together of the interests of low and high earners in a common enterprise, before they know who will need help, is the essence of social insurance (Mashaw and Marmor 1996). Privatization will convert the current insurance form of SS to an every-man-for-himself arrangement of private accounts that will make retirement income dependent on how much and how well individuals invest (Lieberman 1997).

Most individuals don't know how long they will live, how long their spouses will live, and how much resources their family will need in retirement years. Sometimes it makes sense to have the government help with such decisions, by forcing workers to put aside a certain amount while working, and by providing benefits for as long as the worker, or the worker's family, lives (Gramlich 1998, 21; Thompson and Upp 1997, 4). Social Security represents our commitment to share risks and to assure basic economic security for every member of our society (Bradley in Kingson and Schulz 1997, 55–6); it is our strongest expression of community solidarity. Through SS, we recognize that "we are all in this together," with everyone sharing responsibility, not only for our families and retirement but also for the protection of everyone else in our society, present and future (Ball and Bethell 1997, 277–8).

Opposing Privatization

Yes, SS has other functions. However, as an investment to create a retirement nest egg, which is the way most Americans see it, SS has become an outright rip-off (Glassman 1997). For the majority of Americans, who rely on SS as their major source of retirement income, it is unfair to force them to invest their retirement money in such low-return options as SS. If social insurance is the major concern, part of the required SS contribution could go to the purchase of private-sector life and disability insurance policies to provide for those contingencies (NCPA 1996).

The current system is basically a fraudulent device to provide social insurance under the guise of pension savings (in Marmor and Mashaw 1988, 7). We need to separate the social insurance function from the pension benefit function of SS. The insurance purpose, like other private insurance policies, can be achieved based on a pooled-risk system. The pension fund, however, must be left for individuals to own, manage, and accumulate. Most Americans demand control over their retirement fund, knowing how much they have and expect to have, so that they can plan their life after retirement accordingly. Ultimately, individuals, not the government, should have responsibility for retirement preparation and disability protection; government intervention should be restricted to situations of extreme hardship (Kingson and Schulz 1997, 50).

A funded system can be achieved while maintaining the insurance function of SS. By allowing individuals to divert only a portion of SS taxes to personal retirement accounts, the government can guarantee that everyone receives a basic amount of pension at retirement or disability. The so-called Basic Pension plan, similar to the one employed in the United Kingdom, would be an example. Under this system, everyone would be protected by a flat-rate Basic Pension, while providing opportunity for all workers to accumulate wealth in their own private accounts (Lilley 1999; ES2000 1999). With this plan (partial privatization), a chunk of SS would be left to cover other insurance purposes as well as providing a safety net for the elderly.

Privatization Will Undermine the Redistributive Function of Social Security

Opposing Privatization

Social Security has an important function of redistributing income. The major reason SS has been so successful in reducing old-age poverty is because of this redistributive character. It deliberately transfers resources from those with high lifetime earnings to those with low earnings (Quinn and Mitchell 1996). Social Security pays the low-income worker an annual income equal to 56.7 percent of one's final wage, compared with 43.9 percent for middle-income workers, and 31.4 percent for high-income workers (Baker 1997). No private savings plan, annuity, or whole-life insurance policy has this redistributive, antipoverty feature (Quinn and Mitchell 1996).

In a privatized system, the benefits one receives would depend on the level of individual contribution and investment performance. If SS were to be fully privatized, therefore, fifteen million elderly Americans would live below the poverty line (Hage 1995), and one in five American families would need supplemental retirement benefits. This would require a huge tax increase to create gigantic new government programs to help these people or increase Welfare and Supplemental Security Income (SSI) spending substantially (Hage 1995; Ball and Bethell 1997, 276).

A privatized system might provide an adequate retirement income for workers with long and steady careers with generous earnings and good luck in the investment arena. But what about people who work part time, those who drop out of the labor force to raise children, who have low wages, and who are less likely to have other private pensions? (Hage 1995; ES2000 1999). The neediest members of the population have less to contribute to the private account, yet depend on SS income the most when they retire. Under the privatized system in Argentina, only 50 percent of the economically active population contribute regularly to the SS system; in Brazil, 57 percent (Kay 1997).

Social Security benefits may be progressive but market return rates are usually favorable to higher-income people who have expertise in investment and pay proportionately lower management fees (PNIS 1998). Moreover, the existing tax policy already offers greater subsidies to the retirement savings of higher earners than lower earners. The home mortgage interest deduction and the nontaxability of IRA, Keogh, 401(k), and defined contribution plans provide much more assistance for wealth accumulation to high earners than to low earners. The redistributive structure of SS pensions somewhat reduces this inequality. A shift to a privatized system, however, would eliminate an important equalizing feature of the overall retirement system (Mashaw and Marmor 1996).

Supporting Privatization

So far, SS benefits have been so generous that they were a better deal than conventional, low-risk, private-sector investments, even for the affluent. In the coming century, however, when SS ceases to be so attractive to average to high income earners, political support for SS could be weakened (Quinn and Mitchell 1996).

Under the current SS system, both the income adequacy and individual equity components are intertwined in one complex set of payroll taxes and retirement benefit regulations (Quinn and Mitchell 1996). Maintaining income adequacy and providing individual equity, however, are fundamentally different functions that cannot be intermingled. Maintaining income adequacy is a welfare function that must be dealt with by the government (Tobin 1988, 64). We already have many welfare programs to provide assistance to those in need from the general federal budget, such as Supplementary Security Income (SSI), Food Stamps, Welfare, and energy and housing assistance. On the other hand, retirement pensions should be actuarially fair to contributing participants, and this can be achieved only through a funded system. The current system is basically a fraudulent device to provide welfare under the guise of retirement pensions (in Marmor and Mashaw 1998, 7). We need to separate the welfare (income adequacy) function from SS. If providing a safety net for the elderly poor is the main concern, we already have a federally funded safety-net program, the SSI, to bring the most impoverished elderly and disabled up to a minimum standard of living (in Ball and Bethell 1997, 259; in Tobin 1988, 61–62).

If separating the welfare function from SS is impossible, we can maintain certain levels of the redistributive function while allowing workers to privatize part of their SS tax. We could create a partially privatized system that requires a minimum level of compulsory contribution to be used for redistribution purposes, while allowing a certain portion of payroll taxes to be invested in private accounts (Tobin 1988, 64; Mashaw and Marmor 1996). Such a plan will not destroy SS's safety net or its redistributive function; it simply adds a second tier to the existing system. The first tier remains everyone's safety net; the second tier will be individual savings accounts (Beard in Beard et al. 1997). With this plan, we can encourage even low-income people to save for their retirement. As President Clinton proposes, the federal government could match contributions of low-income contributors on a progressive basis, allowing them to accumulate proportionately more savings than they otherwise would (Clinton 1998). The government could also make contributions on behalf of disabled workers through age 65 (Kotlikoff 1998).

Pushing redistribution too far, at the expense of the interest of the middle- and high-income earners, would turn SS into a welfare program, and would undermine political support for SS among middle- and high-income workers (Ball and Bethell 1997, 266–7).

The Costs of Changing to a Privatized System (Transition Costs) Are Too High

Opposing Privatization

If SS were fully privatized, workers would stop paying SS contributions to the government, yet the government must pay benefits to those who are already retired. Since older workers must receive the promised benefit and younger workers would be going into accounts for their own retirement, there would be a generational hole in the financing of public retirement costs (Kay 1997; Gramlich 1998, 61). A change to privatization, therefore, would require the transitional generation to pay twice for retirement; their own retirement through a fully funded system and that of the currently and near-retired through the old pay-as-you-go system (Bosworth 1997, 185). Privatization advocates propose plans to provide funded plans to those below a given age, while the already retired continue to receive benefits under the old system. Several plans propose using age 55 as the cut-off point. But ten years to retirement age is not long enough to build up a private pension savings plan (Ball and Bethell 1997, 284).

Even with a partial privatization plan, transition costs will be a serious problem. In the absence of new taxes, it is simply impossible to shift even two percentage points from SS to private accounts unless benefits are reduced substantially (Ball and Bethell 1997, 283; Dreyfuss 1996).

The SS Administration estimates that the government would have to come up with a staggering $8 trillion in new revenues to maintain the system until personal retirement accounts take over (Hage 1995). How can we pay for this transition cost? These costs have to be financed through a combination of tax increases, benefit reduction, and additional government borrowing (AARP 1999). According to the SS Advisory Council's estimation, it would require an extra 52 percent payroll tax, imposed over seventy-two years, beginning in

1998, plus about one trillion dollars in borrowing over the next forty years to finance this transition cost (Mashaw and Marmor in Beard et al. 1997). The Chilean government, in order to pay for their transition cost, even with a budget surplus, had to cut spending on redistributive programs like health care and education. Argentina, which passed a partial privatization law in 1993, is dealing with the revenue shortfall by cutting basic benefits (Kay 1997).

Supporting Privatization

The transition to a privatized system will be costly, but the cost can be minimized, and, in the long run, the benefits from privatization would override the cost of transition. We can minimize transition costs by phasing in the funded system gradually over a generation (Lilley 1999; Tobin 1988, 66). For instance, the Personal Security Account (PSA) plan, suggested by a group of SS advisory council members, would keep workers age 55 and over on the present system and put all workers under age 25 on an entirely privatized system, with those between 25 and 54 on a hybrid system, which includes their accrued benefits under the current system at the time of transition and the proceeds of their personal security accounts (Gramlich 1998, 61; Quinn and Mitchell 1996).

When privatized systems such as the PSA plan have been adopted in other countries, the middle-aged workers have simply been given the benefit credits they have built up under the previous system, financed out of the existing government budget (Gramlich 1998, 61, 79). Those who opted out of the system in Great Britain received a tax rebate sufficient to finance a private pension at least equivalent to that which they would have been entitled to in the old system (Lilley 1999). In Chile, transition costs are handled through large, permanent infusions of general tax revenues to pay for a substantial minimum benefit and for credit for past work under the old system (Ball and Bethell 1997, 283).

Transition costs would be high in the beginning, leading to a large amount of new governmental spending and borrowing. It will eventually, however, taper off as middle-aged workers gradually move on (Gramlich 1998, 61). In addition, as the new system matures, SS benefits can be reduced substantially, because the private savings will offset the reduction in benefits (Francis 1998d).

The expected federal budget surpluses could help fund transition costs. The booming economy, along with budget restraints, created a federal surplus in 1998, and this trend is expected to continue for at least fifteen years. This surplus could ease the transition costs (Miller 1998; Gergen 1998; Mitchell 1998a).

Most of all, the transition costs of privatization would be considerably less than the cost of fixing SS problems. Keeping the current system in place and trying to maintain it on sound footing would be a lot more costly than transition costs. In the long run, any cost of transition would turn out to be a good investment and money worth spending (Mitchell 1998a).

Privatization Would Be
Good for the Economy

Supporting Privatization

The existing pay-as-you-go system depresses national savings by discouraging people to save on their own (Feldstein in Gramlich 1997, 151–2). Workers regard their payroll tax contributions as retirement savings, and the prospect of future SS benefit spares them the need to save for retirement on their own. The government, on the other hand, treats SS taxes just like any other revenue and spends them. They are not channeled, directly or indirectly, through the capital markets into investments in productive capital assets. Economist Feldstein estimates the national capital stock to be trillions of dollars greater under a funded system (in Tobin 1988, 55; in Marmor and Mashaw 1988, 7).

Economists from across the political spectrum have long complained that low levels of savings undermine economic growth (Mitchell 1997). The low saving rate causes low investment and slow growth in productivity and living standards (Poterba 1990, 38). There is also widespread agreement that record payroll taxes hinder job creation and reduce wages (Mitchell 1997).

If SS were privatized, it would lead to higher national savings. Higher rates of saving will produce higher rates of investment, and the economy would be strengthened by a massive increase in long-term investment funds (in Baker 1998; Holley 1999; in Baker 1997; Lilley 1999). It would also boost the creation of jobs by sharply reducing the tax penalty imposed on employment. The resulting increase in economic growth would add thousands of dollars to the average family's income (Mitchell 1997). An extra 1 percent investment yield would generate pensions 30 percent higher (Lilley 1999). Over time, privatization would increase the economy's output by roughly 15 percent and the capital stocks by roughly 40 percent (Kotlikoff 1998). National saving rates for Chile have risen significantly since pension reform (Gramlich 1998, 80). Chile now has Latin America's highest savings rate (Rotella 1998).

Opposing Privatization

A privately funded system would create a source of national saving, only if the government does not have to borrow or increase taxes to supplement the loss in SS revenues (Bosworth 1997, 166; Mashaw and Marmor in Beard et al. 1997). Most plans for privatization take money that is now invested in government securities and put it into private securities. However, if the government continues to tax and spend at the same rate, it will simply have to borrow, at the same rate, from elsewhere. National savings can increase only if overall private savings go up at a rate not equaled by government borrowing. Changing the form of SS Trust Fund holdings will not do the trick, nor will relocating those holdings into private security accounts (Mashaw and Marmor 1996). All the privatization plans call for the government to continue to pay SS benefits to current recipients and those about to retire; therefore, spending would be exactly the same after privatization as it was before (Baker 1998).

The rate of national savings and economic growth reflects a variety of factors—public and private investment, technology, employment, human capital, business profits—not just the rate of personal savings (Mashaw and Marmor 1996). National saving rates for Chile have risen significantly since pension reform, but it is difficult to tell how much of the rise was due to pension reform and how much was due to other factors, such as economic boom (Gramlich 1998, 80).

In fact, privatization could negatively affect the national economy. In 1998, Americans were delighted that, for the first time in nearly thirty years, the federal budget was in balance. It was in balance because each year the Treasury borrowed $80 billion from the SS Trust Fund surplus, and covered the deficit in the rest of the federal budget. If a big piece of SS contributions go into private accounts, the Trust Fund surplus will disappear, and the federal budget will plunge back into deficit, causing serious economic troubles in the future (Editors, *The Nation* 6-1-98).

Privatization Will Prevent Government Diversion of Social Security Surpluses

Supporting Privatization

Since the 1983 SS reform, which included a payroll tax hike and the taxing of SS income, the SS agency has been collecting about 20 percent ($60 billion) more than it needs to pay retirees. This reserve would build to $3.3 trillion by 2020 (Ball and Bethell 1997, 271). However, instead of setting this money aside to pay for the retirement of baby boomers, the government has been borrowing this money to finance other government programs and to reduce federal budget deficits. When the surplus is needed with the retirement of baby boomers, the government will have to either borrow the money from somewhere or raise taxes (Bosworth 1990, 31; Editors, *The Nation* 6-1-98).

Instead of raising the payroll taxes in 1983, if we had allowed the baby boomers to set aside the increased portion of their payroll tax in private accounts, we would not be talking about SS problems today. The government cannot have access to private accounts invested in private sectors; the money would definitely be there when the baby boomers retire. Moreover, the individual accounts would have grown a lot more than SS due to the higher-than-average stock market performance since the late 1980s.

Social Security's looming surpluses pose an irresistible target for the government. While taxpayers may operate on the assumption that SS taxes fund only SS spending, "a tax is a tax," when it comes to the government's tendency to spend (Crain and Marlow 1990, 133–4). So far as SS remains in its current form, there is no guarantee that the government will not be tempted to use the money for other purposes. The only way to prevent the government's misuse of the SS surplus is to privatize it. It is better to eliminate the surplus by reducing tax than the current decision to use the reserve to finance government consumption on other programs (Bosworth 1990, 32–3).

Opposing Privatization

The option of setting aside the surplus to add to national savings has enormous appeal from an economic view. It provides a means of responding to the inadequate national saving and to the excessive trade deficit (in Bosworth 1990, 31–2). Moreover, this surplus is economically desirable as a way of anticipating a demographic shift that will produce a significant deficit when baby boomers retire (in Nordhaus 1990, 179; Bartlett 1997, 228–9).

Even with some government diversion, if the government can pay it back with interest, it would not harm the Trust Funds, and could actually be a benefit to all Americans. Thanks to SS surplus, for the first time in thirty years, we were able to achieve a federal budget surplus in 1998. If a big portion of SS contributions go into private accounts, the Trust Fund surplus will disappear, and the federal budget will plunge back into deficit again, causing more serious economic troubles in the future (Editors, *The Nation* 6-1-98).

If preventing the government misuse of SS surplus is the goal, we don't have to take such drastic measures as privatizing SS. It can be done simply by separating the SS Trust Funds from the unified federal budget, thus preventing the government from using the surplus (AFL-CIO 1995). The "lock box" bill the House passed in May 1999 would serve this purpose (Lipman 1999).

Privatization Would Hurt Women

Opposing Privatization

Social Security is a vital safeguard against poverty and depravation for aging women. Women tend to earn less than men; they tend to work more intermittently or part-time than men (ADSS 1999; Diamond in Kiefer 1998). So far as an individual pension fund is a function of how much workers contribute, women in general would have lower account balances than men at retirement. Moreover, women tend to live longer than men—on average seven years longer, and therefore, women depend on SS more than men do, and they are in greater danger of outliving their resources of retirement income. On the contrary, it is impossible to outlive one's SS benefit (Tzemach 1999).

Under the current SS system, women receive higher rates of return than men do because of the progressive benefit formula and longer life expectancy. For median female retirees, SS replaces 54 percent of average lifetime earnings, compared with 41 percent for the median male. Social Security provides extra benefits to spouses with low lifetime earnings, even if spouses did not work at all outside the home. Social Security provides benefits to elderly widows; 74 percent of elderly widows receive benefits based on the earnings of their deceased spouse. Social Security provides benefits to spouses of any age who care for children under age 16 if the worker (other spouse) is retired, becomes disabled, or dies; women represent 98 percent of recipients receiving benefits as spouses with a child in their care (Tzemach 1999). The system is designed in such a way that the income discrepancies between men and women would be at least in part compensated in favor of women. The totally privatized system will not have any of these features.

Supporting Privatization

The current SS system is not all that advantageous to women as opponents of privatization claim. There are significant disparities in the current benefit packages for men and women. Women receive lower benefit pay-backs than men do, not only because women earn typically less than men but also because women's status under the SS system depends on a variety of factors including work history, marital status, and work habits. A widow, for instance, who has worked in a two-earner household receives less than a widow who has no work record (ADSS 1999). Single and divorced women fare poorly under the existing system. The benefit rates for divorced women are the same as for a spouse living with a marriage partner, although it goes to a person living alone and is frequently inadequate in that situation (Ball and Bethell 1997, 268; Editors, *The Nation* 6-1-98).

Individual accounts would be better suited to the needs of today's women than the current system. The current system, designed in a time when fathers were the breadwinners and stay-at-home mothers were the norm, is outdated and unfair to today's working women. While the current system does offer spousal and survivor benefits to women for their years out of the workforce, it does little to enable working women to maximize the return on their payroll tax investment during their years in the workforce. By enabling working women to keep a portion of their SS taxes in a personal account, these women could create a nest egg of their own that would make them more secure and independent during retirement (Dunn in Tzemach 1999). If male contributors die before retirement, under the privatized system, any nonannuitized portion of their retirement account balance would go to their spouse, who is also entitled to the survivors' benefit. The privatized plan, therefore, would increase the survivor's protection, which usually helps women more than men (Kotlikoff 1998).

Privatization Would Hurt Low-Income People

Opposing Privatization

Privatizing SS will hurt low-income and part-time workers, who currently benefit from the progressive and redistributive features of the present system. Low-income workers typically have small account balances, potentially subjecting them to higher fees because asset-based revenues cannot begin to cover the costs of maintaining these accounts. Thus, they are likely to earn lower returns than higher-income workers who make the same investment choices. The administrative costs for IRAs currently range from $35 to $45 per account per year. Flat-rate costs of this type are most disadvantageous to low-wage workers, because these charges consume a larger percentage of the investment in small accounts than of the investments in larger accounts (Kijakazi and Greenstein 1998).

Lower-income workers tend to be more timid and inexperienced investors, lacking expertise, and tend to invest conservatively to avoid risks. If SS were privatized, this behavior could produce huge differences in the size of retirement nest eggs, thereby intensifying the income inequality of the elderly population (Dentzer 1997; Mashaw and Marmor 1996; PNIS 1998; Century Foundation 1999).

Supporting Privatization

In appearance, SS benefits seem redistributive; they give low-wage workers better return on their life-time earnings. The true formula, however, is not quite as redistributive as it appears. First, low-income workers pay proportionately more tax than high-income workers, because the payroll tax is not progressive, and there is an income cap of $72,600 subject to payroll tax. Consequently, the burden of payroll taxes on the low-income earners is much greater than the high-income earners. Lower-income workers typically start working at an earlier age than higher income workers do because they do not go to college, and thus contribute to the system for longer years. Lower-income people, as a group, have shorter life expectancy than higher income people, and thus receive fewer life-time benefits (Ball and Bethell 1997, 265; Kotlikoff 1998; ES2000 1999; Murdock in ADSS 1999).

Under a funded system, all workers have the chance to accumulate wealth. Working longer and saving more pay off because whatever people save would be reserved for their retirement only. Low-income people, who start working early and die early in general, would thus benefit from the privatized system. Even if they die early, they can give the unused portion of their retirement savings to their children (ES2000 1999).

Privatization Would Encourage People to Work Longer

Supporting Privatization

The current SS system encourages workers to retire early and discourages the retirees from working part-time after retirement (Quinn and Mitchell 1996). As SS benefits increased, Americans have been retiring at an earlier age. In 1950, nearly half of all American men aged 65 and over were in the labor force; in 1997, fewer than one in six were (Quadagno and Quinn 1997, 128). The average age for receiving SS benefits declined from 69 in 1950 to 64 in 1990 (Bosworth 1997, 161).

Privatization, on the other hand, would increase the incentives to delay retirement and to work after retirement, because one's own contributions would be directly linked to her pension accumulations and eventual benefits. The longer one works, and the more one saves, the greater one's retirement nest egg would be (Quinn and Mitchell 1996). Given the demographic changes on the horizon, and the increasing health and longevity of older Americans, this may be just what we need (Quadagno and Quinn 1997, 146).

Opposing Privatization

It is not SS that encouraged people to retire early; it is the robust economy and higher productivity. The simplest economic explanation for the postwar early retirement trend is that we have grown wealthier over time. Therefore, we can afford to start work later, work fewer hours per year, and retire earlier than we once did. Recent cohorts of retirees have enjoyed a generally robust economy and dramatic increase in the value of their real estate holdings, which allowed them to retire early (in Quadagno and Quinn 1997, 135).

It is not SS that discourages work, but it is the earnings test that does. By eliminating the earnings test, which discourages work and earning money among retirees, those who can work after age 65 would be better motivated to continue to work without being penalized (Clinton 1999). We can encourage people to work longer simply by eliminating this earnings test instead of privatizing the system.

Centralized Investment of Social Security Trust Funds

As an alternative to privatizing SS, some lawmakers proposed investing part of the SS Trust Funds in private equities (called Centralized Investment) to achieve higher rates of return than the current Treasury securities in which the

Trust Fund is presently invested, while maintaining the SS's defined-benefit structure as is. The contributions of the baby boom generation have led to the buildup of a significant reserve. Especially since the 1983 SS reform, the agency's revenues exceed expenditure by about $60 to $100 billion per year, which is about 20 percent over the needed expenditure (Weaver 1998; Quinn and Mitchell 1996; Baker 1998; Francis 1998b; Century Foundation 1998), and the agency expects the reserve to build to about $3.3 trillion by 2020 before it starts to go down (Ball and Bethell 1997, 271). The Social Security Advisory Board suggested investing 14.6 percent of the surplus in private equities (Greenstein 1999); President Clinton, up to 25 percent (Clinton 1999); Ball's plan (Maintenance of Benefit Plan), up to 40 percent (Ball 1996). The following sections summarize the supporting and opposing views of this centralized investment option.

Centralized Investment Would Bring Higher Rates of Return Than Treasury Securities, with Lower Risks Than Private Accounts

Supporting Centralized Investment

The centralized investment plan would bring higher rates of return than the Treasury securities, without exposing workers to the risks that follow individual investment, because the risks of the stock market would be shared by all participants (Kiefer 1998; Greenstein 1999; PNIS 1998). In the past, SS has never developed a large reserve for advanced funding, so the rate of return on the small contingency reserve has made little difference in long-range financing. Now the fund is becoming quite large, increase in the rate of return will make a major difference (Ball 1996).

Since 1926, Treasury issues have yielded an annual average return of about 2 to 5 percent, compared with 6 to 11 percent for stocks (Kiefer 1998). Studies of investment returns on stocks versus bonds over many decades indicate that stocks consistently outperform bonds (Barnhart 1999). It would be unfair to mandate people to invest their retirement money in funds that generate low returns when there are higher-return options available. Investing a portion of the Trust Funds in private equities can generate market-rate interests that would help reduce the projected deficit, greatly improve the contribution-to-benefit ratio for young workers, and thereby preserve SS as a good deal for tomorrow's young workers (Ball and Bethell 1997, 275; Ball 1996).

This centralized investment option would also be more cost-effective than the privatized system. Investing collectively through the government would result in significant administrative savings compared with investing through 150 million small individual accounts, because it would have lower management fees and no additional annuity conversion fees (Aaron in Greenstein 1999; Kijakazi and Greenstein 1998). The administrative costs associated with centralized investing of SS reserves are projected to consume less than 1 percent of the amounts invested, compared with 20 to 30 percent in the privately funded system (Greenstein 1999; Kiefer 1998).

Opposing Centralized Investment

Investing the Trust Funds in stocks may bring slightly higher returns than the Treasury issues, but at the expense of higher risks (Diamond in Kiefer 1998). Stock market risks are stock market risks. Centralizing them, sharing them, or spreading them out won't make them go away (Weaver 1998). In a Depression like the 1930s, if the government funds had been in equities, they would have lost well over half the value of their common stock portfolio (Ibbotson in Barnhart 1999). This fear is not ancient history. Just in the last few years, the stock market in Japan, which faces its own enormous retirement income needs, suffered a 50 percent loss (Barnhart 1999).

The volatility of returns of stocks far exceeds swings in bond yields. Since 1926, one-year returns of blue-chip stocks have gyrated between a 54 percent profit and a 43 percent loss. Government bonds, by contrast, gained 40 percent in their best year but lost only 9 percent in their worst year (Barnhart 1999). If the stock market experienced a sharp or prolonged drop, resulting in substantially lower investment earnings than anticipated, would the government increase SS taxes or reduce benefits? Some proponents suggest that the government would just ride out the ups and downs in the market, but persistent underfunding or overfunding of a defined-benefit plan necessitates changes in taxes or benefits (Weaver 1998). Proponents of centralized investment do not suggest that SS beneficiaries accept reduced benefits if stock prices slide over a long stretch. That means taxpayers would be called on to bail out SS whenever stocks failed to meet pay-out requirements (Barnhart 1999).

Supporting Centralized Investment

The proposed plans for centralized investment retain the substantial majority of its reserves in Treasury bonds. These bond holdings would equal the full cost of several years of SS benefits. Between the ongoing revenue from payroll taxes, the interest and dividends earned on bonds and equities, and the revenue from redeeming bonds, the SS system would be able to ride out an extended stock market downturn without having to sell off stocks when stock prices were down (Greenstein 1999).

This is precisely what corporate and public-employee pension funds do—diversify their assets. They place a portion of their portfolios in equities to take advantage of the higher rate of return, while placing other portions of their portfolios in investments that do not fluctuate as much as equities do. This generally enables these pension funds to avoid liquidating stock holdings during bear markets. In fact, the SS Administration's proposal is quite cautious in this regard—only 14.6 percent of SS reserves would be invested in equities. By contrast, large corporate pension funds place more than 40 percent of their assets in equities; state and local public employee pension funds invest more than 60 percent of their assets in equities (Greenstein 1999).

Centralized Investment Is Dangerous to the Economy

Opposing Centralized Investment

Although touted as a safe way to take advantage of the high returns produced by stocks, centralized investment plans would do little to improve the retirement security of workers, while posing great dangers to the economy. If the government invested $1 trillion of Trust Funds in equities by 2015, the federal government could become the largest shareholder in the United States (Weaver 1998), owning one-seventh of the stock market (Miller 1998). Having a government as the largest investor in the market gives one shareholder far too much influence (Diamond in Kiefer 1998). It could become a government monopoly, providing services for which there are no precise private market counterparts (Weaver 1998). It is politically impossible to insulate such huge funds from government direction (Greenspan in Barnhart 1999); there will be influences on corporations (Pozen in Barnhart 1999). Depending on which index funds or stocks the government chooses, it would funnel tens of billions of dollars into large, well-established companies and would ignore small and newly formed ones. Any decision the government makes would alter the distribution of wealth and ownership in the economy (Weaver 1998). The government's job must be to regulate and stabilize the economy, not to accentuate the booms and the busts (Barnhart 1999).

Supporting Centralized Investment

Investing SS reserves in equity securities will not roil capital markets, so long as investments are limited to broad index funds. These funds would be managed solely in the interest of beneficiaries, and the government would be only a passive shareholder (Mashaw and Marmor 1996).

The speculation that the proposed Trust Fund investment would pump so much money into the equities market that it would distort the market or cause a stock market bubble that could burst, injuring investors and the economy, is highly unlikely. Under the SS Administration's proposal, the investment of a portion of Trust Fund reserves in equities markets would occur gradually over fifteen years. Even at full implementation, the infusion of Trust Fund reserves into the equities market would be small, totaling less than 4 percent of the market. This is much too small to cause serious market distortion (Greenstein 1999; Barnhart 1999; Ball 1996).

Centralized Investment Will Be Affected by Political Influence

Opposing Centralized Investment

Any proposal for public investment of Trust Funds in private equities immediately raises concerns about who would make the decisions and how the capital might be allocated among competing projects. Imagine a group of legislators and public officials trying to decide how to invest a massive fund in corporate stocks. Unless carefully circumscribed by Congress, every aspect of every investment decision—including who to name to the investment board, which stocks to buy and in what proportions, when to buy and sell, and how to exercise shareholder rights—could be based on political rather than economic factors (Weaver 1998).

Consider also the conflicts of interest the government would find itself in as a major investor and owner of the U.S. capital stock—conflicts between its role as fiduciary for SS participants and as a regulator of business in the interest of public welfare. Also consider the problems of corporate governance. Somebody, somehow, would have to vote the shares of all those companies held by the Trust Funds (Weaver 1998).

One can easily imagine the pressures that would come to bear on the government to ban investments in politically unfavorable companies—perhaps tobacco companies, or companies moving plants abroad, or companies involved in labor disputes—and direct money toward politically favored companies (Weaver 1998).

Supporting Centralized Investment

There are ways to ensure complete neutrality in investments and in matters of corporate governance and provide layers of protection against political interference. There can be an independent body that will oversee the investment of the funds, and then the funds themselves will be invested by private sector money managers, not by the government (Greenstein 1999). This would remove management of the funds from the government or Congress and transfer it to an independent, nonpolitical, professional management board. This independent board would contract with private fund managers selected through competitive bidding. These managers would invest a portion of SS reserves in broad index funds in the equities market (Greenstein 1999).

We could establish procedures to further ensure that the independent board would have no ability to influence corporate decisions by exercising voting rights on shares the board holds. These voting rights would be sterilized so they have no effect on corporate decision making. This way, the executive branch and Congress would be walled off from the investment process, just as they are walled off from Federal Reserve Board decisions on interest rates (Greenstein 1999).

REFERENCES

AFL-CIO. 1995. "Statement by the AFL-CIO Executive Council on Social Security." 22 February. (http://www.aflcio.org/estatements/ssecur.htm).

Allen, Jodie. 1999. "The exaggerated death of Social Security." *U.S. News & World Report.* 10 May.

American Association of Retired Persons (The) (AARP). 1999. "Social Security." *Where We Stand.* 1 January. (http://www.aarp.org/wherewestand/standsocsec.html).

Americans Discuss Social Security (ADSS). 1999. "Women and Social Security." 1 March. (http://www.policy.com/issues/issue252.html).

Baker, Dean. 1998. "Nine misconceptions about Social Security." *The Atlantic Monthly* 282, no. 1 (July):34–39.

———. 1997. "The privateers' free lunch." *The American Prospect* 32 (May–June):81–84.

Ball, Robert M. 1996. "A secure system." *The American Prospect* 29 (November–December):34–35.

———. and Thomas N. Bethell. 1997. "Bridging the centuries: The case for traditional Social Security." Pp. 258–94 in *Social Security in the 21st century*, edited by Eric R. Kingston and James H. Schulz. New York: Oxford University Press.

Bartlett, Dwight K. 1997. "Financing and work issues: Another view." Pp. 225–30 in *Social Security in the 21st century*, edited by Eric R. Kingston and James H. Schulz. New York: Oxford University Press.

Barnhart, Bill. 1999. "Stock market gamble on Social Security: Big payoff, big risk." *Chicago Tribune.* 21 January.

Beach, William W., and Gareth E. Davis. 1998. "Social Security's rate of return." The Heritage Center for Data Analysis, no. 98-01, 15 January. (http://www.heritage.org).

Beard, Sam, Theodore R. Marmor, and Jerry L. Mashaw. 1997. "Is there a social security crisis?" *The American Prospect*, no. 30 (January–February):16–19.

Bishop, Matthew. 1998. "From Chile, with a pinch of salt." *The Economist.* 24 October.

Bosworth, Barry. 1997. "What economic role for the Trust Funds?" Pp. 156–77 in *Social Security in the 21st century*, edited by Eric R. Kingston and James H. Schulz. New York: Oxford University Press.

———. 1990. "Social Security, budget deficits, and national saving." Pp. 29–34 in *Social Security's looming surpluses: Prospects and implications*, edited by Carolyn L. Weaver. Washington, D.C.: The AEI Press.

Center on Budget and Policy Priorities (CBPP). 1999. "Administrative and other costs consume more than 40 percent of included accounts in the United Kingdom, new study finds." Center on Budget and Policy Priorities. For Immediate Release: 16 March. (http://www.cbpp.org/3-16-99socsec-pr.htm).

Century Foundation (The). 1999. "Social Security: The real deal." Issue Brief #1. 19 March. (http://www.tcf.org/Issue_Briefs/Social_Security/The_Real_Deal.html).

———. 1998. "Policy in perspective: Social Security reform." *A Century Foundation guide to the issues*. New York: The Century Foundation Press. (http://www.tcf.org/Publications/Basics/Social-Security).

Chen, Yung-Ping, and Stephen C. Goss. 1997. "Are returns on payroll taxes fair?" Pp. 76–90 in *Social Security in the 21st century*, edited by Eric R. Kingston and James H. Schulz. New York: Oxford University Press.

Clinton, Bill. 1999. "Saving Social Security now and meeting America's challenges for the 21st century." (http://www.whitehouse.gov/WH/SOTU99/sss.html).

———. 1998. "Address by the president to a national forum on Social Security." (In Kansas City, Missouri, 7 April.) The White House, Office of the Press Secretary.

CNN News. 1999. "Clinton upset over reports GOP dropping Social Security reform." 23 April.

Corn, David. 1998. "Anti-Social Security." *The Nation* (Digital Edition). 24 August. (http://www.thenation.com).

Crain, W. Mark, and Michael L. Marlow. 1990. "The causal relationship between Social Security and the federal budget." Pp. 119–34 in *Social Security's looming surpluses: Prospects and implications*, edited by Carolyn L. Weaver. Washington, D.C.: The AEI Press.

Crutsinger, Martin. 1999. "Answers about Social Security plan." *Yahoo News*. 7 February.

Dentzer, Susan. 1997. "Fair play in Social Security." *U.S. News & World Report*. 27 January.

Dreyfuss, Robert. 1996. "The biggest deal: Lobbying to take Social Security private." *The American Prospect*, no. 26 (May–June):72–75.

Economic Security 2000 (The) (ES2000). 1999. "Arguments: Pay-as-you-go vs. a funded system." 10 March. (http://www.economicsecurity2000.org/PressRoom/apgvsfs.html).

Feldmann, Linda. 1998. "Linking Social Security to stocks: A good idea?" *Christian Science Monitor*. 10 September.

Francis, David. 1998a. "Problems with taking Social Security private." *Christian Science Monitor*. 20 April.

———. 1998b. "Social Security bailout: Is a 'big fix' needed?" *Christian Science Monitor*. 30 April.

———. 1998c. "Battle brews on Social Security." *Christian Science Monitor*. 22 June.

———. 1998d. "Beware Privatization." *Christian Science Monitor*. 27 July.

Friedman, Milton. 1999. "Social Security chimeras." *New York Times*. 11 January.

Gergen, David. 1998. "Save Social Security. Now!" *U.S. News & World Report*. 14 December, 76.

Glassman, James K. 1997. "Do-it-yourself Social Security." *U.S. News & World Report*. 6 October, 50.

Goldstein, Amy, and George Hager. 1998. "Social Security investment plans weighed." *Washington Post*. 8 December, A01.

Graetz, Michael J. 1988. "Retirement security policy: Toward a more unified view." Pp. 91–118 in *Social Security: Beyond the rhetoric of crisis*, edited by Theodore R. Marmor and Jerry L. Mashaw. Princeton, N.J.: Princeton University Press.

Gramlich, Edward M. 1998. *Is it time to reform Social Security?* Ann Arbor, Mich.: University of Michigan Press.

———. 1997. "How does Social Security affect the economy?" Pp. 147–66 in *Social Security in the 21st century*, edited by Eric R. Kingston and James H. Schulz. New York: Oxford University Press.

Greenstein, Robert. 1999. "Should a portion of Social Security benefits be invested in equities?" Center on Budget and Policy Priorities. 23 February. (http://www.cbpp.org/equity.pdf).

Hage, David. 1995. "Privatizing Social Security." *U.S. News & World News*. 3 April, 47.

Holley, David. 1999. "Poles' pension money starts to play the market." *Los Angeles Times*. 8 January.

Hurd, Michael D. 1997. "Adequacy and equity issues: Another view." Pp. 219–24 in *Social Security in the 21st century*, edited by Eric R. Kingston and James H. Schulz. New York: Oxford University Press.

Jaffe, Charles. 1998. "Overhauling social security." *Boston Globe*. 23 November, C05.

Kay, Stephen J. 1997. "The Chile con: Privatizing Social Security in South America." *The American Prospect*, no. 33 (July–August):48–52.

Kiefer, Francine. 1998. "Social Security: How to privatize?" *Christian Science Monitor*. 28 July.

Kijakazi, Kilolo, and Robert Greenstein. 1998. "How would various Social Security reform plans affect Social Security benefits?" The Center for Budget and Policy Priorities. 8 September. (http://www.cbpp.org/9-8-98socsec.htm).

Kingson, Eric R., and James H. Schulz. 1997. "Should Social Security be means-tested?" Pp. 41–61 in *Social Security in the 21st century*, edited by Eric R. Kingson and James H. Schulz. New York: Oxford University Press.

Kotlikoff, Lawrence. 1998. "Privatizing Social Security." *Idea House*. National Center for Policy Analysis Policy Report, no. 217. July. (http://www.ncpa.org/studies/s217.html).

Krauss, Clifford. 1998. "Social Security, Chilean style." *New York Times*. 16 August.

Lieberman, Trudy. 1997. "Social insecurity: The campaign to take the system private." *The Nation*. 27 January.

Lilley, Peter. 1999. "Social Security reforms in Britain: The principles of effective privatization." *Backgrounder*. The Heritage Foundation, no. 1259. 2 March. (http://www.heritage.org/library/backgrounder/bg1259.html).

Lipman, Larry (Cox News Service). 1999. "House passes 'lock box' bill." *Dayton Daily News*. 27 May.

Longman, Phillip J. 1998. "Bait and switch on Social Security." *U.S. News & World Report*. 20 April, 25.

Marmor, Theodore R., Fay Lomax Cook, and Stephen Scher. 1997. "Social Security politics and the conflict between generations: Are we asking the right questions?" Pp. 195–207 in *Social Security in the 21st century*, edited by Eric R. Kingson and James H. Schulz. New York: Oxford University Press.

———. and Jerry L. Mashaw, Eds. 1988. "Introduction." Pp. 3–13 in *Social Security: Beyond the rhetoric of crisis*, edited by Theodore R. Marmor and Jerry L. Mashaw. Princeton, N.J.: Princeton University Press.

Mashaw, Jerry L., and Theodore R. Marmor. 1996. "The great Social Security scare." *The American Prospect*, no. 29 (November–December):30–37.

Miller, Matthew. 1998. "Rebuilding retirement." *U.S. News & World Report*. 20 April, 20–26.

Mitchell, Daniel J. 1997. "A brief guide to Social Security reform." *Talking Points*. The Heritage Foundation, no. 22, 7 August.

Mitchell, Daniel J. 1998a. "Social Security's $20 trillion shortfall: Why reform is needed." *The Backgrounder*, The Heritage Foundation, no. 1194. 22 June.

———. 1998b. "Totally privatized system would work best for seniors." *Dayton Daily News*. Community Forum. 30 July.

Nation (The) (electronic edition). Editors. 1998. "Social (in)security." 1 June. (http://www.thenation.com).

National Center for Policy Analysis (NCPA). 1996. "Social Security reform: Other countries are leading the way." *Brief Analysis* 212. 30 August. (http://www.adss.org/poll_data/poll_intl.cfm).

New Republic (The). Editors. 1998. "Payroll payback." 26 January.

Nordhaus, William D. 1990. "Protecting the Social Security surplus through institutional or fundamental reform?" Pp. 179–84 in *Social Security's looming surpluses: Prospects and implications*, edited by Carolyn L. Weaver. Washington, D.C.: The AEI Press.

Orszag, Peter. 1999a. "Administrative costs in individual accounts in the United Kingdom." Center on Budget and Policy Priorities. 16 March. (http://www.cbpp.org/3-16-99socsecexec.htm).

———. 1999b. "Individual accounts and Social Security: Does Social Security really provide a lower rate of return?" (Executive summary) Center on Budget and Policy Priorities. (http://www.cbpp.org/3-11-99socsec.htm).

Policy News & Information Service (The) (PNIS). 1999. "Social Security at the crossroads" The Issue of the Week. (http://www.policy.com/issuewk/1999/0306_60).

———. 1998. "Issue of the week: Social Security." 1–7 June. (http://www.policy.com/issuewk/98/0601/index.html).

Poterba, James M. 1990. "Boosting national saving through U.S. fiscal policy." Pp. 35–38 in *Social Security's looming surpluses: Prospects and implications*, edited by Carolyn L. Weaver. Washington, D.C.: The AEI Press.

Quadagno, Jill, and Joseph Quinn. 1997. "Does Social Security discourage work?" Pp. 127–46 in *Social Security in the 21st century*, edited by Eric R. Kingston and James H. Schulz. New York: Oxford University Press.

Quinn, F. Joseph, and Olivia S. Mitchell. 1996. "Social Security on the table." *The American Prospect*, no. 26 (May–June):76–81.

Quinn, Jane Bryant. 1998. "Should we go private?" *Newsweek*. 7 December, 89.

Rosenbaum, David. E. 1999. "House Republicans end bid to revamp Social Security." *New York Times*. 23 April.

Rotella, Sebastian. 1998. "Taking a hard look at Chile's privately managed system." *Los Angeles Times*. 6 December.

Shapiro, Joseph P., and Ben Wildavsky. 1998. "Time to fix Social Security." *U.S. News & World Report*. 14 December, 18–22.

Smith, Nick. 1998. "Congressman Nick Smith's plan for saving Social Security." (http://www.house.gov/nicksmith/social/ssapg5.htm).

Steuerle, C. Eugene. 1997. "Social Security in the 21st century: The need for change." Pp. 231–38 in *Social Security in the 21st century*, edited by Eric R. Kingson and James H. Schulz. New York: Oxford University Press.

Tzemach, Gayle. 1999. "Women weigh in on Social Security." ABCNews.com. 2 March.

Thompson, Lawrence H., and Melinda M. Upp. 1997. "The social insurance approach and Social Security." Pp. 3–21 in *Social Security in the 21st century*, edited by Eric R. Kingson and James H. Schulz. New York: Oxford University Press.

Tobin, James. 1988. "The future of Social Security: One economist's assessment." Pp. 41–68 in *Social Security: Beyond the rhetoric of crisis*, edited by Theodore R. Marmor and Jerry L. Mashaw. Princeton, N.J.: Princeton University Press.

Wasow, Bernard, and David Smith. 1995. "Fixing Social Security." *Washington Post*. (http://epn.org/tcf/xxssec01.html).

Weaver, Carolyn L. 1998. "How not to reform Social Security." American Enterprise Institute. (http://www.teleport.com/~prf/ss/jan99).

Zuckerman, Mortimer B. 1998. "Investing the wrong way." *U.S. News & World Report*. 11 May, 72.

Zuckerman, Mortimer B. 1999. "Retirement without worry." *U.S. News & World Report*. 8 March.

CHAPTER

9 School Voucher Programs

The widespread belief that our public school system is in grave need of reform has led people from all walks of life to promote school choice by means of vouchers. School choice would give parents the authority to choose the schools their children attend, instead of relying on school districts to assign children to schools based on residential areas.

Proposals to create school choice in one form or another have been around for a long time. The original idea of school choice was the voucher plan proposed by Milton Friedman. In his plan, the per-pupil cost of education would be provided in the form of a voucher to be used to purchase education in either public or private schools. Friedman believed that providing parents with vouchers would foster competition among private and public schools, providing an incentive for better performance and improved academic achievement (Viteritti 1996; Witte 1990, 32).

During the 1960s and 1970s, however, Friedman was a lone voice in the policy wilderness. It was not until the 1980s that this idea of school choice broke through the surface of politics. In the early 1980s, disappointed by the declining quality of public education, politics shifted its emphasis away from public education and tilted toward private education and school choice. The conservative Reagan administration proposed tuition tax credits and vouchers to help parents pay private school tuition, but Congress refused to adopt the plan. Nevertheless, the voucher movement continued to gain increasing momentum among policymakers across the ideological spectrum. By the 1990s, public funding of private schools was at the center of the school choice debate as a major option of school reform (Cookson 1994, 28–36).

The recent support for the voucher movement is coming not only from the conservative camp but also from the liberal Democrats (Toch 1991, 67–8; Dougherty and Sostre 1992, 38). For a long time, politically active African Americans and Democrats have looked on vouchers as a poison apple intended to kill off public education. With inner-city schools in a state of permanent crisis, however, lower-income African Americans are being drawn increasingly to vouchers as a last best hope for getting at least some of their kids out of their periled public schools. Because of the potential appeal to African American voters, vouchers, which had largely been a Republican cause, grew from a small-scale educational experiment to a sizable political issue (Lacayo 1997, 72).

Types of School Choice Programs

There are many versions of school choice; most of them fall under two broad categories. First is public school choice, where choice of school is limited to public schools (including magnet schools). This public school choice can be either intradistrict or interdistrict. Second is all school choice (or full school choice), in which choice of schools can include private as well as public schools. Choice of private schools can be limited to nonsectarian schools only (as in Maine and Vermont) or include all religious and parochial schools (as in Florida; Milwaukee, Wisconsin; and Cleveland, Ohio). This form of choice can be provided either with vouchers or tax credits.

Vouchers can be either universal (the same amount of per-pupil cost is provided to every family, regardless of income level); means-tested (vouchers are provided only to low-income families); or progressive (vouchers are provided in proportion to family's income—more to lower-income families and less to higher-income families).

Existing School Choice Programs

The public-school-choice program is already widespread throughout the United States, in various forms, such as magnet schools, charter schools, and open enrollment systems. As of 1999, nine states permit public school choice throughout the state, and twenty-one states within some districts. Open enrollments are offered in eight states, and thirty states have operating or approved charter schools. States such as Minnesota and Arizona have introduced choice initiatives through various tax credits or deduction processes (CER 1999).

The school choice option that is gaining the greatest attention and creating controversy is the all-school-choice program, which provides parents with a portion of the public educational funding to allow their children to attend public or private schools. The longest running full-school-choice program is in Vermont. In order to meet the demand of parents who live in towns too small to support a local public school, the state has been paying tuition expenses for these children to attend any public or nonsectarian private schools (including schools outside the state) for more than a century. Families in Maine, who live in towns without public secondary schools, may send their children to any public or nonsectarian private schools, with the state-provided voucher (CER 1999; Sharp 1999). However, in both states, parents cannot choose religious schools. In June 1999, the Maine state law that bars the state from reimbursing students' tuition at religious schools was upheld by a federal appeals court (V. McCarthy 1999).

In 1990, the Milwaukee Parental Choice Program was enacted allowing up to 1 percent of economically disadvantaged pupils in the public schools to attend nonsectarian private schools. In 1995, it was expanded to include religious schools (CER 1999). In 1998, 6,200 Milwaukee students attended fifty-seven religious and thirty secular private schools with vouchers that were worth $4,900 each (Toch and Cohen 1998). In 1996, the Cleveland voucher program allowed about 4,000 low-income students to receive publicly funded vouchers to attend grades K–3 in private schools of their choice including religious schools (Murphy et al. 1997; J. McCarthy 1999). The Milwaukee and Cleveland voucher programs, however, are limited to children from low-income families. In April 1999, Florida became the nation's first and only state to provide a state-wide voucher program to allow students to attend private schools at taxpayers' expense. All students in Florida's worst public schools, regardless of family income or their grades, are eligible for vouchers of about $4,000 a year to help pay for private or parochial school tuition (CER 1999).

Discussion in this chapter is limited to the most controversial issue of school choice, the voucher program that includes religious schools as well as out-of-district public schools. The first point includes discussion of whether our public education system has problems that are serious enough to require voucher programs.

Our Public Education System Has Failed; We Need a Major Reform

Supporting Vouchers

Our cities' public schools are in trouble. Partly as a result of the government-mandated desegregation policy started in the 1960s, which led to a massive "white flight," students at risk, especially low-income minority students, are disproportionately concentrated in urban areas. Schools in low-income neighborhoods often exhibit low levels of expectations for their students, deplorable levels of course failure and retention in grades, and low levels of graduation and basic skills achievement (Moore and Davenport 1990, 188; Carter 1999; Schmoke in Viteritti 1996). A steady stream of reports from the nation's public schools has documented a 25 percent high school dropout rate, high proportion of high school graduates who are functionally illiterate, and three decades of falling test scores (Beers and Ellig 1994, 19). Especially in inner-city schools, the problem is even more pronounced. Fifty-seven percent of central-city fourth graders in public schools cannot read (Carter 1999). Over the years, due to economic changes and technological development, most jobs require at least ninth-grade levels of reading, writing, and math. However, a large percentage of urban high school graduates are not reaching even this minimum skills level and are thus unemployable (Moore and Davenport 1990, 187–8). Parents and community leaders have voiced outrage that the public schools are not only failing in their educational mission but are increasingly becoming breeding grounds for a host of social problems including crime, drug abuse, gang activities, pregnancy, and violence (Beers and Ellig 1994, 19).

What is even more alarming is the fact that this failure of public education occurred despite massive government support for public education. The national average public school per-pupil cost per year has tripled since the 1960s and reached $5,363 in 1997, compared with $1,499 of average Catholic school tuition. In most large inner cities, the cost is well over $6,000 per pupil (Carter 1999; Kim 1997; Hakim et al. 1994). The average public school teacher salary increased by 50 percent, adjusted for inflation, averaging $3,900 in 1998, compared with about $2,900 in private schools (Beyerlein 1999; Toch 1991). Public schools' average class size has fallen by a third since the 1960s, to about twenty-five, which is about the same as in private schools (Toch and Streisand 1997; Beers and Ellig 1994, 19). Under the Title I program, which provides aid to poor children's education, we have spent more than $100 billion since 1965, and Congress reauthorized the Elementary and Secondary Education Act in 1999, a $13 billion program that will be used for inner-city K–12 public education (Carter 1999). If the declining quality of public education continues, it is certainly not for the lack of reform efforts or funding (Beers and Ellig 1994, 19; Hakim et al. 1994, 4).

Opposing Vouchers

American public education is often perceived as failing, yet the pessimism is overstated and exaggerated by media distortion and political manipulation. Careful examinations by many scholars show just the opposite: American public education is not failing. On virtually every measure available, American education is making gains. Test scores are not declining, but advancing. Dropout rates are not increasing—they have held steady for the past two decades. The reason SAT scores appear to be dropping is largely because of the changing demographic characteristics. Since the mid-1970s, largely due to the availability of college scholarships and loans especially to minority students, many more students are taking the SAT, many of whom in the past could not even dream of going to college. An increased number of immigrants, whose native language is not English, are also taking the exam. If 1990 SAT scores were weighted to reflect the demographic makeup of the 1975 pool of test takers, scores actually improved by 30 points in fifteen years (Smith and Meier 1995, 121–2).

The truth is, except for big city schools, people are generally satisfied with their public schools (Kirst in Brown 1992, 185). We must not assume that the problems of American public education are similar across districts or that all American public schools are in crisis or failing. The problems vary in substance and gravity, depending on the districts and geographic areas, and the differences must be taken into account when looking for policy solutions. There will not be a single, simple solution. Vouchers are not going to be a panacea (Witte 1992, 120). Even the problems we see in urban schools have existed in the same place for several generations. Actually, in modern times, urban schools are not all caught in an inescapable spiral of decay but are actually making progress in the face of horrific social and financial challenges (Smith and Meier 1995, 122; Witte 1992, 121).

It is not unusual that urban schools' operating costs exceed those of either private or suburban schools. Their buildings are usually older than suburban schools, thus requiring higher maintenance costs; they need more extensive security measures, such as metal detectors and security officers; they have greater student population who need subsidies, such as free lunch and breakfast, transportation, and special education needs; they have to pay higher salaries to attract qualified teachers willing to teach despite the challenges.

Supporting and opposing views of vouchers can vary depending on the types of vouchers—whether the vouchers are universal or means-tested. In the following, supporting and opposing views of universal vouchers in general are discussed, followed by means-tested vouchers.

School Vouchers Give Parents of All Income Levels Freedom of Choice

Supporting Vouchers

Traditionally, children are assigned to public schools according to where they live. People of means have always had school choice, because they can afford to move to an area with high-quality public schools, or they can choose to enroll their children in private schools. Parents without such means generally have no choice of school and have to send their children to the school assigned to them by the district, regardless of the school's quality or appropriateness for their child (CER 1999). In 1954, in *Brown v. Board of Education*, the Supreme Court promised equal educational opportunities for all children. The equal opportunity in education, however, has been available only for the financially well-off families who could move to better school districts or send their children to private schools (Reinhard 1997; Witte 1990, 43). Vouchers will give families of all income levels the option to choose which school they want their children to attend, public or private, religious or secular. If parents have the right to choose so many other basics in their lives, such as where they live, where they go to church, where they work, then they also ought to have the right to choose which school their children should attend. We might expect a communist society to assign children to state schools to receive a uniform education, but America is the land of freedom, diversity, and choice. Our educational system should reflect those values and welcome choice and competition (Vanourek 1996).

The diversity of school choice is reflected in the diversity in private-sector schools. There are single-sex schools, religious schools, specialized schools, such as technology, music, fine arts schools, and Afrocentric academies. There are day schools, boarding schools, independent prep schools, and Montessori schools. There is greater diversity in the private sector of education as compared with the public sector, thus greater options to choose from (Toch 1991, 67).

Opposing Vouchers

Choice has always existed in American education. The principal choice strategies have been: 1) selection of neighborhood which determines the school; and 2) the option of private schools. Choices in education, like many other choices in our society, do not come for free. Many parents take great pains and effort to earn sufficient income to afford a home in a good school district or to send their children to private schools. They pay a lot of property tax or private school tuition to support their children's good education (in Barulich 1996). It won't be fair to offer the same privilege that they earn through hard work to others who did not earn it. It violates the American spirit, the value of hard work, achievement, and competition.

Parents do not have the real choice under the voucher system, only an illusion of choice. The real choice remains with the private school admissions officers who decide whom to enroll, how many to enroll, and whether to participate in a voucher program at all (Sikes 1997). Admission decisions are often based on students' family backgrounds, past performance, and test scores of students, which indicate potential success in school (NEA 1996). Many private schools have entrance exams, and usually reject two of every three students who apply (Chase 1997).

Vouchers Increase Parental Involvement in Children's Education

Supporting Vouchers

One of the most important outcomes of school choice is a sense of shared ownership and pride in the schools they have chosen. Choice is a form of empowerment. There is something dignified about being allowed to choose a school rather than being compelled to attend a particular school (Cookson 1994, 97). This means more interest, concern, and participation by the owners, leading to consumer-driven improvements in education (duPont 1994, 128; Coleman and Hoffer 1987; Bauch and Goldring 1995; Fliegel in Beers and Ellig 1994). Many educators share the belief that parental choice is a key factor in determining parental involvement in students' education, and parental involvement is powerfully linked with students' achievement (Bast and Harmer 1997; Cookson 1994, 98).

An important feature of most private school voucher programs is that they pay only partial tuition, usually half. Parents have to pay the rest, either in cash, or, if the school agrees, in volunteer services. When parents have to scrimp and save to pay for tuition, they think of education as an investment. They take charge. They pay attention to whether they are getting their money's worth. The children take school more seriously when they know their parents are sacrificing for the sake of their future (Meyerson 1999).

Choice plans increase not just parental involvement but also parental satisfaction in schools. Studies found that parents in choice schools were more satisfied with their children's education than parents of students in zoned schools. They believed more strongly that their children enjoyed school, were academically challenged, and had better teacher-student relationships than in the matched schools (Driscoll 1993; Cookson 1994, 87; Witte 1993).

Opposing Vouchers

Parental involvement does not automatically increase simply because children change to private schools. The extent to which parents can participate in school activities depends heavily on parents' work status and availability of transportation. A study of the Cincinnati choice program discovered that parental involvement in choice schools (specialty and magnet schools) was not higher than in zoned schools. For some parents, this was due to lack of transportation, and for others, it was because of their work schedules (Goldring 1997, 98). In other countries with choice programs (Australia, the Netherlands, Canada, and England), there was no improvement in parental involvement among parents whose children moved to choice schools, and parental involvement was not higher in the selected choice schools than in the zoned schools (Brown 1992, 183).

In British Columbia's experiment with choice, the private schools, upon receiving public funds, were required to follow government-mandated regulations, and thus lost their religious character and autonomy, and parents' satisfaction with their private schools decreased as a result (Brown 1992, 183).

Vouchers Foster Competition and Accountability

Supporting Vouchers

Many public school systems are centralized and bureaucratic monopolies. Their customers are assigned to them by virtue of geography, not choice. Customers must pay regardless of whether they are satisfied with the service or product, or whether they choose an alternative such as private schooling. As a result, school systems have few incentives to deliver quality education (Beers and Ellig 1994). By extending parents' opportunities to seek a better education, vouchers will force the public system to respond to a competitive market in much the same way that private schools already do. Increased competition will compel public schools to become more efficient and effective in order to stay in business (Doyle 1996; Reinhard 1997; Carter 1999).

Following the basic economic law of supply and demand, parents and students will be attracted to schools that fulfill those educational needs. Those schools, public or private, doing the best job of meeting the demands of their potential customer base will be rewarded with increased revenue. The schools that do not respond to the demands of the marketplace will be punished (Chubb and Moe 1990).

Choice programs thus far have shown that when public schools are faced with the possibility of a large student transfer and a corresponding loss of funding, they have shown a willingness to make improvements both in how and what they teach. Using the Department of Education data, Hoxby found that in areas where public schools compete heavily for the same students, overall student test scores rose 3 percentile points, in areas where public and private schools compete for the same students, 8 percentile point improvement. In areas where the public school suffered no financial loss for losing students, public school spending remained the same; whereas in areas where several public schools vie for the same students, the overall per-pupil expenditures decreased by 17 percent (Hoxby in Rees 1999).

With vouchers, families become powerful consumers who hold the fate of schools in their hands. Teachers and administrators will face greater accountability and will be motivated to produce tangible results (Viteritti 1996).

Oppposing Vouchers

The claim that public schools do not have any competition is not entirely true; competition already exists under the current school system. Parents are able to choose their residence based on the quality of local schools and, therefore, public school districts have a lot of incentive to improve their outcomes, which is directly related to the attractiveness of their community. One of the major factors that determine people's decision to purchase a house is the school district. If a school's performance falls, some families will leave, and it will become more difficult to attract newcomers to the community. Property values will fall, and other local businesses would be hurt. Rational managers of local public schools have every incentive to keep such a trend from developing in the first place (Peterson 1990, 69). In two separate studies in the New Jersey and Los Angeles area, analysts discovered that as the performance of high school students' standardized tests improves, so do the property values of the community (Rosen and Fullerton in Peterson 1990, 68).

There is great danger in placing public schools in a complete market situation based on competition. Education is not and cannot be a consumer good; it is a public good that communities must provide for all children (Shanker in Boyer 1994, xii). Some of the marketplace problems cannot be accepted in an educational setting. For instance, markets punish companies that do not respond to the market with bankruptcy. If a school closes because it fails to meet the demands of parents, what happens to the students who are attending the school (Smith and Meier 1995, 28)? What traumatic experience would that be for the students? In 1995 in Milwaukee, two of the city's voucher schools shut down in the middle of the school year, leaving their students literally standing outside their doors (NEA 1996).

A market-based competition would motivate public schools to improve only if the money is provided on a per-pupil base rather than on common services. If not, public schools have no incentive to recruit more students. Ironically, however, in order to make less popular public schools improve, the government is obligated to provide more resources to the less popular schools, which undermines the basic argument of competition providing incentives.

If schools are forced to compete to survive, business interests might override students' interests in the nature of education. Some schools might become a business of making profits off students instead of schooling. Not only do companies have an incentive to respond to market demands, but they also have the incentive to respond to this demand by using as few resources as possible so as to maximize profits. Schools might do the same. Some schools might promise more than they can deliver and cut costs in areas where the impact on performance is not readily noticeable (Smith and Meier 1995, 28).

A market approach to schools would encourage schools to put price tags on students. Children with special needs and disabilities come with high price tags. They may be perceived as difficult to provide for and expensive in terms of time and resources, and less attractive than other students (Evans and Vincent 1997). If survival is linked to high performance, no school would want students with lower academic or profit potential. The market might well become a cruel place for physically, socially, and academically handicapped children (Smith and Meier 1995, 127).

Public schools and private schools cannot compete because they are not on a level playing field. Private schools can, and a majority of them do, handpick their student bodies, and, formally or informally, dismiss students who do not meet their academic or disciplinary criteria. The majority of private schools have entrance exams, and require that students successfully finish their previous grade level (Sikes 1996; Shanker and Rosenberg 1994, 62). With vouchers, public schools, instead of improving, would face the danger of becoming a "dumping ground" for all the academically, socially, and physically handicapped children (Smith and Meier 1995, 61; Cookson 1994; Crain 1993; NEA 1996).

Choice, by itself, does not adequately enhance the information required for the parents to be intelligent consumers in education (Elmore 1990). It is difficult and costly to provide adequate information about the quality of schools in a comparable pattern (Hirschman in Weeres 1990, 234). To make matters worse, there is no consensus on what constitutes good quality schools. What makes a good school is not just the academic achievement of the students. Many studies have found that parents' criteria for assessing schools are wider than academic performance (Glatter et al. 1997, 202). Many studies of choice programs, in the United States and in other countries (the Netherlands, Australia, Canada, and England), have shown that most parents select schools based on nonacademic qualities, such as religious affiliation, social class and race of peers, convenience of location, learning climate, availability of supplementary day care, proximity of school to parent's job, and availability of athletic or special education programs (Brown 1992, 176–8; Wells 1993; Witte 1993; Carnegie Foundation 1992, 51–2). In the Carnegie Foundation's Milwaukee voucher program study, only 16 percent of the parents cited "academically related" reasons for making choices (Carnegie Foundation 1992, 13, 50–51). African American parents often keep their children in low-status schools to avoid the pain of exposing their children to racism and thereby possibly damaging their self-esteem (Wells and Crain 1992).

The purpose of education is not merely to teach math and reading but also to prepare citizens for a democratic society (Peterson and Greene 1998). Life requires developing one's talents to the full; yet, life also requires getting along with all different types of people. Schooling must be a balance between social and an academic preparation for life (Jones 1990, 243). Once we include all these nonacademic qualities of schools, rating schools and providing school information to parents in a comparable format becomes almost an impossible task to achieve.

Probably for these reasons, many studies have found no empirical evidence that increased school choice and competition result in increased effectiveness of service in education (Elmore 1990; Brown 1992, 175–84; Wells and Crain 1992). The British school choice programs have shown that the schools have limited ability to respond to the external changes, and thus, competition and market force do not necessarily bring about academic improvement (Levin and Riffel 1997, 55; Edwards and Whitty 1997, 40). In other countries with a choice system (the Netherlands, Australia, Canada), researchers found a uniform curriculum in all schools, private and public, and an almost total absence of innovation (Brown 1992, 183). Most choice schools were unaware of the parents' views and demands and were unprepared to change their practice to take account of the demands and views (Hughes 1997, 84; Levin and Riffle 1997, 44).

It is not the market-type competition that makes a good school (Smith and Meier 1995, 130). There are hundreds of public schools that have shown dramatic improvements in producing quality education. Their spirit of renewal, however, has arisen not from the threat of competition but from the schools' own commitment to improve. What makes good schools are the high academic standards and accountability displayed by devoted and caring teachers and their willingness to improve the quality of education with the support of parents (Boyer 1994, 140; Doyle 1996; Murphy et al. 1997; Rothstein 1993, 20).

Competition Can Be Created within the Public School System

Opposing Vouchers

If the goal is to create a market-type competition, we don't need vouchers that support private schools. It is possible, as many states and school districts have tried, to provide choice among public schools, thus public schools can compete among themselves (Boyer 1994, 142). Many states and school districts offer public school choice in the forms of magnet schools (schools specializing in particular disciplines like art or science), charter schools (publicly funded for-profit schools), and special program schools, either interdistrict or intradistrict. The basic goal is to create diversity and choice among public schools without creating inequality. Every school would become attractive; students would choose schools based on their individual interests, style, and career goals (Hirsch 1997; Glatter et al. 1997).

Supporting Vouchers

It is not established whether most parents want a diverse system, as distinct from a high-quality one, and it is certainly not clear whether specialty schools are appropriate for secondary education (Glatter et al. 1997, 195). Early specialization would be undesirable for the majority of primary- and secondary-level school children. Children are not sure what they want to study; they need to try many different things before they can decide what they want to focus on. It is better to have uniformity among schools emphasizing the mastery of the basics and leave the specialization to higher education (Jones 1990, 257).

One of the reasons Catholic schools achieve high academic standards is because they stick to the basics rather than spending a lot of money in fancy equipments, elective courses, and extracurricular activities. They push students to take advanced courses in math and English rather than in all kinds of vocational or other specialized courses (Toch 1991, 71).

The cost of operating magnet schools has been horrendous without achieving much academic improvement. According to Carnegie Foundation's study, on a per-student basis, magnet school projects have been the most expensive federally subsidized programs in the nation. They involve massive school busing to transport students to schools of their choice, often far away from their neighborhoods, and additional administrative staff to oversee the program (Carnegie Foundation 1992, 24).

In areas where the magnet school approach was implemented, magnet schools quickly became popular schools of choice, as opposed to unpopular zone schools, creating inequality among schools (Hirsch 1997).

Vouchers Violate the First Amendment Requirement for the Separation of Church and State

Opposing Vouchers

Providing tax-funded vouchers to private schools creates a legal problem when it involves religious schools. About 90 percent of the nation's 26,000 private schools claim a religious identity; many are parochial, that is, they are run by churches, parishes, synagogues, or mosques (Laconte 1999). Providing government funds to religious schools, either directly or indirectly, violates the First Amendment requirement for the separation of church and state (Viteritti 1996; Lee and Foster 1997, 152).

Public funds must be used for public schools only. Public dollars carry the responsibility for providing public access, governance, and accountability (National PTA 1997; Bolick 1998). The 1973 Supreme Court ruling in the *Nyquist* case found it unconstitutional for the states to pay religious school tuition, and that ruling remains the law of the nation (Shields and Mincberg 1998).

Voucher supporters say that it is all right to fund religious schools as long as parents, not the government, do the choosing. That argument does not stand. When you give tax dollars to a parent to pass on to a school, it is still tax money flowing to a religious ministry (Lynn in LaPolt 1998). Taxpayers have no control over private school policies and practices. It is unconstitutional to ask citizens to pay taxes to support privately held institutions that report only to privately selected boards and church committees (Sikes 1996).

Religious schools are not just public schools with a pinch of prayer added. They are pervasively sectarian institutions created exclusively to serve a private purpose by educating young people in the faith. In most cases, these schools' primary mission is driven by faith and doctrine. The religious mission shapes the curriculum, sets priorities, and emphasizes faith-based principles such as creation theology in science classes. This is clearly "promoting" religion, which is against our Constitution. The government may not promote religion, and it cannot escape its constitutional responsibility simply by passing the money to parents (Shields and Mincberg 1998).

Supporting Vouchers

The state-provided vouchers do not "establish" or "promote" a religion as long as parents are free to use them to send their children to any school—Catholic, Protestant, Jewish, Muslim, or secular (Peterson and Greene 1998; Vanourek 1996). Giving money to parents and kids is not the same as giving it to schools. Aid to students and families is a matter of providing government benefits. It is not a religious establishment (Lee and Foster 1997, 152).

Parents who choose to have their children attend sectarian schools are entitled to the same rights and privileges as those who do not (Viteritti 1996). Currently, parents who send their children to private schools must pay twice for their children's education—the private school tuition and property tax that supports their area public schools. Most parents who choose private schools do so out of religious conviction; they want their children to learn religious beliefs and values as a part of education. This double payment for education is a high price to pay to exercise a constitutionally guaranteed right to freedom of religion (Bast and Harmer 1997). Vouchers would allow them to exercise their religious rights and educational choices without being penalized. For these parents, vouchers are simply the money that they have earned and given to the government in the form of taxes to be used for their children's education (Cookson 1994, 106). Not allowing them this right would be a discrimination against people of faith who are only trying to give their children an education that reflects their religious beliefs. It is clear that once a state decides to fund private education, it must do so with neutrality. They cannot discriminate against religious schools and punish parents who hold religious beliefs (V. McCarthy 1999).

In every case since the *Nyquist* decision in 1973, the Supreme Court has sustained programs that made aid available to parents or students who may direct it to religious schools. In the 1983 *Mueller v. Allen* case, the Court upheld a state income tax deduction for educational expenses, even though the vast majority of deductions were used for religious school expenses. The Court noted that the public funds are transmitted to religious schools "only as a result of numerous choices of individual parents of children" (Bolick 1998). The Wisconsin Supreme Court in 1998 held that Milwaukee's voucher program did not violate Wisconsin's Constitution because funds are funneled to students, not schools; one religion is not favored over another; it does not promote religion or link church and state; and children were the primary beneficiaries and the benefit to school is indirect (Bolick 1998; Toch and Cohen 1998; LaPolt 1998). In

November 1998, the U.S. Supreme Court declined to review a Wisconsin Supreme Court's decision upholding Milwaukee's Parental Choice Program (Lewin 1999).

Private Schools Are Better
Than Public Schools

Supporting Vouchers

Catholic schools have been especially effective in educating inner-city, minority students. Students in urban Catholic schools achieve at much higher levels and have lower dropout rates than do students in public schools in the same area, despite the fact that the Catholic schools accept students just like the ones attending public schools (Shanker and Rosenberg 1994, 59; Viteritti 1996). Coleman et al. compared Catholic and public schools' academic performances, controlling for selection effect, and concluded that Catholic schools produce better learning environments and higher academic achievement than public schools (1982). Convey's series of studies, based on National Assessment of Educational Progress data, documented consistently higher scores of Catholic school students compared with public school students (1992). Greeley's analysis of data from longitudinal study showed superior performance among whites, African Americans, and Hispanics in Catholic schools, compared with students in public schools, in every single category (in Doyle 1996). The 1990 Rand Corporation's study of New York City's public and Catholic schools produced the same result (Hanks 1996). Neal's study showed that while 62 percent of minority students at urban public schools graduate, the graduation rate for similar students of a corresponding background in Catholic schools is 88 percent (CER 1999; Hanks 1996). In 1993, the New York State Department of Education found that Catholic schools with 81 to 100 percent minority composition outscored New York City public schools with the same percentage of minority enrollment (Hanks 1996). Although they had similar percentages of students from troubled families with low incomes, Catholic schools expelled far fewer children than did public schools (Byrk in Hanks 1996).

It is not just the level of academic performance that was different. Greene found that private schools produce students with higher degrees of political participation, social capital, and tolerance than do public schools. Private schools also provide better racial and class diversity than do public schools (Rees 1999).

Private schools and parochial schools, by and large, are more cost-effective than public schools. On average, they operate at a cost between 50 and 60 percent of the average per-pupil cost of public schools (Viteritti 1996). The average Catholic school tuition was $1,499 in 1997, which is less than one-third of the average annual per-pupil cost of public schools, which was $5,363 in 1997 (Carter 1999; Fox 1999).

Opposing Vouchers

Public schools and private schools cannot be compared because they are not on a level playing field. Private schools are allowed to handpick their student bodies; they are also free to get rid of students who do not work out, who generally end up in the public schools (Shanker and Rosenberg 1994, 62; Sikes 1996). For example, 71 percent of Catholic high schools require an entrance exam, as do 43 percent of other religious schools and 66 percent of independent schools; 80 percent require that entering students have successfully completed their previous year of school (Shanker and Rosenberg 1994, 62). While students at private schools score higher on achievement measures, this is just as likely to reflect selective screening as the ability to provide superior education services (Witte 1992; Smith and Meier 1995, 124).

When controlled for family background and screening effect, most research leans heavily toward the view that the apparent superiority of some private schools is due more to the relative preparedness and family background of their student bodies than to characteristics stemming from their private control (Cookson 1993). According to the 1990 National Assessment of Educational Progress, there is virtually no difference in the performance of public and private schools when family background is controlled (Shanker and Rosenberg 1992, 129–130). Jencks reanalyzed Coleman et al.'s data and concluded that the differences Coleman et al. found between public and private school children's achievement were not substantial (1985). Lee and Byrk found that, after accounting for individual student differences, variations in achievement gains were the results of racial and socioeconomic school composition, average number of advanced courses taken, amount of homework assigned, and staff problems in the school. Whether a school was private was virtually insignificant (1989).

What makes a good school is not whether it is private or public. Any school that exhibits the same cluster of attributes—high expectations, high standard of conduct, accountability, a focused curriculum, good order and discipline, and caring teachers and staff committed to producing tangible results—will have successful outcomes (Doyle 1996; Murphy et al. 1997; Rothstein 1993, 20).

Government Vouchers Will
Entail Government Regulations

Opposing Vouchers

Government money always comes with strings attached. Whenever government money flows, regulations follow. Voucher programs could become a Trojan horse for government meddling in private education, thereby undermining the quality and autonomy of private schools (Laconte 1999; Dewey 1997).

The Supreme Court is unlikely to approve public funding to private schools unless private schools are willing to implement state-mandated regulations governing admissions, curriculum, student discipline, and religious activities (Brown 1992, 186). In Milwaukee, in order to participate in voucher programs, religious schools had to make major concessions—all participating schools must loosen their admission policies and allow voucher students to opt out of religious activities (Laconte 1999). When Milwaukee private schools received more applications than they could accommodate, students were chosen by lottery. The admission process is what makes it possible to evaluate whether a child and her family would be comfortable with a religious institution. The whole philosophical framework of religious schools could be ruined and children would be confused if families were opposed to what schools teach and emphasize. The leaders of National Religious School Associations, though supportive of vouchers, mostly reject government-imposed conditions on admissions. Almost all religious schools prefer accepting students of parents who subscribe to the mission of their schools (Laconte 1999).

The Milwaukee voucher program's second concession, an opt-out provision, is just as controversial. It prevents schools from requiring students to participate in any religious activity that they or their parents find objectionable. If parents are not backing what schools teach, there is no foundation on which education can be built (Zellmer in Laconte 1999). It is impossible to separate school's discipline policies from Christian commitment. Christian school teachers are not using behavioral management techniques; good behavior is an expression of faith (Rahn in Laconte 1999). Most schools would not be happy with an opt-out provision (Zwiebel in Laconte 1999). The Department of Education report found that 86 percent of private schools surveyed would balk at a voucher program that allowed exemptions from religious instruction (Laconte 1999).

The Washington, D.C. voucher bill required that no part of the voucher be used for religious purposes. Voucher-redeeming religious schools must certify that their curriculum was "religion free." This is a stab at the heart of what makes private education a desirable choice—the religious mission (Dewey 1997).

When vouchers become available, the laws that currently protect public school students from discrimination based on sex, race, religion, sexual orientation, pregnancy, or any kind of physical, emotional, or academic disability, would be extended to participating private schools (Laconte 1999). If the changes do not come through legislation, they will come through litigation, when individuals begin filing a host of discrimination lawsuits against private schools (Doyle in Laconte 1999). If voucher programs expose these classrooms to new layers of government oversight and threat of lawsuits, few sectarian schools would want to participate in voucher programs. Whether religious schools would endorse voucher programs depends on how the law would be written and how much government regulation it entails (Hoyt in Laconte 1999).

In the Netherlands, which has had school choice since the 1920s, in Australia, which began school choice in 1973, and in parts of Canada with school choice programs, private schools with state funding were significantly deprivatized and became de facto public schools. Private schools were subjected to increasing government regulation and centralization, and, as a result, the distinction between private and public schools disappeared (James in Dewey 1997; Brown 1992, 183). The regulations typically included specifying hiring and firing procedures, credentials and salaries of teachers, criteria for selecting students, price and expenditure per student, and participants in the school's decision-making structure. In addition, vouchers raised teachers' and staffs' salaries and other administrative costs while lowering private-sector donations and contributions (Dewey 1997).

Religious schools have a specific mission that is not just academic; they assert moral and transcendent alternatives to our secularized public schools (Laconte 1999). Their independence and autonomy, therefore, is critical for their success in educating children. Voucher programs, if designed poorly, could destroy their mission and make them less private, less parochial, and more like public schools (Riley in Laconte 1999). Vouchers are supposed to create competition by breaking up the public school monopoly. However, if private schools lose their autonomy and distinctive identity and become part of the government sector, there is no "free-market" case for school choice (Dewey 1997; Laconte 1999).

Supporting Vouchers

The current proposals for school choice are designed to ensure that the voucher is legally regarded as a grant to the individual child or his guardians, not a direct aid to the schools. Under this scheme, not one cent of public money flows directly from the state to a sectarian private school, thus it does not give the government the power or right to regulate private school policies any more than it already does now. On the part of the private schools, participation in voucher plans is never mandatory; they are free to remain outside the program if they believe the accompanying regulations are too burdensome (Bast and Harmer 1997; Laconte 1999).

Even without vouchers, state governments may, and already do, regulate private schools at will. State governments often mandate academic curricula, hours of study, qualifications of teachers, facilities, student evaluations, students' attendance, health and safety codes, and other intimate details of private schooling (Laconte 1999; Bast and Harmer 1997). What prevents excessive regulation is not the absence of a "cash nexus" between private schools and the state but the legal design of the voucher program and the strength of opposition to such regulations on the part of private schools (Bast and Harmer 1997).

So far, the opt-out provision has not caused any problems in Milwaukee classrooms. About 6,300 low-income students are using the voucher program, attending mostly Catholic, Protestant, and Islamic schools, yet, no one is opting out of the schools' mandatory prayer services. Officials say they know of no students being excused from religious activities. It is evident that parents, when they have the choice, choose religious schools because they want the infusion of values in their children's education (Schmeling in Laconte 1999).

To a certain extent, and in some areas, government regulation is necessary to make sure the public money is not used to undermine the base of our democratic ideals and common goals. Nobody wants our public money to be used to indoctrinate children in communist or fascist ideology or to teach superiority of one race over another (Cline 1997). In a society so diverse as America, a decentralized system of school choice could produce schools that are highly unequal in resources and discriminatory toward low-power groups. Centralized checks are necessary to prevent abuse of civil rights and liberties. This is the price we have to pay to maintain true and safe school choice (Merelman 1990, 90).

Vouchers Will Intensify the Existing Inequalities and Segregation among Schools

Opposing Vouchers

Any form of school choice, such as open enrollment, magnet schools, vouchers, and tax credits would inevitably result in inequality of schools, stratified by social class, race, or other family backgrounds. Schools, in order to survive in competition, would be forced to attract and select the most academically prepared students, those with the most supportive and involved parents, leaving the most disadvantaged, hard-to-educate, and at-risk students behind in the troubled traditional public school system (Peterson and Greene 1998; Smith and Meier 1995, 61; Cookson 1994; NEA 1996; Crain 1993).

Private schools can and do select their students. About 71 percent of Catholic high schools require an entrance exam, as do 43 percent of other religious schools and 66 percent of independent schools. About 80 percent of Catholic schools require that entering students have successfully completed their previous year of school. Private schools are also free to get rid of students who do not work out, who generally end up in the public schools (Shanker and Rosenberg 1994, 62).

For a school choice to be a viable option of school reform, a fair admission policy for all schools must be guaranteed (Glatter et al. 1997, 197). The major question is whether private schools would be willing to subject themselves to government regulations regarding their admissions procedure (Adler in Glatter et al. 1997, 200). A lottery system could produce a system of choice that is relatively equitable. However, even the lottery system, as it happened in New York City, cannot prevent selective biases. Many studies have documented that the more educated, concerned, and informed parents are, the more likely they will choose schools, and the more likely their children will do better academically (Bauch in Cookson 1994; Willms and Echols in Cookson 1994, 92; Wells 1993; Carnegie Foundation 1992; Witte 1993; Crain in Cookson 1994, 93).

Even with the public school choice, there is strong evidence that choice has benefited more advantaged families and resulted in inequality. In twenty-nine states with public school choice, students competed for limited places in sought-after schools, such as magnet schools; schools also sought students who were most articulate, most informed, and least in need of improvement (in Viteritti 1996; Plank et al. 1993; Moore and Davenport 1990, 189). In experimental school choice schemes in New York (in 1984–1985), Chicago (in 1986), Philadelphia (in 1987–1988), and in Boston (in 1984–1985), there was an overwhelming bias toward establishing procedures and standards at each step in the admission process that screened out problem students and admitted those with good academic records, good attendance, good behavior, and no special learning problems. These admission policies drained the neighborhood schools of their highest-achieving and best-behaved students, leaving the nonselective schools to deal with an even higher concentration of students with the most serious learning problems. Frequently, choice schools, formally or informally, sent students who did not meet their expectations back to their neighborhood schools (Moore and Davenport 1990, 201–5).

Unless a school system makes and carries out a fundamental commitment to improve educational services in all schools and for all student subgroups, school choice would inevitably increase inequality (Moore 1990). In other countries with choice systems, choice policies did not reduce racial and social class segregation, or improve urban schools, or help racial, ethnic, and language minority students (Brown 1992, 185). The British school choice policy has created a highly stratified two-tier system in which elite schools provide the model against which other schools are judged (Edwards and Whitty 1997, 40). In Australia, experience with private and public school choice resulted in a dual educational system, one for the poor and one for the rich (Brown 1992, 184). In the Netherlands, Australia, England, and Canada, "white flight" has left some area public schools racially and ethnically segregated (Brown 1992). One of the problems the British school choice program faced was finding places for children who had been expelled from their choice schools for behavior problems. Most likely, they were sent to their local schools in their neighborhood zones, and this made many local schools unattractive to many residents (Mayet 1997, 174).

If the goal is to help disadvantaged children, school choice seems to have the opposite effect (Carnegie Foundation 1992). School choice seems to exacerbate the inequality and segregation based on a combination of race, income level, and previous school performance (Moore and Davenport 1990, 198).

Supporting Vouchers

Once we decide to implement school choice with vouchers, there are a number of ways to reduce the creaming effect. First, vouchers can be either means-tested (provided to low-income families only), or progressive (provide more for the poor and less for the well-off). These options would make it easier for lower-income families to use vouchers. The recently established voucher programs in Cleveland and Milwaukee target at-risk children exclusively from low-income families who are often academically disadvantaged (CER 1999).

Second, skimming and creaming can be reduced by tightly controlling the admissions policy. Random selection by means of lottery or banding (students of all different levels of ability and backgrounds are assigned to each school) would significantly reduce potential skimming and creaming effects. Schools can be required to reserve certain percentages of their seats for disadvantaged students (Coons in Witte 1990, 32). Another option is a controlled choice, currently used in many states with public school choice. This plan provides parents with choices while maintaining the racial and socioeconomic balance in all schools. Parents influence selection by making ranked choices of schools, but the final assignments are made by administrators following prearranged rules that factor in racial balance, students' ability, family background, neighborhood, special student needs, and siblings (Witte 1990, 33).

From the inception, public education was meant to be the greatest equalizer, providing equal opportunity of education to everyone. In recent years, however, the public school system, instead of being more egalitarian and integrated, is becoming more racially segregated and isolated (Cookson 1994, 90–110). In contrast, today's private school students are less racially isolated than their public school counterparts. According to 1992 Department of Education data, 37 percent of private school students are in classrooms whose share of minority students is close to the national average, compared with only 18 percent of public school students. Forty-one percent of private school students are in highly segregated schools (either more than 90 percent white or more than 90 percent minority), as compared with 55 percent of their public school peers (Peterson and Greene 1998; Doyle 1996).

Private school students also report having more positive relationships with students from other racial and ethnic groups. According to the 1992 Department of Education survey, they are significantly more likely to have cross-racial friends than are students at public schools. Students, teachers, and administrators at private schools all report fewer racial problems than they do in public schools (Peterson and Greene 1998). Most important of all, students in private schools have more internal integration than students in public schools. All students study the same demanding curriculum, and thus, students of different backgrounds are more likely to be in classes together than those in public schools, where African American and Hispanic students are often tracked into less demanding classes (Powell in Toch 1991, 73).

In fact, people who are most supportive of vouchers are the central-city minorities. A national survey in 1997 by the Joint Center of Political and Economic Studies found the greatest support for vouchers among African Americans, 57 percent, as compared with 47 percent of white respondents. For blacks ages 26 to 35, the figure is 86 percent (Peterson and Greene 1998; Lacayo 1997, 74).

Vouchers Would Cost Too Much

Opposing Vouchers

Voucher programs would be extremely costly. Not only will taxpayers be forced to foot the bill for the vouchers themselves, but they will have to pick up the tab for a whole new bureaucracy and hidden costs like transportation (Chase 1997). Public schools, when they lose a few students to private schools, still face the same cost of operation as before, because certain overhead costs of maintaining the buildings and staff are fixed. However, part of the public tax money that previously supported public schools would be diverted to private schools in the form of vouchers. The Cleveland public school system had to eliminate its full-day kindergarten program for more than 4,000 students, (almost 70 percent of all students) in 1996–1997, so that 834 children, who were funded through the voucher program, could attend full-day kindergarten at private schools, at two and a half times the cost (Murphy et al. 1997).

Students who already attend private schools without vouchers (about 12 percent of the student population) would also become eligible for vouchers and draw on the public fund, thus causing an additional burden on public school resources. In short, vouchers will force taxpayers to support two entire education systems—public and private—costing the taxpayers more than ever before (Chase 1997; Freeney 1994, 44).

The voucher plans would require a massive school busing (Weeres 1990, 235). If no transportation is provided, many lower-class parents, who often do not have means of transportation or who must work, cannot choose schools other than the assigned ones in the neighborhood. However, if we do provide transportation to voucher students with public money, how can we justify not providing the same transportation to those students who already attend private schools? The government might end up providing transportation to all students who attend private schools, because not providing transportation to them would be discriminatory.

Supporting Vouchers

Voucher programs could be cheaper than the current public school system. In 1997, the national average public school annual per-pupil costs was $5,363; in most large cities, it is well over $6,000. Private schools, on average, operate at a cost between 50 and 60 percent of the per-pupil rate of public schools. The average annual tuition at Catholic schools was only $1,499 in 1997 (Carter 1999; Toch 1991, 71; Fox 1999; Hakim et al. 1994, 4; Viteritti 1996). In Cleveland, vouchers covered up to 90 percent of private school tuition, up to a maximum of $2,250. This maximum amount was a little more than a third of the pupil cost of Cleveland public schools, which was $6,507 in 1997. These numbers clearly reveal that with only one half the per-pupil cost we spend on public schools, we can cover most of private school tuition with vouchers (Carter 1999).

Americans make a massive investment in public education. Yet, much of that money is being wasted in public school bureaucracy and inefficiency. Most cities are trying to fix their schools with more or less of the same ingredients that have already failed for over three decades—more money and greater centralized control (Carter 1999). Public schools have grown larger, stronger, and more expensive to operate during the past two decades. Between 1980 and 1990, real per-pupil spending on public schooling rose 33.5 percent, 35.5 percent between 1970 and 1980 (Fox 1999). Through vouchers, we can channel that money to schools that work, forcing public schools to become more efficient and cost-effective (Carter 1999).

It Is Better to Improve Public Schools Than to Support Private Schools with Vouchers

Opposing Vouchers

There is no question that many inner-city school systems have problems. However, it would be a mistake for the states to walk away from the failing urban public school systems and turn to private schools. To do so would be a severe blow to the foundation principle of the government's responsibility for delivering education in common, government-oriented nonsectarian schools, open to all (AJC 1999). Private schools perform a needed service in our society, but there is no substitute for a strong public school system that is capable of accommodating the broad-based needs and wishes of the mainstream community (Sikes 1996).

If the goal is to help inner-city, underprivileged children, we need to support their schools with additional, compensatory funding and organizational reforms (Brown 1992, 185). Vouchers would help only a fraction of the poor students to get out of their troubled public schools; the majority of the poor children will not be able to take advantage of them. On the other hand, improving the existing public school system would benefit all the public school children as well as their community (Lacayo 1997, 73).

When public schools are given the freedom and resources to test bold new ideas, successes can happen. There are many examples of such schools all over the nation; East Harlem in New York is one of many examples (Rothstein 1993, 20). Many charter schools, which are publicly funded schools free of some of the bureaucratic rules, have been successful also (Lacayo 1997, 74). What makes a good school is not whether it is private or public. Rather, it is characteristics such as a high standard of conduct and achievement, a culture of shared mission and service, motivated leadership and accountability, and devoted teachers committed to making a tangible difference (Murphy et al. 1997; Archer 1998, 5; Toch 1991; Chubb and Moe 1990; Rothstein 1993, 20).

The nation's public schools are the backbone of our democratic system, weaving our diverse background into one nation and helping young people grow into responsible citizens. Public education values having a society that is not fragmented by divisions imposed by segregated or exclusive upbringing. It has an important function of uniting the children of different social, cultural, ethnic, racial, economic, and religious backgrounds under common goals and ideals, promoting limitless lifestyle options and respect for all differences (Rabkin 1999; Chase 1997). On the contrary, private schools serve people with particular views and backgrounds, such as those who want a religiously based education, socially exclusive environment, or an educationally distinctive atmosphere geared to a focused curriculum or a unique pedagogy. If vouchers are allowed on a large scale, the question of how to appropriate and modify private school principles to maintain such public educational goals would become a critical issue (Jones 1990, 243–54). If not, the common school tradition will be lost as educational diversity increases. Despite the fact that vouchers would ease the tuition burden for many Jewish parents and expand enrollment in Jewish schools, many Jewish organizations, such as American Jewish Committee and American Jewish Congress, firmly oppose vouchers that support religious schools, because it threatens the public education's ideal of religious tolerance (Rabkin 1999).

Supporting Vouchers

For over three decades, we have spent an enormous amount of money trying to improve our public school quality. Per-pupil expenditure in public schools has tripled since the 1960s, reaching $5,363 (national average in 1997) (Kim 1997), in comparison with Catholic schools' average tuition of $1,499 (Carter 1999; Hakim et al. 1994, 4). The average public school teacher's salary increased by 50 percent, adjusted for inflation, averaging $39,099 in 1997 (Beyerlein 1999), compared with approximately $29,000 in the private school system (Toch 1991, 73). Public schools' average class size has fallen by a third since the mid-1960s to about twenty-five, which is about the same as in private schools (Toch and Streisand 1997). To help the children of poor families, we spent over $100 billion since 1965 in Title I programs alone, and Congress reauthorized an additional $13 billion in 1999 (Carter 1999).

What is the result? Fifty-seven percent of central-city fourth graders in public schools cannot read (Carter 1999). Student performance in the nation's public school systems has continuously declined from 1961 to 1991. Median SAT scores have fallen almost 80 points over the past thirty-year period (Chubb and Moe 1990). If the public school system is not improving, it is not because we did not try to reform it, or we did not spend enough money. Clearly, spending more money is not the answer. Japan spends about 50 percent less per student than the United States, yet Japanese students consistently rank higher than U.S. students (Hakim et al. 1994, 4).

The U.S. public educational system is growing bigger and bigger. While the average school district in 1930 served only 200 students and 300 in 1950, by 1970, the average district served more than 2,500. As schools and school districts grew in size, they became more centralized and bureaucratic, parental influence diminished, funding was shifted from the local community to statewide jurisdiction, and it became more centralized and bureaucratic (Peterson 1990, 61–2). The public schools' large, centralized monopolistic system, where most administrative decisions are made by the school district, prohibits innovation, accountability, and efforts by the service providers—the principals and teachers (Hakim et al. 1994, 9). It cannot be responsive to the demands of parents and students. The system is designed to serve the legislature and school boards, not parents and children (Chubb and Moe 1990, 30–5).

Private schools, on the other hand, are governed by the market instead of hierarchical bureaucracies, and thus enjoy a lot more autonomy and innovation and can be more responsive to parents' and students' demands (Chubb and Moe 1990, 564). With greater autonomy and authority given to teachers and principals, private schools provide a professional environment for teachers concerned with producing tangible results (Chubb in Hill and Chubb 1991). They have been successful in paring down bureaucracy and handing over staffing and other matters to principals and teachers. The archdiocese of Washington, D.C., for instance, runs its 50,000-student school system with a central administration of just seventeen people. By contrast, the D.C. public schools support their 81,000-student enrollment with a headquarters bureaucracy of 1,500 (Toch 1991, 71).

Given the large size and rigid institutional structure of our big city public schools, it is virtually impossible for public schools to apply the lessons of private schools. The only way to innovate our public school system is to bring it to a market system, where schools are rewarded or punished based on their ability to enroll students. Currently, the bad public schools are not permitted to close;

instead, they are rewarded with more money. Only the market system that includes private schools would motivate public schools to improve (Chubb in Hill and Chubb 1991).

The School Effect Is Limited

Opposing Vouchers

When children's academic performance declines, the school is always the first to be blamed. For decades, however, virtually all research done on students' performance have repeatedly shown that family background is the main determinant of students' performance, not the quality of schools, or the amount of money schools spend on educating children (Coleman et al. 1966; Jencks et al. 1972; Chubb and Moe 1990; Smith and Meier 1995, 21; Witte 1992, 121). The harsh truth is that, in most situations, the family is a far more critical institution than the schools in determining a student's academic outcome, yet the family is far more imperiled than the schools are. Increasingly, schools are blamed and teachers are asked to do what parents have not been able to accomplish, such as motivating and disciplining students. Today, the nation's public schools are called on to stop drugs, reduce teenage pregnancy, feed students, improve their health, and eliminate gang violence, while trying to meet academic standards. If they fail anywhere along the line, we condemn them for not meeting our expectations (Boyer 1994, 138).

We cannot expect schools to solve all problems by themselves, because the most serious education problems are directly and immediately affected by adverse environment, such as poverty, family dissolution, poor employment prospects, drug and alcohol abuse, crime and delinquency, and discrimination (Witte 1992, 121; Weeres 1990, 238). When children are distracted by unfavorable surroundings not conducive to learning, they lack motivation, study habits and skills, educational expectations, and self-esteem, which are critical to academic achievement. When they do not improve academically, they are more likely to be drawn to crime, delinquency, drugs, alcohol, and pregnancy, thus creating a vicious cycle of underachievement (Witte 1992, 121).

A Carnegie Foundation's study reported that one-third of kindergarten students come to school not prepared to learn because of poor health, inadequate nurturing, and language deprivation. Other studies identified lack of parental support, child abuse, violence, and drug problems as serious deterrents to learning among older students (Boyer 1994, 138–9).

Improving the quality and facility of schools is not going to be sufficient to bring up educational standards. School problems must be solved in conjunction with other problems in our society, especially the family dissolution, urban blight, drugs, social inequality, and poor employment prospects (Hakim et al. 1994, 3). The danger of continuously blaming schools for failing to solve problems is that, in so doing, the real problems threatening education are being ignored (Smith and Meier 1995, 122).

Supporting Vouchers

Coleman and his colleagues in 1966 found that school effects were minimal: Factors like race, income, and parents' education level were more important than school characteristics as predictors of academic performance (1966). Later in 1981, however, he reopened the argument with other research data and demonstrated that which school a child goes to does matter; better a good school than a bad school. He concluded that even when family background factors are controlled, private schools do a better job educating students, particularly poor minority students, than public schools do (Coleman 1981; Coleman et al. 1982; Convey 1992; Doyle 1996; Cookson 1994, 80).

In most central-city public schools, students' average test scores fall as students advance through public schools. For example, when New York City public school students were matched against the statewide average, controlling for students' racial and income status, New York City students scored 3 percentile points behind the statewide average in third grade, but 6 points behind in sixth grade, and as much as 15 points behind in high school (Peterson and Greene 1998). If schools really don't matter, why do inner-city public school students' average test scores fall farther behind the statewide average as students advance in grade levels?

If school effects really were only weak (or worse yet, if they did not exist at all), the whole rationale of vouchers and school choice would come tumbling down. Indeed, if schools don't matter, there is no point in worrying about the right way to educate children, private or public (Doyle 1996).

Private Schools Cannot Accommodate All the Voucher Students

Opposing Vouchers

If vouchers were offered on a sustained basis, the existing private schools must expand their facilities or new private schools must be built, causing the price of vouchers and tuition to increase. Across the nation, there are about three times as many low-income children waiting in line to attend the private school of their choice as there are scholarships available to place those children in school. In New York City alone, more than 22,000 children want a shot at one of the 1,200 grants now offered by the School Choice Scholarship Foundation (Carter 1999). How can private schools accommodate all these students, unless they expand their facilities or build new schools? The price of vouchers is bound to go up.

Catholic schools are the most affordable private schools in the inner city, in part because they are the most heavily subsidized. The national average Catholic tuition of $1,499 covers only 62 percent of the total cost of the education. The rest is paid for by the church, either at the parish or diocesan level. At this level, no new schools will be built anytime soon. What sized voucher then could increase capacity (Carter 1999)?

Supporting Vouchers

Private schools, especially Catholic schools, have shown remarkable ability of innovation and adaptation. Many pioneers in privately funded vouchers have already developed a model that would enable inner-city churches to open new schools at rock bottom prices. Pat Rooney's Safe Haven schools in Indianapolis and Bernie Miller's in Chattanooga are just a few examples. The CEO America Horizon project in San Antonio is planning to provide vouchers to up to 14,000 low-income children to attend private schools. Already two new schools have been created by the program and some existing schools have opened up new classrooms (Carter 1999).

Since the 1960s, the cost of education has increased so rapidly for both public and private schools that many Catholic schools found it increasingly difficult to maintain their enrollment (Peterson 1990, 70). The flight of middle-class Catholics to the suburbs and increased tuition hikes have left many inner-city Catholic school classrooms empty. Nationally, Catholic school enrollment has plunged from 5.7 million in 1964 to 2.5 million in 1991 (Toch 1991, 71). The number of Catholic schools in the nation dropped by 50 percent since the 1970s (Brown 1992, 175). Sister Sheehan of the U.S. Catholic Conference laments that public schools have students with no buildings, whereas Catholic schools have buildings with no students (in Toch 1991, 71).

According to the U.S. Department of Education report, there are more than 3,100 private schools serving 22 urban communities with the most overcrowded public school systems. About a third of these private schools operate below 70 percent of their full capacity. The report estimates that there are between 150,000 to 185,000 private school spaces available in these urban districts alone (Carter 1999).

While the demand is staggering, at least three times as many private school seats are available as there are children waiting in line to fill them. Limits in capacity are not an obstacle to school choice at its current level (Carter 1999). In order for private schools to actively invest in expanding their facilities, there must first be large and sustained demand for private school education created by vouchers (Porath in Carter 1999). Inner-city public schools spend over $6,000 a year per pupil to educate their children. If we can spend half of that money on voucher programs, private schools could easily solve the capacity problem (Carter 1999).

Voucher Programs Will Strengthen the Inner-City Community

Supporting Vouchers

School choice would not only improve the quality of public schools, but also have beneficial community effects. Schools are social organizations; they have a strong influence on the community as a whole (Cookson 1994, 98). One of the major reasons why people leave the central cities for the suburbs is because of the poor quality of inner-city schools. A Calvert Institute survey of people who had moved out of Baltimore found that among families with school-age children, more than half of them cited the poor quality of the school was a primary reason to leave. Of those, 51 percent said that they might have stayed in the central city if all-school-choice options were available (Carter 1999).

Good schools, whether private or public, are the lifeblood of our cities (Doyle in Carter 1999). Catholic schools are important for the city because they serve as "neighborhood anchors," promoting a high quality of life for the whole community (Varady and Raffel in Carter 1999). The Hope Academy in Cleveland became an anchor for the local community, leading to a community effort among people who did not even have children in the school. It pulled the neighborhood together to eradicate the bad influence that had been disturbing the community (Morris in Carter 1999). The prospect of having strong Catholic schools in the neighborhood with a widespread school choice program would create a positive neighborhood effect that might go a long way toward revitalizing our central cities (Carter 1999). Young parents with children entering school will forgo the expensive move to the suburbs and pick instead a local private school suited to their needs. Other families will give up their suburban homes to live closer to their jobs. Businesses will open, so their employees can bring their children with them on their daily commute. The central city will pick up, property values will rise, racial integration will increase, and the students' test scores will rise (Peterson and Greene 1998).

Opposing Vouchers

The all-school-choice program includes not just the inner-city Catholic schools but also the suburban public and private schools. Once vouchers are provided, there is no guarantee that the inner-city children will attend inner-city Catholic schools only. What kind of community effect can we expect to see in inner cities when a large number of relatively well-off and concerned parents take their children, money, and loyalty to suburban schools away from their own neighborhood? Parents may become involved in their children's school of choice in a different neighborhood, and they may become less attached to their community as a result.

In order for a community to be revitalized, community members must support their public schools first. The public schools represent their community, more so than private schools do. Strong public schools will attract families and businesses; availability of private schools should remain as a secondary factor, because private schools serve primarily specific subgroups of the population.

Means-Tested Vouchers

The supporting and opposing views discussed thus far apply to universal vouchers in general, which provide the same amount per-pupil cost of education to all parents, regardless of income level, who wish to send their children to private schools. Means-tested vouchers, on the other hand, provide aid only to low-income parents who wish to send their children to private schools, such as the existing voucher programs in Cleveland and Milwaukee. The following sections summarize supporting and opposing views of means-tested vouchers.

Vouchers Must Be Means-Tested

Supporting Means-Tested Vouchers

Vouchers must be means-tested, providing aid only to the disadvantaged children of the lower-income families. They are the ones who need them the most, and they are the ones who could benefit most from them (Meyerson 1999). Poor children need a better education more than children from the well-off families. Nevertheless, the schools they attend, particularly in inner-city areas, are the least successful of all public schools (Peterson and Greene 1998). Many well-off families already exercise their choice either by sending their children to private schools or by purchasing homes in areas with high-quality public schools. What we need is a program that would extend these opportunities to parents and children who are not as fortunate (Witte 1990, 43).

In all likelihood, vouchers will not be enough to cover the whole tuition at private schools. Most existing vouchers cover about half of private school tuition (Chase 1997). As a result, universal vouchers would only make it easier for middle- and upper-income families to send their children to private schools (many of whom already do), but not lower-income families who have limited means of financing additional tuition costs and transportation (Chase 1997).

It has been more than forty years since we promised an equal opportunity of education in the historic *Brown v. Board of Education* decision of 1954. However, our country still does not provide an equal opportunity of education to underprivileged children. To force children into inadequate schools is to deny them any chance of success. To do so simply on the basis of their parents' income is unconscionable.

Opposing Means-Tested Vouchers

Under the name of vouchers or scholarships, what we are creating in reality is another form of government handouts to the poor, the "school stamp." Once created, just like other government entitlement programs like Food Stamps, Welfare, and Medicare, voucher programs will create problems of dependency and will grow by leaps and bounds (Bast and Harmer 1997). It will make the poor ever more dependent on government handouts, and it will create a vast system of government contractors and parents with "school stamps," a massive Medicare-style lobby for ever-increasing subsidies (Dewey 1997). The more numerous public subsidies become, the more is there generated in citizens the notion that everything is to be done for them, and nothing by them (Spencer in Bast and Harmer 1997). A hundred years ago, most Americans would have though it incredible that the federal government would one day systematically relieve individuals of their responsibility to save for their retirement and families of their duty to take care of their elderly parents (Dewey 1997). With means-tested vouchers, we are trying to relieve parents of their responsibility to pay for their children's education. Where does this end? How can we expect our children to learn the value of responsibility and accountability when their parents expect the government to take care of their food, housing, health care, and education?

Currently, parents who choose a private school for their children's education are forced to pay more than their share of their children's education; they pay their children's private school tuition in addition to the local property taxes that fund local public schools. With means-tested vouchers, they would end up paying higher federal income taxes to support poor inner-city children's vouchers.

Most suburban families who live in the public school district of their choice are reasonably happy with their schools. They took great pains to earn sufficient incomes and saved frugally to afford a home in a good school district, primarily to get away from the unhealthy influences of some of the inner-city children who bring their neighborhood problems to school. To these parents, means-tested vouchers mean busloads of inner-city youths who might bring the problems of ghetto streets that they desperately try to get away from. These parents are not welfare recipients; they pay taxes exceeding the public school's costs of educating their children. Have they exercised any less fiscal responsibility than parents who receive free vouchers in addition to welfare and food stamps? It is not fair to provide the same privileges that these people earn through hard work to others who did not earn it. It violates the American value of hard work, competition, and achievement. Choice in education, like many other choices in our society, does not come free. If you want your child to get a good education, you must work hard to get it, and that is what we need to teach our children of all income levels, the value of hard work, not the idea that the government can always bail you out.

Means-Tested Vouchers Have Been Successful

Supporting Means-Tested Vouchers

Although it is still too early to examine the full impact of means-tested voucher programs, there is plenty of evidence that they enhance the academic achievement of lower-income children. In Milwaukee, students applying for choice were assigned to a test or control group by means of lottery. Students enrolled in choice schools had only modest improvement in the first two years; but by years three and four, choice students began outstripping their peers in the control group. It should not be surprising that student performance does not improve considerably until the third and fourth years. Education does not happen overnight; it takes time to adjust to a new teaching and learning environment. The disruption of switching schools and adjusting to new routines and expectations may hamper improvement in test scores in the first year or two in a choice school (Peterson and Greene 1998). Another study found that the choice program in Milwaukee was responsible for a dramatic increase in aspiration levels among voucher students. A significant number of dropouts returned to school, and students' satisfaction with schools increased from 25 percent to 75 percent (Nathan 1991, 144).

In Cleveland, test scores in mathematics and reading showed large gains for voucher students attending private schools, which enrolled approximately 25 percent of the student body coming from public schools with means-tested vouchers. Between the beginning of the school year in September 1996 and May 1997, these students on average gained 5 percentile points on the reading test and 15 percentile points in math, relative to the national norm. Improvements in these test scores were experienced by students in all grades (Greene et al. 1997). Clearly, private school vouchers are the key to educational success for students who are financially trapped in failing inner-city public school systems (Greene and Peterson 1996).

Opposing Means-Tested Vouchers

Despite the intensity of the debate, there is no conclusive evidence that means-tested vouchers improve academic performance of lower-income students. There are equal numbers of studies, if not more, which indicate that voucher students did not perform higher than nonvoucher students who were left behind. Voucher advocates have embraced the view of Paul Peterson, a Harvard University political science professor, whose research indicated that voucher students scored higher than their public school peers. The same Milwaukee data, when evaluated by others, however, have shown that the difference Peterson found was negligible. The four-year evaluation of the Milwaukee voucher program conducted by Professor John Witte showed that voucher students did not achieve any better than their public school counterparts (Murphy et al. 1997; Witte 1992; Toch and Cohen 1998; Sikes 1997). A study conducted six years after the implementation of the program by an independent researcher has shown no improvements in students' learning among those who received vouchers compared with similar students in public schools (NEA 1996). A much anticipated study in Cleveland, supported by the state, has found that voucher recipients in parochial schools have not done any better academically than their public school counterparts (*U.S. News & World Report* 3-30-98, 5). The overall results of means-tested vouchers are disappointing, or mixed at best.

It once again supports the belief that the school effect is limited, that is, which school children attend has only a marginal influence on the academic achievement of the children. We need a broader approach to solving the inner-city school problems. Clearly, means-tested vouchers are not the most ideal option. This program tends to drain public resources out of the public school system; it exacerbates the existing problems of school inequality; it helps only a few students at the expense of the majority who are equally deserving; and it is not effective in improving the academic performance of the students or the quality of public schools, despite the high costs of implementing it.

REFERENCES

American Jewish Congress (AJC). 1999. "American Jewish Congress says Ohio Supreme Court's decision to void voucher program would be better if it had been based on the Constitution, not a technicality." (http://www.prnewswire.com).

Archer, Jeff. 1998. "Voucher proponents claim victory in Albany." *Education Week*. 17(22):5.

Barulich, David. 1996. "Vouchers: No, but . . . Taxpayers help to parents will advance separation." *Education Liberator* 2(8). October.

Bast, Joseph L., and David Harmer. 1997. "The Libertarian case for vouchers and some observations on the anti-voucher separationists." In "Vouchers and educational freedom: A debate," *Cato Policy Analysis*, no. 269, 12 March.

Bauch, P. A., and E. B. Goldring. 1995. "Parental involvement and school responsiveness." *Education and Evaluation Policy Analysis* 17(1):1–22.

Beers, David, and Jerry Ellig. 1994. "An economic view of the effectiveness of public and private schools." Pp. 19–38 in *Privatizing education and educational choice: Concepts, plans, and experiences*, edited by Simon Hakim, Paul Seidenstat, and Gary W. Bowman. Westport, Conn.: Praeger.

Beyerlein, Tom. 1999. "Looming teacher shortage makes local educators fret." *Dayton Daily News*. 24 May.

Bolick, Clint. 1998. "Are school vouchers constitutional?" *National Center for Policy Analysis. Brief Analysis*, no. 272. (http://www.ncpa.org/ba/ba272.html).

Boyer, Ernest L. 1994. "Blending the neighborhood school tradition with 'choice within schools.'" Pp. 137–44 in *Privatizing education and educational choice: Concepts, plans, and experiences*, edited by Simon Hakim, Paul Seidenstat, and Gary W. Bowman. Westport, Conn.: Praeger.

Brown, Frank. 1992. "The Dutch experience with school choice: Implications for American education." Pp. 171–89 in *The choice controversy*, edited by Peter W. Cookson, Jr. Newbury Park, Calif.: Corwin Press.

Carnegie Foundation for the Advancement of Teaching. 1992. *School Choice*. Princeton, N.J.: Carnegie Foundation.

Carter, Casey. 1999. "A question of capacity." *Policy Review*, no. 93 (January–February).

Center for Education Reform (CER). 1999. "Answers to frequently asked questions about school choice." (http://www.edreform.com).

Chase, Bob. 1997. "Voucher system would hurt schools not help." *Minneapolis Star*. 30 September.

Chubb, J. E., and T. M. Moe. 1990. *Politics, markets, and America's schools*. Washington, D.C.: Brookings Institute.

Cline, Andrew. 1997. "School choice would fare better under vouchers than tax credits." John Lock Foundation. (http://www.johnlocke.org/issues/primary_secondary_education/school_choice_and_competition/voucher.html).

Coleman, James. 1981. "Public schools, private schools, and public interest." *The Public Interest*, no. 64 (Summer).

———, and T. Hoffer. 1987. *Public and private high schools: The impact of communities*. New York: Basic Books.

———, T. Hoffer, and S. Kilgore. 1982. *High school achievement: Public, Catholic, and private schools compared*. New York: Basic Books.

———, Ernest Q. Campbell, Carol J. Hobson, James McPartland, Alexander M. Mood, Frederick D. Weinfeld, and Robert L. York. 1966. *Equality of educational opportunity*. Washington, D.C.: Government Printing Office.

Convey, John T. 1992. *Catholic schools make a difference: Twenty-five years of research*. Washington, D.C.: National Catholic Education Association.

Cookson, Jr., Peter W. 1994. School choice: The struggle for the soul of American education. New Haven, Conn.: Yale University Press.

———. 1993. "Assessing private school effects: Implications for school choice." Pp. 173–84 in *School choice: Examining the evidence*, edited by Edith Rasell and Richard Rothstein. Washington, D.C.: Economic Policy Institute.

Crain, Robert L. 1993. "New York city's career magnet high schools: Lessons about creating equity with choice programs." Pp. 259–68 in *School choice: Examining the evidence*, edited by Edith Rasell and Richard Rothstein. Washington, D.C.: Economic Policy Institute.

Dewey, Douglas D. 1997. "Separating school and state: A prudential analysis of tax-funded vouchers." In "Vouchers and educational freedom: A debate," *Cato Policy Analysis*, no. 269. 12 March.

Dougherty, Kevin J., and Lizabeth Sostre. 1992. "Minerva and market: The sources of the movement for school choice." Pp. 24–45 in *The choice controversy*, edited by Peter W. Cookson, Jr. Newbury Park, Calif.: Corwin Press.

Doyle, Denis P. 1996. "The social consequences of choice: Why it matters where poor children go to school." *The Backgrounder* (The Heritage Foundation), no. 1088. 25 July.

Driscoll, Mary Erina. 1993. "Choice, achievement, and school community." Pp. 147–72 in *School choice: Examining the evidence*, edited by Edith Rasell and Richard Rothstein. Washington, D.C.: Economic Policy Institute.

duPont IV, Pierre S. 1994. "A 'GI Bill' for educating all children." Pp. 121–36 in *Privatizing education and educational choice: Concepts, plans, and experiences*, edited by Simon Hakim, Paul Seidenstat, and Gary W. Bowman. Westport, Conn.: Praeger.

Edwards, Tony, and Geoff Whitty. 1997. "Marketing quality: Traditional and modern versions of educational excellence." Pp. 29–43 in *Choice and diversity in schooling: Perspectives and prospects*, edited by Ron Glatter, Philip A. Woods, and Carl Bagley. New York: Routledge.

Elmore, Richard F. 1990. "Choice as an instrument of public policy: Evidence from education and health care." Pp. 285–318 in *The theory of choice and control in education*. Vol. 1 of *Choice and control in American education*, edited by William H. Clune and John F. Witte. New York: The Falmer Press.

Evans, Jennifer, and Carol Vincent. 1997. "Parental choice and special education." Pp. 102–15 in *Choice and diversity in schooling: Perspectives and prospects*, edited by Ron Glatter, Philip A. Woods, and Carl Bagley. New York: Routledge.

Fox, Jonathan. 1999. "Sending public school students to private schools." *Policy Review*, no. 93 (January–February).

Freeney, Tom. 1994. "Why educational choice: The Florida experience." Pp. 39–58 in *Privatizing education and educational choice: Concepts, plans, and experiences*, edited by Simon Hakim, Paul Seidenstat, and Gary W. Bowman. Westport, Conn.: Praeger.

Glatter, Ron, Philip A. Woods, and Carl Bagley. 1997. "Review and implications." Pp. 191–205 in *Choice and diversity in schooling: Perspectives and prospects*, edited by Ron Glatter, Philip A. Woods, and Carl Bagley. New York: Routledge.

Goldring, Ellen B. 1997. "Parental involvement and school choice: Israel and the United States." Pp. 86–101 in *Choice and diversity in schooling: Perspectives and prospects*, edited by Ron Glatter, Philip A. Woods, and Carl Bagley. New York: Routledge.

Greene, Jay P., and Paul E. Peterson. 1996. "The effectiveness of school choice in Milwaukee: A secondary analysis of data from the program's evaluation." *American Political Science Association Panel on the Political Analysis of Urban School Systems*. August–September.

Greene, Jay P., William G. Howell, and Paul E. Peterson. 1997. "An evaluation of the Cleveland scholarship program." (http://www.edexcellence.net/issuepl/subject/choice/paulp.html).

Hakim, Simon, Paul Seidenstat, and Gary W. Bowman. 1994. "Introduction." Pp. 1–18 in *Privatizing education and educational choice: Concepts, plans, and experiences*, edited by Simon Hakim, Paul Seidenstat, and Gary W. Bowman. Westport, Conn.: Praeger.

Hanks, Dorothy. 1996. "How Milwaukee's choice program helps poor children succeed in school." *The Heritage Foundation, F.Y.I.*, no. 120. 23 September. (http://www.heritage.org/library/categories/education/fyi120.html).

Hill, Paul, and John Chubb. 1991. "Can public schools survive?" *U.S. News & World Report*. 9 December, 78.

Hirsch, Donald. 1997. "Policies for school choice: What can Britain learn from abroad?" Pp. 152–65 in *Choice and diversity in schooling: Perspectives and prospects*, edited by Ron Glatter, Philip A. Woods, and Carl Bagley. New York: Routledge.

Hughes, Martin. 1997. "Schools' responsiveness to parents' views at key stage one." Pp. 71–85 in *Choice and diversity in schooling: Perspectives and prospects*, edited by Ron Glatter, Philip A. Woods, and Carl Bagley. New York: Routledge.

Jencks, Christopher. 1985. "How much do high school students learn?" *Sociology of Education*. 58:128–35.

———, M. Smith, H. Avery, M. J. Bane, D. Cohen, J. Gintis, B. Heyns, and S. Michelson. 1972. *Inequality: A reassessment of the effect of family and schooling in America*. New York: Basic Books.

Jones, Thomas H. 1990. "The politics of educational choice." Pp. 241–62 in *Choice in education: Potential and problems*, edited by William Lowe Boyd and Herbert J. Walberg. Berkeley, Calf.: McCutchan Publishing Co.

Kim, Eun-kyung (Associated Press). 1997. "New Jersey per-pupil cost tops." *Dayton Daily News*. 19 September.

Lacayo, Richard. 1997. "They'll vouch for that." *U.S. News & World Report*. 27 October, 72–75.

Laconte, Joe. 1999. "Paying the piper." *Policy Review*, no. 93 (January–February).

LaPolt, Alisa (AP). 1998. "Court opens door for schools." *Dayton Daily News*. 11 June.

Lee, Susan, and Christine Foster. 1997. "Trustbusters." *Forbes*. 159(11):146–52.

Lee, Valerie E., and Anthony S. Byrk. 1989. "A multilevel model of the social distribution of high school achievement." *Sociology of Education*. 62:172–92.

Levin, Benjamin, and J. Anthony Riffel. 1997. "School system responses to external change: Implications for parental choice of schools." Pp. 44–58 in *Choice and diversity in schooling: Perspectives and prospects*, edited by Ron Glatter, Philip A. Woods and Carl Bagley. New York: Routledge.

Lewin, Nathan. 1999. "Are vouchers constitutional?" *Policy Review*, no. 93 (January–February).

Mayet, Gulam-Husien. 1997. "Admissions to schools: A study of local education authorities." Pp. 166–77 in *Choice and diversity in schooling: Perspectives and prospects*, edited by Ron Glatter, Philip A. Woods, and Carl Bagley. New York: Routledge.

McCarthy, John. 1999. "Cleveland voucher plan struck down." The Associated Press. AP–NY. 28 May.

McCarthy, Vince. 1999. "Maine school voucher case to be appealed to U.S. Supreme Court." American Center for Law and Justice. BW1197. 3 June 3. (http://www.aclj.org).

Merelman, Richard M. 1990. "Knowledge, educational organization, and choice." Pp. 79–85 in *The theory of choice and control in education*. Vol. 1 of *Choice and control in American education*, edited by William H. Clune and John F. Witte. New York: The Falmer Press.

Meyerson, Adam. 1999. "A model of cultural leadership." *Policy Review*, no. 93 (January–February).

Moore, Donald R. 1990. "Voice and choice in Chicago." Pp. 153–98 in *The practice of choice, decentralization, and school restructuring*. Vol. 2 of *Choice and control in American education*, edited by William H. Clune and John F. Witte. New York: The Falmer Press.

———, and Suzanne Davenport. 1990. "School choice: The new improved sorting machine." Pp. 187–224 in *Choice in education: Potential and problems*, edited by William Lowe Boyd and Herbert J. Walberg. Berkeley, Calif.: McCutchan Publishing Co.

Murphy, Dan, F. Howard Nelson, and Bella Rosenberg. 1997. "The Cleveland voucher program: Who chooses? Who gets chosen? Who pays?" American Federation of Teachers (AFT). (http://www.aft.org/research/reports/clev/contents.htm).

Nathan, Joe. 1991. *Free to teach: Achieving equity and excellence in schools*. New York: Pilgrim.

National PTA. 1997. "Public school choice." *Our Children*. May/June.

NEA, Center for the Advancement of Public Education. 1996. "Vouchers." In Brief. November. (http://www.nea.org/info/vouch.html).

Peterson, Paul E. 1990. "Monopoly and competition in American education." Pp. 47–78 in *The theory of choice and control in education*. Vol. 1 of *Choice and control in American education*, edited by William H. Clune and John F. Witte. New York: The Falmer Press.

Peterson, Paul E. and Jay P. Greene. 1998. "Race relations and central city schools: It is time for an experiment with vouchers." *The Brookings Review*. 16, no. 3 (Spring): 33–37.

Plank, Stephen, Kathryn S. Schiller, Barbara Schneider, and James S. Coleman. 1993. "Effects of choice in education." Pp. 111–34 in *School choice: Examining the evidence*, edited by Edith Rasell and Richard Rothstein. Washington, D.C.: Economic Policy Institute.

Rabkin, Jeremy. 1999. "A choice for the chosen." *Policy Review*, no. 93. (January–February).

Rees, Nina S. 1999. "Public school benefits of private school vouchers." *Policy Review*, no. 93 (January–February).

Reinhard, David. 1997. "Send out the children." *Portland Oregonian*. 22 June.

Rothstein, Richard. 1993. "Introduction." Pp. 1–28 in *School choice: Examining the evidence*, edited by Edith Rasell and Richard Rothstein. Washington, D.C.: Economic Policy Institute.

Shanker, Albert, and Bella Rosenberg. 1994. "Private school choice: An ineffective path to educational reform." Pp. 59–74 in *Privatizing education and educational choice: Concepts, plans, and experiences*, edited by Simon Hakim, Paul Seidenstat, and Gary W. Bowman. Westport, Conn.: Praeger.

———, and Bella Rosenberg. 1992. "Do private schools outperform public schools?" Pp. 128–45 in *The choice controversy*, edited by Peter W. Cookson, Jr. Newbury Park, Calif.: Corwin Press.

Sharp, David (AP). 1999. "Religious school subsidy ban upheld." *Dayton Daily News*. 2 June.

Shields, Carole, and Elliot Mincberg. 1998. "The case against school vouchers." *Dayton Daily News*. 30 November.

Sikes, Mary Ellen. 1996. "What is so bad about school vouchers?" *WASHline*. October. (http://www.softdisk.com/comp/shume/politics/vouchers.html).

Smith, Kevin B., and Kenneth J. Meier. 1995. *The case against school choice*. Armonk, New York: M. E. Sharpe.

Toch, Thomas. 1991. "The exodus." *U.S. News & World Report*. 9 December, 66–77.

———, and Betsy Streisand. 1997. "Does class size matter?" *U.S. News & World Report*. 13 October, 22–28.

———, and Warren Cohen. 1998. "Public education: A monopoly no longer." *U.S. News & World Report*. 23 November, 25.

Vanourek, Gregg. 1996. "The choice crusade." *Network News & Views*. (http://www.edexcellence.net/library/crusade.html).

Viteritti, Joseph P. 1996. "Stacking the deck for the poor: The new politics of school choice." *The Brookings Review* 14, no. 3, (Summer):10–13.

Weeres, Joseph. 1990. "Is more or less choice needed?" Pp. 225–40 in *Choice in education: Potential and problems*, edited by William Lowe Boyd and Herbert J. Walberg. Berkeley, Calif.: McCutchan Publishing Co.

Wells, Amy S. 1993. "The sociology of school choice: Why some win and others lose in the educational marketplace." Pp. 29–48 in *School choice: Examining the evidence*, edited by Edith Rasell and Richard Rothstein. Washington, D.C.: Economic Policy Institute.

Wells, Amy Stuart, and Robert L. Crain. 1992. "Do parents choose school quality or school status? A sociological theory of free market education." Pp. 65–82 in *The choice controversy*, edited by Peter W. Cookson, Jr. Newbury Park, Calif.: Corwin Press.

Witte, John F. 1993. "The Milwaukee parental choice program." Pp. 69–110 in *School choice: Examining the evidence*, edited by Edith Rasell and Richard Rothstein. Washington, D.C.: Economic Policy Institute.

———. 1992. "Public subsidies for private schools: What do we know and how do we proceed?" Pp. 103–27 in *The choice controversy*, edited by Peter W. Cookson, Jr. Newbury Park, Calif.: Corwin Press.

———. 1990. "Choice and control: An analytical overview." Pp. 11–46 in *The theory of choice and control in education*. Vol. 1 of *Choice and control in American education*, edited by William H. Clune and John F. Witte. New York: The Falmer Press.

10 Welfare Reform

Assistance to low-income households in the United States is provided through numerous programs supported by federal, state, and local governments. Four major programs are the Food Stamp Program, Aid to Families with Dependent Children (AFDC), Supplemental Security Income (SSI), and Medicaid. The Food Stamp Program provides assistance to help low-income households obtain a nutritious diet. AFDC provides cash assistance to households with children. SSI is designed to provide assistance to low-income people who, because of age or disability, cannot work. The Medicaid program is designed to ensure access to adequate health care by low-income households who are aged, blind, or disabled, and those who receive AFDC (Ohls and Beebout 1993, 3).

In constant dollars, federal, state, and local welfare spending rose from $158 billion in 1975 to $324 billion in 1993. Welfare spending in 1996 was 8.4 times greater than it was in 1965 when the War on Poverty began (Rector 1996). According to a figure available from the House Ways and Means Committee, 17 percent of the federal budget was targeted for welfare-related programs in 1994 compared with 6.4 percent in 1968 (MacLeish 1997), although it dropped to 12 percent in 1999 (U.S. GPO 1999). More than 3.5 trillion dollars have been spent on welfare since 1965, but poverty, illegitimacy, and other social problems have increased. It is because of this rise in welfare spending and the increase in poverty and welfare dependency that many Americans and politicians feel that the current welfare system needs to be reformed.

When people talk about welfare reform, AFDC is the program people usually have in mind, and legislation about welfare reform usually focuses on this program. The AFDC program accounts for only about 1.5 percent of total federal spending (not including the states' spending on AFDC), but it receives a much greater share of public attention because of the common perception of AFDC recipients as young, never married, single mothers with children (Bane and Ellwood 1994, x).

AFDC began in 1935 (it was then called Aid to Dependent Children) as part of the Social Security Act. The program provided cash payments to families with children whose father or mother was absent, incapacitated, deceased, or unemployed. The original object of this program was to reduce poverty without forcing mothers, primarily widows, into the labor force. Since then, however, numerous changes in the social landscape have occurred. Many women poured into the labor market; the cost of welfare increased; the number of single-parent families headed by unwed mothers grew. The concern about long-term reliance on welfare has undermined the 1930s view that welfare should provide an alternative to work. The focus of welfare reform has shifted from reducing poverty to reducing dependency (Tanner 1995; Sidel 1996, 86).

In 1996, approximately five million families (about thirteen million people) received AFDC. Nearly one out of every seven American children was in a family receiving such aid. About 92 percent of families on AFDC had no father present. The average family size was 2.9 persons, down from four in 1969 (Tanner 1997, 94). In 1994, the amount of AFDC benefits ranged from a high of $924 per month in Alaska to a low of $120 per month in Mississippi (not including other benefits, such as Food Stamps and Medicaid); the national average was $339 per month (Tanner et al. 1995).

There was little effort to reform welfare until the late 1980s when President Reagan and many other conservatives asserted that AFDC and other federal welfare programs had grossly failed to help the poor. President Reagan attempted, on a program-by-program basis, to restrict eligibility to the truly needy. States were required to set eligibility and income-verification standards. In the 1980s, a number of states established workfare programs aimed at correcting the shortcomings of federal programs and at making serious efforts to prepare welfare clients for employment. Massachusetts ET Choices Program, the Baltimore Options Program, and California's GAIN program are some of the examples (Bane and Ellwood 1994, 21–23). Nevertheless, the total number of welfare recipients continued to grow although the benefit level (per recipient) declined in many states since 1972 (Whitman 1992; Tanner 1995).

The Family Support Act (FSA) of 1988 was the first major attempt at welfare reform since the passage of the Social Security Act in 1935. The centerpiece of that effort was the Job Opportunities and Basic Skills (JOBS) Training Program, a combination of job-training and job-search initiative. States were allowed to mandate that individuals participate in job searches and could require some participants to perform community service as a prerequisite for receiving benefits (Tanner 1995; Bane and Ellwood 1994, 1). Unfortunately, the FSA requirements came into effect during a very difficult time for states. During the late 1980s, a national recession led to increasing welfare caseloads and decreasing state revenues. Providing the education, employment, and training services mandated by FSA required state money (the federal government paid only about 60 percent of the cost), and many states did not have it. Overall, only 16 percent of nonexempt AFDC recipients (or 7 percent of all adult AFDC recipients) participated in JOBS programs four years after FSA started (Bane and Ellwood 1994, 25; Whitman 1992).

In August 1996, President Clinton signed the Personal Responsibility and Work Opportunity Reconciliation Act. The purpose of this bill was to end the federal entitlement to cash assistance (AFDC) and hand it over to the states. Each state receives a block grant instead (up to $15 billion a year), and can set eligibility criteria and benefit levels on its own. Under this bill, recipients are allowed to receive benefits for two years at a time without working, with a lifetime limit of five years. This bill requires each state to enact work requirements into its welfare program (Sidel 1996; Church 1996; Rector 1996; Tanner 1995; Casse 1997).

What are the arguments surrounding welfare and welfare reform? Is welfare the right way to help the poor? Does our welfare policy need to be reformed? Or, do we need a welfare program at all? The following sections discuss supporting and opposing arguments of welfare, welfare reform, as well as different welfare reform policies.

Welfare Discourages Work and Creates Dependency

Supporting Welfare Reform

The current welfare system offers each single mother with children a paycheck under the condition that she does not work and does not marry an employed male (Rector 1996). This type of welfare system undermines the basic values of work, responsibility, and independence. Welfare actually made the poor worse off in the long run by encouraging dependency (Murray 1984). In 1996, five million families depended on welfare, and 30 percent of these recipients had remained on it for eight years or more (Gibbs 1994). These numbers will continue to rise unless the system is reformed.

This type of welfare system is unfair to everyone: to taxpayers, who must pick up the bill for failed programs, and to the poor themselves, who are trapped in a system that destroys opportunity for them and hope for their children (Tanner 1995). In addition, this system is unfair to other equally poor, yet hardworking parents who are not entitled to the same benefit. It rewards people for being unemployed and bearing children out of wedlock (Crittenden 1995, 16).

Opposing Welfare Reform

In all fifty states, AFDC benefits are well below the poverty line, ranging from Mississippi where benefits are an incredibly low 13 percent of the poverty line to Alaska where they amount to 79 percent (Sidel 1996, 88). Those who argue that welfare discourages work fail to recognize that even when the value of Food Stamps was added to the AFDC, total benefits were only an average of $629 a month in 1991, or 28 percent below the poverty level. If welfare dependents can find jobs that pay better than this poverty level of welfare, they would much rather work than remain on welfare (Peterson and Peterson 1994). In fact many people on welfare want to work, but they are in a situation in which they cannot work due to family responsibilities or mental or physical problems, or they are unable to find work that pays enough to make ends meet due to lack of education and training. There is a severe shortage of full-time jobs for low-skilled, entry-level workers that pay decent wages with health and other benefits, especially in inner-city and rural areas where most of the welfare recipients live (Wilson 1987; White 1996; Whitman 1992; Sidel 1996, 108).

Welfare Pays Too Much

Supporting Welfare Reform

Many people believe that welfare provides a minimum subsistence level of assistance to low-income families. That popular misconception results from examining only one federal welfare program, AFDC. The truth is that there are at least seventy-seven means-tested federal programs for the poor. State, county, and municipal governments operate additional welfare programs (Tanner et al. 1995). AFDC recipients are automatically eligible for a host of other federal, state, and local benefits, such as Food Stamps, Medicaid, Housing Assistance, Utilities Assistance, and Special Supplemental Food Program, just to mention a few. The pre-tax value of the total package of benefits relative to a job providing the same after-tax income exceeds the poverty level and the amount a recipient could earn in an entry-level job in every state. In twenty-one states, the total welfare benefits package exceeds 150 percent of the poverty level; in Hawaii, Alaska, Connecticut, and Massachusetts, the benefits package is more than 200 percent of the poverty level. This suggests that recipients of aid are likely to choose welfare over work, thus increasing their long-term dependence (Tanner et al. 1995). In 1989, New York City sent letters to 100,000 AFDC clients urging them to volunteer for job training and job search assistance, and only one percent signed up (Whitman 1992). Any welfare reform effort must recognize that individuals are unlikely to move from welfare to work as long as welfare pays as well as or better than working. That suggests that the most promising welfare reforms are those that substantially cut back on the level of benefits (Tanner et al. 1995).

Opposing Welfare Reform

The problem is not that welfare pays too much, but that jobs available to these less-skilled workers do not pay enough. If we really want to encourage these people to work, we should increase the minimum wage and provide decent jobs with medical and other benefits, rather than reducing welfare benefits. As long as work pays so poorly, many people will become long-term dependents on welfare (Bane and Ellwood 1994, 122–3).

Welfare income has declined steadily over the last twenty years (by 42 percent), and the current benefit is, for most recipients, not enough to make a decent living. Many recipients of welfare keep informal sources of income to survive. Some work part-time baby-sitting or cleaning houses, and others rely on family members or other charity organizations for help (Sidel 1996, 89).

Many of the welfare recipients truly cannot work for various reasons. Some must care for young children or sick family members, others suffer from mental illnesses or physical handicaps. Many others have alcohol or drug dependency problems, and many more are functionally illiterate or seriously lack education and work experience that their chances of getting decently paid jobs are very slim. It is too cruel and unfair to punish these people and their innocent children by reducing welfare benefits simply to encourage a few others to get off welfare. Those who truly need help must have an adequate level of income provided by the government until they can become self-sufficient.

Welfare Costs Too Much Taxpayers' Money

Supporting Welfare Reform

The welfare system was originally developed to provide temporary help for the poor until they could pull themselves out of poverty. However, over the years it has produced a growing number of families that rely solely on the system and its benefits for an indefinite number of years. As a result, welfare spending increased by more than eight times from 1975 and 1995. Total welfare spending in the United States in 1995 exceeded $324 billion, which was over $3,400 for each taxpaying household in the United States (Rector 1996). About 39 percent of the families with children received federal benefits in 1994, about one in seven American children was on AFDC (Hage et al. 1995).

Opposing Welfare Reform

Most welfare reform efforts target primarily the AFDC program. The majority of legislation about welfare reform also focuses on this program. What many people do not realize is that the $24 billion spent on AFDC benefits in 1994 represented only 1 percent of the federal budget and 3.4 percent of the average state budget. Even when the Food Stamp Program costs are included, less than 5 percent of the federal budget goes to assist the poor (Abramovitz 1995). Contrary to widespread impressions, AFDC benefits have declined 42 percent in real terms from 1975 until 1995. The percent of federal spending allocated to AFDC declined from 1.5 percent in 1975 to 1.1 percent in 1992 (Sidel 1996, 89).

Congress funds more than 125 programs that subsidize private businesses. This so-called corporate welfare—subsidies and tax breaks intended to protect particular industries—is estimated to cost the federal government a minimum of $85 billion annually in direct spending and billions more in foregone tax revenues (Moore and Stansel 1995). According to Congress's Joint Committee on Taxation, corporate tax breaks in the 1995 fiscal year reached $60 billion. Ralph Nader's group, Public Citizen, estimates corporate welfare as more than $167 billion (Sidel 1996, 110). During the congressional hearing in July 1999, critics of corporate welfare produced a laundry list of alleged abuses, ranging from $300,000 in government help to improve the 3,000 rockets set off nightly in Disney theme parks to $268 million given to IBM, General Motors, and General Electric as part of the Department of Commerce's Advanced Technology Program (Ackerman and Loftus 1999).

There are many other examples of welfare for the middle-class and the affluent—a wide array of personal and professional tax deductions, veteran's benefits, Medicare, unemployment compensation, workers' compensation, and educational scholarships and loans, just to name a few (Sidel 1996, 111). Nevertheless, not too many people are concerned about these government subsidies and benefits. Why are the poor being targeted when many others receive more benefits than they do?

Welfare Mothers Should Work

Supporting Welfare Reform

The primary purpose of AFDC, when it was created in 1935, was to allow widows to keep their children under their care instead of under the care of public institutions and to allow these women to avoid working outside the home. However, since the 1960s, millions of women from every social class have combined work and parenting. Indeed, a combination of work and family responsibilities is now the most common lifestyle for American women. Few women spend their entire lives at home caring for their children, even if their husbands are present in the household (Teles 1996).

About half of the single mothers on AFDC have no preschool children under the age of 5. Work should be imposed on single mothers with children over the age of 5. In addition, if an AFDC mother gave birth to another child after her enrollment in AFDC, that should not exempt her from work requirements even if the child is under age 5. This rule is needed to prevent mothers from having additional children to escape the work requirements (Rector 1996).

Opposing Welfare Reform

Raising children is a difficult and expensive task, which generally requires the efforts of the mother and father bound by the commitment of marriage. It is very difficult for a single parent to find the time and emotional resources needed to raise a child while also working to support the family. In cases in which one parent is missing for whatever reason, for the sake of the innocent children, the other parent should not be expected to do the work of two—providing child care and being the full-time breadwinner (Bane and Ellwood 1994).

The importance of marriage and the contribution of both parents is intensified in the case of parents with low skills and earning capacities. Forcing poor women to work makes it harder for them to supervise their children. Especially in neighborhoods plagued by poor schools, lack of health care, substandard housing, and in some cases drugs, crime, and violence, parental guidance is critically needed (Abramovitz 1995).

Even in the 1990s, most women would prefer to stay home to care for their children if they could. A 1992 Roper Poll showed that 53 percent of all women and 64 percent of married women in the United States preferred to stay home if they could. Only a third of married women worked full-time throughout the year in 1992, and only 23 percent of them had children under the age of three, even though they had a male partner to help juggle earner-parent roles. The right to care for one's own children at home should not be reserved for two-parent affluent families. Single welfare mothers, burdened with caring for children without the help of a partner, should have the same right (Mandell 1995).

Welfare Encourages Illegitimate Births

Supporting Welfare Reform

Across the nation, the welfare system has destroyed the family structure in low-income communities. The availability of welfare encourages women to choose single parenthood and divorce over intact family by making those choices economically viable (Rector 1996; Bane and Ellwood 1994, 74). Between 1960 and 1993, the proportion of out-of-wedlock births among teenagers rose from 15 percent to 71 percent, with the absolute number of out-of-wedlock births rising from 89,000 to 369,000 (Besharov and Gardiner 1996). In 1960, only 5.3 percent of all births were out of wedlock. By 1990, 28 percent of all births were out of wedlock (Tanner 1995). As a result, the marital status of AFDC recipients has changed. In 1973, the typical recipient was a women who was divorced or separated from the father of her children. By 1990, 54 percent of the children on AFDC had mothers who had never been married to the fathers of their children (Bane and Ellwood 1994, x). About 59 percent of women receiving AFDC in 1996 were 19 years old or younger when they had their first child (Besharov and Gardiner 1996). Single mothers make up the largest proportion of long-term recipients, averaging 9.33 years on welfare and making up 39 percent of all recipients on welfare for ten years or longer (Tanner 1995). Because so many unwed teen mothers drop out of school and have poor earning prospects in general, they are more likely to become long-term recipients (Besharov and Gardiner 1996; Bane and Ellwood 1994, 61).

Women may not get pregnant just to get welfare benefits, but welfare has taken away a major incentive to avoid such pregnancies (Tanner 1995; Rector 1996). Without the money, they are going to be more careful, use contraception, or at least have second thoughts about having a child. Many studies have shown that the availability of welfare plays an important role in influencing a woman's decision to have a child out of wedlock (Rector 1996; Winegarden 1988; Tanner 1995; Murray 1984; Mead 1986; Gibbs 1994). From society's perspective, having a baby that one cannot care for is profoundly irresponsible, and the government should not subsidize it (Murray 1984).

Opposing Welfare Reform

The causes of teen pregnancy are much more complex and multifaceted than people think. This complexity and the multicausal nature of teenage pregnancies have been largely overlooked in the current welfare debate. First of all, there is a very strong link between early sex and achievements, both present and expected achievements. Teenagers are more likely to have babies when they see no other future for themselves. Those who seek higher education or fulfilling careers are much less likely to have babies as compared with those who drop out of high school. That is why teenage childbearing is concentrated among young women who are poor and disadvantaged in many ways (Hayes 1987, 100; Mandell 1995).

Sexual mores have clearly changed. There is a sharp increase in reported premarital sexual activity, and there is strong evidence that attitudes toward giving birth to a child out of wedlock have softened over time (Bane and Ellwood 1994, 115). As more adolescents have sexual intercourse at an earlier age than before, the pregnancy rate among teenagers is bound to rise (Sidel 1996, 125). In addition, as more teens become sexually active at an earlier age, their lack of knowledge and thought regarding contraceptive use are certain to be major factors that affect the increase of out-of-wedlock births among teens (Horowitz 1995). Simple elimination or reduction in welfare is not going to change the pattern of teen pregnancy or solve the problems related to teen pregnancy.

Welfare Destroys Family Values

Supporting Welfare Reform

The vastly superior alternative to welfare is family restoration. The only way to solve our welfare problem and the harsh social fallout it produces is to focus more on preventing nonworkable single-parent families from forming in the first place. We need to encourage young low-income mothers and fathers to get married and maintain intact families. We need legal and social changes to discourage divorce and abandonment. In particular, we need measures to reduce the number of illegitimate births, including welfare benefits (Zinsmeister 1995).

Opposing Welfare Reform

Traditional family values are being destroyed, not by the misguided social welfare programs, but by the economic structure that is not congruent with family values. Economic factors play an important role in influencing many women's decisions as to whether they should get married, stay married, or to have children out of wedlock. Unfortunately, there are neither enough good jobs nor enough husbands who could provide women with enough money to support the family. Over the years, there has been a substantial decline in wages of millions of male low-skilled workers, and that economic situation discouraged marriages and encouraged divorce for many women. When men's prospect of becoming breadwinners is bleak, women are less likely to marry them. When men cannot fulfill their role as breadwinners, their ties to their families become weakened leading to higher rates of divorce (Sidel 1996).

If we want to restore family values, we need to provide decent jobs to men who are unemployed or underemployed. We need to expand education and job training opportunities for these many underprivileged men. Unless men are gainfully employed and earn enough money to support their families, women are less likely to get married or stay married.

Those who advocate restoration of family values fail to realize the fact that about 50 percent of welfare mothers ran away from abusive husbands, ex-husbands, boyfriends, parents, and step-parents. A 1992 study in Washington state found that 55 percent of welfare mothers had been hit, kicked, punched, or beaten by their boyfriends or spouses. Many women are worried about abuse not only for themselves but for their children (Whitman et al. 1995).

Family is not always a source of loving and caring relationships. More often than people imagine, family is a place of conflict, hatred, violence, and abuse. Women and children, who are more likely to be victims of domestic abuse, need an alternative life-support system in case their lives are threatened by their family members. Welfare enables women who are battered and abused to have choices other than to remain in the same dwelling with the abuser. Cutting welfare benefits would undercut women's economic independence by depriving women of a small but critical alternative to abusive men in their lives. Without the backup of welfare, many women face hard times protecting their children and have more trouble resisting an abusive relationship and exploitative jobs (Ehrenrich 1994; Sidel 1996, 85; Abramovitz 1995).

Poverty and Economic Injustice Should Be Blamed, Not Welfare

Opposing Welfare Reform

According to the conservatives, welfare is blamed for all the social problems we see in society, including illegitimate births, high rates of divorce, delinquent child support, family breakdown, high rates of violence and crime, and the cycle of welfare dependency. What they fail to see is that the underlying cause of all these problems is the poverty that arises from the lack of well-paying jobs, not welfare. There are few job options available in our society for less-educated and less-skilled workers to earn sufficient money to make a living and buy medical coverage. These unfair economic conditions create poverty, inequality, and sense of injustice and resentment among the poor. Fair and equitable economic conditions are the only way to solve these problems, not the elimination of welfare (Horowitz 1995, 232).

Economists and policymakers report permanent loss of low-skilled manufacturing jobs in the United States due to the changing structure of the economy. Manufacturing jobs are disappearing due to technological development and global competition. U.S. manufacturing companies are moving overseas in search of cheaper labor; those that remain in the United States move to suburban areas for a safer and less expensive environment. Our economic system simply does not provide enough decent-wage jobs for low-skilled workers, either male or female, especially in inner-city areas (Mandell 1995; Horowitz 1995; Sidel 1996, 15; Wilson 1987; Wilson and Neckerman 1986).

In addition, during the 1980s and 1990s, we have seen a massive concentration of wealth and income in the hands of the richest among us. Income inequality has increased and reached the greatest in the mid-1990s ever since data have been collected. While the rich have become significantly richer, the poor and the working class have lost ground. Between 1979 and 1989, the real average hourly wages of male high school dropouts declined 18 percent, 13 percent for male high school graduates. Even males with some (less than three years) college education experienced more than an 8 percent drop in income. Only workers who had completed four years of college experienced a slight increase in income. During this same time, many working-class and middle-class families have fallen into poverty (Sidel 1996, 15–16).

The central problem our society must deal with is not the character of poor women and the structure of the welfare system. The real problem is poverty that arises from economic injustice. We must realize that people are poor not because of their character defects but because of the economic and structural limitations they face, and that the poverty they face makes them hopeless, helpless, and dependent. Welfare reform punishes the poor for being poor. Our responsibility as a civilized society is to end poverty as we know it, not welfare (MacLeish 1997; Sidel 1996).

Supporting Welfare Reform

Economy and personal behavior are always closely related. Economy, however, is not the only cause of poverty. We have to admit that lack of personal responsibility is another factor that is closely related to poverty and welfare dependency. Without personal responsibility, no one is going to succeed regardless of their economic situation. The current welfare system failed because the system gives money to people and does not ask for a single thing in return. There is no deal like welfare in the real world. No one gets money for nothing. People must take responsibility for their own actions, and government policies must be formulated in such a way that it would encourage people to be responsible for their actions (Thompson 1994).

Welfare dependents must "quit being a victim" (Hillary Clinton in Whitman 1992) and quit blaming others or the economy. The poor, once they are given chances to bring themselves out with temporary help, have nothing else to blame but themselves. It is time that we should emphasize personal responsibility and accountability of one's own actions, instead of blaming others.

The economy cannot be blamed for everything. During the mid-1980s when the unemployment rate plummeted in many cities, welfare dependency did not decline. During this time, unemployment rates among young black males with little education declined sharply, yet AFDC rolls edged upward in many states (Whitman 1992).

Reform Costs More Than the Welfare Benefits

Opposing Welfare Reform

Providing incentives to get welfare recipients to work is much more complicated and costly than many people think. Providing employment and training services or community work experience to welfare recipients requires investing a substantial amount of money and staff time. Some costs are obvious, such as job training classes, child care, and transportation. In addition to that, there are other hidden costs, such as staff costs for assignment and monitoring (Bane and Ellwood 1994, 26; Roberts 1995). Job training alone could cost around $6,000 a year per person. Providing basic monitoring for each workfare enrollee (in government-provided community service jobs) could cost an additional $3,300. On top of that you have to add a huge bill for the cost of tools, supplies, and work-stations, plus the expense of day care for the children, all in addition to the amount of the welfare grant (Zinsmeister 1995). The Congressional Budget Office projects that the average annual cost of filling a thirty-five-hour-a-week workfare position in 1999 will be roughly $8,000, about half of which will go for child care. That is more than ten times the welfare cost per client on average (Whitman et al. 1995). Moreover, a lot of money and time go into eligibility hearings. It is safe to assume that no publicly employed bureaucrat in welfare agencies will lose his or her job as a result of welfare reform. In fact, the number of paper shufflers will probably increase (Klein 1996).

If there is a guarantee that these recipients will become self-sufficient as a result of this expensive reform effort, it could be worth trying it despite the high cost. However, previous efforts to train and educate welfare recipients have not been successful in reducing welfare dependency, despite the large amount of money the government has spent (Besharov and Gardiner 1996; Tanner 1995; Rich 1993; Zinsmeister 1995).

Supporting Welfare Reform

In order to save money in the long run, we must spend more in the short run. Governor Tommy Thompson of Wisconsin, who slashed the state's welfare rolls by 58 percent, had to spend $383 million in health and child care to enable single mothers to work. He increased funds for training, job placement, and child care fivefold, and spent $1,400 a year per person in addition to welfare benefits helping each parent prepare for work. After a few years of heavy invest-ments, however, the state has saved $1.5 billion by shrinking its welfare rolls; the state now saves $2 in benefits for every $1 it spends making them employ-able (McCormick and Thomas 1997; McCormick 1995).

Governor Thompson says that it usually takes eighteen months of the state's patience and spending to prepare a person to leave the dole for good. We just cannot ask a welfare mother to get a job if she has to give up the medical insurance she gets on welfare, if she has no training or bus ticket to get to work, or if she cannot find a safe place to leave her children (Alter 1996).

Welfare reform, if planned carefully, can save money immediately through better planning, management, and effective targeting. Although there are some hardcore long-term dependents who may need extensive training and help, there are many others who are fairly competent. This group of women simply needs a little help in finding jobs. It does not cost the state a lot of money to get these people out of welfare (Governors Weld and Engler in Alter 1996). The high cost of reform applies mostly to potential long-term dependents with limited education and work experience. The reform should target these poten-tial long-term dependents early and provide extensive help for them. If we can make these people self-sufficient, even if the immediate cost is high, it is worth spending the money (Alter 1996).

We Must End Welfare Benefits to All Able-Bodied Adults

Supporting Welfare Reform

It is time to recognize that welfare does not work; welfare should be ended. The entire welfare system for individuals who are able to work should be eliminated. That includes AFDC, Food Stamps, subsidized housing, and all the rest. The only way to prevent people from entering the failed system is to abolish the program that insulates individuals from the consequences of their actions. Individuals unable to support themselves through the job market should fall back on the resources of family, church, community, or some other private charity (Tanner 1995; Murray 1984; Bennett 1997).

This is tough love on a large scale; end welfare, and young girls considering having a baby out of wedlock would face more deterrents, greater social stigma, and more economic penalties arrayed against them if they have babies. There would be far fewer births to unwed mothers, and far greater life opportunities for those girls (Bennett 1997). This tough love is actually for their own good. These cuts in assistance and services may be painful at first, but in the long run these harsh measures will enable the next generation to "stand on their own two feet" (Bennett 1997; Murray 1984).

Opposing Welfare Reform

Cutting welfare benefits to the poor violates their rights. Food, shelter, and health care must be recognized as a constitutional right. The government has a responsibility to protect and provide its citizens, especially the poor and the most vulnerable, such as the elderly, sick, and children, with a minimum level of food, shelter, and health care (in Gest 1995). In 1970, the Supreme Court declared, in *Kelly v. Goldberg*, that welfare benefits were "an entitlement protected by the due process clause of the Constitution" (in Tanner 1995).

There is no legal justification in barring welfare for teens who give birth out of wedlock. Any rule that attempts to impinge on parents' sexual relations and the nature of a household is wrong (Melnick in Gest 1995). Without welfare, millions of desperate women would have no hope, no place to go, or no other way to care for their children (Sidel 1996, 85). Support for single mothers was originally based on a moral consensus that women who were unable to support their children because of the death of their spouse should be able to care for their children at home. Supporting widows through a larger program of insurance and leaving those single mothers, incapable of supporting their children because of desertion, out is unfair and discriminatory (Teles 1996, 40).

Even the toughest welfare administrators recognize that some welfare recipients face long-term obstacles to work, such as substance abuse, learning disabilities, emotional and physical problems, and personal crises. For these people, who may not meet strict disability criteria, some fallback system is needed to protect their children (Gueron 1994).

Welfare Reform Will Increase Poverty

Opposing Welfare Reform

Welfare reform and other cuts in welfare benefits will make the lives of poor women and children more miserable and tear apart the meager safety net that existed for them (Mandell 1995). According to the Urban Institute's estimate, the reform bill of 1996 would throw 1.1 million children into poverty. Many families would be pushed out on the street, and the crime rate could go up. There are some recipients who need a little bit of push to be independent, but there are many others who cannot work for many different reasons and truly need help. We cannot allow these truly needy to suffer so that a few others may pull themselves out of dependency (Alter 1996).

Supporting Welfare Reform

Since the start of the War on Poverty in 1965, the United States has spent more than $3.5 trillion trying to ease the plight of the poor. The result of that massive investment has primarily been more poverty (Tanner 1995). The underclass is much larger, more violent, more poorly educated, and have more out-of-wedlock births (Bennett 1997). According to the Census Bureau, in 1993, 15 percent of all people in the United States still lived below the poverty line (Sidel 1996, 69). It is apparent that welfare, which was created to reduce poverty, actually created more poverty since the 1960s.

Innocent Children Will Suffer
under Welfare Reform

Opposing Welfare Reform

The children, whose financial status in society is beyond their control, would suffer if welfare benefits are reduced. These children did not ask to be born to welfare parents and did not do anything wrong to be punished by poverty. According to a report from the Children's Defense Fund (CDF), one in four children were below the poverty level in 1994. An Urban Institute study predicted that the number would increase by 12 percent as a result of the 1996 welfare reform bill (Kaus 1996; Church 1996; Ehrenreich 1994, 92). These various types of welfare reform efforts, such as elimination of AFDC, time limits, child cap, and work requirements are experiments on real people's lives. No one knows what the long-term impact is going to be like, especially on innocent children's lives in years to come. Experimenting on people's lives is unethical and cruel (Whitman 1992).

Supporting Welfare Reform

Children suffer more from welfare than from poverty. Children growing up in welfare-dependent neighborhoods are actually the true victims of America's social welfare policy. Children raised in homes in which welfare is the primary source of income find welfare, out-of-wedlock births, and unemployment normal and acceptable ways of life (Bane and Ellwood 1994, 80; Tanner 1995). When the parents are paid for not working, their children will grow up without learning work as being an essential part of life. They have no role models who get up early in the morning, go to work, and work hard to make a living. Without role models, they do not learn the work ethic, discipline, and responsibility they need to be self-reliant when they grow up. This work ethic and discipline is equally, if not more, important as food on the table and clothes to wear (Olasky 1995). Children born out of wedlock and raised on welfare are three to four times more likely to be poor, be on welfare, and have children out of wedlock than children from intact families when they become adults. Women raised in single-parent households are 164 percent more likely to bear children out of wedlock than those who grew up in two-parent households (Tanner 1995; Hill and O'Neill 1990; Zuckerman 1994; Rector 1996).

Many single mothers are too young, too poor, immature, and too unloved to be responsible mothers; their children are often neglected, abused, and even abandoned (Senator Bradley in Sidel 1996, 39). As a result, children raised in single-parent families are more likely to drop out of school, do poorly while they are in school, be physically, emotionally, and sexually abused, and be victims of violent crime than children from intact families (Bennett 1997). They have lower levels of educational achievement, lower economic achievements, increased psychological and behavioral problems, and a greater propensity to substance abuse, juvenile delinquency, and crime. One half of all juvenile offenders were raised by only one parent who received welfare (Rector 1996; Tanner 1995).

Opposing Welfare Reform

Millions of children from single-parent families are not neglected, abused, or abandoned, and they do not become drug addicts, dropouts, or criminals. Many single mothers do a heroic job in transmitting values and raising their children well against great odds (Sidel 1996, 40). The source of the problem is not welfare but the widespread poverty amidst incredible affluence; massive hopelessness and alienation among those who feel that they are outside the boundaries of society. Crime and violence are reflections of the deeply felt despair among the poor. Children who grow up in poverty are more likely to be asocial or violent, not because of welfare but because of their resentment against inequality, injustice, and hopelessness they observe as they grow up. Children who grow up with middle-class single mothers do not suffer from the same disadvantage and do not show the same asocial problems (Sidel 1996, 31).

Welfare Reform Efforts Have Been Successful

Supporting Welfare Reform

Many new reform programs have shown positive results. Across the country, welfare rolls have been declining since the peak in 1994, and even more rapidly in the two years since a federal overhaul became law in 1996. By the end of September 1998, just under 8 million people were collecting AFDC, 44 percent down from 14.3 million in 1994, and that is the lowest level in thirty years (Meckler 1999, Hammonds 1998). Even in one of the poorest states, Mississippi, welfare rolls have fallen by a fifth, despite an average unemployment rate of 13.2 percent (DeParle 1997).

The strong economy in the 1990s obviously helped, but it is not a complete explanation. In the sixty-year history of welfare, through many prosperous economic times, we have never had such a drop in caseloads as since the 1990s (Alter 1997).

Opposing Welfare Reform

The initial drop in the welfare roll since the reform efforts started could be the result of what poverty researchers call the smoke-out effect—elimination of welfare abuse and fraud cases—rather than the effectiveness of the reform programs per se (Glastris 1997; Zuckerman 1995). The law's tough provisions may be chasing away, or smoking out recipients who can more or less afford to leave the dole at least temporarily because they have undisclosed or unofficial incomes—from family, friends, or under-the-table jobs (Glastris 1997). In Wisconsin, Governor Thompson discovered that about 20 percent of welfare recipients had undisclosed jobs. Welfare researcher John Pawasarat of the University of Wisconsin estimates that much of the 27 percent decline in the state's welfare caseloads since 1996 has come from recipients leaving the rolls because they did not have time to keep their unreported job and still comply with mandatory thirty- to thirty-five-hour-a-week work assignments (Glastris 1997). Edin and Lein, in their study of 214 welfare mothers, discovered that three in four of them had financial help from family and friends, and nearly half had worked at some sort of unofficial job during the previous year, such as baby-sitting or housecleaning (in Glastris 1997). In 1994, random fingerprint tests showed that about 25 percent of the 1,500 recipients tested were double dipping in both New York and New Jersey (Zuckerman 1995). The success of welfare reform was not so much due to the effectiveness of job training but because it eliminated welfare fraud and abuse cases. Better screening and eligibility tests can eliminate these people from the roll much more effectively than expensive reform programs. Effective screening in New York City in 1995 (Guiliani Program) found that nearly 60 percent of the 18,000 who applied during the three-month period were ineligible (Zuckerman 1995).

A part of the reform's success includes those who were forced to leave welfare as a penalty for not showing up for job training classes. Many states have withheld benefits from recipients who did not attend classes or accepted offers of employment. In Mississippi, between 1995 and 1997, about 19 percent of the recipients lost their benefits for violating these welfare rules (DeParle 1997).

This so-called success of reform programs occurred during the robust economy, evidenced by an average of 5 percent unemployment rate, which created strong demands for entry-level workers. No one knows what will happen to this reform program when the economy goes into recession. Welfare mothers who found it easy to be employed during prosperous times may find it next to impossible to be put on payrolls when recession strikes. Some may lose jobs they found earlier and go back on the dole (Hammonds 1998; Church 1996).

Moreover, even for those who leave welfare for a job, the retention rate is very low. About 70 percent of those who find jobs either quit or are fired within a year (Whitman et al. 1995; DeParle 1997). The focus of policy ought to be not just getting people off the rolls but also making it possible for them to stay off (Bane and Ellwood 1994, 11). We need to track down those who left welfare until they become truly independent before we can call the welfare reform a success.

The following sections discuss supporting and opposing views of various welfare-related policies and programs.

Private Charity Welfare versus Government Welfare

Supporting Charity Welfare

We need to reduce government welfare and increase private-sector charity welfare (Rector 1996). The government welfare system should be replaced with a network of charitable organizations that would care for the poor by stressing the importance of family bonds, employment, and spiritual guidance (Olasky 1995). There is widespread recognition that government welfare has failed in the sense that the government has been the least effective institution in aiding the poor. The government welfare agencies are too large, bureaucratic, slow, inflexible, inefficient, and corrupt. The role of the government should not be to actually run antipoverty programs but only to subsidize those who do them well— smaller private charities (Newt Gingrich in *Newsweek* 10-7-96). We need to re-channel a major portion of current funding into private, either secular or religious, charities, which function with greater efficiency than government programs can do (Rector 1996). The reduced size, greater flexibility, and hands-on management style that distinguish many private-sector charities permit them to monitor the behaviors of the poor and incorporate innovative methods for helping the poor (Olasky 1995; Newt Gingrich in Shapiro and Seter 1995).

Traditionally, Americans have been extremely generous in donating time and money to charities (Tanner 1995). Before the advent of government welfare programs, America's private and religious charities met the needs of the poor. Unlike the current welfare system, these charities were successful in reducing dependence and helping people work their way out of poverty. As a result of large government welfare programs since the 1960s, however, personal involve-ment in charity is down and cynicism is up. Many of us would like to contribute more of our money and time to the poor, but we are weighed down by heavy tax burdens. Many Americans justifiably feel that they already pay enough taxes that help the needy (Olasky 1995). The proliferation of welfare ended the golden age of "neighborhood helpfulness" (David Beito in Shapiro and Seter 1995). Reducing the size of government welfare will rekindle that American tra-dition of generosity (Newt Gingrich in Shapiro and Seter 1995). It is time to give that role of helping the poor back to charities. Churches, synagogues, com-munity volunteers, and neighborhood help groups can be much more effective in helping the poor than the impersonal and inefficient government bureau-cracy that is already too large and costly.

Opposing Charity Welfare

The government has a responsibility to help needy citizens, and only the gov-ernment has the resource capacity to meet the poor's basic needs. Few churches and charities have the private income necessary to provide long-term housing, social services, and especially steady income to support poor families in any number (Krammer 1995).

The share of the burden private charities assume has increased steadily since the 1980s, despite the increase in government welfare. In 1993, even with generous governmental welfare policies, Catholic Charities served 10.6 million people of every social, economic, ethnic, and religious background. Nearly 7 million people sought emergency services—primarily food and shelter—includ-ing 1.7 million children. That number is growing every year, while government support is decreasing (Krammer 1995). In 1995, private charities already helped

700 percent more people with emergency services than in 1981 (Krammer 1995).

Nationally, charities get about 30 percent of their funding from the government, and many programs get more than half their money from the government. The proposed government cut in funding will hit hard on charities (Shapiro and Seter 1995). The Independent Sector, a Washington-based group that keeps track of nonprofit organizations, estimates that such nonprofit organizations would need a 120 percent increase from contributions in seven years just to maintain their existing programs (Milbank 1995). The number of people who need emergency aid and other services will grow, and charitable organizations will be unable to make up for the annual loss of $15.1 billion in government funding in seven years. Private donations totaled about $12 billion in 1995. The charities will have to double their fund-raising and add an additional $3 billion to make up for the cuts (Krammer in Hundley 1997).

Work Requirements (Workfare) in Exchange for Welfare Benefits

Supporting Work Requirements

The reform bill passed by Congress in 1996 includes work requirements for welfare recipients, called workfare. Up to 40 percent of the AFDC caseloads will be required to work or become self-sufficient by 2002. Recipients who do not obtain private-sector jobs will be required to perform community service in exchange for benefits (Rector 1996; Whitman 1998). The purpose of this workfare is to integrate the obligation to work into welfare. Welfare recipients must realize that the benefits are not free. The benefits are provided under the condition that they must try to become self-sufficient, and if they cannot become self-sufficient during a reasonable time period, they must pay for the benefit by performing public services provided by the government. If we truly want welfare recipients to become self-sufficient in the real world, we need to make them learn that everybody has to pay for what they receive. Work requirements will also give the recipients much needed work experience and incentive to get off welfare. Through the required work, they could learn work ethics, discipline, punctuality, and other interpersonal skills that they need to be self-sufficient (Mead in Teles 1996, 150; Thompson 1994).

Opposing Work Requirements

The idea of making welfare recipients work for their benefit is nonsensical. If a person is capable of working, she should not be on welfare from the beginning.

If an employable person is on welfare, that is welfare fraud. Instead of requiring them to work, we should simply cease all payments. Welfare must be provided only for those who truly cannot work (Martin Anderson in Tanner 1995).

The type of employment envisioned under most workfare programs is unlikely to give recipients the experience or job skills necessary to find employment in the private sector. For example, New York Mayor Rudolph Guiliani required welfare recipients to perform such jobs as scrubbing graffiti and picking up trash from city streets. It is difficult to imagine that those types of work experiences will teach them skills needed to put them in demand by private-sector employers (Tanner 1995).

Performing community service is work within the welfare system that still carries the same stigma as receiving welfare. Even if they do the same work as workers outside of welfare, their work sets them apart from the rest of society with a separate group identity as welfare recipients. Community service jobs as payback are degrading and do not promote social values related to real work outside of welfare and, therefore, would not solve the problems related to the welfare subculture (Teles 1996).

Providing community service jobs for these less-skilled and inexperienced workers is a very difficult and costly task. Public-sector jobs are expensive to create and maintain. The primary problem is that large-scale, government-run work programs generate large-scale administrative headaches—even when the jobs are as simple as stabbing trash with a stick. Often the government must provide transportation, child care, proper attire for the workers, supplies needed for work, and even wake-up calls in the morning (Whitman 1998). The Congressional Budget Office estimates that each public-service job for welfare recipients costs $3,300 in monitoring costs. That does not include potential child-care outlays of up to $3,000 per participant, if mothers with young children are included (Tanner 1995). Many of those assigned to the program refuse to cooperate fully, obliging the government to set up a separate process to review the cases of families threatened with sanctions (Whitman 1998).

Welfare-to-Work Partnership Program

Supporting Welfare-to-Work Partnership

There are two strategies that might be used to connect the work norm with public assistance: getting people to work within the welfare system, such as community service, or setting up a system of work and income support outside of the welfare system (Teles 1996, 171). President Clinton's welfare-to-work partnership is an example of the latter. It involves economic incentives for private companies that hire welfare recipients. Private-sector employers can get federal tax credits of up to $8,500, in addition to state and local incentives, for each welfare recipient they hire (Hammonds 1998). A survey of companies shows that in 1996, 135,000 welfare recipients have been hired by U.S. companies, 70 percent of them full-time with health benefits (Alter 1997, Meckler 1997).

In American society, work gives citizens a social standing, dignity, and recognition. Private-sector work, outside of the welfare system, supports this set of social values and therefore is more likely to serve a socially integrative function, whereas work within the welfare system can only amount to working off a welfare check (Teles 1996, 172–3).

Opposing Welfare-to-Work Partnership

To raise the employment prospects of welfare clients, the government is offering deep subsidies to businesses. Employers pay just $1 an hour for the first six months, while the state provides $4.15 to bring clients up to the minimum wage (DeParle 1997). Welfare-to-Work Partnership takes federal money that once went in cash grants to welfare parents to subsidize the wages employers pay to welfare clients whom they hire. It helps private companies more than welfare recipients. Why do the companies get paid for the work welfare recipients perform? It is not fair that they pay less wages and also get the government subsidies (Church 1996).

A major hurdle to the strategy of work outside welfare is finding the jobs and ensuring that the recipients with jobs stay on their jobs. Most private-sector jobs require highly specialized skills and training. Often companies look for specific people with specific skills, not just anyone. It is not fair for the private-sector industry to be forced to hire unqualified workers, and it is not fair for other qualified workers who try to find jobs yet cannot because the priority is given to the welfare recipients (Meckler 1997; Teles 1996, 174).

In places where this Welfare-to-Work Partnership is implemented, union representatives fear that their members will be displaced and their wages might drop in competition with welfare recipients (Klein 1996; Samuelson 1997; Whitman et al. 1995).

Time Limits on Welfare Benefits

Supporting Time Limits

People must understand that welfare is only temporary help, not a permanent entitlement. Too many people are staying on welfare for too long, or find themselves needing welfare again and again throughout their lives. Almost one quarter of those who ever use AFDC end up collecting it for ten or more years (Bane and Ellwood 1994, 96). Single mothers make up the largest proportion of long-term recipients, averaging 9.33 years on welfare and making up 39 percent of all recipients on welfare for 10 years or longer (Tanner 1995).

People can change while on welfare. People who might have gotten off more readily at first could become conditioned by welfare and have a harder time leaving it after being on it a few years. They may become stuck in welfare because they have become passive or unmotivated, or because they lose confidence in themselves (Bane and Ellwood 1994, 34–5, 100).

Allowing people to be on welfare for two years at a time and a total of five years in one's lifetime will adequately cover the poor people's economic emergencies. There is no need for a person to be on welfare for more than two years. That is more than enough time for him to get training and find a job. If for any reason he loses his job, he will have another chance to try with the total lifetime limit of five years. Strict deadlines and time limits are necessary to give recipients an extra push toward self-sufficiency and discourage dependency (Roberts 1995).

Opposing Time Limits

The two-year time limit is too punitive, particularly for students who are trying to finish high school or college. About 80 percent of teen mothers are high school dropouts. Two years of education and job training are unlikely to prepare them to obtain work in a competitive private-sector economy (Tanner 1995, 105). Experiments have shown that it is almost impossible to get everybody to work in that short period of time (DeParle 1997). The time limit may push people who are not prepared to work into low-paying, dead-end jobs. If they are rushed into a job that they are not prepared for, they may not be able to maintain the job for long. The time limit will lower the job retention rate for welfare mothers, which is already less than 50 percent (Whitman et al. 1995; DeParle 1997).

A lifetime limit of five years is overly punitive to the many who, for many reasons, cannot work. This time limit might help those who are able to work, yet need a little push. The hard cases—those with disabilities, mental or physical problems, substance abuse problems, or those with sick family members—are most likely to end up on the streets after the deadline (Alter 1996).

Welfare recipients are not a homogeneous group of people. Every case is different and deserves individual attention. Not everyone will be prepared to work after two years of training. Some need more time than others, and some may never be able to work at all. Cutting the unemployable off welfare without providing other means of support is too cruel. The goal of welfare reform should not be to cut them off the rolls regardless of the cost but should be to help them to rebuild lives the best way they can. As a civilized nation with resources, it would be a mistake to simply cut them off knowing that they will not have means of survival.

Family (Child) Cap

Supporting Family (Child) Cap

The reform bill passed in 1994 (Work and Responsibility Act) includes a family cap. Mothers already enrolled in AFDC will not receive an automatic increase in federal benefits if they give birth to an additional child while on welfare (however, states will be permitted to enact legislation to opt out of this requirement). Under the previous welfare system, if a mother enrolled in AFDC gave birth to additional children, she received an automatic increase in AFDC and Food Stamp benefits. No other family in the United States receives an automatic increase in income by having more children. There is no reason to provide expanded welfare benefits to single mothers who have additional illegitimate children while already dependent on welfare (Rector 1996). This practice encourages women to have more children while on welfare to receive more money. It encourages teenage mothers to have children, drop out of high school, and permanently depend on public assistance. We need to stop children being born illegitimately and into poverty. No one should have children unless they can support them. The only way to stop it is to be tough on people who have children they cannot support (Friedman 1995; Rector 1996).

Opposing Family (Child) Cap

This regulation is based on the false assumption that women on welfare have children to receive more welfare. On average, women receive an additional $64 in AFDC benefits a month when they have another child. It is hard to imagine that a person would have another child simply to get $64 a month (Whitman 1992).

Women's decision to have children hinges on complex cultural forces such as peer pressure, family backgrounds, future prospective, and subcultural norms. Simply withholding benefits or punishing them for having additional children will not make them more responsible. New Jersey froze benefits for additional kids in 1992, yet the number of illegitimate births did not decline significantly (Friedman 1995). It is naive to believe that government programs and modest shifts in policies will somehow solve the problem of illegitimacy once and for all (Whitman 1992).

Family cap also denies women's reproductive rights. The government does not have the right to interfere with such intimate and private decisions such as women's decision to bear children (Sidel 1996, 53; Abramovitz 1995).

Moreover, such regulation would unfairly punish children for their parents' behavior and, therefore, discriminates against the children of the poor. The government has a responsibility to protect children of all backgrounds and birth statuses. It was not the children's fault that they were born illegitimate or to welfare mothers (Sidel 1996, 53; Gest 1995).

REFERENCES

Abramovitz, Mimi. 1995. "Welfare and women's lives." *Democratic Left.* May/June.

Ackerman, Elise, and Margaret Loftus. 1999. "What money can't buy: Critics of 'corporate welfare' are finding new allies during this presidential cycle." *U.S. News & World Report.* 12 July, 46.

Alter, Jonathan. 1997. "A real piece of work." *Newsweek.* 25 August.

———. 1996. "Washington washes its hands." *Newsweek.* 12 August.

Bane, Mary Jo, and David T. Ellwood. 1994. *Welfare realities: From rhetoric to reform.* Cambridge, Mass.: Harvard University Press.

Bennett, William J. 1997. "Welfare reform must address the crisis of illegitimacy." In *Welfare reform,* edited by Charles Cozic. San Diego, Calif.: Greenhaven Press.

Besharov, Douglas J., and Karen N. Gardiner. 1996. "Paternalism welfare reform." *Public Interest.* Winter.

Casse, Daniel. 1997. "Why welfare reform is working." *Commentary.* 104(3):36–42.

Church, George J. 1996. "Ripping up welfare." *Time.* 12 August , 18–22.

Crittenden, Ann. 1995. "A humane plan to help working and welfare parents." *Working Woman.* 16 June, 1.

DeParle, Jason. 1997. "Welfare reform creates new hardship in Mississippi." *New York Times.* 16 October.

Ehrenreich, Barbara. 1994. "Real babies, illegitimate debates." *Time.* 22 August, 90.

Friedman, Dorian. 1995. "The flawed premise of welfare reform." *U.S. News & World Report.* 11 September, 32.

Gest, Ted. 1995. "Courts: The next arena." *U.S. News & World Report.* 16 January.

Gibbs, Nancy. 1994. "The vicious cycle." *Time.* 20 June, 24–30.

Glastris, Paul. 1997. "Was Reagan right?" *U.S. News & World Report.* 20 October, 30–31.

Gueron, Judith M. 1994. "The route to welfare reform." *Brookings Review.* Summer.

Hage, David, David Fischer, and Robert Black. 1995. "America's other welfare state." *U.S. News & World Report.* 10 April, 34–37.

Hammonds, Keith H. 1998. "Welfare-to-work: A good start." *Business Week.* 1 June.

Hayes, Cheryl D., ed. 1987. *Risking the future: Adolescent sexuality, pregnancy, and childbearing.* National Research Council. Washington, D.C.: National Academy Press.

Hill, M. Anne, and June O'Neill. 1990. *Underclass behaviors in the United States: Measurement and analysis of determinants.* New York: City University of New York, Baruch College.

Horowitz, Ruth. 1995. *Teen mothers: Citizens or dependents?* Chicago, Ill.: University of Chicago Press.

Hundley, Wendy. 1997. "Welfare: Mandated changes a cause for concern." *Dayton Daily News.* 10 April.

Kaus, Mickey. 1996. "Clinton's welfare endgame." *Newsweek.* 5 August.

Klein, Joe. 1996. "The role of a lifetime." *Newsweek.* 7 October.

Krammer, Fred. 1995. "Compassion alone won't do the job." *Insight.* 3–10 April.

MacLeish, Rod. 1997. "The (un)worthy poor." *Christian Science Monitor.* 17 January, 19.

Mandell, Betty Reid. 1995. "Shredding the safety net." *New Politics.* Summer.

McCormick, John. 1995. "Missing the point on welfare." *Newsweek.* 14 August.

———, and Evan Thomas. 1997. "Family: From welfare to work." *Newsweek.* 26 May.

Mead, Lawrence. 1986. *Beyond entitlement: The social obligations of citizenship.* New York, NY: Free Press.

Meckler, Laura (Associated Press). 1999. "Welfare rolls at lowest level in 30 years." *Dayton Daily News.* 25 January, 5A.

———. 1997. "Reform to change lives, jobs." *Dayton Daily News.* 30 June.

———. 1988. "Welfare reform model." *Dayton Daily News.* 20 August.

Milbank, Dana. 1995. "U.S. charities fear Republican welfare cutbacks." *Wall Street Journal.* 7 November, 24A.

Moore, Stephen, and Dean Stansel. 1995. "Put an end to corporate welfare." *USA Today*. 11 September.

Murray, Charles. 1984. *Losing ground: American social policy, 1950–1980*. New York: Basic Books.

Ohls, James C., and Harold Beebout. 1993. *The Food Stamp Program: Design tradeoffs, policy, and impacts*. Washington, D.C.: The Urban Institute Press.

Olasky, Marvin. 1995. "The new welfare debate: How to practice effective compassion." *Imprimis*. September.

Peterson, Janice L., and Carol Dawn Peterson. 1994. "Single mother families and the duel welfare state." *Review of Social Economy*. (Fall):321–29.

Rector, Robert. 1996. "Welfare reform." In *Issue '96: The Candidate's Briefing Book*, edited by Stuart M. Butter and Kim R. Holmes. Washington, D.C.: The Heritage Foundation.

Rich, Spencer. 1993. "Training programs can work, but they can't work miracles." *Washington Post National Weekly Edition*. 22–23 February.

Roberts, Steven V. 1995. "Wisconsin's lesson in welfare reform." *U.S. News & World Report*. 3 July, 56.

Samuelson, Robert, J. 1997. "Judgment calls: Economic mythmaking." *Newsweek*. 8 September.

Shapiro, Joseph P., and Jennifer Seter. 1995. "Welfare: The myth of charity." *U.S. News & World Report*. 16 January, 39–40.

Sidel, Ruth. 1996. *Keeping women and children last: America's war on the poor*. New York: Penguin Books.

Tanner, Michael. 1997. "Welfare should be eliminated." Pp. 92–103 in *Welfare reform*, edited by Charles P. Cozic, San Diego, Calif.: Greenhaven Press.

———. 1995. "Ending welfare as we know it." *USA Today*. March.

———, Stephen Moore, and David Hartman. 1995. "The work vs. welfare trade-off." *Cato Policy Analysis*. 19 September.

Teles, Steven M. 1996. *Whose welfare? AFDC and elite politics*. Lawrence, Kans.: University Press of Kansas.

Thompson, Tommy G. 1994. "Response and responsibility: Welfare reform that works." *Commonsense*. Spring.

U.S. Government Printing Office. 1999. "A citizen's guide to the federal budget: Budget of the United States government fiscal year 1999." (http://www.access.gpo.gov/su_docs/budget99/guide/guide.02.html/spending).

White, Jack E. 1996. "Let them eat birthday cake." *Time*. 2 September, 45.

Whitman, David, Dorian Friedman, Mike Tharp, and Kate Griffin. 1995. "Welfare: The myth of reform." *U.S. News & World Report*. 16 January, 30–39.

Whitman, David. 1998. "Despite tough talk; states avoid workfare." *U.S. News & World Report*. 12 January, 26–27.

———. 1992. "War on welfare dependency." *U.S. News & World Report*. 20 April, 34–40.

Wilson, William J. 1987. *The truly disadvantaged*. Chicago, Ill.: University of Chicago Press.

Wilson, William J., and Katherine M. Neckerman. 1986. "Poverty and family structure: The widening gap between evidence and public policy issues." In *Fighting poverty: What works and what doesn't*, edited by Sheldon Danziger and Daniel Weinberg. Cambridge, Mass.: Harvard University Press.

Winegarden, C. R. 1988. "AFDC and illegitimacy rates: A vector autoregressive model." *Applied Economics*. (March:1589–1610).

Zinsmeister, Karl. 1995. "Chance of a lifetime." *American Enterprise*. January/February.

Zuckerman, Mortimer B. 1995. "Showing the way on welfare." *U.S. News & World Report*. 22 May, 72.

———. 1994. "Starting work as we know it." *U.S. News & World Report*. 4 July, 72.

INDEX

Abortion, 1–26
  access to, 14–15
  adoption as an alternative to, 11–12
  dangers of illegal, 13–14
  extent of, in the U. S., 4–5
  father's (of the fetus) consent in, as
    requirement, 20
  government funded, 2, 16–18
  history of legalization of, 1–3
  late–term (partial–birth), 21–22
  legal vs. moral perspectives on, 8–9
  mandatory waiting period for, 3,
    18–19
  parental consent for, 2, 19–20
  parental notification of, 2, 19–20
  partial–birth (late–term), 21–22
  public opinion about, 4
  rape and, 15–16
  reasons of seeking, 5
  religious views on, 3
  unwanted pregnancy, 9–10
Academic performance of students
  effects of school on, 254–255
  factors that affect, 254–255
  family background and, 254
Affirmative action policy, 27–49
  as a compensatory remedy, 29–30
  as a group–focused remedy, 29–30
  as reverse discrimination, 34–35. See
    also Reverse discrimination
  class-based vs. race-based, 46
  college admission policy and, 34–35
  continued need for, 37–38
  cultural diversity and pluralism
    promoted by, 32–34
  definition of, 27
  effectiveness of, 36–38, 41–43, 44–45
  effects of, on minority underclass,
    44–45
  history of, 27–29
  increased opportunities for minorities,
    created by, 30–31
  minority role models created by, 32

racial tensions, increase created by, 40–
    41. See also Racial tension
  stigmatization of minorities as a result
    of, 39–40
  Supreme Court decisions on, 27–29
  unfairness of, 31, 34–35
  voluntary vs. forced, 46–47
  workforce, declining quality as result of,
    38–39
African Americans
  bifurcation (polarization) among. See
    Black bifurcation
  college dropout rate of, 31
  college enrollment rates of, 28–29,
    34–35
  death penalty and, 60–62
  disadvantages of, 37–38
  education level of, 36
  educational qualification of, 34–35, 42
  employment qualification of, 42–43
  homicide rates of, 61
  improved status of, 36–37
  middle class, increase of, 31, 44–45
  poverty and, 37
  out-of-wedlock birth rates of, 37, 42–43
  professionals, 36
  victim-focused identity of, 30
Aid to Families with Dependent Children
    (AFDC), 266
  average amount of, 267, 268–269
  cost of providing, 266–267, 270
  declining benefits of, 270
  employability of women who receive,
    272, 278
  goals of, 266–267, 271
  history of, 266–268
  recipients of, 267
All-school-choice programs, 231–232
American Bar Association, death penalty,
    51
Anti-abortion movements, 3
Assault weapons, 93–94
  banning, effectiveness of, 94

Assault weapons, *continued*
   banning of, 93–94
   crimes committed with, extent of,
      93–94
   dangers of, 93–94
   definition of, 94
   threats to police officers, 94

Baby boom generation, and Social
   Security, 185
Bartley-Fox Amendment in Massachusetts, 89
Black bifurcation (polarization), as a result
   of affirmative action policy, 45
Black underclass. *See also* Minority
   underclass
   affirmative action policy and, 44–45
   definition of, 38
   growing size of, 38
   situation of, 44–45
Brady Law, 77, 89
   definition of, 95–96
   effectiveness of, 95–96

Capital punishment. *See* Death penalty
Capitation payment method in health
   insurance, 118
Catholic schools. *See also* Religious
   schools and Private schools
   as community anchors, 257
   causes of higher academic standard in,
      240–241, 243
   cost-effectiveness of, 243
   declining enrollment in, 256
   effectiveness of, 243–244, 256
   funding of, 256
   screening of students in, 244
Centralized investment of Social Security
   Trust Funds, 221–226
   dangers of, 221–226
   definition of, 221–222
   effects of, on national economy,
      224–225
   higher rates of return with, 222–224
   lower investment risks with, 222–224

CEO America Horizon Project, 256
Charter schools, 231, 240
Chimeras, 152, 157
College admission standards
   race as a plus factor in, 35–36
   standardized tests as, 28–29
   top-ten percent law as, 28–29
   unfairness of, in the past, 35–36
Compassion in Dying, 166
Corporate welfare, 271
Cost-sharing, in health insurance,
      129–130
   benefits of, 129
   definition of, 129
   increase of, 129
   need for, 129
   problems of, 130
Cost-shifting, in health care, 112–113
   definition of, 112
   extent of, 112–113
   managed care and, 121–122
   necessity of, 112–113
   rationales of, 112–113
Crime rates, in the U. S., 71
Criminals, as victims of the environment,
      67–68
Cultural diversity, 32–34. *See also* Racial
      diversity
   benefits of, 32–33
   business appeals of, 33
   in education, 33–34
   in public-sector workforce, 33
Cultural pluralism. *See* Cultural diversity

Deadbeat dads. *See* Delinquent child
      support
Death penalty, 50–74
   as a cruel and unusual punishment,
      54–56
   as a justified killing, 68–69
   brutalization effects of, 69
   cost of, compared to life imprisonment,
      65–66
   cost-cutting measures of, 65–66
   deterrence effects of, 56–60
   due process of the law in, 55

Eighth Amendment, as violation of, 54–56
execution, certainty of, 59–60, 66
executions, delayed, 58–59
executions, number of, 50–51
executions of. *See* Executions of the death penalty
for the innocent, 58–59, 64–65
history of, 50–51
indigent defense of, 62–63
in other countries, 51–52, 70–71
incapacitative effects of, 57
juvenile offenders and, 50–51
life imprisonment as an alternative to, 71–72. *See also* Life imprisonment
lighthouse effects of, 57
overturned convictions of, 63–64
poor and, 62–63
post conviction appeals in, 58–59, 65–66
public opinion about, 51, 69–70
racial biases in, 60–62
restitution as a rationale for, 52–54
retribution as a rationale for, 52–53
role of penance in, 68
state laws regarding, 50–51
unfairness of, 60–63
Death row inmates
innocent, 63–65
number of, 50
on probation, parole, and pretrial release, 72
racial backgrounds of, 61–62
socioeconomic status of, 62–63
Death with Dignity Act, in Oregon, 166
Defensive medicine, 110–111
Delinquent child support, and abortion, 20
Discrimination, against minorities, 43
Due process of the law, in capital punishment, 55

Economic injustice. *See also* Income inequality
changing economic structure, cause of, 275–276

welfare and, 275
Employment Retirement Income Security Act (ERISA), 125
Euthanasia, passive vs. active, 169–170
Executions of the death penalty
innocent and, 63–64
methods of, 50
number of, 50–51
state laws regarding, 50–51
types of, 50
Experience (risk) rating, in health insurance. *See* Underwriting

Family (child) cap, in welfare, 288
definition of, 288
need for, 288
problems with, 288
unfairness of, 288
Family Support Act (FSA) of 1988, 267
Family values
economic factors, influence on, 274
poverty and, 42–43
restoration of, 42–43
welfare and, 273–274
Fear of crime, among Americans, 71
Federal budget surplus, and Social Security, 197
Federal Firearms Act of 1938, 76
Fee-for-service system of health care, 107–108
abuses in, 107–108
benefits of, 108
Firearm violence. *See* Gun violence
Firearms Owner's Protection Act of 1986, 76–77
Firearms
as self-defense, 85–88
child-resistant features in, 99
criminals' access to, 92
defensive use of, 86–88
domestic violence and, 86, 91
easy access to, and crime rate, 82–83
manufacturing industry. *See* Gun manufacturing industries
ownership. *See* Gun ownership
safety features of, 99

Firearms, *continued*
 stolen, extent of, 92
 suicide rates and, 83–84, 86
Food Stamp Program, 266
Fourteenth Amendment, and abortion
  right, 1
Full privatization of Social Security. *See
  also* Privatization of Social Security
 benefits of, 199
 definition of, 199
 problems of, 199–200

Gag clauses, applied to managed care
  doctors, 118
Gag rules, on abortion, 2–3
Genetic engineering, 151–152, 155–156
 benefits of, 155
 cloning technology, use in, 151–152
 potential risks of, 155–156
Government-controlled health care
  systems, 134–136
 need for, 135–136
 private system vs., 134–136
Government regulations, of private
  schools, 246–247
Government-operated welfare, 282–284
 inefficiency of, 282–283
 private charity welfare vs., 282–284
Gun Control Act of 1968, 76
Gun control laws
 assault weapons and, 93–94
 federal vs. state and local, 98
 general, 76, 92–93
 handguns and, 95
 state and local, 78
 targeted, 76, 91–92
 types of, 76–78
Gun control, 75–103
 applied to criminals, 88–89
 crime control vs., 81
 crime rate and, 89–90
 controlling crime, effectiveness of,
  88–89
 history of, 76–78
 in other countries, 89–90
 laws. *See* Gun control laws

 public opinion about, 78
 Second Amendment and, 79–80
Gun dealers
 federal licensing of, 97
 local licensing of, 89
 straw intermediary, 88–89
Gun manufacturing industries
 lawsuits against, 77, 99–100
 regulating, 99–100
 responsibilities of, 100
Gun ownership
 among high school students, 82
 among law abiding citizens, 91–92
 crime rate and, 82–83, 91
 domestic violence and, 91
 in the U.S., 75
 legal purposes of, 91–92
 modern purposes of, 80
 reasons for, 75
 residency requirement of, 97
 self-defense and, 85–88
 suicide and, 83–84
 types of, 75
Gun violence
 cost of treating victims of, 75
 in schools, 82
 in the U.S., 75
 injuries from, 75, 81
 non-firearm violence vs., 81
 victims of, 75
Gun-related accidents
 among children, 84–85
 fatal, 84–85
 frequency of, 84–85
 preventing, 85
Guns. *See* Firearms

Habeas Corpus petition, in death penalty
  cases, 58–59
Handguns
 banning of, 95
 dangers of, 95
 for self-defense, 95
 in crimes, 95
Health care costs, 104–115
 fee-for-service system and, 107–108

good quality care and, 114–115
health care insurance and, 106–107
high administrative costs and, 107
in other countries, 105
in percent of GDP, 104
mal-practice lawsuits and, 110–111
medical specialists, large share, and, 109–110
medical technology, development of, and, 113–114
physicians' high income and, 108–109
rise of, 105–106, 108–114
Health care insurance
administrative costs of, 140–141
cost of, 105
cost-shifting and, 112
employer-based, 140–142
individual (consumer)-based, 142–144
percent of population without, 111
portability of, 141
private managed care firms, as providers of, 117
third-party indemnity, 106–107
Health care rationing, 130–132
dangers of, 131–132
definition of, 130
in Britain, 131
in Oregon, 131
need for, 130–131
unfairness of, 131–132
Health care reform, 104–147
history of, 104
mandated employer-based health insurance as option of, 140–142. See mandated-employer-based health insurance
mandated individual (consumer)-based health insurance as option of, 142–144. See Mandated individual (consumer)-based health insurance
National Health Insurance (NHI) as option of, 136–138. See also National Health Insurance (NHI)
National Health Service (NHS) as option of, 138–140. See also National Health Service (NHS)
need for, 105–115
single-payer plan as option of. See National Health Insurance
socialized medicine as option of. See National Health Service
universal health care system as option of, 132–134
Health Maintenance Organizations (HMOs), 104, 115–116. See also Managed care
Hispanic Americans. See Minorities
Hospice programs
as alternative to physician-assisted suicide, 177
availability of, 177
effectiveness of, 177
role of, 177
Human cloning, 148–164
as asexual reproduction process, 162–163
definition of, 148
Feinstein-Kennedy proposal on, 149
First-Bond proposal on, 149
history of, 148–150
individuality issue regarding, 161–162
in genetic engineering, 151–152
medical benefits of, 152–153, 154, 155, 156–157, 158
methods of, 150–151
moral issues regarding, 160
partial (tissue and organ reproduction), 151, 154–155
potential risks of, 153, 154–155, 155–156, 157, 159
religious groups' views on, 150, 161
techniques used in transgenics, 152
U.S. Government's moratorium on, 149
whole, 151, 152–153
World Health Organization's (WHO's) position on, 149–150

Illegal abortions, dangers of, 13–14
Illegitimate births
abortion and, 17
among minorities, 37, 42–43
among welfare recipients, 272–273

Illegitimate births, *continued*
   causes of, 273, 288
   increase of, 272
   welfare and, 272–273
   welfare of the children born, 279–280
Income inequality
   increasing, 275
   welfare spending, increase caused by,
      275–276
Income redistribution function of Social
   Security, 212–214
Indigent defense, in capital cases, 62
   cost of, 62
   problems of, 62
Inequality among schools
   magnet schools, as creators of, 241
   vouchers and, 247–250
Infant mortality rate, as a measure of
   quality of health care, 114–115, 139
Interstate gunrunning, 97

Late-term abortions, 21–22
Legal cases
   Adarand Constructors v. Pena, 28
   Bakee v. University of California, 27–28
   Brown v. Board of Education, 234, 258
   *Cruzan v. directors, Missouri Department
      of Health*, 165
   Doe v. Bolton, 1
   Furman v. Georgia, 50, 57
   Gregg v. Georgia, 50
   *Hopwood v. University of Texas School of
      Law*, 28
   Kelly v. Goldberg, 278
   Mueller v. Allen, 242
   Planned Parenthood v. Casey, 3, 20
   Roe v. Wade, 1, 2, 18
   Sheet Metal Workers v. EEOC, 28
   Vacco v. Quill, 166
   Washington v. Glucksberg, 166
   *Weber v. Kaiser Aluminum and Chemical
      Corp.*, 28
   Webster v. Reproductive Health Services, 2
Lex talionis, 53
Liberty interest
   in abortion, 5–6, 9–10

   in physician-assisted suicide, 168
Life expectancy at birth, 114–115, 139
   as a measure of quality of health care,
      114–115
   effects of increased, on Social Security,
      185–186
Life imprisonment
   as alternative to death penalty, 71–72
   cost effectiveness of, 72

Magnet schools, 231, 240–241
   cost of operating, 241
   creating school inequality, 241
Mal-practice medical lawsuits, 110–111
   abuse of, 110
   benefits of, 110–111
   costs of, 110–111
   frequency of, 110
Managed care, 115–127
   competition created by, 116, 119–120
   cost-cutting measures used by, 117–118
   cost-shifting created by, 121–122
   creating inequality of health care,
      121–122
   definition of, 115–116
   growth of, 115–116
   health care decision-making within, 118
   health care savings created by, 116–
      117, 121
   history of, 115–116
   increasing premiums of, 116–117
   limited choices under, 123–124
   membership figures of, 104
   patients' complaints against, 118
   patients' right to sue, 126–127
   physicians' autonomy in, 122
   pre-existing condition restrictions
      within, 121
   preventive care in, 123
   quality of health care under, 117
   share of, in health care industry,
      115–116
   subscribers' satisfaction rate with,
      119, 126
Managed care reform, 124–127
   cost of, 125–127

history of, 124
need for, 124–125
Mandated employer-based health
    insurance, 140–141
    administrative cost of, 140–141
    lower-income families and unfairness
        of, 142
    benefits of, 140
    definition of, 140
    limited choices under, 141
    portability of, 141
    problems with, 140–141
Mandated individual (consumer)-based
    health insurance, 142–144
    benefits of, 142–143
    definition of, 142–143
    problems with, 143–144
Means-tested school voucher programs,
    231, 249, 258–261
    definition of, 231, 249, 258
    mixed results of, 260–261
    need for, 258
    problems of, 259
    success of, 260–261
    unfairness of, 259–260
    universal voucher programs vs., 259
    welfare function of, 258–259
Medicaid, 104, 266
Medical Savings Account (MSA), 142–
    143, 144
    benefits of, 142–143
    problems with, 143–144
Medical technology
    cost of, 113–114
    high-cost low benefit versus low-cost
        high benefit, 113–114
Medicare, 104
Milwaukee Parental Choice Program, 232
Minorities. *See also* African Americans,
    Hispanic Americans
    college dropout rates of, 31, 42
    corporate executives, 37–38
    discrimination against, 43
    economic status of, 37–38
    educational qualification of, 34–35,
        41–42
    educational status of, 36–38

employment test scores of, 38–39
enrollment in higher education, 28–29,
    34–35
improved status of, 36–38
in poverty, 38
income levels of, 36–37
increased opportunities for, 30–31
negative stereotypes of, 39–40
out-of-wedlock birth rate of, 37, 42–43
role models, need for, 32
scapegoating of, 40
single-parent families among, 42–43
standardized test scores of, 34–35,
    38–39
stigmatization of, with affirmative
    action policy, 39–40
underclass, 38. *See also* Underclass
    minorities
under-representation of, 41–43
unemployment rate of, 38
victim-focused identity of, 30
Minority underclass. *See also* Black
    underclass
affirmative action policy and, 44–45
definition of, 38
growing size of, 38
situation of, 44–45

National Health Insurance (NHI),
    136–138
    benefits of, 136–137, 138
    cost-effectiveness of, 136–137
    definition of, 136
    disadvantages of, 137–138
    of Canada, 136–137
    quality of care under, 137–138
National Health Service (NHS), 138–140
    cost-effectiveness of, 139
    definition of, 138–139
    in Britain, 139–140
    problems with, 139–140

Old-Age, Survivors, and Disability
    Insurance (OASDI), 184. *See also*
    Social Security

Omnibus Crime Control Safe Street Act
of 1968, 76
Open enrollment system, 231
Out-of-wedlock births. *See* Illegitimate
births

Partial human cloning. *See also* Human
cloning
definition of, 151
medical benefits of, 154
potential risks of, 154–155
Partial privatization of Social Security. *See
also* Privatization of Social Security
benefits of, 199–200
definition of, 199–200
problems of, 199
Partial-birth abortions (Late-term
abortions), 21–22
Patients' Bill of Rights Act, 124–127
Pay-as-you-go system of Social Security,
184, 188–189, 190–191
Permissive licensing policy (of guns), 76,
91–92. *See also* Targeted gun control
Personal Responsibility and Work
Opportunity Reconciliation Act of
1996, 268
Physician's role, in physician-assisted
suicide, 176–177
Physician-assisted suicide, 165–183
abuse of, in the Netherlands, 172–173
better terminal care vs., 170–171,
178–179
definition of, 166
Fourteenth Amendment, rights
protecting, 168–169
frequency of, in the U.S., 167
history of, 165–166
hospice program as an alternative
to, 177
in Australia, 166
in the Netherlands, 166, 171, 172–173
in Oregon, 166
irrationality in requesting, 180–181
legal issues regarding, 168–170
medical professionals' view of, 167
moral issues regarding, 173–174

need for, as a result of modern
technology, 170–171
physicians' role in, 176–177
potential risks of allowing, 174–
175, 181
public opinion on, 167
reasons for requesting, 171, 180–181
religious groups' views on, 167, 174
slippery slope effects of, 172–173,
174–175
Point-of-Service (POS) plans, 116. *See also*
Managed care
Poverty
among children, 43
among minorities, 43
as a cause of capital crimes, 67–68
Pre-existing condition restrictions
(exclusions), 120, 128–129, 142–143
Preferred Provider Organizations
(PPOs), 104, 116. *See also* Managed
care
membership figures of, 104
Prepaid Group Plans (PGPs). *See*
Managed care
Preventive care, 123
Private charity welfare, 282–284
effectiveness of, 282–283
funding of, 283–284
government welfare vs., 282–284
increased burden on, 283–284
Private schools. *See also* Catholic schools
admission criteria for, 235, 247
autonomy of teachers in, 253
availability of, with vouchers, 255–256
cost-effectiveness of, 252–253
costs of education in, per-pupil, 233
de-privatization of, with vouchers,
245–246
effectiveness of, in educating students,
253, 255
government regulations of, with
vouchers, 244–247
public schools vs., 238, 243–244, 252–
253, 255
screening of students by, 247–248
Private system of health care, 134–136
benefits of, 134

dangers of, 134–135
government-controlled health care
    systems vs., 134–136
Privatization of Social Security, 198–221
    administrative costs with, 207–209
    benefits of, 204–205
    centralized vs. de-centralized manage-
        ment of funds under, 202–203
    definition of, 198–199
    full vs. partial, 199–200
    government diversion of Social Security
        Trust Funds and, 217–218
    higher rates of return with, 206–207
    in Britain, 203, 207–208
    in Chile, 198–199, 203, 208, 217
    in other countries, 203–204
    income redistribution function of Social
        Security under, 212–214
    low-income people and effects of, 220
    mandatory vs. voluntary, 201–202
    national economy and effects of,
        216–217
    retirement age and, 221
    risk factors with, 209–210
    social insurance function of Social
        Security under, 210–212
    substitutive vs. supplementary, 201–202
    transition cost under, 214–215
    types of, 199
    women and effects of, 218–219
Public opinion polls
    on abortion, 4
    on gun control, 78
    on gun ownership, 75
    on Patients' Bill of Rights, 125
    on physician-assisted suicide, 167
    on school voucher programs, 250
    on the death penalty, 51, 69–70
    on working motherhood, 272
Public schools
    choice within, 240–241
    competition within, 240–241
    diversity within, 240–241
    dropout rates in, 232
    goals of, 251–252, 254
    high costs of, 233, 250–251, 252–253
    importance of supporting, 251–252

improvements in, 233–234, 240,
    251–252
lack of competition and accountability
    in, 237–240
large size of, 253
market approach, dangers of using,
    237–240
private schools vs., 238, 243–244,
    252–253
problems of, 232–233, 252–253
role of, as an equalizer, 249
segregation, increased, 249–250

Quality of education
    factors that affect, 244, 251–252, 254
    improved, with competition, 240
    money and, 252–253
    problems of defining, 239–240
Quality of health care
    high cost of health care vs., 114–115
    improved, 114–115

Racial bias, in the death penalty, 60–62
    against African Americans, 60–62
    race of the victim and, 60–61
Racial diversity, 32–34. *See also* Cultural
        diversity
    benefits of, 32–33
    in colleges, 28–29
    racial representation vs., 34
Racial inequality
    affirmative action policy and, 41–43
    causes of, 41–42
Racial segregation
    in college campuses, 40–41
    in workplaces, 40–41
    increase of, 40–41
Racial tension
    affirmative action policy and, 40–41
    in college campuses, 40–41
    increase of, 40–41
Rehabilitation (as a punishment rationale)
    capital punishment and, 67
    effectiveness of, 67–68

Religious schools. *See also* Catholic
    schools
  admission processes in, 245
  autonomy of, 244–246
  educational curriculum of, 241–242
  educational goals of, 241–242, 246
  independence of, 244–246
  opt-out provisions in, 245, 246–247
  special missions of, 246
Restitution (as a punishment rationale),
    53–54
  vengeance vs., 54
Restricted gun control, 76, 92–93. *See also*
    Restrictive licensing policy
Restrictive licensing policy, 76, 92–93. *See
    also* General gun control
  effectiveness of, 92–93
Retirement age
  increased, and Social Security, 196–197
  Social Security, privatizing and, 221
Retribution, as a punishment rationale,
    52–53, 54
Reverse discrimination, 34–35
  as a result of affirmative action policy,
    34–35
Right to bear arms, 79–80. *See also* Second
    Amendment
Right to life
  criminals', 54–55
  fetuses', 6–7, 16, 22–24
Right-to-die, with the help of physicians.
    See Physician-assisted suicide
Roman Catholic Church, on abortion, 3

"Safe Haven" schools, 256
School choice
  by means of vouchers. *See* School
    voucher programs
  controlled, 249
School effect, on academic performance
  limits of, 254–255
  environmental effects vs., 254
  family background vs., 254
School voucher programs, 230–265
  community revitalizing effects of, 257
  cost of providing, 250–251

  court decisions on, 241
  definition of, 230
  dual education system, created by,
    248
  effects of, on the inner-city community,
    257
  First Amendment and, 241–242
  freedom of choice with, 234–235
  history of, 230–231
  in Australia, 245–246, 248
  in Britain, 236, 248
  in Canada, 237, 245–246, 248
  in Cleveland, 232, 249, 250, 251,
    260–261
  in Florida, 232
  in Maine, 231–232
  in Milwaukee, 232, 238, 245, 249,
    260–261
  in the Netherlands, 245–246, 248
  in Vermont, 231
  in Washington D.C., 245
  increased competition and accountabil-
    ity with, 237–240
  increased government regulation of
    private schools with, 244–247
  increased parental involvement with,
    235–236
  means-tested, 231, 249, 258–261. *See
    also* Means-tested school voucher
    programs
  need for, 232–234
  private schools, availability, 255–256
  progressive, 231, 249
  school inequality created by, 247–250
  screening and selecting effects of,
    247–250
  separation of church and state and,
    241–242
  types of, 231
  universal, 231
Second Amendment, and gun control,
    79–80
Single-payer plan. *See* National Health
    Insurance (NHI)
Smart-gun technologies, 100
Social Security Act of 1935, 184
Social Security Amendment in 1983, 184
Social Security benefits

cuts as a reform option, 193–194
increased, 186
means-tested, 194–195
Social Security shortfall, expected,
184–185
causes of, 185–188
exaggeration of, 187–188
major overhaul solutions for,
189–191
minor adjustment solutions for, 188–
189, 190–198
Social Security reform, 184–229
centralized investment of Social
Security Trust Funds as, 221–226
federal budget surplus, use of in, 197
major overhaul options as, 189–191
means-tested benefit cuts as, 194–195
minor adjustment options for, 188–189,
191–198
need for, 185, 188–189, 189–191
payroll tax increase as, 191–192
privatization as. See Privatization of
Social Security
raising (or removing) income cap
subject to Social Security tax as,
192–193
reducing cost-of-living adjustment as,
195–196
reducing Social Security benefits as,
193–194
retirement age increase as, 196–197
Social Security Trust Funds
centralized investment of. See
Centralized Investment of Social
Security Trust Funds
government diversion of, 186–187,
197–198, 217–218
projected depletion of, 185
Social Security
average payment of, 184
cost of, 184
definition of, 184
history of, 184–185
income redistribution function of,
212–214
pay-as-you-go system of, 184, 188–189,
190–191
payroll tax increase, 191–192

payroll tax, 184–185
privatizing, See Privatization of Social
Security
recipients of, 184
shortfall, expected, 185. See also Social
Security shortfall
social insurance function of, 210–212
welfare function of, 212–214
Socialized medicine. See National Health
Service (NHS)
Standardized test scores
as a college admission standard, 28–29,
34–35
as an academic achievement predictor,
35, 39
causes of declining, 233–234
declining, 253
employment and, 38–39
importance of, 35, 39
of minority students, 34–35
worker productivity and, 38–39
Straw intermediaries (strawmen), of gun
buyers, 88–89, 92
Suicides
among teens, 83
availability of guns and, 83–84
in Japan, 84
methods of, 84
Sullivan Law, 76, 89, 98
Supplementary health insurance, 133
in other countries, 133
under universal health care system, 133
Supreme Court decisions
on abortion, 1–2
on affirmative action policy, 27–28
on Cleveland school voucher
program, 242
on federal funding of abortion, 2
on mandatory waiting period for
abortion, 18
on Milwaukee school voucher program,
242–243
on passive euthanasia, 166
on physician-assisted suicide, 165–166
on state funding of religious schools,
241, 242
on the death penalty, 50–51
on welfare rights, 278

Targeted gun control policy, 76, 92–93
Time limits on welfare, 286–287
  need for, 286–287
  problems with, 287
Tiered health care system, 133–134
  dangers of, 133–134
  definition of, 133
  in other countries, 133–134
  justification for, 133
Top-ten percent law, in college
  admissions, 28–29
Transgenics, 152, 156–157
  benefits of, 156–157
  potential risks of, 157
  with cloning technology, 152

Underwriting, in health care insurance
  definition of, 127
  need for, 128
  unfairness of, 127–128
Uninsured people (without health
  insurance)
  as percent of population, 111, 132
  background of the, 111, 132
  health care benefits available for the,
    111–112
  health care outcomes of the, 112, 132
Universal health care system, 132–133
  definition of, 132
  impossibility of achieving, 133
  rationales of, 132–133

Victim's right activism, 53–54
Violent Crime Control and Law Enforcement Act of 1994, 77

Welfare dependency, 268–269
  causes of, 268–269
  duration of, 268, 286–287
  economic (structural) causes of,
    275–276
Welfare programs. *See also* Aids to families
  with dependent children (AFDC)
  corporate, 271
  cost of providing, 266–267, 270
  creating dependency, 268–269

  discouraging work, 268–269
  economic injustice and, 275–276. *See
    also* Economic injustice
  effects of, on children, 279–280
  family values and, 273–274. *See also*
    Families values
  for the able-bodied, 278
  for abused women, 274
  for the affluent, 271
  generous benefits of, 269
  government provided, 282–284. *See also*
    Government welfare programs
  illegitimate births and, 272–273. *See also*
    Illegitimate births
  need of, for single mothers, 272, 274
  personal responsibility and, 275–276
  private charity versus government
    provided, 282–284. *See also* Private
    charity welfare
  recipients' employability, 270, 278
  right to receive, 278
  types of, 266, 269
  work opportunities and, 269–270
Welfare reform, 266–290
  cost of, 276–277
  effective screening as an option of,
    281–282
  effects of, on children's welfare,
    279–280
  effects of, on economy, 282
  effects of, on poverty, 279
  family (child) cap as an option of, 288.
    See also Family (child) cap
  history of, 266–268
  in Wisconsin, 277, 281–282
  long-term benefits of, 277
  smoke-out effects of, 281
  success of, 281–282
  success of, in Wisconsin, 277
  time limit as an option of, 286–287. *See
    also* Time limits on welfare
  welfare-to-work partnership as an option
    of, 285–286. *See also* Welfare-to-work
    partnership
  workfare as an option of, 267, 284–285.
    See also Workfare programs
Welfare-to-work partnership program,
  285–286

definition of, 285–286
effectiveness of, 285–286
problems of, 286
socially integrative function of, 286
unfairness of, 286
White flight, 232, 248
Whole human cloning. *See also* Human
    cloning
definition of, 151
for infertile couples, 152–153
medical benefits of, 152–153

risk of abuse with, 153
Women's right, in abortion, 5–6
Work requirement for welfare benefits.
    See Workfare programs
Workfare programs, 284–285
benefits of, 284
cost of providing, 285
examples of, 267
problems with, 284–285
with community service, 284–285